CONTRACT AND POWER

European Contract Law and Theory Series, Volume 9

# CONTRACT AND POWER

Ideologies, Inequalities, and Marginalisation in European Contract Law

*Edited by*

Lucinda Miller
Pietro Sirena

INTERSENTIA
LEFEBVRE GROUP

Intersentia
Lefebvre Belgium SA
Avenue Jean Monnet, 4
1348 Louvain-la-Neuve
Belgium
Email: contact@larcier-intersentia.com

*Distribution for the UK, Ireland and*
*Rest of the World (excl. France, Belgium and Luxembourg)*
Ingram Publisher Services UK
1 Deltic Avenue, Rooksley
Milton Keynes MK13 8LD
United Kingdom
Tel: +44 1752 202 301 | Fax: +44 1752 202 331
Email: ipsuk.customercare@ingramcontent.com

*Distribution for France and Other Countries (excl. Ireland and the UK)*
Interforum Editis
92 avenue de France
75013 Paris
France

*Distribution for Belgium and Luxembourg (excl. France, Ireland and the UK)*
Larcier-Intersentia
Avenue Jean Monnet, 4
1348 Louvain-la-Neuve
Belgium

Contract and Power


Artwork on cover: Mural from the Temple of Longing (1922), Paul Klee (German, 1879 - 1940) - Artvee

ISBN 978-1-83970-602-8
D/2026/06040/0058
NUR 822

British Library Cataloguing in Publication Data. A catalogue record for this book is available from the British Library.

# CONTENTS

# LIST OF AUTHORS

*Felix Aiwanger*
Senior Research Fellow, Max Planck Institute for Comparative and International Private Law Hamburg, Germany

*Greta Berardi*
Research Assistant in EU Law, University of Groningen, Law Faculty, The Netherlands

*Aurelia Colombi Ciacchi*
Professor of Law and Governance, University of Groningen, Law Faculty, The Netherlands

*Niamh Connolly*
Associate Professor, University College London, Faculty of Laws, United Kingdom

*Alma-Cristina Onaie*
Research Assistant in EU Law, University of Groningen, Law Faculty, The Netherlands

*Orit Gan*
Senior Lecturer, Sapir College School of Law, Israel

*Martijn W. Hesselink*
Professor of Transnational Law and Theory at the European University Institute, Florence, Italy

*Tom Hick*
Senior Research Fellow at the Max Planck Institute for Comparative and International Private Law, Hamburg, Germany

*Stefanie Jung*
Professor of Corporate Law at the Technical University of Munich, TUM School of Management (Heilbronn Campus), Germany

*Pascal Lokiec*
Professor at Sorbonne University, Paris, and former President of the French Association for Labour Law and Social Security law, France

*Maria Rosaria Marella*
Professor of Private Law, Roma Tre University, Department of Law, Rome, Italy

*Giovanni Marini*
Professor of Jurisprudence and Comparative Law, Link-Campus University, Rome, Italy

*Francesco Mezzanotte*
Professor of Private Law, Roma Tre University, Department of Law, Italy

*Lucinda Miller*
Associate Professor, University College London, Faculty of Laws, United Kingdom

*Pietro Sirena*
Professor, Bocconi University (Milan), Dean of Bocconi Law School, Milan, Italy

*Lyn KL Tjon Soei Len*
Associate Professor in the Department of Women's, Gender and Sexuality Studies at The Ohio State University, Columbus, Ohio, The United States of America

# INTRODUCTION

## Contract and Power: Ideologies, Inequalities, and Marginalisation in European Contract Law

Lucinda MILLER and Pietro SIRENA



This collection of essays emerges from the SECOLA conference held at University College London in the spring of 2024. The aim of the conference was to interrogate the topic of 'contract and power', using the breadth of this theme to encourage exploration of the wide variety of sources, types, dynamics, impacts, expressions and distributions of power that arise within, bear down on, extend beyond, or are reproduced by contracts, contractual governance, and contractual relationships. Naturally, the law, legal actors and legal discourse were also central to our enquiries, whether that be in their role of constituting and shaping power, obscuring manifestations of power, or in their potential to constrain and govern power and resulting inequalities.

At the same time, it was hoped that the very broad theme of contract and power could be refracted through the particular lens of inequalities and marginalisation. In that respect, we were interested in exploring how power, in its multiple guises and in its interactions with contracts, contractual relationships, and the law may have gendered or racialised dynamics, or may be experienced distinctly by people from marginalised or vulnerable communities. We are grateful to all participants of the conference and to authors of this edited volume for their rich contributions and for engaging so directly with the conference theme. The essays included in this volume address the theme not just from a breadth of perspectives but also from a range of legal jurisdictions – common law, civil law and the EU legal system itself. The book clearly does not reflect all there is to say on power and contract, for that would be an impossible task. Instead, the essays collectively bring insight to key issues in the relationship of contract and power, many of which tend to be sidelined by dominant accounts of the law.

This introduction offers an intellectual map of some of the themes of power and contract which are especially relevant to the contributions in this volume, bringing together some of the issues explored in the subsequent chapters.

## 1. THE CONCEPT OF POWER

When we use the term 'power' in everyday language, we think we know what we are talking about.[1] But, whilst intuition might be a preliminary guide, power is a complex and multi-dimensional phenomenon with a variety of diverse, contested and often politicised views about its meaning, including how it is, and should be, theorised and addressed by the law. Despite the concept pervading analysis[2] of the normative foundations of private ordering and of European contract law, and despite it being increasingly recognised that contractual relationships are important sites of power,[3] it is not generally considered to be a legal concept at all.[4] There is certainly no legal definition on which to ground analysis, in contract law or in any other legal domain.[5] Legal scholarship must grapple with the plural and indeterminate nature of the concept and its many shifting forms and 'mechanisms of production and reproduction'.[6] These generate continually evolving power dynamics which may both transcend as well as attach themselves to specific disciplinary fields, subfields and factual constellations.

---

1 S. Lukes, *Power: A Radical View*, Palgrave Macmillan, Basingstoke 2021, p. 66.

2 Both implicitly and explicitly. See S. Grundmann, 'Societal Order and Private Law', in S. Grundmann, H.-W. Micklitz and M. Renner (eds.), *New Private Law Theory. A pluralistic approach*, Cambridge University Press, Cambridge 2021, pp. 131 et seq.; G. Bachmann, Private Ordnung: *Grundlagen ziviler Regelsetzung*, Mohr Siebeck, Tübingen 2006; D. Poelzig, *Normdurchsetzung durch Privatrecht*, Mohr Siebeck, Tübingen 2015; A. Hellgarth, *Regulierung und Privatrecht: Staatliche Verhaltenssteuerung mittels Privatrecht und ihre Bedeutung für Rechtswissenschaft, Gesetzgebung und Rechtsanwendung*, Mohr Siebeck, Tübingen 2016. For an overall account, see M. Renner, 'Private Ordering', in S. Grundmann, H.-W. Micklitz and M. Renner (eds.), *New Private Law Theory. A pluralistic approach*, ibid., pp. 484 et seq.

3 See, for example, the contribution of P. Lokiec in this volume.

4 H-W. Micklitz, *The Politics of Justice in European Private Law: Social Justice, Access Justice, Societal Justice*, Cambridge University Press, Cambridge 2018, p. 329.

5 Although, see Article 102 TFEU and the notion of abuse of a dominant position.

6 See the contribution of M.R. Marella and G. Marini in this volume, section 1.

From a civilian perspective, the traditional private law has adopted a purely conceptual and axiologically neutral definition of power, thereby rendering the concept entirely useless: if power is identified in the private autonomy which is granted to each subject (for example, to conclude any contract they wish), then the very concept of legal power dissolves into a fiction and ultimately obscures the reality of facts.[7] Conversely, private law (especially contract law)[8] has traditionally refrained from addressing contexts in which power emerges *de facto*—power that is embedded in socio-economic relations, in disparities of role or gender, or within organised structures, beginning with enterprises vis-à-vis workers or consumers, but also vis-à-vis small and medium-sized businesses.[9] In this sense, the contribution of European (private) law can be regarded as fundamentally important, since it has compelled national legal systems to move beyond a purely legal and, so to speak, micro-sectoral concept of power. Instead, attention has shifted to a conception of *de facto* power, one that arises from socio-economic relations and which is 'measured' on a macro-social scale against the overall structures of society (at least, insofar as a single market is concerned).[10] Ordoliberal thought, which forms the intellectual matrix of European law, has in fact been explicitly hostile to such situations of *de facto* power,[11] viewing them primarily as an obstacle to the functioning of

---

7 Pioneering in the critique of this conceptual framework was the contribution of L. Raiser, 'Die Aufgabe des Privatrechts', (1955) *JuristenZeitung*, pp. 209–216.

8 Here we refer to both civilian and common law traditions.

9 Seminal contributions in this direction were offered by C.M. Bianca, *Le autorità private*, Giuffrè, Milan 1977 (*de facto* powers within relations of employment law, family law, etc.); C.-W. Canaris, 'Die Bedeutung der iustitia distributiva im deutschen Vertragsrecht' *AcP* 1972, pp. 201 et seq. (pure commutative justice is not sufficient to neutralise the *de facto* inequalities between the parties).

10 H.-W. Micklitz, 'The Public and Private - European Regulatory Law and Financial Services' (2014) 10 *ERCL* 473; H.-W. Micklitz, 'The Visible Hand of European Regulatory Private Law-The Transformation of European Private Law from Autonomy to Functionalism in Competition and Regulation' (2009) 28(1) *Yearbook of European Law* 3. With specific regard to the financial sector, see O.O. Cherednychenko, 'Financial Consumer Protection in the EU: Towards a Self-Sufficient European Contract Law for Consumer Financial Services' (2014) 10 *ERCL* 476; Y. Svetiev and A. Ottow, 'Financial Supervision in the Interstices between Private and Public Law' (2014) 10 *ERCL* 496; H. Marjosola, 'What Role for Courts in Protecting Investors in Europe - A View from Finland' (2014) 10 *ERCL* 545; F. della Negra, 'The Private Enforcement of the MiFID conduct of business rules. An overview of the Italian and Spanish experiences' (2014) 10 *ERCL* 571; F. Möslein, 'Third Parties in the European Banking Union: Regulatory and Supervisory Effects on Private Law Relationships Between Banks and their Clients or Creditors' (2015) 16(3) *EBOR* 545; M. Andenas and F. della Negra, 'Between Contract Law and Financial Regulation: Towards Europeanisation of General Contract Law' (2017) 28(4) *European Business Law Review* 499.

11 Path-breaking was F. Böhm, 'Privatrechtsgesellschaft und Marktwirtschaft' (1996) 17 *Ordo* 75. On ordo-liberalistic thought and power, see C.-W. Canaris, 'Verfassungs- und europarechtliche Aspekte der Vertragsfreiheit in der Privatrechtsgesellschaft', in P. Badura and R. Scholz (eds.), *Wege und Verfahren des Verfassungslebens. Festschrift für Peter Lerche zum 65. Geburtstag*, C.H. Beck, Munich 1993, pp. 85 et seq.; K.-H. Ladeur, *Der Staat*

the market economy and ultimately as a political danger as well.[12] It is therefore evident that the neutralisation of asymmetries between 'strong' and 'weak' actors has been regarded as an indispensable element for the establishment and functioning of the European single market and, indirectly, for the promotion of peace and democracy in the Member States.[13]

As will be discussed below, one of the recurring themes that emerges from the essays collected in this volume is that the concept of power requires both an evaluative perspective based on the analysis of socio-economic relations, and an approach that cuts across the different branches of the legal system. For the legal culture of civil law countries, particularly, this represents a radical challenge, since the tradition of private law is rigorously formalistic, axiomatically neutral, and grounded in a sharp distinction between the sphere of private law and that of public law.

Another thematic thread that unites the essays is the contingent and values-driven nature of power. Power is an 'ineradicably value-dependent'[14] concept, in the sense that where (and if) power is visible, the way it is defined, and normative positions on its (il)legitimacy are rooted in (often unacknowledged) value-assumptions[15] and intellectual, moral or ideological positions, all of which are entangled within prevailing and countervailing social, political, economic and legal narratives of the time. For instance, a neoliberal perspective will provide different evaluations of (and responses to) power from a viewpoint rooted in social justice, or from a 'law and political economy' approach.[16]

---

*gegen die Gesellschaft. Zur Verteidigung der 'Rationalität der Privatrechtsgesellschaft,'* Mohr Siebeck, Tübingen 2006; K. Riesenhuber (ed.), *Privatrechtsgesellschaft*, Mohr Siebeck, Tübingen 2007. On European (private) law and power, see K. Meyer and J. Scheinpflug, *Privatrechtsgesellschaft und die Europäische Union*, Mohr Siebeck, Tübingen 1996, pp. 11 et seq., pp. 75 et seq.; S. Grundmann, 'The Concept of the Private Law Society: After 50 Years of European and European Business Law' (2008) 16(4) *ERPL* 2008553; S. Grundmann, 'Societal Order and Private Law', in S. Grundmann, H.-W. Micklitz and M. Renner (eds.), *New Private Law Theory. A pluralistic approach*, above n. 2, pp. 131 et seq.

12 F. Möslein (ed.), *Private Macht*, Mohr Siebeck, Tübingen 2016; K. Barker, S. Degeling, K. Fairweather and R. Grantham (eds.), *Private Law and Power*, Bloomsbury, London 2017; P. Sirena and A. Zoppini (eds.), *I poteri privati e il diritto della regolazione*, RomaTre Press, Rome 2018; G. Resta, 'Poteri privati e regolazione', in *Enc. dir.*, I tematici, V-2023, *Potere e costituzione*, a cura di M. Cartabia and M. Ruotolo, Giuffrè, Milan 2023, pp. 1008 et seq.

13 S. Grundmann, 'Privatrecht und Regulierung', in M. Auer, H.C. Grigoleit, J. Hager et al. (eds.), *Privatrechtsdogmatik im 21. Jahrhundert. Festschrift für Claus-Wilhelm Canaris zum 80. Geburtstag*, de Gruyter, Berlin 2017, pp. 930 et seq.

14 S. Lukes, above n. 2, p. 34.

15 Ibid., p. 34.

16 E.g. J. Britton-Purdy et al., 'Building a Law-and-Political-Economy-Framework: Beyond the Twentieth-Century Synthesis' (2020) 129 *Yale L.J.* 1784; P.F. Kjaer (ed.) *The Law of Political Economy: Transformation in the Function of Law*, Cambridge University Press, Cambridge 2020.

Moreover, as two of the chapters in this volume demonstrate,[17] adopting an intersectional lens to questions of power will yield different insights on domination and the experiences of 'multiple marginalised' people.[18]

The definitional complexities and value-laden nature of power complicates the task of properly discerning the concept and unearthing its patterns and effects. Yet, doing so is important because what is considered to count as power (and, equally, what is not), how we measure it, and where the sources of power are believed to lie, determine whether we respond to it, in what way, and for what purposes. Moreover, a clearer conceptualisation of the operation of power helps defend change in the interests of those who may experience its oppressive effects.[19] Each of the chapters that follow highlight the importance of context in unearthing patterns and effects of power. They remind us that analyses must be sensitive to the localised, on-the-ground, and informal dimensions of power and the ways in which patterns of power are constituted through an 'interplay of social, economic, cultural and legal power', and may differently impact on the most vulnerable members of society.[20]

It is helpful to frame the authors' chapters in this volume by setting out two meanings of power, both of which are rooted in social and political theories of power that emerged in the mid 20$^{th}$ century,[21] but which are nevertheless highly relevant to contract and to the issues raised in this book. The first is encapsulated by the notion of 'power *to*' and the second as 'power *over*'. Whilst we will separate these two forms of power for reasons of exposition, both are tightly interrelated and it will often be the case, although not always, that both meanings are concurrently tied to the same factual circumstances being analysed, albeit viewed from opposing perspectives.

## 2. POWER 'TO'

This conceptualisation of power can be initially aligned with the power-conferring nature of the legal system which grants individuals the ability to voluntarily create their own mutually beneficial and legally binding agreements. In this way, power 'to' signifies the *capacity* to create and change legal relationships,[22] and to organise exchange in a legally binding form.

17 See the contributions of M. Hesselink and L. Tjon Soei Len, Chapter 9, and of M.R. Marella and G. Marini, Chapter 10, in this volume.

18 See the contribution of M. Hesselink and L. Tjon Soei Len in this volume.

19 As Marella and Marini point out, section 1.4.

20 See I. Ramsay, 'Consumer Credit Law, Distributive Justice and the Welfare State' (1995) 15 *Oxford Journal Legal Studies* 177, 188.

21 S. Lukes, above n. 2, pp. 35–42.

22 Lukes notes that 'power to' indicates a 'capacity' a 'facility', and an 'ability', above n. 2, p. 39.

In principle, the legal system grants this legal power to all persons – natural and legal – an approach that can be associated with the social and legal evolution that began in the 19th century and which saw a shift from a legal order founded on status-based rights, enjoyed only by the aristocratic members of society, towards the principle that rights and duties were to be granted to all, regardless of class or privilege.[23] As such, the conferral of contractual power to all citizens marked the end of the *Ancien Régime* and enshrined the notion of (formal) equality within private law systems.

The power to enter into agreements and thus to use contractual mechanisms to change one's legal relationships can be conceptualised as having productive value for the holder of those rights for whom the breakdown of rigid social hierarchies provided new opportunities for economic activity and personal liberties. This empowering or enabling feature of contract might be broadened even further to embrace a wider range of legal subjects. The starting point for Felix Aiwanger in Chapter 6 is that nature too is a rights-holder, a legal subject in charge of its own interests and to be viewed as an equal partner with whom to negotiate. This is not an absurd notion, as Aiwanger points out: jurisdictions around the world have been experimenting with the granting of legal rights to nature, whether that be through the path of granting constitutional rights, or by deploying private law mechanisms (e.g. compensatory damages in tort law). And so, nature as the subject of contractual rights fits with this evolution.

Extending the power 'to' beyond natural and legal persons in this way is valuable, Aiwanger argues, since nature is then able to negotiate for itself more favourable contractual terms and ceases to be simply an object of 'discretionary human powers' and a 'resource to be exploited'. In this context, power becomes a positive force in society, shifting the discourse about the protection of nature towards an empowering 'ecocentric'[24] model of cooperative mutual negotiations with space for shared meaning and dialogue.

This paints a particularly favourable image of contracting – a terrain in which parties come together for cooperative, mutually advantageous and empowering interactions. And, in some part, this may be true. As the liberal narrative of contract theory tells us, contract offers the power to shape an individual's 'own ideas of desirable interpersonal relationships, whether they be intimate or at arms length'.[25] For some communities, the normative force of contract may feel especially liberating. In flattening hierarchies and 'democratising'[26] the manner in which social and economic goods are distributed in society, contract may be viewed as granting choice and freedom to those previously alienated from the

---

23 H. Maine, *Ancient Law: Its Connection with the Early History of Society, and its Relation to Modern Ideas*, Cambridge University Press, Cambridge 2013.

24 See the contribution of F. Aiwanger, in this volume.

25 See the contribution of M. Hesselink and L. Tjon Soei Len in this volume, section 4.4.

26 Ibid., section 4.4.

market because of, for example, gendered and racialised restrictions. From this perspective, the account of contract law as constituting an empowering space for arrangements between equal individuals seems compelling.

In retelling her own experience of her encounters with contract law, Patricia Williams provides us with a stark reminder of the empowering force and agency that the formalities, (or, as she puts it, the 'tonalities') of contract law may offer.[27] Williams recounts how contract law grants her, a Black woman, the opportunity to engage in the market as an equal subject of law – as a bearer of contractual rights and duties – and gives her the tools to present herself as commercially trustworthy. As just mentioned, this has particular potency for those members of society that were previously excluded from the market because of their race or gender, or worse, whose participation in the market was not as a legal *subject*, but as legal *object* – the object of a legal contract between two others during the period of slavery in the USA.[28] Williams' writing highlights the importance of local, autoethnographical accounts of power which might otherwise be lost in the dominant – white, male, heteronormative, etc. – narratives of power. As Williams herself observes in her narration, her white male colleague navigating an identical market exchange – the rental of accommodation – experiences societal power very differently from the Black female and so will view their own relationship with the law very differently too. For the more privileged in society, the power 'to' contract may at times be a less valuable, perhaps even a dispensable,[29] legal tool.

Not all contributors take such a positive view of the power that contractual rights provide. Martijn Hesselink and Lyn KL Tjon Soei Len (Chapter 9) are more critical and adopt what they themselves present as a radical position. Deploying an intersectional lens, they reveal ways in which private law creates and maintains injustices along intersectional vectors of oppression. Contract law's complicity with oppression provides the basis for rejecting the very idea of contract as a necessary way of organising social and economic relations. The only way to ensure a more just future, they argue, is to abolish the institution of contract law itself. In practice, this stance would mean the elimination of such things as: contract law's bilateral and thus inward-regarding orientation which excludes consideration of collective interests; self-interest as the core of exchange; violent coercion by the state in enforcing contracts, to name just a few of the elements that the authors cite as a consequence of this radical proposal. Importantly, it would mean abandoning the private law orthodoxies and fixed ideas about how to organise the social order, and in doing so release

27 P. Williams, 'The Pain of Word Bondage', in *The Alchemy of Race and Rights*, Harvard University Press, Cambridge 1991, Ch. 8 'The Pain of Word Bondage', pp. 146–165.

28 Ibid., pp. 17–19.

29 An informal arrangement may be considered more conducive to the trust-based bonds that support the exchange relationship.

those from marginalised communities from the task of having to engage with a legal system that is constructed on extractive, gendered, racialised, etc. forms of oppression.

It should be highlighted that the authors take very seriously Williams' defence of contractual rights mentioned above, and it makes them cautious in their agenda. However, their argument remains that ultimately a society where *nobody* has private law rights would be a more just one overall, since it would not be a society in which the law can be used for intersectional oppression and marginalisation. Importantly, it would be a society in which marginalised people would not be forced to engage with racialised, gendered systems of power.

Even if one does not fully embrace the idea of the abolition of contract law, Hesslink and Tjon Soei Len provide a salutary reminder of the ways in which contracts and the institutions of contract law may reinforce dynamics of power – state power as well as individual private power – and may harm those from the most marginalised communities.[30] Indeed, our productive account of power 'to' has so far sidestepped discussion of how the end of status-based rights and the shift to a new era of equality and freedom in contractual relations was only equality in the very thinnest of senses. Liberal theories of contract might proclaim that the transactional terrain is one of equality for all in neutral, pre-political markets, but this misses the point that more powerful individuals come to contract law with more than others. From this perspective, the notion of 'equality' is a purely formal one that masks social inequalities and the power that some have over others. Power 'to', therefore, may enable power 'over' others. We return to these issues in the next section.

This brings us to an important point about the scope of the notion of power 'to'. We have noted that, in principle, all persons are conferred with the power to participate in economic and social life utilising the instruments of contract law. But we should clarify that more carefully by making a distinction, a distinction that is more explicit in civil law jurisdictions, between the ability to *hold* rights and the ability to *exercise* legal rights. In practice, not everyone is equally able to exercise those rights and enter into contractual relationships.

Perhaps the most obvious restriction is on the legal rules relating to 'incapacity'. The incapacity rules establish restrictions concerning which individuals are deemed not capable of binding themselves to contractual obligations and are in effect 'the gateway to involvement in the operations of a market economy'.[31] They can be conceptualised as limits to the notion that all are equal – and that all enjoy capacity – under the law. Generally speaking,

---

30 We take this point up below.

31 S. Deakin, 'Capacitas: Contract Law, Capabilities and the Legal Foundations of the Market', in S. Deakin and A. Supiot (eds.), *Capacitas; Contract Law and the Institutional Preconditions of a Market Economy*, Hart Publishing, Oxford 2009, p. 2.

the categories that most European legal systems include within the incapacity rules are minors, persons with mental illness or with temporary impairment due to drink or drugs, and unincorporated associations. These groups of persons are deemed not to be able to understand the consequences of their actions and so are protected from the contractual responsibility to which they might otherwise find themselves subject. As an 'ultra-interventionist'[32] set of rules which operate as exceptions to contractual freedom and which have the potential to increase uncertainty within the law, the recognised categories have been narrowly drawn, increasingly so, in all Western legal systems.[33]

The incapacity rules might seem to establish the formal boundaries of the scope of the power 'to'. Yet, there are other restrictions on an individual's ability to participate fully in economic life which set limits to the exercise of power 'to'. For example, the scope of the power to engage in contractual relations is contingent on the precise size of the terrain within which private ordering can take place. Limits on an individual's freedom to organise their social and economic relations as they see fit are set by the law and are guided by collective policy goals and considerations of public morality.[34] Whilst the conceptual relationship between these legal rules and the rules on incapacity is not well formulated,[35] both shape the scope of the power for individuals to organise exchange through contract. Further restrictions on the power to exercise contractual rights might arise from the lack of material resources and/or insufficient economic leverage that may prevent access to the market, a restriction that is often experienced most acutely by the more disadvantaged in society. All these components elucidate which persons are legally and materially empowered to enter into legal agreements.

But limits also occur through less visible, and often less legitimate encroachments into the space of private ordering. For example, the power to engage in contractual relations may be greatly reduced by means of our increasingly automated society which can eliminate the very *raison d'être* of contracting as a tool for allocating risk and resolving uncertainty. Here we refer to what Shoshana Zuboff defines as 'uncontract', viz., a private space of unilateral execution by machine rather than a space for contractual relations. Where corporations find economic benefits in dealings through machine rather than contract then this diminishes opportunities to engage in the 'expressions of solidarity and human agency that have been gradually institutionalised in the notion of "contract" over the course of millennia'.[36] Gone are 'promises,

32 See the contribution of P. Lokiec in this volume, section 2.2.

33 And have been increasingly narrowed over the years.

34 For example, rules against the enforcement of certain types of immoral or illegal contract.

35 S. Deakin, above n. 31, p. 4.

36 S. Zuboff, *The Age of Surveillance Capitalism: The Fight for a Human Future at the New Frontier of Power*, Profile Books, London 2019, p. 220.

dialogue, shared meaning, problem solving...'.[37] and instead we are left with a space of 'uncontract' where the power to engage in contractual relations is denied.

As this last example highlights, restrictions in the ability to organise through contract will often be intimately related to and captured in the second understanding of power – power 'over' – since the corollary of being the object of domination will often be the reduction in capabilities, or 'power to'. It is to this second form of power that we now turn.

## 3. POWER 'OVER'

The second, albeit closely related meaning of power lies in the idea of *domination*, or power 'over'. This understanding of power brings to the fore the more relational and sometimes conflictual aspects of power[38] that are not captured by the meaning of power that was detailed in the section above. It suggests a less positive, more malign form of power since it articulates the idea that the dominating effects of the exercise of power may mean that one party is acting against their will and/or against their own interests. In this respect, Pascal Lokiec's contribution (Chapter 1) characterises power as '... the ability to impose one's will on others'. Lokiec's own analysis focuses specifically on the contractual instrument as the site through which various patterns of inter-party power play out, and which place one party in a position of domination over the other. But a different general definition may be required if we are to also capture wider forms of power 'over'. For example, instances of power that are discursive in nature and which shape norms and ideas and which, as we will later see, may normalise and reproduce inequalities. We also need to capture forms of power (and here is specifically meant *economic* power) such as that held by a corporation in a monopoly position and which may influence whole markets and, thus, the broader conditions within which contracting takes place. Further, power may such that it secures compliance with the goals of the power-holder, not by overcoming their will but by altering their internal desires in ways that subvert what they actually want.[39] Perhaps power 'over' might therefore be more generally defined as the ability to affect the physical and mental state of another, or of the world around us.[40] This definition also has the advantage of embracing instances of power that are

---

37 Ibid., p. 220.

38 S. Lukes, above n. 14, p. 39.

39 See the contribution by N. Connolly in this volume.

40 For this definition, see K. Barker, S. Degeling, K. Fairweather and R. Grantham (eds.), *Private Law and Power*, above n. 12, p. 7.

productive or emancipatory, such as the disciplining force of the law when it corrects unequal power relations and protects the more vulnerable.

## 3.1. POWER AT THE NEGOTIATION STAGE

Power over another may arise and have coercive effects at the negotiation state, just as much as during the life cycle of the contract, including at the enforcement stage. Two chapters focus on the negotiation stage as an important site of power. Tom Hick in Chapter 7 highlights the power dynamics during negotiations which prevent a contract from ever coming into being, what he describes as a 'no-contract' situation. Hick's focus is on commercial contracts where the market dominance of one negotiating party means that their perceived 'disagreement point'[41] (perhaps better described in this context as the 'threat point') is weighted so far in their favour that they are in the position to be able to reject the offer from the counterparty and choose not to contract with them. The greater the economic dominance of the firm, the more that the threat of 'no-contract' is felt and the more detrimental impact is felt by the less dominant firm, sometimes preventing access to markets completely.[42]

The power dynamics that are at play in the no-contract scenario are given very little analytical attention in contract law scholarship.[43] This is because, as Hick points out, the situation of no-contract is not immediately troublesome for contract law and its foundational principles: 'freedom of contract' is understood as embracing the key principle that parties are free *from* contract and this legitimises the ability of the dominant firm to walk freely away from the negotiations. Thus, 'the absence of a contract is a perfectly acceptable outcome' for the law.[44]

Hick's chapter reveals the way that dominant accounts of the law and the language through which the law's organising features and paradigms are presented may obscure or even reinforce phenomena of power. This *discursive*

---

41 See R. Stone, 'Inequality of Bargaining Power', in M. Chen-Wishart and P. Saprai (eds.), *Research Handbook on The Philosophy of Contract Law*, Edward Elgar Publishing, Cheltenham 2025, describing this as 'the state of affairs that would result should the parties fail to reach an agreement' (p. 165).

42 Of course, economic dominance will not always end up in a 'no-contract' scenario and may instead significantly reduce the bargaining power of the weaker party so that resulting contracts are heavily disadvantageous.

43 Aside from regulatory obligations in certain utilities sectors such as water and energy supply.

44 See the contribution of T. Hick in this volume, section 2.1. For recent judicial confirmation of this position, see the UK Supreme Court decision of *Pakistan International Airline Corporation* v *Times Travel (UK) Ltd* [2021] UKSC 40 para. 26; 'Equally, a party in a strong bargaining position, such as a monopoly supplier, may refuse outright to enter into a contract which the weaker party desires.'

power of the law is something to which we will shortly return in more detail but for now we note Hick's point that in prioritising freedom *from* contract, an individualist understanding of contract law is prioritised and, at the same time, the freedom *to* contract of the counterparty becomes de-prioritised and made invisible. The reductive characterisation of freedom of contract renders opaque material manifestations of power at the negotiating stage and may end up normalising exploitative behaviour by the holder of economic power. Moreover, the resultant position is that 'corrections' to the law's starting point – a starting point that gives primacy to a liberal and individualist orientation to the law – must then be applied to account for its harmful consequences. However, these corrections[45] are not just inadequate,[46] they also require classification of the counterparty as *dependent* on the contract and, importantly, as an *exception* to the normal operation of legitimate legal rules. As Marella and Marini observe,[47] this sort of rule-exception relationship establishes hierarchies of power, marginalising and subordinating the 'exception' in preference to the 'rule' and establishing a legal discourse that constitutes and reproduces dynamics of power.

In Chapter 8, Stefanie Jung takes a gendered lens to the issue of salary negotiations where the power dynamics at play between employers and applicants – typically, a relationship of unequal power hierarchies[48] – as well as differences (actual and perceived) in the negotiating behaviour of men and women may result in employment contracts that pay women far less than their male counterparts. This results in what is commonly known as a 'gender pay gap'.[49] Jung's chapter draws attention to the complexity in understanding the causal factors for this pay gap, which in turn problematises the design of effective regulatory interventions. In evaluating the potential of EU legislation (specifically, the Directive on Pay Transparency[50]) for reducing this gap, she observes how the Directive restricts freedom of negotiation in order to rebalance power at this pre-contractual stage. Transparency requirements (such as under Art. 5(1)) and bans on employers questioning applicants about their current and previous remuneration (Art. 5(2)) aim to readjust informational deficits and rebalance bargaining power. The strategy is one typical of neoclassical accounts of bargaining inequalities which aim to correct informational asymmetries between the parties.

---

45 Hick gives examples of such 'corrections' in sections 2.2 and 2.3.

46 This prompts Hick to recommend a 'no-contract law' that provides a response to these power imbalances.

47 Chapter 10.

48 As Jung makes clear.

49 As Jung highlights, this is at a troubling level of 12.7% (as an EU average in 2022).

50 Directive (EU) 2023/970 of 10 May 2023 to strengthen the application of the principle of equal pay for equal work or work of equal value between men and women through pay transparency and enforcement mechanisms [2023] *OJ* L 132/21.

Yet, as Jung argues, the Directive does not address the more deeply embedded gendered dynamics that shape negotiations. Power imbalances at the bargaining table are not simply the product of missing information but are also conditioned by cumulative social and legal norms that construct gendered identities. Stereotypes of 'appropriate' negotiating behaviour for women, for instance, influence both employer expectations and female applicants' self-perceptions, while deviations from these norms risk sanctions through what scholars call the *backlash effect*. These cultural scripts can therefore translate into gender-differentiated pay outcomes, even when formal transparency measures are in place.

By highlighting these layers, Jung demonstrates both the promise and the limits of regulatory intervention. The Directive may reduce some disparities by targeting information deficits, but it does not neutralise the broader social and institutional hierarchies that continue to shape negotiating behaviour and outcomes. The persistence of these dynamics underscores the challenge of closing the gender pay gap through transparency measures alone.

## 3.2. INEQUALITY OF BARGAINING POWER

As both Hick and Jung remind, dynamics of power at the negotiation stage will impact whether a contract emerges at all from negotiations and, if it does, the content of its terms. The notion of 'inequality of bargaining power' is deployed to describe the underlying power issues at play in both these situations. The term describes the situation where the position of one party vis-à-vis the other is more dominant in some way and thus gives them the power to shape the bargaining process in ways that better serve their own interests. To state that transactions are not negotiated in a terrain of identically positioned individuals should not be overly surprising, despite the orthodox account of contract law as embodying a space in which parties come together as equals. The reality instead is that parties come to the bargaining table with a whole range of different experiences, personal and physical attributes, 'situational vulnerabilities',[51] structural or systemic (dis)advantages, and so forth, and the realities of those differences (as well as the perceptions of what each party is set to gain or lose through the transaction) will always give one party some sort of an advantage over the other. In other words, bargaining imbalances are an

51 This refers to inequality that arises from the contracting circumstances and so is a distinct, contextual form of vulnerability, see J.M. Paterson, 'Responses to Unequal Bargaining Power in Consumer Contracts', in J. Gardner, A. Goymour, J. O'Sullivan and S. Worthington (eds.), *Politics, Policy and Private Law: Volume II Contract, Commercial and Company Law*, Hart Publishing, Oxford 2025, p. 152.

inevitable part of the richness and diversity of societal relations and a 'a core feature of market relationships'.[52]

We have thus far hinted that some of the sources which account for inequalities of bargaining power may be found in social, political and economic forces.[53] As Orit Gan sets out in her analytical mapping of the principle (Chapter 2), one source of power imbalance between the parties may emerge from factors that are specific to their particular relationship, those which Gan classifies as 'inter-party' vectors of power. Here she includes differences rooted in particular physical attributes (such things as intelligence, strength or attractiveness) or in 'relational-specific' factors,[54] such as the information held by one party, or their risk averseness. These differences allow, to a greater or lesser extent, one party to mould the bargaining process in their favour.

More broadly, Gan stresses that bargaining power should be understood not as a binary opposition between the powerful and the powerless, but as dynamic, fluid, and context-dependent, operating along a continuum. Her analysis of *Thorne v. Kennedy* (High Court of Australia) illustrates this approach. In that case, she shows how interpersonal pressures, systemic gender and class inequalities, and immigration law as a state instrument intersected to coerce a weaker party into an unfair agreement. For Gan, the Court's refusal to classify these converging forces as duress exposes the risks of maintaining an unduly narrow conception of the doctrine. Building on this, Gan positions duress law squarely within the broader project of policing abuses of bargaining power. She argues that neither courts nor legislators can approach duress in isolation from the wider structures of inequality that shape contractual negotiations. The enduring vagueness and incoherence of duress doctrine, she suggests, stem from the absence of a clear account of what constitutes bargaining power, how it should be assessed, and when its exercise becomes illegitimate coercion.

The wider significance of Gan's contribution lies in her contention that duress law can—and should—serve as a vehicle for distributive justice. By requiring courts to attend not only to immediate threats but also to the social and legal contexts that condition parties' ability to consent, she reimagines duress as an instrument for correcting unjust bargaining outcomes and for challenging the institutionalisation of power in private law. In doing so, her chapter dismantles the myth of contract law as a neutral sphere of equal bargaining and instead reveals it as a system that both reflects and reproduces social hierarchies. By insisting that duress must explicitly account for inequalities across interpersonal, systemic, and state dimensions, Gan offers

52 M. Auer, 'Bargaining with Giants and Immortals: Bargaining Power as the Core of Theorizing Inequality' (2024) *Law and Contemporary Problems* 54, 58.

53 K. Barker, S. Degeling, K. Fairweather and G. Grantham (eds.), *Private Law and Power*, above n. 12, p. 9.

54 See the contribution of O. Gan in this volume.

a sharper theoretical framework and a practical tool for exposing the ways in which the ideal of 'freedom of contract' often masks coercion.

In Chapter 3, Niamh Connolly explores a different form of inter-party power. Connolly is interested in the gendered dynamics of power that arise from the ties of intimacy between partners in a romantic relationship.[55] The deep affection that a woman[56] feels for her partner, Connolly argues, may mean that she internalises the imperative to serve and prioritise his needs and interests. This may leave her in a position of subordination and vulnerability vis-à-vis the man and increase the likelihood of transactional outcomes in which she is disadvantaged.

The power at play here may be easily missed. For example, there are no coercive acts that force the woman to act against her own will. Nor does the power imbalance within the relationship depend on any specific and identifiable characteristic (such as infirmity, poor education, or economic dependence). Instead, power arises in the context-specific nature of the intimate relationship in which the woman's devotion to her partner means that she may 'freely' make a transactional decision that is entirely 'shaped by [her] understanding of the other person's interests'.[57] In this way, 'affective power' steers what the woman *herself* actually wants,[58] supressing her own desires and self-interest in favour of other-regarding motivations. From this perspective, although one might describe transactional decisions as being based on the woman's *own* choices and values and the result of genuine consent, they are nevertheless driven by imperceptible patterns of relational power. Connolly's study demonstrates the need to be wise to a wider range of context-specific vulnerabilities which may be the source of inequalities in power.

Moving away from this form of situational or relational vulnerability, we come to a different form of vulnerability and power inequality that could be said to describe 'a *universal* state of defencelessness and susceptibility':[59] 'digital vulnerability'.[60] In European legal discourse, this term tends to refer to consumer digital markets in which structural patterns of asymmetry between consumers and business facilitate novel technologically driven forms of exploitation and oppression. Such things as data harvesting, dark patterns,

55 Connolly also acknowledges that similar dynamics of power might be present in the parent-child relationship, as well as relationships in which cultural norms play a part.

56 As Connolly observes, it tends to be the woman, rather than the man, that finds themself in the less dominant position.

57 See the contribution of N. Connolly in this volume, section 3.1.

58 Ibid., section 3.1.

59 See the contribution of M.R. Marella and G. Marini in this volume, section 5 (emphasis added).

60 See, for example, M. Growchoski, 'Digital Vulnerability in a Post-Consumer Society. Subverting Paradigms?', in C. Crea and A. De Franceschi (eds.), *Digital Vulnerability in European Private Law*, Nomos Publishing, Baden-Baden 2024.

and personalisation of the transactional environment – e.g. personalised 'persuasion profiles',[61] a personalised range of choices that consumers may have access to, personalised contractual terms such as withdrawal rights, and even personalisation of remedies[62] – all these corporate strategies make power a far more pressing problem. They enhance opportunities for extractive practices and (re)produce vulnerabilities and inequalities.

In Chapter 4, Aurelia Colombi Ciacchi, Greta Berardi and Alma-Cristina Onaie highlight the problem of 'algorithmic discrimination' – what they describe as direct and indirect discrimination through powerful private and public parties' use of algorithmic decision-making. One of their central claims is that the grounds of this technology facilitated discrimination are most commonly on the basis of sex, gender, race, or ethnicity. Technology, therefore, becomes yet another vehicle through which corporations exacerbate inequalities for already marginalised groups and, as the chapter argues, infringe on individuals' fundamental rights. Algorithms capture data to automate decision-making in relation to such things as an individual's creditworthiness, about gig workers' reliability, about to whom advertising should be targeted and the prices at which goods should be offered. Although algorithms appear to adopt neutral predictive criteria for decision making appears, the process fails to take account of context and an individual's particular circumstances. This results in indirectly discriminatory effects (price and access discrimination, discriminatory allocations of working shifts for platform workers, to name just two) which may be gendered and racialised and may also have additional intersectional impacts. As technological improvements continue to gather pace and the personalisation of contracting reaches new levels of sophistication, the sort of inequalities and discriminatory practices identified by the authors are likely to be exacerbated still further.[63]

The power imbalances between consumers and employees,[64] on the one hand, and corporations, on the other, that are the focus of their chapter point to structural inequalities in the market framework. Consumers are inherently in a position of inferiority in comparison to firms and these hierarchies create imbalances of bargaining power which may then end up being reproduced and reinforced in contractual relationships. More generally, structural and systemic inequalities arise from the background distribution of resources and opportunities in society that privilege some more than others. These inequalities

---

61 See the contribution of M.R. Marella and G. Marini in this volume, section 5.

62 See M. Artigot Golobardes, 'Algorithmic Personalisation of Consumer Transactions and the Limits of Contract Law' (2022) *Journal of Law, Market & Innovation* 18.

63 See also M. Grochowski et al., 'Algorithmic Price Discrimination and Consumer Protection: A Digital Arms Race?' (2022) *Technology and Regulation* 36.

64 The legal status of platform workers may fall outside the legal definition of 'employee' in some jurisdictions.

may be grounded not just in economic distinctions, but also political and social distinctions, with racialised, gendered, heteronormative, and able-bodied social hierarchies exacerbating inequalities and influencing the ability of one party to secure transactional advantages over the other. Importantly, and as we will now explore, the law may also play a role in constituting and reinforcing these inequalities.

## 4. THE LAW AND DYNAMICS OF POWER

Naturally, all of the chapters centre law and legal institutions in their exploration of power and contract. As the authors demonstrate, the law's relationship with power is multi-dimensional: (re)producing, constraining, normalising and making invisible various manifestations of power. It is clear that the law plays a role in the distributive outcome of transactions and (re)configures the relative bargaining power of contracting parties. If by 'law' we mean public law (and we can include regulation for our purposes here), this may seem a trite observation since power is at the very core of this area of the law. Several of the chapters in this volume analyse the way that public law and regulation attempts to rebalance inequalities between parties and discipline power. However, contributions also unearth the (re)distributive role that *contract* law itself plays, most notably in the shape of its rules and doctrines and in the way that its language and framing of paradigms shape understanding and legitimise power imbalances. In doing so, analysis challenges orthodoxies rooted in the idea that contract law is an apolitical neutral system of rules and that any pursuit of distributive objectives is both illegitimate and ineffective.

To begin, social and economic hierarchies of power may be favoured in the design of the basic operational rules and institutions of private law, allowing the law to provide an institutional means through which power can be legitimately exercised over others. Reigniting the early Realist critique of the law (most notably, Hale[65]), Marella and Marini (in Chapter 10) explicitly engage with the foundational rules of contract and property law and their contribution to structural inequalities. These rules, as the authors powerfully remind, endow individuals with legal rights that establish the foundations for their bargaining power. Property law allocates rights of ownership, creating both owners and non-owners,[66] and in doing so gives owners the right to exclude all others from appropriation. It then gives remedies for defending those rights.[67] These entitlements establish the framework within which individuals arrive at the

65 R. Hale, 'Bargaining, Duress, and Economic Liberty' (1943) 43 *Columbia Law Review* 603.
66 See the contribution of M.R. Marella and G. Marini in this volume, section 1.2.
67 Ibid., section 1.2.

bargaining table and the starting positions for negotiations concerning the transfer of property. Contract law then sets the rules through with initial property rights can be legitimately exchanged,[68] ensuring sanctity of these arrangements through its enforcement mechanisms.[69]

These 'rules of the game'[70] have constitutive power in setting the framework in which social and economic relations take place and in doing so determine which groups and individuals start off in a position of strength and the outcomes that are available to them. It is an *ex ante* distribution of wealth that favours those who start off with entitlements, creating the conditions for ever greater accumulation of wealth for those that are already privileged.[71] Even the seemingly neutral legal mechanism of enforcement of the contract involves the state stepping in to lend its coercive power to enforce the bargain at the request of one of the parties.

All this works to the advantage of those already in positions of privilege. And yet, the foundational nature of these rules seems to imbue them with an almost incontrovertible status which makes them difficult to challenge. Relationships of power become embedded as simply the natural way of doing things. What is more, resistance to challenge is buttressed by the manner of their portrayal in the dominant, classical account of private law. Contract law's self-understanding is that of a system of neutral, apolitical rules which prioritises the contractual freedom of equal parties. From this perspective, the distributive effects of the system are made invisible and any redistributive 'interventions' into the market are shunted to *ex post* regulatory and public law mechanisms. Moreover, enforcement of the contract is viewed as simply respecting the consensual bargain of equal parties. The hierarchies of power that are constituted by the mechanisms of contractual enforcement whereby one contractual party is granted public power to reinforce a private bargain, are hidden within the legal narrative that enforcement is simply respecting freely agreed bargains arrived at by equal parties.

And so, this understanding of contract law as a neutral space of voluntary private ordering, free from any intervention from the state, masks the distributive nature of the system and ends up legitimising and normalising

---

68 M.R. Cohen, 'The Basis of Contract' (1933) 46 *Harvard Law Review* 553, 582.

69 As Hale put it many years ago, '[t]he market value of a property or a service is merely a measure of the strength of the bargaining power of the person who owns the one or renders the other, under the particular legal rights with which the law endows him, and the legal restrictions which it places on others'; R. Hale, 'Bargaining, Duress, and Economic Liberty' (1943) 43 *Columbia Law Review* 603, 625.

70 See the contribution of M.R. Marella and G. Marini in this volume, section 1.2.

71 Building on this, Katharina Pistor makes the more recent argument about the way that private law selectively 'codes capital' and thereby acts as a crucial building block for creating and reinforcing wealth and inequality; K. Pistor, *The Code of Capital: How the Law Creates Wealth and Inequality*, Princeton University Press, Princeton 2019.

the exercise of power over others. We might view this legitimising narrative of contract law as itself a form of power – discursive power – which works to exert its influence through norms and ideas which create structural contexts from which a discipline and its actors understand themselves.[72] Freedom of contract, consent, equality – all these notions at the heart of contract law might sound benign but in practice they make invisible underlying realities of inequality and oppression experienced most acutely by the less advantaged participants of the transactional environment. Contractual freedom is a misleading label to ascribe to a regime that gives structurally advantaged individuals the ability 'to legitimately exercise forms of economic pressure on others'.[73] The notion of consent too is as an empty construct when one of the parties is in a position of dependence, or where, for example, sellers burden consumers with decisions they cannot meaningfully make and a simple click of a box is a proxy for assent to a complex set of legally binding terms. Moreover, describing this as 'consent' internalises the idea that the contract is a result of free will, making it easier to explain away exploitative terms as consensual rather than an exercise of power.[74] Equality too has little substance if a legal regime is based on formal ideas of equality and ignores the many structural and systemic inequalities which establish hierarchies that determine the position of persons when they come to the bargaining table. All these terms are ideological constructs that make power more invisible and far more difficult to challenge.

In addition to the foundational rules of the system, we can also point to the ground rules of contract law as having great significance for the balance of power between parties. By 'ground rules' we mean here the substantive doctrines that govern the subject matter of the contract and thus the contractual relations between parties. The precise shape of these rules has distributive consequences for the parties and for subsequent power imbalances. All of these rules, including their interpretation and application by adjudicative bodies,[75] although of a seemingly technical or apolitical character[76] nevertheless determine such things as the boundaries between consent and coercion; the sort of advantage-taking that is deemed permissible; the extent to which a firm can design their contract to 'seduce' weaker market actors;[77] whether contingent

72 D. Fuchs and A. Hennings, 'Governance by Contract from a Perspective of Power: The Case of Land Grabbing', in A.C. Cutler and T. Dietz (eds.) *The Politics of Private Transnational Governance by Contract*, Routledge, Oxon 2017, p. 61.

73 See the contribution of M.R. Marella and G. Marini in this volume, section 1.2.

74 See M. Auer, above n. 52.

75 See the contribution of O. Gan in this volume, section 3.3. For analysis of how contract law adjudication in the common law courts has contributed to market inequality, see J. Spooner, 'Contract Law When the Poor Pay More' (2024) 44 *Oxford Journal of Legal Studies* 257.

76 D. Kennedy, 'The Political Stakes in "Merely Technical" Issues of Contract Law' (2002) 10 *European Review of Private Law* 7.

77 O. Bar-Gill, *Seduction by Contract*, Oxford University Press, Oxford 2012.

charges are permissible;[78] what sort of inequalities in bargaining power are of legal relevance, and so forth. None of these legal ground rules are apolitical. All will have relevance for the power dynamics between the parties, reproducing and reinforcing hierarchies of power with deeply distributive consequences.

We have highlighted how the organising features and doctrines of contract law may constitute, stabilise and even reinforce societal inequalities and render invisible a variety of forms of oppression. Taking this further, Marella and Marini argue for the importance of looking *beyond* the 'doctrines or rules in the foreground, that is those directly applied to the contract' and analysing the broader matrix of legal rules that may shape societal identities and hierarchies and ultimately generate inequalities in bargaining power.[79] Using the example of family law and its framing of housework as *reproductive* work, they demonstrate how the law produces gender identities which inform the way that women are treated in the marketplace. The 'law of social reproduction' (as they call it) constitutes reproductive work as unpaid work (and thus legally re-defines it as *non*-work) and as an essential part of marriage. In doing so, family law institutions remove reproductive work from the sphere of bargaining and place it outside of the market (and of contract law). Reproductive labour is rewarded by rights in marital property which can be easily waived. The authors argue that the law is not 'just' gendered in its distributive effects. It also reinforces genderised identities by defining (e.g. in divorce cases) women as the 'weaker' spouse *by nature* and obscuring the ideological role that the law plays as a vehicle for channelling women into conjugal regimes of unpaid care work. What is more, the subjugation of women in this way is itself a catalyst for producing hierarchies of power both within intimate relationships as well as outside: women's capacity to enter and remain in the labour market becomes less possible and less appealing.

There are connections here with both Jung and Connolly. In respect to Jung's concern with the gender pay gap, it becomes evident that the social hierarchies created by the law as it undervalues reproductive care work defines the 'essential' nature of women – cooperative, caring, compassionate, etc. These stereotypes position women inferiorly in the 'cut and thrust' of the market and is likely to have an impact on women's value in the labour market and consequently in salary negotiations. In relation to Connolly's preoccupation with power dynamics within intimate relationships, it becomes clear that legal rules that shape genderised identities and constitute women as caregivers, or as cooperative, will reinforce subjugation and reinforce the potential for women to subjugate their own desires for those of their partner.

---

78 J. Spooner, above n. 75.

79 See the contribution of M.R. Marella and G. Marini in this volume, section 3.

Many of the contributions focus on the way in which legislative and regulatory rules may be purposively harnessed to exert a disciplinary force over contractual relationships of inequality in which power may be exercised over another. One way it may do this is by protecting structurally 'weaker' parties in the contractual relationship, bringing bargaining power directly into the law's disciplining gaze. Regulatory rules that govern consumer contracts, or those that govern employment or tenancy agreements, can be conceptualised as emancipatory legal regimes that have as their central protective concern the correction of structural imbalances of power between contracting parties and are a well-documented contribution to the so-called 'materialisation' of contract law.

In governing these contract types distinctly, the law creates categories of individuals – consumers, tenants, employees – for the purpose of assigning private rights, obligations and remedies through legislative interventions that depart from the general rules of contract law. In doing so, a status-based orientation to contract law is reintroduced. In other words, a shift 'from status to contract [and back] to status [again]'[80] can be tracked, thereby exposing the falsity of the 19th century promise of equality which promised identical rights to all individuals.

These sorts of legal protections have been described as recognising the 'human being' rather than the legal construct of 'person'.[81] But, as Hesselink and Tjon Soei Len argue in Chapter 9, the law[82] is 'highly selective as to the material features of persons and relationships it chooses to consider'[83] and which fall within its protective gaze. The regulatory lens is skewed very firmly toward a certain type of human, viz., the consumer, or the employee. The law's 'fixation'[84] on the structural power imbalances that arise in these particular contract types and its disregard for the experience of multiple marginalised persons as they come to private law relationships is itself constitutive of power. The 'colourblind materialisation' of (European) private law might present itself as neutral, but this makes invisible oppression and marginalisation and (re)produces and reinforces the experiences of the already privileged (white, male, heteronormative) sectors of society.

The law's categorisation of persons (consumer, employee, tenant) also makes invisible the heterogeneous identities of individuals that constitute these

---

80 K.I. Schmidt, 'Henry Maine's "Modern Law": from status to contract and back again?' (2017) 65 *The American Journal of Comparative Law* 145.

81 H.-W. Micklitz, 'Person, Civil Status and Private Law', in S. Grundmann, H.-W. Micklitz and M. Renner (eds.), *New Private Law Theory. A pluralistic approach*, above n. 2, p. 344 (citing H. Sinzheimer, 'The Politics of labor legislation in Germany' (1920) 40 *The Annals of the American Academy of Political and Social Science* 35-40).

82 The authors' particular focus is on European private law.

83 See the contribution of M. Hesselink and L. Tjon Soei Len in this volume, section 3.1.

84 Ibid., section 5.6.

groups. As Marella and Marini argue,[85] there is an ideological underpinning to law's categorising practices here. In fusing individuals together as, for example, a unitary 'consumer' group, the law flattens hierarchies within that same group and ignores the richness of the social, economic and material contexts which distinguish individual consumers and their differing capabilities for accessing and navigating markets. This homogenised categorisation is too crude a tool to allow legal 'operators' (judges, lawyers and the state) to direct attention to the factors that affect consumer decision-making and which would identify those particular individuals that might need differentiated protections.[86] Further, when the law categorises in this way and dismisses the diversity of consumers and their individual vulnerabilities, the law's image of the (average) consumer may be such that the protective mechanisms it designs (strategies of information provision and transparency) only empower those that are already privileged.

Other chapters also remind that it is not solely the rules of contract law, broadly defined, which purport to control power and establish 'who gets what' from the transaction. As discussed earlier, Jung analyses the potential effectiveness of the EU Pay Transparency Directive[87] in shaping the power dynamics at the pre-contractual negotiation stage and reducing the gender pay gap. Colombi Ciacchi, Berardi and Onaie (Chapter 4) explore how a combination of the direct horizontal effect of provisions of the EU Charter of Fundamental Rights (namely Art. 21(1))[88] and the Fundamental Rights Impact Assessment prescribed in Article 27 of the EU Artificial Intelligence Act[89] might overcome some of the limits of EU Anti-Discrimination Directives in respect to more effectively tackling algorithmic discrimination. One advantage to this approach, they argue, is that the EU Anti-Discrimination Directives pose structural obstacles in instances of indirect discrimination, since this form of discrimination offers an open-ended justification regime: an indirectly discriminatory provision, criterion or practice can be objectively justified if it serves a legitimate aim and the means of achieving that aim are appropriate and necessary.

Two chapters in this volume analyse the effectiveness of contract law as a vehicle for controlling instances of power as compared to alternative disciplining legal rules. In Chapter 5, Francesco Mezzanotte draws the reader's attention to the issue of 'planned obsolescence', a *de facto* power available

---

85 See the contribution of M.R. Marella and G. Marini in this volume, section 5.

86 Ibid., section 5.

87 Above n. 50.

88 Article 21(1) provides that '[a]ny discrimination based on any ground such as sex, race, colour, ethnic or social origin, genetic features, language, religion or belief, political or any other opinion, membership of a national minority, property, birth, disability, age or sexual orientation shall be prohibited'.

89 Regulation (EU) 2024/1689 of the European Parliament and of the Council of 13 June 2024 laying down harmonised rules on artificial intelligence.

to technology holders that enables them to design hardware or software components to deliberately reduce the life span of manufactured goods. This practice facilitates the extraction of ever greater surplus from consumers who are forced to replace their goods far earlier than would otherwise be required. Yet, the power dynamics in this context radiate beyond the relationship between the firm and consumer since by removing from the market products with a longer life the technique of planned obsolescence also removes more sustainable goods from the market and, in doing so, gives firms the power over important collective issues such as the circular economy and sustainable development. It is a form of private power that allows firms to manipulate the framework of the market to suit their own economic imperatives.

Mezzanotte's aim is to reflect on the proper tools for the regulation of this technological power, proposing a distinction between two different models of legislative control: measures that control 'power *in* the market' and measures that control 'power *and* the market'. The former recognises existing manifestations of power within the market and aims to correct the harmful or inefficient impacts of that power through 'second-order' interventionist measures. EU consumer contract law follows this model. The latter responds to a form of power that generates a different and more complex issue: private economic power that allows producers to determine those 'first-order' decisions related to what falls within the scope of the market logic itself. As the practice of planned obsolescence reveals, this form of power can supplant decision-making that belongs in the public realm and throws up wider regulatory challenges that would seem to naturally lie in public law responses. And so, if this sort of power is to be properly constrained then measures of contractual governance which respond to market failures[90] are poorly suited to the challenge of ensuring that powerful private actors are not able to structure entire markets in ways that determine and degrade non-economic, collective goals such as sustainability.[91]

In Chapter 1, Pascal Lokiec is interested in the control of the different manifestations of power that arise within contractual relationships – he distinguishes these powers as 'factual', 'contractual' and 'extra-contractual'. These three types of power correspond to three different stages in which power

[90] Such as those explored in his chapter, section 3.

[91] The healthcare sector in the US is a particularly striking example of how power can control entire markets, this time in ways that might be especially detrimental to already vulnerable individuals – the clinically sick and poor. It is a sector engineered not around optimal health outcomes, but around the economic priorities of business, including insurance providers, resulting in a market offering products and services that are poorly attuned to the clinical needs of patients (consumers). This provides a vivid illustration of how societal inequalities that give the elites (providers of healthcare services) power create ever greater distributional injustices. For this example, see discussion in D. Markovitz, B. Richman and R. Van Loo, 'Consumer Law as an Axis of Inequality' (2022) *Boston University Law Review* 1169, 1174–1175.

is gradually untethered from its contractual roots and ultimately leads to a legal regime that is properly *emancipated* from contract: a regime that Lokiec defines as 'the law of power'. In this way, Lokiec advocates for power within contractual relationships to be regulated by a regime that is separate from contract law. As he observes, the two logics of contract and power are diametrically opposed to each other: contract is rooted in a legitimising register of agreement and consent, and power is characterised as the unilateral imposition of decision-making on another. If a contract is legitimised by the law as the expression of a voluntary, and free commitment, and individuals arriving at the negotiating table are conceived as equally autonomous and consenting partners, power is not presumptively something that has any place within this area of the law. This means that the contractual control of power must rely on a range of misleading fictions which may obfuscate the very existence of power and render control less effective. It is only if the contractual veil is lifted and power is emancipated from contract that a proper regime of control can be put in place.

## 5. CONCLUSION

The observations made in this introductory chapter alert us to the importance of centring power within analyses of contract and of contract law. Power emerges from a range of different sources, both external and internal to the law, and its impact will be felt by us all as we go about our everyday lives. Some of its consequences may be more visible than others and individuals from marginalised communities or in more vulnerable positions may be differently and more harshly exposed. The law – both public law as well as contract law – has a role to play in redressing some of the consequences of power. Careful consideration is required to determine normative questions about when it is desirable for the law to step in and control power: what are the factors that render power problematic, and for whom? And what sort of controls are necessary? Further, which sphere of law – public or private – and which institutions – judicial or legislative – are most appropriate for the task? Perhaps most pertinently for the purposes of this volume, it is crucial that the law's role in constructing, reinforcing and legitimising dynamics of power is laid bare. As we have outlined in this introduction, contract law has been influential in these processes and yet its foundational principles (consent, equality, autonomy, neutrality, etc.) can mask underlying phenomena of power that reside in social, legal, and economic relations and which are then reproduced in contractual relationships. For this reason, contract scholars have an important role to play in making visible the many ways in which power imbalances and inequalities are not at the periphery of our discipline, but very much at its centre.

# CHAPTER 1
# CONTRACT AND POWER

Pascal Lokiec



## 1. INTRODUCTION

Contract and power is the meeting of two logics that nothing predestined to meet.[1] Everything opposes them. A contract is an agreement of will. Power is characterised by the ability to impose one's will on others. Their justifications are opposed. The contract draws on the register of will, power on that of the common good. The act of power can obviously find its cause neither in the will of its author (that would be tyranny), nor in that of its addressee (the person on whom a unilateral act is imposed does not consent to it). This does not preclude the claims of the contract to be the basis of power, and

1 P. Lokiec, *Contrat et pouvoir*, LGDJ, Paris 2021. 'Regulating the Employer's Power', *Industrial Law Journal*, dwaf015, https://doi.org/10.1093/indlaw/dwaf015.

that of common agreement to justify power. These claims are exacerbated in a contemporary world built on the philosophy of contract, and on the idea that nothing is more legitimate than what is agreed. Numerous powers to impose one's will on others are thus imposed by contract, from the power of the employer conferred by a geographical mobility clause to the power of platforms to delete content in application of their general conditions of use, right up to the power of the state if we follow the theory of the social contract.

But agreement is not enough to justify power, which is only legitimate if it is exercised for the common good, not in the selfish interest of the one who owns it, even if they hold this power through legal channels. Although the control of power is inherent in public law, whose DNA is none other than the power of the state, it is not in the genes of modern private law, both in civil law and common law countries. Through a kind of fiction of equality, it was believed that contract would oust power, which was omnipresent before the development of contract (in France, before 1804), and that relationships between private persons, 'civilised' by the effect of contract, would merge into what would be called, *a posteriori*, the theory of the autonomy of will.

The fiction is long gone! It is true that virtually all relationships between private individuals, right up to employment relationships, even though they are built entirely around the idea of subordination, have been understood, and still are today, as contractual relationships. However, the fiction of equality gradually gave way to the reality of power, and the common good competed with consent as the justification for the parties' commitment in contractual relationships.

The meeting of contract and power is the consequence of the increasing recognition of the existence of power relationships within contractual relationships. It has taken three forms, corresponding to three stages in the process of 'emancipation' of power from contract. The three stages that will be described in this article represent, indeed, a movement towards the emancipation of power from contract, in other words a gradual dissociation of power from its contractual source. In stage 1, power is not recognised as such, but as a fact that upsets the balance of contract. The control of power is thus exercised, indirectly, under the guise of contract. Stage 2, based on the control of contractual power, is an intermediate stage, in the sense that unilateral prerogatives are certainly validated but controlled by means of non-specific legal mechanisms. Stage 3 marks the emancipation of power from the contract, in the sense that the control over the decisions of contracting parties, at this stage, falls entirely outside the scope of the law applicable to contracts. The decisions taken during the course of the contractual relationship are therefore considered independently of the contract that gave rise to that relationship.

Between these phases, we should not look for a chronology that would be common to the whole of private law. Some branches of law are now broadly in the first stage (consumer law, insurance law), while others have reached the third (employment law, company law) and still others are about halfway (distribution law, competition law notably). It is unlikely that all of them will fully emancipate power from contract. Emancipation of power depends, indeed, mostly on choices regarding the intensity of control over power and the characteristics of power that may significantly vary from an area of law to the other.

## 2. STAGE 1. THE PROTECTION OF THE WEAKER PARTY (FACTUAL POWER)

The recognition of power in contractual relationships is reflected, at the first stage, in what is known as the protection of the weaker party.[2] At this stage, power is a factual relationship in which the 'strong' party imposes his intention on the 'weak' party. It is only recognised indirectly by the law which reacts to the effects of power by mechanisms designed to govern the contract.

Faced with this factual power which disturbs the balance of contractual relations, private law adopts two sets of reactions; one, voluntarist, which consists in protecting the free consent of the weaker party to the contract; and the other, interventionist, which aims at limiting the scope of consent, and therefore that of the contract, by the creation of a so-called 'protective' public policy.

### 2.1. PROTECTING CONSENT

In the first place, as a consequence of the inequality of bargaining power between the stronger and the weaker party, the consent of the latter must be sufficiently protected to ensure that the contract reflects the intention of both parties. The mechanism of defects in consent is the traditional way of doing so, with notable developments in the direction of taking greater account of factual power.[3] Since the admission of fraudulent misrepresentation and the emergence of duties to provide information together with a system of burden of proof which favours the weaker party, the mechanism of fraudulent misrepresentation can be ranked among the mechanisms that enable the

---

2 H. Rösler, 'Protection of the weaker party in European contract law: standardized and individual inferiority in multi-level private law' (2010) 18 *European Review of Private Law* 729.

3 I.R. Macneil, 'Unconscionable Contracts and the Doctrine of Inequality' (1965) 32 *The University of Chicago Law Review* 367; H.G. Beale, 'The Doctrine of Unconscionability and the Protection of Weaker Parties in Contract Law' (2000) 20 *Oxford Journal of Legal Studies* 345.

control of knowledge-power. Market power, for its part, is the target of the mechanism of economic duress, albeit with a scope that bears no comparison with that of the mechanisms of competition law.

The most significant advances are to be found outside the traditional route of defects in consent, under the impetus of special laws and European Union law that has multiplied directives on consumer credit, package holidays, travel and tours, distance selling, and the supply of electricity and natural gas. Consumer law is a model in this respect, with strong mechanisms aimed at protecting the consent of the consumer. The major advance over traditional defects in consent lies in the creation of genuine contractual procedures, far from the simple meeting of minds which, in contract law, is generally sufficient to form a contract. Electronic contracts are formed in stages, following verification of the order by the customer, confirmation of acceptance by the professional offering the service and acknowledgement of receipt by the professional offering the service. The cooling-off and withdrawal periods ensure that contracts are concluded over time, as in the case of life insurance, doorstep selling, optional contracts, individual provident schemes, consumer credit and mortgages.

In the process of improving consent protection, one mechanism has undergone remarkable development, to the point of sometimes interfering with the defects in consent, with which it maintains complex links: the duty to inform.[4] After being enshrined in case law and having been deployed in specific areas of law, such as consumer law, the duty to inform has incorporated the general law of contract. As important as it is to inform the weaker party to the contract, we must beware of the temptation to respond to power in contracts by giving the weaker party information so that, supposedly, they consent with full knowledge of the facts. The factual power that inhabits most contracts is not just a knowledge-power. It is also, among other things, an economic power that calls for responses others than a simple duty to inform. Unfortunately, legislators have a tendency to be satisfied with this type of duty, aided by a whole body of legal economic analysis which reduces power in contracts to asymmetries of information. It is thus essentially through information duties that the law has chosen to protect consumers against tacit renewal of the contract, by obliging the professional to inform them within a certain period of time of the right not to renew the contract.

The law is capable of mobilising many other techniques to protect consent, such as formalism, a duty to negotiate before concluding a contract, and administrative or judicial approval of the agreement. However sophisticated modern techniques for protecting consent may be, protecting the freedom of consent of the weaker party is not enough where the contract is made up of

---

4 M. Fabre-Magnan, *De l'obligation d'information dans les contrats*, LGDJ, Paris 2014; J.E. Stiglitz, *The Economics of Information: A Guide to the Theory and Practice of the Market for Information*, Cambridge University Press, Cambridge 2000.

non-negotiable clauses determined in advance by one of the parties. This is what the French Civil code calls, since 2016, 'adhesion contracts'. 'A contract of adhesion is one that includes a set of non-negotiable clauses determined in advance by one of the parties', provides Article 1110 of the Civil code. The recognition of such a contract carries two main consequences: first, in an adhesion contract, 'any non-negotiable clause, determined in advance by one of the parties, which creates a significant imbalance between the rights and obligations of the parties to the contract is deemed unwritten'.[5] The second element specific to contracts of adhesion relates to a specific rule of interpretation. The civil code provides that 'in case of doubt, ... the contract of adhesion shall be interpreted ...against the party who proposed it'.[6]

Even when protected, the assent of the weaker party remains constrained by power relationships. The protection of consent needs, as a consequence, to be completed by a second approach.

## 2.2. LIMITING CONTRACTUAL FREEDOM

If controlling the sincerity of the meeting of minds were sufficient to guarantee that a contract conforms to the common good, private law could be reduced to mechanisms for controlling contractual consent. This is clearly not the case,[7] and public policy has rapidly established itself as the principal technique for integrating the common good into contractual relationships, to the extent that some have seen it as 'the legal configuration of the common good'.[8] Just because a person has consented to an injustice, with full knowledge of the facts, does not mean that it is no longer an injustice.

The most radical mechanism devised in the name of public policy consists of measures of defiance towards the weaker party, with the idea that the power of the strong party prevents him from committing himself in full knowledge of the facts. This ultra-interventionist approach, which protects by limiting the legal prerogatives of the protected person, if necessary by requiring judicial authorisation, is essentially confined to the system of incapacities. More traditionally, public policy consists of prohibiting agreements and contractual clauses that are contrary to the common good, because they undermine free competition, physical integrity or the environment. Article 6 of the Civil Code, which states that agreements must be consistent with public policy

---

5 Code civil, Art. 1171.

6 Code civil, Art. 1190.

7 H. Collins, *Regulating Contracts*, Oxford University Press, Oxford 1999; M. Fabre-Magnan, *L'institution de la liberté*, PUF, Paris 2018; D. Tiplady, 'The Judicial Control of Contractual Unfairness' (1983) 46 *Modern Law Review* 601.

8 P. Malaurie, *L'ordre public et le contrat*, Matot-Braine, Paris 1953, 37.

and morality, defines the principle that contracts must be consistent with the common good. Another example, among many, is the legislation regulating unfair terms in consumer contracts which allows the eradication of clauses that confer abusive power on consumers. What could have been a control of prerogatives conferred by the consumer contract to the stronger party (stage 2) is, most of the time, a more classical control of the validity of the clause. In this regard, the legislation on unfair contract terms will not control the abuse in the exercise of the prerogative (e.g. a clause allowing the professional to unilaterally modify the terms of the contract) granted by the clause but will simply remove that very clause based on its unfairness.[9]

Public policy may appear to be antithetical to contracts, the scope of which it limits by various means, but in reality, it is inseparable from them. It is essentially conceived in relation to contract, as the 'police of contracts'[10] or 'contractual public policy'.[11] This is what leads a French author whose thesis was devoted to public policy, to say that 'public policy and contract lead a parallel existence: they both find their *raison d'être* in the common agreement between the parties, one limiting it and the other proceeding from it. But even if the contract were to detach itself from the intention of the parties, public policy would continue to control the contract'[12]. It is therefore understandable that the expansion of public policy over the years has never called into question the hegemony of contract in private law.

It is only when it is sufficiently developed to lead to the drafting of statutes or where the legal relationship is extra-contractual in nature (extra-patrimonial family relationships for example) that public policy has been able to extricate itself from contractual supervision. Apart from the special case of civil servants, the statute has not ousted the contract. It merely brings together the rules of public policy applicable to different types of contracts, without calling into question the existence of an employment contract. Typically, the status of employment is applicable to relationships that arising from contract.

---

9 L. Miller, *The Emergence of European Contract Law: Exploring Europeanization*, Oxford University Press, Oxford 2011; R. Bradgate, 'Unreasonable Standard Terms' (2003) 60 *Modern Law Review* 582; E. Brant and J. Marie Paterson, 'Consumer Redress Legislation: Simplifying or Subverting the Law of Contract' (2017) 80 *Modern Law Review* 895.

10 J. Carbonnier, *Flexible droit*, 7th ed., LGDJ, Paris 1992, 292. G. Farjat, *L'ordre public économique*, LGDJ, Paris 1963, nos. 7, 14.

11 G. Viney and P. Jourdain, 'Les conditions de la responsabilité', in J. Ghestin (ed.), *Traité de droit civil*, 2nd ed., LGDJ, Paris 1998, 387.

12 Malaurie, above n. 8, p. 19.

## 2.3. THE COLONISATION OF CONTRACT

The contract expresses the intention of the parties, statute law the common good. The equation seems simple. The cursor moves to one side or the other according to arguments of an essentially political nature: should the intention of the parties to configure their relationship prevail, which will favour the contract? Or should it be the common good, which will give the prominent role to statute law?

This classical pattern is being challenged by a powerful movement towards the colonisation of contract, which is seeing the common good integrated into the contractual field. This original model for regulating private law relationships, halfway between public policy and the classic contract, between state interventionism and the protection of consent, aims to give the contract a new legitimacy. It is no longer a question of giving it a content such as the parties intended, but such as they should have intended, but also and above all of the common good. Rebalanced by the judge, the contract here finds a new legitimacy, at the risk, however, of forging an act that no longer resembles, either closely or remotely, what the parties intended![13] For it is one thing to subject contracts to higher values, notably in the name of public policy. It is quite another to reshape it in the name of these same values, with the often denounced risk of forcing the contract.

Even if the phenomenon has tended to run out of steam at the beginning of the 21st century, we are not dealing here with a mere 'fashion phenomenon' even if the attention given by the doctrine to contractual solidarity in the 2000s has since declined. The phenomenon is far more important and traditional in common law systems that incorporate into contracts a large number of terms on the basis of consideration on implicit will but also fairness or reasonableness.

There exist several colonisation techniques. Interpretation is one of them, where the judge interprets the contract on the basis of considerations other than the will of the parties, in particular contractual justice. Incorporating implied terms into the contract is undoubtedly the main technique, although it is less usual in France than in the UK. It is interesting to note that where French employment law multiplied legal texts, English judges incorporated implied terms into contracts due to the lack of applicable legislation.

---

[13] P.S. Atiyah, *The Rise and Fall of Freedom of Contract*, Oxford University Press, Oxford 1979; E. McKendrick, *Contract Law*, Hart Publishing, Oxford 2023; H. Collins, *The Law of Contract*, Cambridge University Press, Cambridge 2003; in France, for the reflexions on *solidarisme contractuel*, see L. Grymbaum and M. Nicod, *Le solidarisme contractuel*, Economica, Paris 2004.

# 3. STAGE 2. THE CONTROL OF CONTRACTUAL PREROGATIVES (CONTRACTUAL POWER)

The recognition of power in contractual relationships leads, at a second stage, to the release of contractual prerogatives. The contract usually defines the rights and obligations of the parties. It may also confer powers on one party or the other, for example the power to unilaterally set the price or to unilaterally modify certain elements of the contractual relationship. These prerogatives are subject to control which, while remaining embedded in contract law, tends to emancipate from it.

## 3.1. THE RECOGNITION OF CONTRACTUAL POWERS

We are, at this stage of the emancipation process, no longer in the presence of a simple factual power, but of a contractual power. This power does not depend on the quality of the contracting party, their position in the contractual relationship, or their economic power, but on the existence of a clause attributing power. The law will recognise, and then control, the prerogative granted to the employer by a geographical mobility clause, the prerogative granted to the lessor by a resolutory clause, the prerogative of the supplier to unilaterally set the price, etc.

Initially confined to the margins of contract law (the power of the agent, the depositor, the client, etc.) or to an exception (the power of unilateral termination in the presence of a resolutory clause or in an emergency), this power has gradually become part of ordinary contract law, with the possibility for a contracting party to intervene alone where, traditionally, recourse to the judge was indispensable. The French regulation of 10 February 2016 reforming contract law thus enshrines a whole series of contractual powers: the power to determine the price in framework and service provision contracts; the power to terminate the contract unilaterally, whether or not there is a resolutory clause; the creditor's power to suspend performance under the non-performance exception mechanism, including by anticipation; the unilateral replacement option, which dispenses with the need to obtain the judge's prior authorisation to have the obligation performed by a third party and to ask the debtor for payment of the sums incurred to that end...

Stage 2 of the emancipation process differs from stage 1 in the mechanisms used to control power, essentially abuse of rights and good faith. Most of all, at this stage, power undergoes a double mutation, which distinguishes it from the factual power that interests the first stage.

Firstly, from being factual, it becomes legal. As a result, the source of power is not a factual situation anymore but a clause attributing power. Such a term, which is generally express, confers on one of the contracting parties a prerogative enabling him to intervene unilaterally in the legal situation of the other contractor. Even if this can lead to the contract being forced, it is theoretically conceivable, at this second stage of the emancipation process, to recognise that contracts contain implicit terms attributing power, and therefore to maintain that the power of termination or unilateral modification (the landlord's notice of termination, changes to working conditions imposed by the employer, etc.) was implicitly 'accepted' when the contract was concluded. This approach is however artificial.

Secondly, the next phase of the emancipation process, i.e. the control of contractual prerogatives, departs from the opposition between a weaker party and a stronger party. Although a contractual prerogative is generally the prerogative of a 'strong' party (the contractual power in employment relationships or in residential leases), it may be held by either a weaker or a stronger party, as in the case of the power conferred by a withdrawal clause. The question no longer arises in terms of a weaker or stronger party. The law does not seek to protect a weaker party, but to control the exercise of power. A power that it no longer seeks to annihilate, because it recognises its usefulness as in the case of unilateral termination of contracts or unilateral price fixing. In this sense, the choice of the legislature or the courts to create or recognise a contractual power rather than requiring the agreement of both parties can be explained by a desire to reduce costs at both the formation and performance stages of the contractual relationship. The cost and duration of negotiation or renegotiation are avoided by allowing one of the contracting parties to decide alone, in other words by granting to that party contractual prerogatives.

## 3.2. AN ANSWER TO THE INCOMPLETENESS OF CONTRACT

Far from the initial myth of the complete contract, the incompleteness of the contract is now widely accepted, that is to say the idea is that it is impossible, in a complex world, to foresee and describe all the events likely to occur in the future, to foresee all the possible scenarios in advance, is widely admitted.

Because the parties have limited cognitive capacities, and because information essential to the proper performance of the contract is sometimes unavailable at the time of conclusion of the contract, they cannot foresee all possible events and calculate precisely what the consequences of their decisions will be. How can a complete contract be drawn up when its purpose is to create a new brand whose success is unknown? Impossible in practice, the completeness of the contract is not necessarily desirable. Even if silence in the contract increases the risk of litigation (the absence of a fixed price when the contract is drawn up encourages subsequent disagreement), an incomplete contract can have advantages in terms of flexibility. Less time is required and less money is spent by drawing up a succinct contract, which reduces transaction costs. The economic argument carries increasing weight, with world rankings such as the 'doing business' ranking that, before its withdrawal in 2021, put pressure, in the name of economic efficiency, on the need to reduce the costs associated notably with judicial intervention. This argument also makes unilateralism an asset! In some cases, the parties will limit the problem of incompleteness by giving their contract a limited duration. The fixed-term employment contract, the term of which is in principle known in advance, although it may be uncertain particularly in the case of replacing an absent employee, thus offers the employer greater predictability than an open-ended contract. The parties may also limit the incompleteness of the contract by defining in advance, sometimes because the law obliges them to do so, the situations in which contractual power may legitimately be exercised: resolutory clause, statutory exclusion (of a company or an association), approval clause, stipulation of a clause allowing the co-contractor to modify the object of his service, etc. In any event, multiple techniques exist to complete the contract: incorporating implied terms into the contract, providing for a renegotiation clause (theories of incomplete contracts give a major role to renegotiation), defining a default rule (for example, if the parties to a contract of sale have not stipulated anything about the guarantee against latent defects, the default rule is that any professional seller is presumed to be aware of the defects with which he is familiar), assigning the power of decision to a third party, whether it be an agent (*clause à dire de tiers*), a judge or an arbitrator. And above all, granting this power to one of the parties!

The use of unilateralism is spreading all the more as it is taking off against a backdrop of criticism – virulent in a field such as employment law – of the judge's interference in the mutual agreement of the parties to the contract. There can be no question of forcing a contract when it is not the judge but one of the contracting parties who is responsible for completing the contract. This in no way means that the judge should refrain from dealing with contractual unilateralism! The fear of arbitrariness that may arise from the waiver of consent in the exercise of the prerogative makes it all the more important for the court to monitor abuses in the exercise of the prerogative, in other words, to exercise effective control over the power.

## 3.3. THE VARIETY OF CONTRACTUAL POWERS

There are many contractual prerogatives. Some relate to the formation of the contract, such as those, increasingly usual in business relationships, which allow either party to put an end to the contractual situation by unilaterally going back on its consent: options to withdraw and to repurchase, Material Adverse Change (MAC) clauses, break-up fees, withdrawal options, etc. Others, even more numerous, relate to its performance, such as the option to choose the terms of performance of the obligation, to modify the subject matter of the contract, to choose the means of performance, to determine the means of exercising a right, to authorise sub-contracting, to implement a non-competition or mobility clause, to call in the guarantor, or to extend the term unilaterally. Lastly, there are other clauses relating to the dissolution of the contract, such as the right to terminate the contract, the right to unilaterally terminate fixed-term contracts, and the right of the client to unilaterally terminate a fixed-price contract, the *intuitu personae* clause allowing the contract to be terminated if the configuration of the contracting legal entity changes, the non-renewal clause if tacit renewal is provided for, the termination for non-performance clause, the depositor's power to demand the return of the property, the power of revocation of the mandate by the parties or the power to terminate the contract if the contracting legal entity changes its configuration.

In these examples, contractual power can be summed up as the attribution of decision-making power to one of the parties. In its most elaborate version, contractual power is attributed to a governance structure. The contract, by definition incomplete, is then responsible for organising an effective decision-making mechanism. The State, in the conception of the social contract, constitutes the most accomplished governance structure, with the contracting parties transferring power to it while retaining control over compliance. Private law groups, whatever their nature, also need a governance structure for their operations, one that will take decisions and, in some cases, have disciplinary powers, as in the case of the Supervisory Board set up by Facebook in 2020 to judge internally the consequences to be given to breaches of its contractual conditions by users, including a recent President of the United States!

## 4. THE PREMISES OF EMANCIPATION

The control of contractual power is a particularly delicate task, interwoven between the agreement of the parties and the need to take into account considerations external to this agreement (the behaviour of the parties, contractual justice, good faith...). Judges will mobilise the mechanisms offered by contract law and, rarely, by tort law (the mechanism of abuse of rights is above all based on fault in French law), if we consider that the exercise of the contractual prerogative is detachable from the meeting of minds on which the contract is based.

French law includes two mechanisms for controlling contractual prerogatives: the duty of good faith and control of abuse of rights. The person exercising contractual power will therefore be penalised if he exercises such power in bad faith or in an abusive manner. These mechanisms are at the heart of the control of contractual prerogatives. However, they have one major drawback, which is that they allow only very modest control of these prerogatives. They were not designed to regulate power.

Far from being specific to French law, the process of emancipation has illustrations in the common law, in a legal system in which contractual reasoning is even more dominant than in civil law countries. Traditionally, the contract is so strong in English law that it is through the prism of implied terms that the control of contractual powers is organised in areas such as employment, distribution or banking relationships (interest variation clauses imposed by a bank on its borrowers, notice requirements in the event of termination of an open-ended employment contract, variable bonuses for employees, exclusive location clauses imposed on franchisees). In the absence of techniques to control contractual prerogatives, such as the duty of good faith, which is only recognised in certain cases (sales, insurance, shipping, bills of exchange, for the most part), or abuse of rights, unknown in common law countries, judges limit the exercise of these prerogatives by adapting the content of the contract, following an apparently purely contractual logic. Unilateral change in the terms on which a non-contractual bridging loan was offered to an employee was a breach of the implied term of his contract of employment that the employer would not act so as to destroy the trust and confidence existing between parties.[14]

This is how the control of contractual power is usually presented in English law, with a source that remains contractual (the implied term) but a regime that is increasingly difficult to link to contract law.[15] Emancipation is in some way in the making but not assumed because of the particular strength of contract in Anglo-Saxon legal thought. Control is therefore exercised mainly by giving the contract an 'implied' dimension. Typical is the Braganza case in which the court implies a term into a contract requiring the relevant party to exercise its discretion in a way which is not arbitrary, irrational or capricious. The reasoning is formally contractual (it refers to an implied term of the contract) but uses an approach built around the control of power, far more familiar in public law.[16]

The next and third step is to recognise and apply the law of power.

---

14 *French v. Barclays Bank plc* [1998] EWCA Civ 1092.

15 H. Collins, 'Discretionary Powers in Contracts', in D. Campbell, H. Collins and J. Wightman (eds.), *Implicit Dimensions of Contracts*, Hart Publishing, Oxford 2003, 253; from the same author, 'Market Power, Bureaucratic Power, and the Contract of Employment' (1986) 15(1) *Industrial Law Journal* 1.

16 *Braganza v BP Shipping Ltd* [2015] UKSC 17.

# 5. STAGE 3. THE APPLICATION OF THE LAW OF POWER (CONTROLLING DECISION-MAKING)

Rather than seeking equality between the 'weak' and the 'strong', which is all the more futile since it is not the law but essentially the fact that creates the asymmetry, is it not better to acknowledge the situation of power and start from a premise of inequality? The idea of 'correcting' the various asymmetries and thus rebalancing the contract is nothing more than the consequence of the fiction of equality of the parties to the contract. From being a presupposition, it has become the – unattainable – objective of the law, albeit somewhat attenuated by the fact that it is more a question of balance than of equality. But can we be satisfied with this corrective logic and accept that the balance of contractual relations depends on an imbalance in the duties imposed on the parties, that 'the modern contracting party … comes to demand contractual equality only to seek, in his own name, the benefits of radical inequality'?[17]

Inequalities can undoubtedly fulfil a function of social justice. It is not appropriate, however, to develop unequal law in the name of equality. When it is no more than a fiction, the supposed cooperation between the parties cannot, in the name of an ideal of solidarity and fraternity, mask the existence of a relationship of power and the inevitable antagonisms that this generates. From this point of view, loyalty, which is intended to apply just as much to the weaker party as to the stronger party – hence the rise in labour law of the breach of loyalty as a disciplinary offence – far from being sufficient to curb power, can sometimes even reinforce it.

## 5.1. THE EMANCIPATION

In the third stage, power becomes completely autonomous from contract. At this point, we are dealing with an extra-contractual power that no longer needs the contract to exist. In principle, this legal power is conferred by law, by means of rules attributing power, and may be delegated under certain conditions. Above all, at this stage in the process of emancipation, the control of power is no longer governed by contract law but by a regime of its own.

Effective control of power requires its emancipation from contract. Once the contractual veil is lifted, power is recognised as such and the ability to impose one's will on others is no longer reflected in unbalanced agreements but in unilateral decisions. Here, the legal system recognises that the weaker party is not expressing a free and informed will, but is having decisions imposed on them. It is no longer a question of correcting imbalances, the asymmetry between the parties to the relationship being a constitutive element of the regime of

---

17 B. Beignier, note sous Cass., 1re civ, 28 mars 2000, *D.*, 2000, Jur., p. 574.

power, but of controlling the latter directly. The change of perspective is radical, because the regime of power is by definition satisfied with an asymmetrical relationship and, far from seeking to conceal power, it protects it.

This paradigm shift is not self-evident, given that the drafters of the Civil Code, backed up two centuries later by a powerful movement towards the contractualisation of law (public law, family law, environmental law, etc.), chose to base almost all relationships between private individuals on the contractual model. Postulating that the firm or the employment relationship are contracts was not enough, however, to erase the very high degree of unilaterality that inhabits these relationships!

Emancipating power serves a dual purpose.

First, it makes it possible to preserve the law of contract by removing its claim to regulate power and by maintaining the links between contract and the intention or expectations of parties. The function of contract law is, by the nature of the contract, the satisfaction of the expectations of individuals in society, not the control of power. Even if the law of power shares with contractual solidarity the search for the common good, the path followed to achieve it could not be more different.

Second, il guarantees effective control of power, much more than the law applicable to contracts. Is it convincing to rely on contract law to control unilateral decisions? Does it make sense to rely on abuse of rights or good faith as a basis for requiring contradiction or checking the reasons for a unilateral decision, or even, as is sometimes envisaged, for combating discrimination? Is it sufficient to reconfigure the contractual relationship to make it one of cooperation, and thus control power by requiring its holder to be loyal to those on whom his decisions are imposed? Power is governed more effectively by a regime of its own. The control of proportionality, the increased importance of adversarial proceedings outside the trial, and the requirements of legitimate grounds which are deployed in a whole area of private law form a coherent regime: the law of power.

## 5.2. THE REGIME

The law of power is built around two series of requirements.

The first is the respect for a fair decision-making procedure. Private law is, indeed, gradually developing an elaborate system for controlling decision-making in situations of power. Can we accept that the person who exercises power should decide without constraints, given that consent cannot, by definition, constitute such a constraint in the case of a unilateral decision? The elimination of this essential guarantee that consent represents explains why it must be replaced by compliance with a procedure. While the mutual agreement is an acceptable way of forming a legal act, unilateral intention, should it be orally expressed, alone cannot be binding.

Several techniques can be used to define an acceptable decision-making process. Firstly, a requirement for consultation, obliging the person making the decision to discuss it with the person on whom they are going to impose the decision. A requirement for advance notice, which makes it possible to delay the effects of the unilateral decision. Requiring the decision maker to express by writing the reasons for his decision constitutes another requirement of procedural fairness. The procedure must be more or less elaborate depending on the importance of the decision to be taken. The termination of an employment contract provides a good example of the application of the procedural requirements of the law of power, since the employer must organise an interview with the employee he wishes to dismiss, apply a notice period and notify in writing the reasons for his decision.

The second is the requirement that the decision should be based on a legitimate reason. A requirement that cannot be based solely on mechanisms aimed at controlling contractual prerogatives (abuse of rights, good faith), and that cannot be confused with a formal notification of reasons for the decision. However satisfactory the development of the duty to formalise by writing the reasons may be from the point of view of controlling private powers, formalising the reasons of the decision is not the same as being required to provide fair reasons, with the possibility of recourse to the judge if the ground is unfair.

The control of justification is based on an indeterminate notion (the decision must be reasonable, legitimate, in the company's interest, etc.), so as not to annihilate power. Anyone who is forced to act without the slightest room for manoeuvre has no power. For example, if an employer is forced to lay off employees as soon as his orders drop by a certain percentage, precisely defined by the law, we can consider that he is deprived of his power. There exist various techniques for checking that the decision is justified, most of them imported from public law, starting with Wednesbury Unreasonableness.

## 5.3. THE EXPANSION

Omnipresent in employment law and company law, this system, built around a dual requirement of procedure and just cause, is becoming increasingly important outside these areas. It is to be found in consumer law, competition law, medical law, etc., with an intensity that differs from one field to another. Outside the traditional areas, understanding private power using the tools of the law of power is useful for framing the power of Big Techs over their users, or algorithmic decision-making. In this sense, recognising that Big Techs, under the contractual envelope of their general terms and conditions, exercise power over our personal and professional lives, is necessary if the decisions they take are to be monitored and subject to the procedural and justification requirements of the law of power. Even if Twitter's exclusion of a user on the grounds that they are calling for violence is justified, it is necessary to place these private powers within a legal framework other than that of the law of contract. Similarly, under the guise of automatic processes, algorithms become part of real decision-making processes, which must be controlled. 'Processing of this kind should be accompanied by appropriate safeguards, which should include specific information for the data subject as well as the right to obtain human intervention, to express his or her point of view, to obtain an explanation as to the decision taken as a result of this type of evaluation and to contest the decision', states the General Data Protection Regulation (GDPR). The European Union Artificial Intelligence Act[18] and, more directly, the Directive on Improving Working Conditions in Platform Work[19] enable a control of algorithmic decisions consistent with the regime of power. The latter Directive ensures that workers receive information and explanations for significant decisions made by algorithms, such as suspensions or dismissals. It also gives them the right to human oversight, to protection against discriminatory algorithmic decisions. In other words, it establishes a fair decision-making process, with the possibility of judicial recourse, which more broadly aligns with the perspective of controlling private powers.

## 6. CONCLUSION

The time has come to recognise that the law of contract coexists with a distinct regime, dedicated to the control of power. A regime whose mechanisms, familiar from public law, are increasingly present in the control of private actors' decisions. Just as the law of contract permeates public law through the well-known phenomenon of contractualisation, the law of power is now permeating private law, through the control of decision-making processes. Locked in the guardianship of the contract, this legal regime has never really been able to emerge in private law, and when it has, it has often been under cover of contractual mechanisms that render opaque, sometimes illegible, the phenomenon of emancipation of power that was taking place. Alongside the contract and status pair, the contract and power pair also coexist as a framework to analyse the evolution of private law.

---

18 Regulation (EU) 2024/1689 of the European Parliament and of the Council of 13 June 2024 laying down harmonised rules on artificial intelligence and amending Regulations (EC) No 300/2008, (EU) No 167/2013, (EU) No 168/2013, (EU) 2018/858, (EU) 2018/1139 and (EU) 2019/2144 and Directives 2014/90/EU, (EU) 2016/797 and (EU) 2020/1828 (Artificial Intelligence Act).

19 Directive (EU) 2024/2831 of the European Parliament and of the Council of 23 October 2024 on improving working conditions in platform work.

# CHAPTER 2
# DURESS LAW AND POWER

Orit GAN



## 1. INTRODUCTION

The doctrine of duress has gained much scholarly attention from different theoretical perspectives. Nevertheless, duress law remains vague and inconsistent. This chapter endorses one theoretical perspective and focuses on duress as a doctrine aimed at policing imbalance of bargaining power between the parties. Therefore, duress law needs a clear and structured view of bargaining power. To that end this chapter provides a map of three vectors of power: the first is interpersonal power between the parties, which is the advantage a party has because of personal traits or relational-specific circumstances; the second is systemic social inequalities, which is the advantage a party has due to their dominant social position; and the third is state power, which is the advantage a party has due to legislation, regulation or a court decision. These vectors of power intersect and work together in each case. Therefore, this chapter provides a structured map to decide duress cases, thereby mitigating bargaining power inequalities. Indeed, courts struggle to apply duress. This chapter shows both how and why courts (and other governmental branches) need to consider imbalance of bargaining power.

The chapter proceeds as follows: section 2 briefly surveys the different theoretical perspectives on duress, focusing on duress as a doctrine aimed at policing bargaining power inequality between the parties. To achieve the goal of mitigating bargaining power imbalance duress law needs a clear notion of what factors build bargaining power, how they are measured, what bargaining power is legitimate, and generally what abuses of bargaining power fall under the doctrine of duress. To that end section 3 provides a map of three vectors of power: interpersonal power between the parties; systemic social inequalities; and state power. Section 3 closes with an analysis of the intersection of these vectors of power. Section 4 uses the map to analyse *Thorne v. Kennedy*,[1] a decision by the High Court of Australia. This section demonstrates how analysis of the vectors of power is used to determine a duress claim in this case.

This chapter makes two contributions. First, mapping the three vectors of power and their intersection enriches the literature on inequality of bargaining power. The concept of bargaining power is difficult to define and measure.[2] The map provided shows what factors are legally relevant and what imbalance of power means. Furthermore, the mapping also enriches the theoretical literature on duress law, focusing on duress as a doctrine aimed at policing abuse of bargaining power. Duress law is still unclear and incoherent despite the rich scholarship on duress.[3] The map provided offers a structured view of the bargaining power imbalance to be applied under duress law.

Second, this chapter enriches the discussion on *Thorne v. Kennedy*.[4] The chapter argues that, based on analysis of the bargaining power imbalance between the parties in this case, the High Court should have invalidated the contract due to duress. The High Court based its decision on undue influence and unconscionability, and left the duress claim undecided.[5] However, based

---

1 *Thorne v. Kennedy* (2017) 263 CLR 85; [2017] HCA 49.

2 R.A. Dahl, 'The Concept of Power' (1957) 2 *Behavioral Science* 201; R. Fisher, 'Negotiating Power: Getting and Using Influence' (1983) 27 *American Behavioral Scientist* 149; R.S. Adler and E.M. Silverstein, 'When David Meets Goliath: Dealing with Power Differentials in Negotiations' (2000) 5 *Harvard Negotiation Law Review* 1.

3 G.M. Giesel, 'A Realistic Proposal for the Contract Duress Doctrine' (2005) 107 *West Virginia Law Review* 443.

4 D. Thampapillai, 'Archetypes of Age and Romance: Unconscionable Conduct and the High Court in *Thorne v Kennedy*' (2018) 37(2) *University of Queensland Law Journal* 299; R. Grossi, 'The Discomfort of *Thorne v Kennedy*: Law, Love and Money' (2019) 44(4) *Alternative Law Journal* 281; S. Thompson, 'Feminist Relational Contract Theory: A New Model for Family Property Agreements' (2018) 45 *Journal of Law and Society* 617.

5 J. Eldridge, 'Lawful-Act Duress and Martial Agreements' (2018) 77 *Cambridge Law Journal* 32; F. Maher, 'Clarity or confusion? Duress, undue influence and unconscionable conduct in the High Court' (2018) 12 *Journal of Equity* 91; C. Carr, 'Lawful act duress in Australia' (2020) 13 *Journal of Equity* 292 (criticising the High Court for not deciding the issue of duress).

on analysis of the inequalities of bargaining power between the parties, this chapter concludes that this decision demonstrates a case of duress due to abuse of bargaining power by the stronger party.

## 2. DURESS LAW AND POWER – THEORY

Duress law has gained much scholarly attention.[6] Scholars have analysed duress law from different theoretical perspectives and offered different rationales. The following is a brief review demonstrating the rich and varied theoretical literature of duress. As this chapter focuses on one theory only, it gives only a short review, rather than a detailed and thorough examination, of the main perspectives in duress literature, providing the necessary background before discussing one theory of duress in detail.

According to will theory, duress is a defect in the formation of contract or an excuse and an exception to the rule of contracts enforcement.[7] It is a defence in cases of involuntary bargains where freedom of contract does not apply due to coercion, threats, pressure, or compulsion. In duress cases, consent to a contract is invalid since it was not freely given. According to economic analysis, duress is a case of coercion leading to inefficient results.[8] Duress may lead to undesirable incentives: wasteful efforts to engage in coercion; inefficient precautions to avoid coercion, and reduced investment motives. Right-based theories distinguish offers from threats.[9] An offer increases and a threat decreases the alternatives open to the other party. This distinction between offers and threats provides a baseline to protect the aggrieved party's right. Fairness theories of contract endorse the equality of exchange principle and are concerned with fair allocation of the contract's benefits and other distributive considerations.[10] After this brief survey of the main theories of

---

6 See e.g., A. Wertheimer, *Coercion*, Princeton University Press 1987; P. Westen, 'Freedom and Coercion – Virtue Words and Vice Words' (1985) *Duke Law Journal* 541.

7 J.L. Hill, 'A Utilitarian Theory of Duress' (1999) 84 *Iowa Law Review* 275; J. Kostritsky, 'Stepping Out of the Morass of Duress Cases: A Suggested Policy Guide' (1989) 53 *Alabama Law Review* 583; R.L. Hale, 'Bargaining, Duress and Economic Liberty' (1943) 43 *Columbia Law Review* 603.

8 R.A. Posner, 'Gratuitous Promises in Economics and Law' (1977) 6 *Journal of Legal Studies* 411, 421–424; O. Bar-Gill and O. Ben-Shahar, 'The Law of Duress and the Economics of Credible Threats' (2004) 33 *Journal of Legal Studies* 391; S. Shavell, 'Contractual Holdup and Legal Intervention' (2007) 36 *Journal of Legal Studies* 325.

9 R. Nozick, 'Coercion' in S. Morgenbesser, P. Suppes and M. White (eds.), *Philosophy, Science and Method. Essays in Honor of Ernest Nagel*, St. Martin's Press, New York 1969, p. 440; R. Nozick, *Anarchy, State and Utopia*, Basic Books, New York 1974.

10 J. Gordley, 'Equality in Exchange' (1981) 69 *California Law Review* 1587; P. Benson, 'Abstract Right and the Possibility of Nondistributive Conception of Contract: Hagel and Contemporary Contract Theory' (1989) 10 *Cardozo Law Review* 1077; H.G. Frankfurt, 'Coercion and Moral Responsibility' in T. Honderich (ed.), *Essays on Freedom of Action*

duress demonstrating the richness of duress law scholarship, I turn to focus on one theory of duress.

This chapter focuses on duress as a doctrine aimed at policing abuse of bargaining power by the more powerful party. This theoretical perspective of duress has been endorsed by scholars. Dawson has argued that 'it is through duress and related ideas that private law has dealt most directly with problems raised by inequality in bargaining power'.[11] He has claimed that economic duress is based on notions of fair exchange and unjust enrichment as 'our courts cannot remain indifferent, in fact are not indifferent, to excessive and unjustified gains that are directly traceable to disparity in bargaining power'.[12] Similarly, Ogilvie has suggested that 'economic duress by threatened breach of contract is the unconscionable abuse of a superior bargaining position to place the victim of the threats in the position of having no commercially viable alternatives to submission to the threats'.[13]
Bigwood has also claimed that

> there are clearly limits to the use of comparative strength in contracting. Ostensibly in the name of fairness considerations, the strong must on occasion become subject to various checks on the exercise of their physical or, more commonly nowadays, economic strength. This especially obtains where the exercise of such strength or power (through the use of 'threats') can be said to actively 'exploit' the weak or vulnerable and to jeopardise the integrity of the bargaining process itself.[14]

Keren has observed that the doctrine of duress polices abuses of imbalance of power by the stronger party.[15] She has advocated expanding the doctrine of duress to protect more disadvantaged parties and to police more cases of inequality of bargaining power. In my previous work, I have also endorsed a view of duress as correcting power imbalances between the parties and have proposed a broader doctrine of duress that includes 'economic imbalance,

---

[1973], Routledge Revivals, London 2015, p. 65; S. Lifshitz, 'Distress Exploitation Contracts in the Shadow of No Duty to Rescue' (2008) 86 *North Carolina Law Review* 315; F.H. Buckley, 'Three Theories of Substantive Fairness' (1990) 19 *Hofstra Law Review* 33; S.N. Thal, 'The Inequality of Bargaining Power Doctrine: The Problem of Defining Contractual Unfairness' (1988) 8 *Oxford Journal of Legal Studies* 17.

11 J.P. Dawson, 'Economic Duress: An Essay in Perspective' (1947) 45 *Michigan Law Review* 253, 253.

12 Ibid., 290.

13 M.H. Ogilvie, 'Economic Duress, Inequality of Bargaining Power and Threatened Breach of Contract' (1981) 26 *McGill Law Journal* 289, 318.

14 R. Bigwood, 'Coercion in Contract: The Theoretical Constructs of Duress' (1996) 46 *University of Toronto Law Journal* 201, 202.

15 H. Keren, *Contract Law from a Feminist Perspective*, The Harry and Michael Sacher Institute for Legislative Research and Comparative Law, Jerusalem 2005, p. 186.

relational dynamics between the parties, and other social factors and circumstances that provide a backdrop to the contract'.[16]

Scholars have also engaged with the issues of imbalance of bargaining power in general.[17] Stone has showed that inequality in bargaining power has legal consequences (such as invalidating the contract due to duress or other doctrines) and is relevant from different theoretical perspectives.[18] Barnhizer has argued that the law should develop an 'inequality of bargaining power' concept that is based on the understanding that power is omnipresent (every party has bargaining power), complex (bargaining power is situational, arising from different sources and taking various forms) and dynamic (bargaining power may change in different circumstances).[19]

Auer has explained that bargaining power impacts how the contract's surplus is distributed between the parties. The legal regulation of market interactions aims to correct bargain inequalities. However, Auer has warned that legal intervention is unlikely to affect the distributive outcomes of capitalist market regimes.[20] Hart has explained that modern contract law has not changed formation of contract, which is still governed by classical law. However, 'contract formation, particularly in the doctrine of mutual assent, is where the power in contracting is created, embedded, and, under modem contract law, largely immunised from effective challenge by the contract policing doctrines'.[21] Therefore, she has warned that modern contract law has not solved but rather expanded the problem of coercion. She has concluded that inequality of bargaining power, rather than freedom and consent, are the cornerstones of modern contract law, and that contract law promotes and privileges these imbalances of power.[22] Inequality of bargaining power is institutionalised and concealed under modern contract law, to the detriment of underpowered parties, since it gives powerful parties licence to coerce and to benefit from unfair bargains with impunity. Helveston and Jacobs have argued that courts and academics take different views on bargaining power

---

16 O. Gan, 'Contractual Duress and Relations of Power' (2013) 36 *Harvard Journal of Law and Gender* 171, 175.

17 D.D. Barnhizer, 'Power, Inequality and the Bargain: The Role of Bargaining Power in the Law of Contract – Symposium Introduction' (2006) *Michigan State Law Review* 841.

18 R. Stone, 'The Inequality of Bargaining Power Principle' in P. Saprai and M. Chen-Wishart (eds.), *Research Handbook on the Philosophy of Contract Law*, Edward Elgar Publishing, 2025, p. 165.

19 D.D. Barnhizer, 'Inequality of Bargaining Power' (2005) 76 *University of Colorado Law Review* 139.

20 M. Auer, 'Bargaining with Giants and Immortals: Bargaining Power as the Core of Theorizing Inequality' (2024) 86 *Law and Contemporary Problems* 53.

21 D.K. Hart, 'Contract Formation and the Entrenchment of Power' (2009) 41 *Loyola University Chicago Law Journal* 175, 182.

22 D.K. Hart, 'Contract Law Now-Reality Meets Legal Fictions' (2011) 41(1) *University of Baltimore Law Review* 1.

but have failed to develop a clear and coherent definition of bargaining power, and therefore legislation and regulation are better positioned to police the advantage-taking of superior bargaining power.[23] This chapter enriches this scholarship on duress as a doctrine aimed at policing imbalances of bargaining power.

## 3. DURESS LAW AND POWER – MAP

This section contributes to the literature on duress as a tool to police imbalances of bargaining power between parties, and to the literature on inequality of bargaining power (discussed in the previous section), by mapping the different vectors of power. Courts and scholars have found it hard to define bargaining power, to determine which imbalances of bargaining power warrant legal intervention, and generally to apply duress law.[24] Courts and scholars also found it hard to draw the line between valid consent and invalid consent due to duress, and both consent and duress remain complex concepts that hard to determine.[25] To help courts determine inequality of bargaining power and duress this section provides a map of the three vectors of power that shape duress law: the first subsection discusses the interpersonal power between the parties; the second subsection discusses systemic social inequalities; and the third subsection discusses state power. The last subsection discusses how these three vectors of power intersect.

### 3.1. INTERPERSONAL POWER IMBALANCE BETWEEN THE PARTIES

The first type of imbalance of power is a case where the stronger party pressures the other party and forces them to accede to their terms. This includes negotiation tactics such as manipulation, extortion, intimidation, threats, bullying, and compelling the disadvantaged party to enter a predatory contract.

Kirgis has discussed leverage, which he defined as power rooted in consequences. 'Leverage encompasses all forms of power based on a party's

---

[23] M. Helveston and M. Jacobs, 'The Incoherent Role of Bargaining Power in Contract Law' (2014) 49 *Wake Forest Law Review* 1017.

[24] *Pakistan International Airline Corporation v. Times Travel (UK) Ltd.*, [2021] UKSC 40 (the difference of opinions between Lord Hodge and Lord Burrows); *Martinez-Gonzalez v. Elkhorn Packing Co. LLC*, No. 19-17311 (9th Cir. 2021) (the difference between the majority opinion and the dissenting opinion).

[25] O. Gan, 'The Many Faces of Contractual Consent' (2017) 65 *Drake Law Review* 615.

ability to confer material benefits or impose material costs on a counterparty',[26] or the 'ability to influence another party through the threat of or the imposition of consequences on that party'.[27] 'Positive leverage derives from a party's ability to satisfy the counterparty's interests'[28] while 'negative leverage is derived from a party's ability to impose costs on the counterparty if the counterparty refuses to agree to a set of terms'.[29]

Parties consent out of respect for the other party, because of the other party's charisma or rank, because of stress,[30] because of psychological reasons, cognitive biases[31] or for moral reasons. A party's power may derive from their physical strength, intelligence, organisational authority, confidence, deadlines, attractiveness, focus, or stubbornness. The power of the party is also determined by the relative financial stakes of each of the parties, a party's dependence on the other party, a party's available alternative options, individual traits (such as willingness to take risks, education, intelligence, courage, persistence, intuition), organisational position, information, and morality.

These factors are specific to the parties' relations; that is, one party may employ coercive tactics due to personal traits and to the particularities of the parties' relations, or one party may mould the parties' bargaining in their favour. These factors are all individually attached to the relations between the parties. These interpersonal factors are related to the strength of one party or to the weakness of the other. In other words, these factors are specific to the parties and their relations, which put one of them in a better position than the other. These factors build a specific imbalance of power between the parties. Because of these factors, the parties do not bargain on an equal footing.

It is important to note that in some cases not all the advantages are solely in the hands of one party. Sometimes it is more complicated, with each party holding some (different) bargaining chips. In these cases, some factors could work to one of the parties' advantage and other factors to the other party's advantage. Therefore, rather than a binary approach, whereby each party is viewed as either powerful agent or powerless victim, the courts should acknowledge power inequality on a spectrum ranging from utmost powerlessness to utmost powerfulness, with many situations in between. Thus, the courts should endorse a nuanced, complex, context-specific approach that considers many (sometimes conflicting) factors of power, and strike a balance between them. Indeed, it is a difficult task to distinguish duress from voluntary

---

26 P.F. Kirgis, 'Bargaining with Consequences: Leverage and Coercion in Negotiation' (2014) 19 *Harvard Negotiation Law Review* 69, 73.

27 Ibid., pp. 69–73.

28 Ibid., p. 74.

29 Ibid., p. 74.

30 H. Keren, 'Consenting Under Stress' (2013) 64 *Hastings Law Journal* 679.

31 L.A. DiMatteo, 'Penalties as Rational Response to Bargaining Irrationality' (2006) *Michigan State Law Review* 883.

consent, which requires a delicate analysis of the circumstances. The courts should look at power as a matter of degree, and at the relative power balance between the parties: who holds what bargaining chips? Therefore, the balance of power between the parties is on a continuum: ranging from only one party holding all the power to equal relative power between the parties, with some division of power between the parties in the middle.

Furthermore, power is not static but rather dynamic and may change over time. For example, a young recording artist may have little power relative to the record company. However, over time, she may become a superstar, holding much more power than she previously had. An entry-level junior employee has limited power; however, she may become tenured and then hold a high-ranking position (and generally be in high demand in the job market), thus shifting the power imbalance between her and the employer in her favour. Therefore, the balance of power between the parties may vary over time on an on-going process, such that the parties' relative positions in their relations may change.

In conclusion, each party usually holds some bargaining power due to their personal traits or to specific attributes of the relations between the parties. The courts need to examine the parties' relative balance of power and address abuses of bargaining power inequality. As power is dynamic, complex, and contextual, this is indeed not an easy task. However, ignoring inequality of bargaining power might result in unfair contracts. Therefore, the court's mission of mitigating bargaining power imbalance and policing abuses of bargaining power is important, both from the perspective of just allocation between the parties and from the perspective of social justice generally.

## 3.2. SYSTEMIC SOCIAL INEQUALITIES

The second type of imbalance of power is a case where the empowered party abuses systemic social inequality. The stronger party takes advantage of their socially dominant position and the other party's subordinate position. The coercer did not create these social conditions, but abuses them for their benefit. The party is thus responsible for exploiting the other party's inferior social position.

Contracts of adhesion (standard form contracts) and consumer contracts are examples of systematic market disparities.[32] In these examples, one party

[32] W.D. Slawson, 'Contractual Discretionary Power: A Law to Prevent Deceptive Contracting by Standard Form' (2006) 2006 *Michigan State Law Review* 853; J.F. Hogg, 'Consumer Beware: The Varied Application of Unconscionability Doctrine to Exculpation and Indemnification Clauses in Michigan, Minnesota, and Washington' (2006) *Michigan State Law Review* 1011.

(the business) takes advantage of their better position in the market, and abuses the marginal position of the other party (consumers and customers) in the market. However, Barnhizer has warned against an equal/unequal binary and argued that consumers, too, have bargaining power.[33] Rather than all or nothing he offered a more sophisticated notion of bargaining power. Systemic inequalities of bargaining power are also found in the employment market.[34] As in the previous examples, employers exploit their position of dominance in the labour market. And here, too, it is important to note that while generally employers enjoy better bargaining positions, some employees are also in a powerful position *vis-à-vis* their employer.[35] Government contracts also demonstrate inequality of bargaining power,[36] with the government party in a position of power over the other party (the contractor).

As Barnhizer has stated, 'the practical conception of bargaining power also includes power relations generated by the background legal, social, political and economic system within which the parties interact'.[37] And as West has showed, people consent because they are subordinated, not in order to enhance their well-being;[38] that is, they do not consent, they submit to authority, and they do not agree, they succumb to the power.

Hart has argued that the 'contract law system is premised on class privilege because class is a structural feature of that system'.[39] Class privilege is both obscured and protected under contract law because of lack of attention to these systemic social inequalities. Therefore, class inequality is perpetuated by contract law.

---

33 D.D. Barnhizer, 'Propertizataion Metaphors for Bargaining Power and Control of the Self in the Information Age' (2006) 54 *Cleveland State Law Review* 69. See also, D.D. Barnhizer, 'Bargaining Power in the Shadow of the Law: Commentary to Professors Wright and Engen, Professor Birke, and Josh Bowers' (2007) 91 *Marquette Law Review* 123.

34 J.F. Harris, 'Economic Duress in United States Employment' (2023) 43 *Comparative Labor Law and Policy Journal* 569; R. Arnow-Richman, 'Cubewrap Contracts and Worker Mobility: The Dilution of Employee Bargaining Power via Standard Form Noncompetes' (2006) *Michigan State Law Review* 963.

35 See e.g., *Alaska Packers' Ass'n v. Domenico*, 117 F. 99 (9th Cir. 1902).

36 B.D. Morant, 'The Salience of Power in the Regulation of Bargains: Procedural Unconscionability and the Importance of Context' (2006) *Michigan State Law Review* 925.

37 D.D. Barnhizer, 'Bargaining Power in Contract Theory' in L.A. DiMatteo, R.A. Prentice, B.D. Morant and D.D. Barnhizer (eds.), *Visions of Contract Theory: Rationality, Bargaining and Interpretation*, Carolina Academic Press, Durham NC 2007, p. 85, pp. 97–98.

38 R. West, 'Authority, Autonomy, and Choice: The Role of Consent in the Moral and Political Visions of Franz Kafka and Richard Posner' (1985) 99 *Harvard Law Review* 384.

39 D.K. Hart, 'Revealing Privilege – Why Bother?' (2013) 42 *Washington University Journal of Law and Policy* 131, 142. See also, D.K. Hart, 'Cross Purposes & Unintended Consequences: Karl Llewellyn, Article 2, and the Limits of Social Transformation' (2011) 12 *Nevada Law Journal* 54.

The same goes for other social hierarchies, for example those based on race and gender[40] and their intersection.[41] Thus, when women and black people negotiate (as do other minorities) they may find themselves in a disadvantageous position due to discrimination against them in society.[42] Though the other party did not create and does not control the social structures, they still benefit from them. Taking advantage of social position is lawful, but is still illegitimate, unconscionable, and unfair. Keren has advocated that duress law should acknowledge power imbalance between women and men in our society.[43] I have also advocated broadening duress law to include pressures experienced by women in society and to include the social context. I argued that 'isolating duress from the context of social and economic inequalities normalises more subtle exploitations of economic vulnerability'.[44] Therefore, 'the courts should engage in much broader and more thorough investigation of parties' social constraints and limited choices in society that influence their ability to consent',[45] and 'the courts' definition of duress should include situations in which privileged parties take advantage of their superior social position in order to exploit the other party'.[46]

Taking advantage of social inequalities leads to unfair distribution of the contract's surplus. And as contract law allows powerful parties to benefit from their social position, this means that 'contract law principles are carefully designed to permit and facilitate inequality in exchanges'.[47] For example, women and minorities pay more than men and white people for the same

---

40 D.K Hart, 'Contract Law & Racial Inequality: A Primer' (2021) 95 *St. John's Law Review* 449.

41 For intersectionality in contract law, see L.K.L.T.S. Len, 'Progress Towards What? On the Need for an Intersectional Paradigm Shift in European Private Law' (2022) 1 *European Law Open* 363; L.K.L.T.S. Len, 'Justifying Racial and Gendered Contract in Europe' (2022) 51 *Netherlands Journal of Legal Philosophy* 25.

42 M. Ertman, 'Legal Tenderness: Feminist Perspectives on Contract Law' (2006) 18 *Yale Journal of Law and Feminism* 545; D.L. Threedy, 'Dancing around Gender: Lessons from Arthur Murray on Gender and Contracts' (2010) 45 *Wake Forest Law Review* 749; D.L. Threedy, 'Feminists and Contract Doctrine' (1999) 32 *Indiana Law Review* 1247; H. Keren, 'Feminism and Contract Law' in R. West and C.G. Bowman (eds.), *Research Handbook on Feminist Jurisprudence*, Edward Elgar Publishing, Cheltenham 2019, p. 406; M.M. Ertman, 'Contract's Influence on Feminism and Vice Versa' in D. Brake, M. Chamallas and V. Williams (eds.), *Handbook of Feminism and Law in the United States*, Oxford University Press, Oxford 2022, p. 531; D. Zalesne, 'Racial Inequality in Contracting: Teaching Race as a Core Value' (2013) 3 *Columbia Journal of Race and Law* 23; B.D. Morant, 'The Relevance of Race and Disparity in Discussions of Contract Law' (1997) 31 *New England Law Review* 889.

43 H. Keren, above n. 15.

44 O. Gan, above n. 16, pp. 187–188.

45 O. Gan, above n. 16, p. 194.

46 O. Gan, above n. 16, p. 201.

47 J.I. Harrison, 'Class, Personality, Contract, and Unconscionability' (1994) 35 *William and Mary Law Review* 445, 449. See also, J.L. Harrison, 'Teaching Contracts from a Socioeconomic Perspective' (2000) 44 *Saint Louis University Law Journal* 1233.

items;[48] that is, class, race and gender influence the fairness of contract and the distributive effects of the contract.[49] Therefore, considering these systemic power inequalities means that contract law engages in distributive justice.[50] The personal factors discussed in the previous subsection require just allocation of the contract surplus between the parties. The social factors discussed in this subsection similarly require that contract law correct social inequalities and advance egalitarian allocation on a social level, not only on the interpersonal level. As I have noted,

> refraining from policing the terms of the contract means leaving aggrieved parties unprotected and perpetuating their vulnerability. Courts' scrutiny of the contract should not be viewed as intervening in the equilibrium set by the contract, but rather as correcting any imbalance of power. By allowing the aggrieved party to rescind the contract, the court not only corrects power imbalances but also provides protection against exploitive contracts.[51]

These factors are social and systemic. One party exploits their better social (rather than individual) position, or the other party's social disadvantaged position. Though not responsible for social inequality, one party takes advantage of and benefits from social hierarchies. The parties do not bargain in a vacuum and therefore social factors, not only individual factors, shape their negotiations. In other words, the parties do not negotiate on an island isolated from society, but rather in a specific social setting. Parties are embedded in social relations which affect their negotiations and the terms of their contracts.[52] The parties' relations are set not only by the parties' specific characteristics but also by social factors and attributes. Not attending to these social inequalities would perpetuate them.

---

48 I. Ayres, 'Fair Driving: Gender and Race Discrimination in Retail Car Negotiations' (1991) 104 *Harvard Law Review* 817; I. Ayres, 'Further Evidence of Discrimination in New Car Negotiations and Estimates of Its Cause' (1995) 94 *Michigan Law Review* 109.

49 J.I. Harrison, above n. 47.

50 A.T. Kronman, 'Contract Law and Distributive Justice' (1980) 89 *Yale Law Journal* 472; A. Bagchi, 'Distributive Injustice and Private Law' (2008) 60 *Hastings Law Journal* 105; A. Bagchi, 'Distributive Justice and Contract' in G. Klass, G. Letsas and P. Saprai (eds.), *Philosophical Foundations of Contract Law*, Oxford University Press, Oxford 2014, p. 193; D. Kennedy, 'Distributive and Paternalist Motive in Contract and Tort Law, With Special References to Compulsory Terms and Unequal Bargaining Power' (1982) 41 *Maryland Law Review* 563; H. Collins, 'Distributive Justice Through Contracts' (1992) 45 *Current Legal Problems* 49; M. Jimenez, 'Distributive Justice and Contract Law: A Hohfeldian Analysis' (2016) 43 *Florida State University Law Review* 1265; J. Choi, 'Distributive Justice as a Function of Contract Law' (2022) 7 *Cambridge Law Review* 155.

51 O. Gan, above n. 16, p. 206.

52 S. Thompson, 'Using Feminist Relational Contract Theory to Build upon Consentability: A Case Study of Prenups' (2020) 66 *Loyola Law Review* 55.

In conclusion, a party may gain power not only from interpersonal attributes but also from their socially dominant position. Power derives from social context and is not limited to interrelational context. Though a party did not create the advantage that is due to social inequality, a party may benefit from it and even abuse it. Therefore, power imbalance may not only lead to unfair contracts and unjust allocation of contracts' benefits, but also to perpetuation of social inequalities.

## 3.3. STATE POWER

The third type of imbalance of power is where the state holds power over the parties. The power relations between the state and the parties impacts the power between the parties. First, the courts have the power to either enforce or invalidate the contract; that is, the court has the power either to accept or reject the duress claim (or another claim such as undue influence). Since the doctrine of duress is limited and rarely accepted, this gives power to advantaged parties.[53] They are allowed to coerce others with no legal consequences. Expanding the doctrine of duress means empowering weaker parties and limiting strong parties' abuse of their power. A narrow doctrine of duress means correcting power imbalance in rare and extreme cases and maintaining the *status quo* of unequal bargaining power between the parties; while a broader doctrine of duress means policing exploitative bargaining and mitigating coercion and extortion in negotiations. Both options mean state intervention; however, the first option favours the stronger party while the second option favours the aggrieved party; the first option perpetuates imbalance of power and the other corrects bargaining power inequality. In both cases the parties depend on the courts. In both cases the state shapes the power between the parties by giving power to one party over the other.

Second, the state holds power over parties through legislation and regulation, not only the judicial system. As Kim has argued, 'background law' – that is the substantive law that governs the subject matter of the contract – affects the parties' power in their contract negotiations.[54] And as Barnhizer has claimed, 'courts and legislatures implicitly identify numerous transaction types involving systemic bargaining power deficiencies, thus justifying state policing of interaction'.[55]

---

53 O. Gan, above n. 16.

54 N.S. Kim, 'Bargaining Power and Background Law' (2009) 12 *Vanderbilt Journal Entertainment and Technology Law* 93.

55 D.D. Barnhizer, above n. 37, pp. 121–122.

Adler and Silverstein have observed that the law may shift the balance of power between the parties.[56] Not only duress (and other doctrines such as undue influence, unconscionability) affects the parties' bargaining power, but also labour law, consumer law and housing law, to name a few. Broadly, anti-discrimination laws prohibiting discrimination empower disadvantaged parties.[57] For example, prohibiting sex discrimination improves women's position *vis-à-vis* men, and thus affects their power in negotiations and the terms of their contract. Likewise, anti-discrimination laws promote race equality, therefore empowering ethnic minorities in their negotiations. Legislation and regulation fighting social systemic inequalities may affect the bargaining power discussed in the previous subsection. Through these the state controls the social surroundings, background and context of the negotiations.

As Hart has showed, the state regulates (or deregulates) and constructs the market.[58] Therefore, she criticised the assumption that the market is self-regulating and largely outside of state control. Furthermore, the state decides which contracts are enforceable based on public policy. Hart has concluded that 'The state is as much a party to each contract as the contracting parties themselves'.[59]

Barnhizer has argued that the legal implications of bargaining power are actually about the law's intervention in the private transaction of the parties.[60] Judges decide whether there is an enforceable promise, no contract at all or a voidable contract. Furthermore, legislation and regulation (for example labour law) also intervene in the parties' bargain. Therefore, at the macro level, bargaining power is constitutive of contract, because an enforceable contract can only occur between parties with bargaining power. However, there are transaction types involving systemic bargaining power deficiencies, thus justifying state policing of the interaction. Administering contextual contract law means discretion for judges to shift bargaining power, removing advantages of the strong party and balancing out the disadvantages of the other party.[61] Therefore, the state regulates the market (such as job market or consumer market) and takes part in legally shaping (either perpetuating or making efforts to eradicate) social inequalities.

In conclusion, by either enforcing or invalidating the contract the state holds power against the parties. The parties depend on the court to either give their contract effect and validation or relieve them of the contract.

---

56 R.S. Adler and E.M. Silverstein, above n. 2, p. 28.

57 O. Gan, 'Contract Law, Equality and the State' (2024) 72 *Cleveland State Law Review* 889.

58 D.K. Hart, above n. 22.

59 D.K. Hart, above n. 22, p. 47.

60 D.D. Barnhizer, above n. 37.

61 D.D. Barnhizer, 'Context as Power: Defining the Field of Battle for Advantage in Contractual Interactions' (2010) 45 *Wake Forest Law Review* 607.

Furthermore, regulation and legislation create background rules which set the power dynamics between the parties. Regulation and legislation may police or limit abuse of power, may determine what is illegitimate in negotiations or in the contract terms. On the other hand, regulation and legislation may allow parties to benefit from advantages by maintaining social inequality rather than intervening in systemic social imbalance. Therefore, the state constitutes, and largely shapes, the parties' relations. The parties bargain in the shadow of the law, and thus the law affects their relations. The state (via court decisions, legislation and regulations) gives power to one party or the other.

## 3.4. TRIAD VECTORS OF POWER

After exploring the three vectors of power this subsection examines their intersection.

The state affects interpersonal power imbalance between the parties. The state decides what power imbalance would invalidate the contract via duress and other doctrines (such as undue influence). The state sets the boundaries of what is allowed in negotiations. For example, on the one hand a party may charge a high price because of the other party's high degree of interest in the contract, or because the item is rare and in high demand. On the other hand, a party may not use illegal or criminal threats to extort better contract terms. These are two extremes and there are many coercive situations in between, however duress law as applied by the courts determines what power a party may use, how and to what extent. Duress law determines what coercion is allowed and therefore shapes negotiations. Parties will be careful not to cross the line set by duress law to avoid the risk of the court setting the contract aside. A narrow doctrine of duress leaves many abuses of power legitimate; while broadening duress law would limit the abuse of bargaining power.

The state also affects social systemic inequalities, as the state sets the social background of the contract. Parties bargain in the shadow of the law. Therefore, through legislation, regulation, and court decisions, the state shapes social inequalities. For example, consumer laws, employment laws and housing laws, and even anti-discrimination laws, shape the relations between parties. The state also regulates (or deregulates) the market. The state intervenes in the relations between the parties by either enforcing contracts or invalidating them; by either regulating or not regulating commerce, employment, and housing. By setting an either narrow or broad duress law and by determining how the market would be regulated, the state shapes the contours of negotiations. The parties' relative positions are determined largely by their social positions, which are constructed by the state.

Interpersonal power inequality may supplement social inequality. In this case, the power that one party has over the other derives not only from individual personal features but also from social structure. The power imbalance is determined not only by the party's interest in the contract, for example, but also by social status. The relations between the parties are influenced by personal as well as social issues. For example, in cases of Jewish men refusing to give their wives a *get* (a decree of divorce under Jewish law), they abuse both their superior social position over their wives under Halachic law and their interpersonal advantages.[62]

Sometimes both power vectors pull in the same direction and sometimes in opposite directions. Though usually one party enjoys both vectors of power, sometimes they do not.[63] For example, the power of an employee in high demand may exceed that of the employer who is usually the systemic powerful party. A woman is not always the weaker party due to gender inequality in society; for example, a woman might have a *personal* advantage over a man, though men enjoy higher *social* status in patriarchal society.[64] Therefore, the court must carefully balance all factors in a nuanced contextual way. The court should not automatically conclude personal inequality of bargaining power because of social inequality, but rather engage in a context analysis specific to each case. At the same time, the court should not ignore social inequalities, as they influence the negotiations.

These vectors of power intersect, and there is no clear division between them. For example, social inequalities may amplify personal advantages. State regulations may limit social inequalities or police individual personal advantage-taking. Therefore, determining imbalance of bargaining power is a complex and nuanced task that must take into consideration many (sometimes conflicting) factors. Duress law should be sensitive to the different vectors of power and their intersection. Granted, this is not an easy task. The next section demonstrates how analysis of the vectors of power may be useful and helpful in determining duress.

## 4. DURESS LAW AND POWER – TEST CASE

This section puts the map into practice by using it to analyse a test case. After a short introduction of a decision by the High Court of Australia this section analyses each of the vectors of power, and closes by exploring their intersection in this case. This section demonstrates application of the map, however the

---

62 *Golding v. Golding*, 581 NYS 2d 4, 5 (NY App. Div. 1992).

63 S. Carsley, 'Surrogacy in Canada: Lawyers' Experiences and Practices' (2022) 34 *Canadian Journal of Women and the Law* 41 (examining power dynamics between surrogates and intended parents).

64 See for example how the High Court described the fact the power imbalance between the parties in *Louth v. Diporse* (1992) 175 CLR 621.

map is general and also applicable to other cases of duress. As scholars have commented on how difficult it is to define and detect duress, coercion, and bargaining power, this map is a tool to help courts apply duress law.

## 4.1. *THORNE V. KENNEDY*

At issue in this case were two agreements entered into between Ms. Thorne and Mr. Kennedy.[65] Ms. Thorne was a 36-year-old Eastern European woman with no substantial assets. Mr. Kennedy was a 67-year-old wealthy Australian property developer. They dated and decided to marry. Mr. Kennedy made clear to Ms. Thorne that she would need to sign a prenuptial agreement before the wedding, or the wedding would be off. 10 days before their wedding Mr. Kennedy took Ms. Thorne to see an independent solicitor to review a prenuptial agreement his solicitor drafted. During that meeting he waited for her in the car. By that time Ms. Thorne's family had already flown to Australia for the wedding, guests were invited, Ms. Thorne's dress was made, and a wedding reception was booked. The independent solicitor explained to Ms. Thorne that the prenuptial agreement was one-sided, protecting only Mr. Kennedy's interests, and advised her not to sign it. A few minor amendments to the prenuptial agreement were made, and Ms. Thorne signed it four days before the wedding. A little over a month after the wedding Ms. Thorne signed another agreement identical to the prenuptial agreement. Before signing the second agreement Ms. Thorne met again with the independent solicitor, who again advised her not to sign the agreement. During that meeting Ms. Thorne received a call from Mr. Kennedy asking her how much longer she was going to take. Slightly less than four years into the marriage Ms. Thorne and Mr. Kennedy separated.

The primary (first instance) judge, Judge Demack, set both the prenuptial agreement and the second agreement aside for duress.[66] The judge concluded that Ms. Thorne had been powerless, believing she had no choice but to sign the agreements, and that there was inequality of bargaining power between the parties. This conclusion was based on the following factors: Ms. Thorne's lack of financial equality with Mr. Kennedy; her lack of permanent status in Australia at the time; her reliance on Mr. Kennedy for all things; her emotional connectedness to their relationship and the prospect of motherhood; her emotional preparation for marriage; and the 'publicness' of her upcoming marriage.

---

65 *Thorne v. Kennedy* (2017) 263 CLR 85; [2017] HCA 49.

66 Ibid., paras. 44–48.

The Full Court of the Family Court of Australia (Strickland, Aldridge and Cronin J.J.) overturned the primary judge's ruling, concluding that the agreements had not been vitiated by duress, undue influence, or unconscionable conduct.[67] The High Court of Australia (the plurality, Kiefel C.J., Bell, Gageler, Keane and Edelman J.J.) held that the agreements were voidable because of undue influence and unconscionable conduct, based on the findings of the primary judge.[68] The plurality held that it was not necessary to consider duress. Nettle J. held that there was no duress.[69]

The next subsections apply the map provided in the previous section and conclude that in this case the High Court should have held the agreements invalid for duress. Indeed, this is a difficult case to determine duress, as evident by the different conclusions of the different judges regarding the validity of the agreements, and by the fact that the High Court did not rule on the issue of duress in this case. The map provided in the previous section could help determine duress in this case (as in other cases).

## 4.2. INTERPERSONAL POWER IMBALANCE BETWEEN THE PARTIES

As explained in subsection 3.1,[70] the first vector of power is due to personal pressure which one party put on the other party. The stronger party forces the other party by their illegitimate coercion. The powerful party abuses their personal advantage over the other party.

In *Thorne v. Kennedy*, Ms. Thorne signed the agreements after receiving independent legal advice;[71] however, that did not mean she was free from the pressures of Mr. Kennedy. She was presented with the agreement, and she signed it shortly before the wedding. She met with her solicitor while Mr. Kennedy waited in the car. The prenuptial agreement was drafted by Mr. Kennedy's lawyer and presented to Ms. Thorne as a non-negotiable contract, and indeed only minor amendments to the prenuptial agreements were made. Not only was the contract presented to Ms. Thorne at the last minute, but Mr. Kennedy made it clear that there would be no wedding unless she signed the prenuptial agreement. Ms. Thorne had little time to reflect or think about the meaning of the agreement. Furthermore, not only did she sign the prenuptial agreement only a few days before the wedding, but also under emotional pressure since her

67 Ibid., paras. 49–53.

68 Nettle and Gordon J.J. held that the agreements should be voidable for unconscionable conduct only.

69 (2017) 263 CLR 85; [2017] HCA 49, para. 70.

70 Section 3.1.

71 F. Maher and S. Puttick, 'Reconsidering Independent Advice: A Framework for Analysing Two-Party and Three-Party Cases' (2020) 43 *UNSW Law Journal* 218.

family had flown to Australia for the wedding and was accommodated by Mr. Kennedy, other guests were invited to the wedding, and she was in the midst of wedding organisations (her dress was ready, and the reception was booked). Mr. Kennedy created the pressure by timing the signing of the prenuptial, by conditioning the wedding on entering into the agreement, and by presenting the prenuptial as a take-it-or-leave-it agreement except for minor changes. At the time Ms. Thorne signed the prenuptial she was emotionally invested in the relationship, in anticipation of the marriage ceremony and the marriage itself, followed by motherhood. Also, she was dependent on Mr. Kennedy since she had moved to Australia from abroad, had no family in Australia, and spoke little English. As her lawyer wrote,

> I believe that you are under significant stress in the lead up to your wedding and that you have been put in a position where you must sign this Agreement regardless of its fairness so that your wedding can go ahead.[72]

This stress was all Mr. Kennedy's doing. He was responsible for her state of coercion. Rather than presenting the prenuptial agreement at the last minute and urging her to sign it shortly before their wedding, he should have given her more time to consider the agreement and her solicitor's legal advice, and to negotiate the terms of the agreement.[73] Though Ms. Thorne had independent legal advice, her consent to the agreement was problematic.

In addition to these factors there was also the age difference between Mr. Kennedy and Ms. Thorne, as well as the wealth disparity. Also, Ms. Thorne spoke little English. Mr. Kennedy used these factors for his advantage. As the primary Judge concluded, 'Mr. Kennedy held "[e]very bargaining chip and every power" and did not create any opportunities to negotiate'.[74]

These power disparities were used by Mr. Kennedy to present the one-sided agreement that protected his interests alone. Ms. Thorne's solicitor's impression was that the agreement was 'entirely inappropriate', 'wholly inadequate'[75] and 'the worst agreement' she had seen.[76] Therefore, she advised her not to sign the agreement. The same holds true for the agreement signed after the wedding, since the terms of the two agreements were identical. Furthermore, though the agreement was signed after the wedding, many of the circumstances causing the stress continued.[77] For example, she knew that the marriage would end

[72] (2017) 263 CLR 85; [2017] HCA 49, para. 9.
[73] Ibid., para. 75.
[74] Ibid., para. 106.
[75] Ibid., para. 55.
[76] Ibid., para. 44.
[77] Ibid., paras. 77, 118.

unless she signed the post-nuptial agreement. Ms. Thorne signed two unfair contracts against her solicitor's advice because of duress.

In conclusion, there was disparity of power between Ms. Thorne and Mr. Kennedy. Some of the factors of this imbalance were caused by personal characteristics such as age and wealth; some factors were cynically caused by Mr. Kennedy (such as the timing of presenting the agreement, his waiting in the car during the meeting with the solicitor, his conditioning the wedding upon signing the prenuptial agreement, presenting a contract drafted by his lawyer, and willingness to make only minor changes); some factors were bluntly abused by Mr. Kennedy (such as Ms. Thorne's emotional state of mind before the wedding and her dependence on him since she was in a foreign country and spoke little English).

## 4.3. SYSTEMIC SOCIAL INEQUALITIES

As explained in subsection 3.2,[78] the second vector of power is due to systemic social inequalities. The stronger party did not create the asymmetries of power, but exploited and benefited from them. One party takes advantage of their better social position and the other party's subordinate position.

In *Thorne v. Kennedy*, in addition to the pressures Mr. Kennedy created, he also exploited Ms. Thorne's socially subordinate position. For example, he was in a better position due to his social class and gender.[79] He was an upper-class wealthy man while she was a woman with little economic means. Furthermore, she was dependent on him for her visa status. This social position influenced Ms. Thorne's consent because her options were few and meagre. Her consent was given from a position of social disadvantage and therefore was defective. As the primary judge put it, 'If the relationship ended, Ms. Thorne "would have nothing. No job, no visa, no home, no place, no community"'.[80] The judge's conclusion that Ms. Thorne was in a position of powerlessness derived not only from the interpersonal relations of power discussed previously, but also from Ms. Thorne's social position *vis-à-vis* Mr. Kennedy. Duress should include not only pressures directed by one party towards another but also exploitation of social constraints and social inequalities. Wrongful behaviour and illegitimate pressure are not limited to coercion tactics that one party employs against the other, but also arise from taking advantage of social inequalities. In this case Mr. Kennedy indeed held all the bargaining chips; however, in other cases women might hold some power and advantage over men. In other words,

---

78 Section 3.2.

79 E. Kuiper, '"What's Mine is Mine": A Socialist Feminist Critique of Binding Financial Agreements in Australia' (2021) 34 *Australian Journal of Family Law* 129.

80 *Thorne v. Kennedy*, above n. 65, para. 100.

other women might not be as powerless as Ms. Thorne. In the same manner, a younger party may have the upper hand over the other, older, party.

In conclusion, in addition to the interpersonal power imbalance there were systemic social inequalities between Mr. Kennedy and Ms. Thorne due to class, gender, age, and legal status in Australia. Mr. Kennedy knowingly and deliberately took advantage of these social inequalities to force Ms. Thorne to sign a contract protecting his interests alone. These social pressures added to his coercive tactics discussed in the previous subsection.

## 4.4. STATE POWER

As explained in subsection 3.3,[81] the third vector of power is the power relations between the parties and the state. Whether the court enforces or invalidates the contract, the court employs judicial power over both parties. It is the dependence of the parties on the court which shapes the power imbalance between the parties.

In *Thorne v. Kennedy* the primary judge set the agreements between Ms. Thorne and Mr. Kennedy aside; the Full Court of the Family Court of Australia enforced the contracts, and the High Court of Australia invalidated the agreements. In each case the court employed its judicial power. Invalidating the contract empowered Ms. Thorne while enforcing it empowered the already powerful Mr. Kennedy. In other words, while the High Court (as did the primary judge) intervened to mitigate the imbalance of power between the parties, the Family Court maintained the inequality between the parties.

In addition to the courts, other government branches have power over the parties. The state influences and takes part in shaping the relations between the parties through legislation and regulation.

In *Thorne v. Kennedy*, the state controls the visa status of non-Australians. According to immigration laws, Ms. Thorne would receive visa status upon marrying Mr. Kennedy. Therefore, she was dependent on him for her legal status. She knew that without signing the agreements there would be no marriage, and if there would be no marriage then she could not stay in Australia. Mr. Kennedy knew that and exploited her dependency. Though he did not *create* the threat of losing her visa, he took advantage of it.

In a similar manner, the Family Law Act also controlled the parties' relations. The parties bargain in the shadow of the law,[82] and therefore the statute regulates financial agreements entered into before and after marriage. The Act sets the requirements of these agreements and allows courts to

81 Section 3.3.

82 R.H. Mnookin and L. Kornhauser, 'Bargaining in the Shadow of the Law: The Case of Divorce' (1979) 88 *Yale Law Journal* 950.

intervene in certain circumstances and set the agreements aside. This Act allowed Ms. Thorne to challenge the agreements she signed. It polices unfair prenuptial/nuptial agreements and empowers dependent and disadvantaged parties. A minimalist intervention approach in these agreements would perpetuate inequalities between spouses; while greater intervention would mitigate inequalities between the parties. The Family Law Act requires independent legal advice before the signing of an agreement. It also requires disclosure of material matters. These requirements empower disadvantaged parties. However, as this case demonstrated, this is not enough, and the disadvantaged party may sign an unfair agreement against legal advice because of duress. Furthermore, this statute does not address the timing of entering into premarital agreements. Requiring that prenuptial agreements be signed a certain time before the wedding would also restrict abuses of bargaining power by one party.

While immigration laws worked in Mr. Kennedy's favour, resulting in a prenuptial agreement to Ms. Thorne's detriment, the Family Law Act evened out the power imbalance and empowered Ms. Thorne, allowing invalidation of the agreement. Though more requirements for valid agreements could be added, the statute mitigates bargaining power between spouses.

In conclusion, in addition to personal and social vectors of power, laws in the background of the parties' bargaining affect their negotiations, as the parties bargain in the shadow of the law. While Mr. Kennedy used immigration law as a bargaining chip in his favour, Ms. Thorne used the Family Law Act to rescind the contract. Each of these laws influenced the power balance between the parties: the former put Mr. Kennedy in a dominant position over Ms. Thorne, while the latter gave Ms. Thorne the upper hand. Furthermore, the Family Court perpetuated social inequalities and allowed coercive negotiation tactics and a one-sided contract, while the High Court promoted social equality between spouses and policed advantage-taking in negotiations. The former perpetuated and the latter corrected the imbalance of power between the parties.

## 4.5. TRIAD VECTORS OF POWER

As explained in subsection 4.1,[83] the High Court did not determine the issue of duress in *Thorne v. Kennedy*. Based on the analysis in the previous subsections, this subpart concludes that the Court should have accepted Ms. Thorne's duress claim.

[83] Section 4.1.

Mr. Kennedy used coercive tactics (such as presenting the prenuptial agreement at the last minute, waiting in the car during Ms. Thorne's meeting with the solicitor) and threats (to cancel the wedding if Ms. Thorne did not sign the prenuptial agreement), and abused his preferable position (presenting an agreement drafted by his lawyer, allowing only minor amendments and refusing to negotiate its terms). Mr. Kennedy also exploited social inequalities that put him in a better bargaining position as a wealthy older man. He used Ms. Thorne's dependence on him for a visa and for economic support. As I explain elsewhere, in the context of spousal agreements the courts need to endorse a broad notion of duress, considering 'economic imbalance, relational dynamics between the parties, and other social factors and circumstances that provide a backdrop to the contract'.[84]

As inequality of bargaining power between parties to prenuptial agreements often exists,[85] it is important that disadvantaged parties be protected from duress. The map applied here provides the courts with a tool to empower disadvantaged parties. Duress law is a doctrine aimed at policing abuse of power by prohibiting coercive practices by powerful parties. It shifts the balance of power in the aggrieved party's favour. As the primary judge aptly concluded, Mr. Kennedy held '[e]very bargaining chip and every power'.[86] The result was one-sided agreements protecting his interests alone. Therefore, the agreements should be invalidated for duress. Duress law polices such abuse of power and prohibits such coercion resulting in unfair agreement.

However, due to the specific inequalities between spouses, this is not sufficient. Therefore, the Family Law Act allows courts to invalidate such agreements. Scholars have analysed why men have the upper hand in negotiating prenuptial agreements,[87] in general in marriage[88] or cohabitation,[89]

---

[84] O. Gan, above n. 16, p. 175.

[85] M. Kaye, L. Sarmas, B. Fehlberg and B. Smyth, 'Prenuptial agreements – What's happening?' (2023) 36 *Australian Journal of Family Law* 38.

[86] *Thorne v. Kennedy*, above n. 65, para. 47.

[87] G.F. Brod, 'Premarital Agreements and Gender Justice' (1994) 6 *Yale Journal of Law and Feminism* 229; L. Guggenheimer, 'A Modest Proposal: The Feminomics of Drafting Premarital Agreements' (1996) 17 *Women's Rights Law Reporter* 147; A.A. Marston, 'Planning for Love: The Politics of Prenuptial Agreements' (1997) 49 *Stanford Law Review* 887; S. Thompson, 'Pre-nuptial Agreements – A Good Route to Autonomy?' (2024) *Financial Remedies Journal* 163.

[88] A.L. Wax, 'Bargaining in the Shadow of the Market: Is There a Future Egalitarian Marriage?' (1998) 84 *Virginia. Law Review* 509; J.E. Hasday, 'Intimacy and Economic Exchange' (2005) 119 *Harvard Law Review* 491, 494; J.T. Younger, 'Lovers' Contracts in the Courts: Forsaking the Minimum Decencies' (2007) 13 *William and Mary Journal of Women and Law* 349.

[89] S. Thompson, 'Cohabitation Contracts and Gender Equality' in R. Probert and S. Thompson (eds.), *Research Handbook on Marriage, Cohabitation and the Law*, Edward Elgar Publishing, Cheltenham 2024, p. 352; O. Gan, 'Nonmarital Contract Law' (2024) 76 *Rutgers University Law Review* 663.

and generally in negotiating with women,[90] resulting in unfair contracts to women's detriment. Duress law, together with protective legislation (and other doctrines such as undue influence) would empower women and level the playing-field of prenuptial/nuptial agreements. Hence, the High Court should have rescinded the contract due to duress. Instead, the High Court invalidated the agreements for undue influence and unconscionable conduct. Therefore, these doctrines are also important tools for policing abuse of bargaining power. Though the differences between the three doctrines and their overlap are beyond the scope of this chapter, it highlights the importance of duress as a tool to battle inequalities of bargaining power.

In conclusion, analysing the three vectors of power showed that Ms. Thorne's duress claim should have been accepted, resulting in the invalidation of the two contracts she signed. Indeed, this is not an easy case, as duress cases are usually difficult to decide. However, applying the map provided in the previous section demonstrates how an analysis sensitive to the different vectors of power and their intersection could determine duress claims.

Other cases, of course, might yield different application of the vectors of power (including their intersection) and different results. This case is but one example, and each case warrants a careful contextual and nuanced application of the map provided in the previous section.

## 5. CONCLUSION

Duress is an important doctrine. It defines what use of bargaining power is acceptable in negotiations; it polices abuse of bargaining power; it empowers disadvantaged parties; and it mitigates inequalities in bargaining power. However, courts struggle to determine duress. To make the application of duress law easier this chapter maps three vectors of power – interpersonal power between the parties; systemic social inequalities; and state power – and their intersection. Analysing these three vectors of power, this chapter provides a structured map to decide duress cases. Determining duress is indeed not easy, as *Thorne v. Kennedy* demonstrates. However, this chapter demonstrates why and how courts (alongside legislators and regulators) need to police and mitigate bargaining power imbalances.

---

90 C.M. Rose, 'Bargaining and Gender' (1995) 18 *Harvard Journal of Law and Public Policy* 547.

# CHAPTER 3

# PRESUMED UNDUE INFLUENCE AND THE POWER TO TAKE ADVANTAGE IN INTIMATE RELATIONSHIPS

Niamh Connolly

## 1. INTRODUCTION

Mrs. Stuart was a wealthy Canadian heiress at the turn of the twentieth century. Her husband of more than 40 years was a shareholder in a paper company. When the company was hundreds of thousands of dollars in debt, Mrs. Stuart agreed to guarantee those debts. She ended up losing everything she owned to the bank. She later sued the bank, alleging that it had caused her husband to exert undue influence on her to give the guarantees.[1] Mrs. Stuart's testimony in the case must have caused concern to her legal representatives. She affirmed that her husband had neither put pressure on her nor made any misrepresentations to her.[2] She knew exactly what she was doing. She 'acted of her own free will to relieve her husband in his distress and … would have scorned to consult any one'.[3] Perhaps fortunately, but presumably gallingly, for Mrs. Stuart, the Privy Council disregarded her evidence and ruled that her property should be returned to her. According to Lord Macnaghten, the plaintiff's protestations 'that she acted of her own free will and not under her husband's influence merely shew how deeprooted and how lasting the influence of her husband was'.[4]

This chapter identifies a significant reason why it is appropriate that the doctrine of presumed undue influence should assist a person in the position of Mrs. Stuart, who knowingly consented to sacrifice her own financial self-interest to assist the person with whom she was in the closest of intimate relationships. Mrs. Stuart deserved to be believed and still to succeed in her legal action. Presumed undue influence protects people from the exploitation of relational vulnerabilities and Mrs. Stuart was vulnerable due to her concern for her husband.

The problem of people being taken advantage of by their spouses or loved ones is a perennial one. There are cases dating back centuries in which wives have challenged gifts that they made to their husbands. Early instances of such

1 *Bank of Montreal v. Stuart* [1911] AC 120; [1910] UKPC 53.
2 Ibid., 136–137.
3 Ibid., 137.
4 Ibid., 137.

cases date from the eighteenth century, notwithstanding the historical doctrine of *coverture*, which limited married women's property rights and contractual capacity. The authorities expose a range of ways in which a husband might take advantage of his wife. These include misrepresentation and coercion but also more subtle pressures and sources of vulnerability. Early cases failed where the wife was not able to prove 'compulsion, fraud or imposition'.[5] As time went by, undue influence law developed the presumption mechanism, arising from relationships of trust, to facilitate proof of influence in contexts other than marital relationships.[6] However, this facility was not extended to wives. In the early twentieth century, *Howes v. Bishop* confirmed that the relationship between a wife and her husband is not one that generally raises a presumption of influence.[7]

The resulting position in English law is that wives may plead presumed undue influence by their husbands, provided they establish on the facts that their individual relationship is one that engenders influence. The same principle applies to other intimate relationships, availing husbands and cohabitees. If the second required element is present, namely a transaction that calls for explanation, this will raise the presumption of influence. The focus will then shift to whether the defendant can rebut this presumption.

Although it is open to people in intimate relationships to prove that their specific relationship is one characterised by influence, the case law seems to overlook a significant, commonplace reason why people are vulnerable to being taken advantage of when they act to benefit their loved ones. Existing law focuses on the existence of a relationship of dependence between partners, which may expand to include a person's general vulnerabilities, in order to establish a *de facto* relationship of 'trust and confidence'. By targeting dependence, the law fails to respond to a central reason why any of us might be taken advantage of by those to whom we are closest. The law then emphasises the quality of information about the transaction that has been provided as the means to ensure that a person in a relationship of influence takes their decision freely. In treating full information and understanding of the transaction as the cure for influence, the doctrine shows a limited appreciation of the nature of the constraint on the decision-making of the influenced person.

The identification and exposition of a key, underappreciated source of vulnerability within the closest intimate and familial relationships is at the core of this chapter. We are all potentially vulnerable to being taken advantage of by the people we care about because we do not act out of pure self-interest when we interact with loved ones and family members. Due to an internalised

---

5 *Grigby v. Cox* (1750) 1 Ves. Sen. 517, 518; 27 ER 1178; *Pawlet v. Delaval* (1755) 2 Ves. Sen. 663; 28 ER 422, 425.

6 *Earl of Chesterfield v. Janssen* (1751) 2 Ves. Sen. 125; 28 ER 82, 100.

7 *Howes v. Bishop* [1909] 2 KB 390; [1908–10] All ER Rep. Ext. 1299, 1302.

commitment to the other person and the relationship, we may prioritise their interests to the detriment of our own. Doing so does not mean that we have outsourced our judgement or fail to understand the consequences of our actions. People may know exactly what the risks are and enter the transaction anyway, due to the intimate or familial relationship.

This mode of behaviour is at odds with the pursuit of rational self-interest that contract law generally assumes. In these relationship cases, one person renounces their self-interest, to promote the interests of the other. The logic that two people will reach agreements that accommodate both their interests does not apply in a scenario where one person prioritises the interests of the other but that second person does not reciprocate their concern. The disparity in the two people's motivations and objectives skews the process, setting the scene for exploitation and substantively unfair outcomes. It confers on the person who benefits from the other's altruistic motivation the power to take advantage of it.

This chapter makes the case that it is appropriate for private law to protect people from this form of advantage-taking in intimate relationships, and that presumed undue influence is the appropriate tool to do so. The doctrine is broad enough to protect people from both active and passive exploitation within relationships. Presumed undue influence should accommodate this widespread form of relational vulnerability by recognising it at the stage of determining whether there is a relationship of influence between two people. The first half of this chapter will examine the doctrine of presumed undue influence from a doctrinal and normative perspective, in order to show that it is an appropriate legal tool to respond to the exploitation of relational power in marital and intimate relationships. The second half will elaborate the proposition that people often act in an other-focused way in intimate relationships, and draw the resultant connections between vulnerability, power and exploitation that justify using the law of presumed undue influence to prevent this form of advantage-taking.

## 2. THE DOCTRINE OF PRESUMED UNDUE INFLUENCE AND INTIMATE OR MARITAL RELATIONSHIPS

### 2.1. RISKS OF EXPLOITATION IN INTIMATE RELATIONSHIPS

Since the 1990s, scholars have highlighted the social problem of 'sexually transmitted debt', or 'emotionally transmitted debt', where a person becomes liable for the debts of their intimate partner.[8] The problem is not limited to romantic relationships; it commonly occurs between parents and children as well.[9] Different dynamics within close personal relationships may place people at risk of exploitation in very different ways.[10] Some cases involve coercion, others the delegation of decision-making, others material or emotional dependence, and others a loving willingness to pursue the interests of one partner. These different dynamics within relationships can provide distinct reasons why the law ought to intervene to protect a person from an obligation to which they have consented.

Equitable case law has long sought to protect people from the risk of exploitation arising from their intimate relationships. Specifically, there is a recurring idea of an 'invalidating tendency'[11] or 'tender' treatment of wives, though Lord Browne-Wilkinson rejects this in *Barclays Bank v. O'Brien* in favour of more broadly applicable principles.[12] This concern for wives has informed several rules, which focus on different sources of risk. Adequate information and misrepresentation are a strong locus of concern. The Australian concept of a 'special equity' for wives, established in *Yerkey v. Jones*, targets the danger that the wife will lack understanding of the effect of the proposed security.[13] Presumed undue influence in English law frequently relies on two potential risks to a wife's decision-making: (a) her deference to her husband in financial matters or, more recently, (b) potential vulnerabilities. Additionally, undue influence may sometimes respond to the exertion of overt pressure within a relationship.

Each of these risks may be present in some marriages, but none will be universally present. More importantly, this identification of sources of risk omits another reason why a wife might agree to a transaction despite knowing that it may harm her individual self-interest. This is the reason identified by Lord Browne-Wilkinson in *Barclays Bank v. O'Brien*: 'the sexual and emotional ties' between people in an intimate relationship.[14] The disadvantage of focusing on knowledge and understanding is that it means the law will stop short of protecting a person who understands the risks but is subject to 'powerful emotional pressure'.[15] Parents who give guarantees for their adult children are

---

8 See e.g. P. Baron, 'The Free Exercise of Her Will: Women and Emotionally Transmitted Debt' (1995) 13 *Law in Context: A Socio-Legal Journal* 23.

9 M. Bailey, 'Sexually Transmitted Debt: Criticisms and Prospects for Reform' (1999) 8 *Auckland University Law Review* 1001, 1002.

10 *Grigby v. Cox*, above n. 5, 518; see also *Hatch v. Hatch* (1804) 9 Ves. Jun. 292; 32 ER 615, 617.

11 *Yerkey v. Jones* [1939] HCA 3; (1939) 63 CLR 649, 675–76.

12 *Barclays Bank v. O'Brien* [1994] 1 AC 180, 190; [1993] UKHL 6.

13 *Yerkey v. Jones*, above n. 11, 683.

14 *Barclays Bank v. O'Brien*, above n. 12, 190.

15 J.L. Cummins, 'Relationship Debt and the Aged: Welfare vs Commerce in the Law of Guarantees' (2002) 27(2) *Alternative Law Journal* 63, 64.

often 'well aware of the improvidence of their decision' but reluctantly agree because of their relationship with them.[16] Understanding the danger is not the issue.

## 2.2. PRESUMED UNDUE INFLUENCE: AN APPROPRIATE TOOL TO RESPOND TO THIS RELATIONAL VULNERABILITY

A broad overview of the equitable doctrine of presumed undue influence suggests that it is the appropriate doctrine to respond to this specific form of relational vulnerability. The core mischief to which undue influence responds is taking unfair advantage of another person.[17] Presumed undue influence protects from exploitation people whose vulnerability exists in the context of particular relationships. Modern case law emphasises this purpose of protecting the vulnerable.[18] Significantly, presumed undue influence responds to more than one type of advantage-taking, including both active and passive exploitation.[19] We see the fundamentally plural nature of the doctrine when we trace the strands of authority dealing with different types of relationship back to the eighteenth century.[20] In the nineteenth century, cases such as *Huguenin v. Baseley*[21] and *Allcard v. Skinner*[22] moved towards generalising and simplifying the doctrine.[23]

Historically, certain categories of relationship have been considered necessarily to raise the presumption of undue influence (e.g. attorneys, solicitors, parents). In addition, it has long been possible to prove that the relationship between two people is one of trust and confidence, that can raise the presumption.[24] Sometimes the relationship is one where a person is an authority figure or adviser. Frequently, a qualifying relationship has been one where one person allows the other to manage financial matters on their behalf.[25] In *Etridge*, Lord Nicholls lists phrases used to denote a relationship of influence: 'trust and confidence, reliance, dependence or vulnerability on

---

16 *Janesland Holdings Pty. Ltd. v. Simon and Others* [1999] ACTSC 35, para. 79.

17 *Royal Bank of Scotland plc v. Etridge (No. 2)* [2001] UKHL 44, paras. 6, 8; *Stavely v. Restis* [2024] EWHC 670, para. 66.

18 *Macklin v. Dowsett* [2004] EWCA Civ. 904; *Malik v. Sheikh* [2018] EWHC 973 (Ch.).

19 D. Capper, 'Undue Influence and Unconscionability: A Rationalisation' (1998) 114 *Law Quarterly Review* 479, 493.

20 *Morris v. Burroughs* (1737) 1 Atk. 398, 403; 26 ER 253, 255; W. Swain, 'Reshaping Contractual Unfairness in England 1670–1900' (2014) 35 *Journal of Legal History* 120.

21 *Huguenin v. Baseley* (1807) 14 Ves. 273; 33 ER 526.

22 *Allcard v. Skinner* (1887) 36 Ch. D. 145.

23 Swain, above n. 20, 134–137.

24 W.H.D. Winder, 'Undue Influence and Coercion' (1939) 3 *Modern Law Review* 97, 101–102; *Bridgman v. Green* (1755) 2 Ves. Sen. 627.

25 *Royal Bank of Scotland plc v. Etridge (No. 2)*, above n. 17, para. 14.

the one hand and ascendancy, domination or control on the other'.[26] He emphasises that none of these descriptors is 'all-embracing'.[27] Different terms point to different sorts of dependence or vulnerability. However, we should not let the terms we use dictate a narrow understanding of the substance of the relationship required. The law should recognise the potential for abuse of influence within a relationship, however that potential arises.

The breadth of undue influence is also reflected in the diversity of forms it can take, as Lord Nicholls explains in *Etridge*.[28] Sometimes, there has been actual pressure (though it may be difficult to prove).[29] Other times, presumed undue influence involves taking advantage of a position of strength in a relationship, regardless of how that power arose. The plurality of rationales in the various distinct streams of undue influence leaves room to question the House of Lords' endorsement in *Etridge* of the unity of undue influence. This is the proposition that all cases resolve to actual undue influence, whether proven with the aid of a presumption or not.[30] There is a difference between cases that involve actual pressure, however proven, and those involving passive exploitation or the mere risk of passive exploitation of an advantage arising from the relationship between the parties.

## 2.3. THE PRESUMPTION SOMETIMES RESPONDS TO DIFFICULT-TO-PROVE COERCION

One distinct function that the presumption of undue influence serves is to capture cases where there has actually been wrongful pressure but it is too difficult to prove in court.[31] Actual undue influence is a limited tool, unsuited to identifying all cases of pressure and control in intimate relationships. Old cases such as *Grigby v. Cox*[32] and *Nedby v. Nedby*[33] refused a remedy to a wife because she had not positively proven compulsion, even though the circumstances raised suspicions. In *Nedby*, Parker VC acknowledged 'circumstances of suspicion in the case', given some evidence that the wife had been 'agitated and distressed'.[34] Without a presumption mechanism, adducing positive proof was too high a hurdle to surmount. Similarly, the wife in *Howes v. Bishop* could

26 Ibid., para. 11.
27 Ibid., para. 11.
28 Ibid., paras. 7–11.
29 Ibid., para. 7.
30 Ibid., para. 93.
31 *Re Craig (deceased), Meneces v. Middleton* [1971] Ch. 95, 104.
32 *Grigby v. Cox*, above n. 5, 518.
33 *Nedby v. Nedby* (1852) 5 De Gex. & Smale 377; 64 ER 1161.
34 Ibid., 1164.

not persuade the judge that there was anything improper in how her husband overcame her resistance.[35]

Coercion in an intimate relationship can use subtle techniques. It is likely to be psychological or emotional as much as violent.[36] Demands can be backed up by an unexpressed and continuing threat of retribution for non-compliance. The wife sureties interviewed by Fehlberg in her research into 'sexually transmitted debt' revealed that they were subject to pressures that 'ranged from subtle forms of pressure inherent in the conjugal relationship, to emotional blackmail and extreme physical abuse'.[37] In addition, controlling behaviour might take place over a long period. It is not a one-off act, directed to compelling the victim to agree to a specific transaction. Modern scholarship emphasises that an accurate understanding of the effects of coercion should incorporate the 'dynamics of power within abusive relationships'.[38] A history of domestic violence has a continuing impact on a person's ability effectively to defend their own financial interests.[39] The judgments in *Chin v. Chin*[40] and *Sollis v. Leyshon*[41] both acknowledge that 'such influence is often exerted clandestinely and over a period of time'.[42] Thus, if the law required a victim to demonstrate threats directly related to the signing of the specific transaction in order to establish undue influence, it would fail to capture the effect on them of longer-term patterns of violence or coercion.

Furthermore, it is frequently difficult for an external observer to perceive whether an intimate relationship is abusive or not. *Louth v. Diprose* illustrates this opacity of personal relationships. A man gave a house to a woman with whom he was infatuated. The trial judge considered that she had manipulated his emotional vulnerability and the High Court of Australia accepted this view of the facts.[43] However, Sarmas reveals that the man's behaviour might have been emotionally and physically abusive, and more akin to sexual harassment than to benign romantic gestures.[44] In *Re Craig*, an elderly widower gave most of his property to the woman whom he employed as his secretary-companion in

35 *Howes v. Bishop*, above n. 7, 1302.

36 B. Fehlberg, 'Money and Marriage: Sexually Transmitted Debt in England' (1997) 11 *International Journal of Law, Policy and the Family* 320, 332.

37 Ibid., 332.

38 R. Chaudhri, 'Tackling Financial Abuse with the Doctrine of Undue Influence' (2020) 33 *Australian Journal of Family Law* 191, 192–193.

39 P. Easteal, L. Young and A. Carline, 'Domestic Violence, Property and Family Law in Australia' (2018) 32 *International Journal of Law, Policy & the Family* 204, 208.

40 *Chin v. Chin* [2019] EWHC 523 (Ch.).

41 *Sollis v. Leyshon* [2018] EWHC 2853 (Ch.).

42 *Chin v. Chin*, above n. 40, para. 126; *Sollis v. Leyshon*, above n. 41, para. 70.

43 *Louth v. Diprose* [1992] HCA 61; (1992) 110 ALR 1.

44 L. Sarmas, 'Storytelling and the Law: a Case Study of *Louth v Diprose*' (1994) 19 *Melbourne University Law Review* 701, 715–717; see also B. Sangha and B. Moles, 'Gendered Stereotypes and the Unconscionability – Can We Trust the Judges to Get It Right' (1997) 1 *Flinders Journal of Law Reform* 145.

the later years of his life. The impression is of a personal relationship in which Craig was emotionally dependent on the defendant.[45] The evidence strongly hints at a controlling relationship, where the defendant cut the widower off from friends[46] and subjected him to instrumentalised threats that she would leave him.[47] Ungoed-Thomas J concluded, based on the fragmentary insights into their relationship, that the donor was 'entirely at her mercy'.[48]

Presumed undue influence has the benefit of addressing the difficulty of proving coercion in intimate relationships. It operates where there is an 'absence of evidence of overt acts of persuasive conduct'.[49] Absence of evidence is not necessarily the same as absence of undue pressure. Ungoed-Thomas J emphasises this in *Re Craig*, noting that 'absence of direct evidence of a gift being obtained by undue influence in circumstances such as those in this case is far from indicating that it did not occur'.[50] This, then, is the vital function of presumed undue influence in one group of intimate relationship cases: capturing cases where there is likely to be wrongful compulsion but it is too difficult directly to prove. The utility of the doctrine to protect against exploitation in relationships is greatly enhanced because the presumption allows the court to provide a remedy *without* establishing the true nature of the relationship.

The hidden coercion that likely underlies some cases of presumed undue influence is distinct from the more common form of relational vulnerability which is the focus of this chapter. The coercion cases involve both impaired consent and a wrong by the stronger party. The focus of this chapter is different: it concerns the passive exploitation by a person (A) in an intimate or familial relationship of the other person (B)'s propensity to prioritise A's interests. This power neither arises from nor requires coercion. This challenges us to examine the normative justification as to why it is legitimate for equity to invalidate a transaction arising from this weaker form of advantage-taking.

## 2.4. RATIONALES FOR PRESUMED UNDUE INFLUENCE

There has been much scholarly debate on the rationales for presumed undue influence. This debate ranges those who argue that it is defendant-sided (a wrong by the defendant) against those who favour a claimant-sided justification (impaired consent). The historical roots of undue influence in

45 *Re Craig*, above n. 31, 109.
46 Ibid., 111–112.
47 Ibid., 113.
48 Ibid., 114.
49 *Royal Bank of Scotland plc v. Etridge (No. 2)*, above n. 17, para. 10.
50 *Re Craig*, above n. 31, 121.

equitable fraud argue in favour of wrongdoing.[51] However, the cases show that liability in undue influence does not depend on any wrongdoing by the person in a position to influence another.[52] *Hammond v. Osborn* affirms that 'unimpeachable' conduct is no answer to presumed undue influence.[53] Although some cases reveal nakedly exploitative conduct,[54] this is not required. Existing influence can be misused without any active pressure.[55] A defendant's conduct need only be wrongful in the sense of passive exploitation. Rejecting the wrongdoing analysis, Birks and Yin argue that presumed undue influence is a response to impaired consent.[56] Due to a person's dependence within a relationship, they lack the 'judgmental capacity' that the law treats people as possessing.[57] However, both the consent and wrongdoing explanations face similar obstacles. There are key cases – such as *Allcard v. Skinner*[58] – in which the gift reflects the intention of the giver and the beneficiary has done nothing wrong to contribute to the forming of that intention.[59]

The impaired consent rationale may have particular difficulty in reaching intimate relationship cases, such as that of Mrs. Stuart, outlined at the start of the chapter, or cases of religious influence.[60] It seems artificial to insist that Mrs. Stuart did not fully intend to guarantee her husband's debts, despite her belief that she was acting of her own free will. In reality, it seems that she understood what she was doing and why. If we characterise presumed undue influence as a response to impaired judgemental capacity, then we may end up distorting the facts to fit them into the 'impaired consent' box or limiting the law's ability to respond to influence and exploitation in close personal relationships.

Chen-Wishart offers a compelling justification that rejects an overly atomistic, individualist view of human beings.[61] She argues that our relationships are intrinsically valuable, providing a space for 'attachment, interdependence, and generosity'.[62] Close personal relationships 'trigger implicit relational norms

---

51 See also *National Westminster Bank plc v. Morgan* [1985] AC 686, 707; *Barclays Bank v. O'Brien*, above n. 12, 189–190.

52 *Rhodes v. Bate* (1865–66) LR 1 Ch. App. 252, 262; *Hammond v. Osborn* [2002] EWCA Civ. 885, para. 45.

53 *Hammond v. Osborn*, above n. 52, para. 32.

54 *Billage v. Southee* (1852) 9 Hare 534, 540; 68 ER 623.

55 *Royal Bank of Scotland plc v. Etridge (No. 2)*, above n. 17, para. 9.

56 P. Birks and C.N. Yin, 'On the Nature of Undue Influence' in J. Beatson and D. Friedman (eds.), *Good Faith and Fault in Contract Law*, Clarendon Press, Oxford 1997, p. 57; see also Capper, above n. 19.

57 P. Birks and C.N. Yin, above n. 56, 67.

58 M. Chen-Wishart, 'Undue Influence: Vindicating Relationships of Influence' (2006) 59 *Current Legal Problems* 231, 237.

59 *Allcard v. Skinner*, above n. 22, 145; M. Chen-Wishart, above n. 58, 237.

60 *Bank of Montreal v. Stuart*, above n. 1; *Allcard v. Skinner*, above n. 22.

61 M. Chen-Wishart, above n. 58, 241.

62 Ibid., 242.

about how people in such relationships treat each other. They determine the appropriate range of behaviour and of outcomes that is implicit in the distinction between "due" and "undue" influence.'[63] The law of undue influence reacts when the person in a position of power fails to respect 'the implicit norms of the relationship of influence he shares with the claimant'.[64] Presumed undue influence does not seek to control the creation of relationships of influence. As Chen-Wishart points out, influence itself is natural and not to be reprehended. In *Allcard*, Kekewich J emphasises that interpersonal influence is 'natural and right' and necessary for society to exist. However, the law must ensure that this influence 'shall not be unduly exercised'.[65] The mischief is not the creation of influence, but its exploitation. This normative explanation of the doctrine of presumed undue influence fits perfectly with applying it in order to counter imbalances in intimate personal relationships.

This analysis is supported by a historical line of cases involving a person who acted as an advisor or manager of another person's affairs. The law treated that person as coming under a 'fiduciary' type obligation towards the person for whom they were acting.[66] The advisor has a duty 'to advise and take care of the donor'.[67] Lord Eldon referred colourfully in *Huguenin* to 'all that care and providence' that an adviser owes the person whom they are advising.[68] Tiplady explained that society and the law regard 'certain relationships, or points within relationships, as transcending mere commercialism'.[69] In some contexts, the law expects us to curtail the pursuit of self-interest that it generally supports. Romilly MR affirmed in *Hoghton v. Hoghton* that the influence that arises in relationships of trust is 'considered useful and advantageous to society' but that it 'should be exerted for the benefit of the person subject to it, and not for the advantage of the person possessing it'.[70] The law expects the person who has the capacity to take advantage of the other not to act in their own pure self-interest.[71] This constraint on exercising the power to pursue one's naked self-interest translates smoothly to intimate relationship cases.

We can observe also that presumed undue influence sometimes serves a prophylactic purpose.[72] We draw this conclusion from the fact that presumed

---

63 Ibid., 249.

64 Ibid., 264.

65 *Allcard v. Skinner*, above n. 22, 157–158.

66 *Tate v. Williamson* (1866–67) LR 2 Ch. App. 55; *Royal Bank of Scotland plc v. Chandra* [2011] EWCA Civ. 192 [24].

67 *Allcard v. Skinner*, above n. 22, 182.

68 *Huguenin v. Baseley*, above n. 21, 300.

69 D. Tiplady, 'The Limits of Undue Influence' (1985) 48 *Modern Law Review* 579, 582.

70 *Hoghton v. Hoghton* (1852) 15 Beavan 278, 299–300; 51 ER 545.

71 D. Tiplady, above n. 69, 580.

72 *Allcard v. Skinner*, above n. 22, 171; P. Ridge, 'The Equitable Doctrine of Undue Influence Considered in the Context of Spiritual Influence and Religious Faith: *Allcard v Skinner* Revisited in Australia' (2003) 26(1) *UNSW Law Journal* 66.

undue influence can invalidate transactions where the recipient has not done anything wrong. The doctrine's purpose goes beyond sanctioning actual advantage-taking by a person in a position of authority to ensure that nobody in such a position *can* take advantage of it. Nourse LJ confirms the prophylactic rationale in *Goldsworthy v. Brickell*, where he says that undue influence 'may never have occurred' in a case where the presumption operates.[73]

## 2.5. HISTORY OF THE CASE LAW ON WIVES CLAIMING UNDUE INFLUENCE

For centuries, wives who retained the capacity to deal with certain property, even as married women, have brought legal actions challenging gifts made to their husbands. These cases reveal the difficulty of proving actual undue influence as between husbands and wives: in many cases, the evidence establishes a strong suspicion of wrongful pressure, but the wives were unable to adduce positive proof of coercion. The diversity of outcomes (sometimes reached using different doctrinal techniques) is also interesting because it indicates a longstanding tension between competing judicial tendencies. Some cases seem to reflect the judges' desire to grant a remedy and their adaptation of doctrinal rules to achieve this. On the other hand, a strong and persistent current in the case law shows judicial reluctance to treat a husband's influence over his wife as invalidating, either because prevailing social norms viewed such influence as normal and appropriate, or in light of the risk of endangering the rights of third-party creditors. Romer LJ exemplifies this dual concern in *Bischoff's Trustee v. Frank*, where he expressed skepticism that 'the ordinary influence that a husband has on a wife' would constitute undue influence.[74]

In *Pawlet v. Delaval* (1755), Lord Hardwicke held that if a wife 'freely and voluntarily' gave a gift to her husband, it would not be invalidated without evidence of 'compulsion, fraud or imposition'.[75] Yet, there is room for nuance. *Milnes v. Busk* reads as a protective decision. A deceased man's heirs claimed that his wife had gifted him her interests in trust property. Lord Loughborough accepted that the transaction only conferred a right to administer her property during their marriage, reasoning that the husband must have intended merely to do what was fair and proper.[76] Lord Loughborough expressed doubt that the law should consider married women in the same light as single women, given

[73] *Goldsworthy v. Brickell* [1987] Ch. 378, 400–401.

[74] *Bischoff's Trustee v. Frank* (1903) 89 LT 188 (unreported) cited at *Howes v. Bishop* [1909] KB 390, 397–398 (the reports of *Howes v. Bishop* differ).

[75] *Pawlet v. Delaval*, above n. 5, 425.

[76] *Milnes v. Busk* (1794) 2 Ves. Jun. 488, 496–497; 30 ER 738.

that marriage is 'so liable to influence'.[77] The courts should apply the usual 'common precaution, that would attend the transactions of persons under a degree of influence'.[78]

One old strand of equity's protection of wives involved the rectification of marriage settlements drawn up in an underhand way or not drawn up as promised.[79] This availed wives where the husband had the legal documents drawn up. These cases reflect the fiduciary logic. *Lovesy v. Smith* holds that a person who takes on the role of an adviser and conveyancer must explain the legal document clearly to the signatory.[80] Moreover, a person acting in a fiduciary role should not be permitted to profit from their wrongdoing.[81] The reasoning in *Lovesy* may explain why later Evershed MR in *Zamet v. Hyman* invoked a fiancé's duty of candour and protection.[82] However, the origins of some of the case law on intimate relationships in cases that are about advisers in a somewhat fiduciary role (recalling *Tate v. Williamson*[83]) may have channelled the law into focusing too narrowly on the specific criterion of being entrusted to manage financial affairs.

Despite the sense that wives were at risk of influence by their husbands, the early cases held that a wife would have to adduce evidence to prove undue influence.[84] In the early twentieth century, there were hints in some cases that the law might become more receptive to claims by wives of undue influence.[85] Two such Privy Council cases seem at odds with the orthodoxy that wives could not avail of a presumption of influence by their husbands. In *Turnbull v. Duval*, the Privy Council invalidated a security given by a wife to secure her husband's debt.[86] She had been pressed to sign it by her husband and misunderstood the nature of the document. The lenders were affected by this pressure and lack of understanding because they had delegated obtaining her signature to the husband. The pressure in *Duval* does not look like wrongful coercion. Rather, it looks like a wife choosing to help her husband out of a difficult situation, because she cares what happens to him.[87] *Bank of Montreal v. Stuart* was another Privy Council case involving a wife guaranteeing her husband's business debts.[88] The Privy Council invalidated the guarantees, characterising

---

77 Ibid., 498.

78 Ibid., 498.

79 *Clark v. Girdwood* (1877) 7 Ch. D. 9; *Lovesy v. Smith* (1880) 15 Ch. D. 655; *Corley v. Lord Stafford* (1857) 1 De Gex. & Jones 238; 44 ER 714.

80 *Lovesy v. Smith*, above n. 79.

81 *Corley v. Lord Stafford*, above n. 79.

82 *Zamet v. Hyman* [1961] 1 WLR 1442, 1444.

83 *Tate v. Williamson* (1866–67) LR 2 Ch. App. 55.

84 *Grigby v. Cox*, above n. 5; *Nedby v. Nedby*, above n. 33.

85 *Turnbull v. Duval* [1902] AC 429; *Bank of Montreal v. Stuart*, above n. 1.

86 *Turnbull v. Duval*, above n. 85.

87 Ibid., 432.

88 *Bank of Montreal v. Stuart*, above n. 1.

Mrs. Stuart as somebody who 'acted in passive obedience to her husband's directions ... She was ready to sign anything that her husband asked her to sign and do anything he told her to do'.[89] The bank, through its solicitor, was answerable for the husband's influence.

In the same period, other case law held firm against wives alleging undue influence by their husbands. In *Howes v. Bishop* (1909), the law crystallised into the exclusion of a general presumption of influence as between husbands and wives.[90] This created an inconsistency: women who were engaged to be married were presumed to be subject to influence by their fiancés but married women were not presumed to be influenced by their husbands.[91] In *Re Lloyds Bank Ltd.*, Maugham J considered that women who were due to marry were more vulnerable in dealing with their prospective husbands even than married women.[92] His reasoning suggests several reasons why an engaged woman does not protect herself financially: because she expects her interests to be combined with those of her husband, and because she has a high level of trust in him.

The somewhat anomalous cases of *Duval*[93] and *Stuart*[94] had a limited impact on the central question of how the law viewed the possibility of influence within marital relationships. In *Howes v. Bishop*, Lord Alverstone CJ understood *Duval* to indicate that there may be exceptions to the general rule that there was no presumption of influence arising from the relationship between a husband and wife.[95] However, *Duval* later influenced the law in common law jurisdictions in two notable ways. In Australia, *Duval* provided the basis for the doctrine of a special equity that protects guarantor wives.[96] Separately, a series of English guarantee cases in the 1980s endorsed *Duval* and *Chaplin v. Brammall*[97] as establishing that where a creditor entrusts to a person the task of obtaining a guarantee from a close family member, the creditor can be in no better position than the person who acted as its agent.[98] In 1994, however, Lord Browne-Wilkinson in *Barclays Bank v. O'Brien* strongly criticised *Duval* as having an

89 Ibid., 136.

90 *Howes v. Bishop*, above n. 7, 1308; *National Westminster Bank plc v. Morgan*, above n. 51, 703.

91 *Page v. Horne* (1848) 11 Beavan 227; 50 ER 804.

92 *In re Lloyds Bank Ltd.* [1931] 1 Ch. 289, 302.

93 *Turnbull v. Duval*, above n. 85.

94 *Bank of Montreal v. Stuart*, above n. 1.

95 *Howes v. Bishop*, above n. 74, 396.

96 *Yerkey v. Jones*, above n. 11; *Garcia v. National Australia Bank* [1998] HCA 48; (1988) 155 ALR 614; J. Gava, 'Another Study in Judging: Sir Owen Dixon and Yerkey v Jones' (2010) 26 *Journal of Contract Law* 248, 269.

97 *Chaplin & Co. v. Brammall* [1908] 1 KB 233.

98 *Avon Finance Co. v. Bridger* [1985] 2 All ER 281; *Kings North Trust Ltd v. Bell* [1986] 1 WLR 119.

'obscure' and probably incorrect basis. He considered that the husband had not committed any wrongful act.[99]

After *Howes v. Bishop*, the rule in English law was that there was no general presumption of influence by husbands on their wives, though it might, in principle, be possible to prove that an individual spousal relationship was one of (undue) influence. *Howes v. Bishop* illustrates that, when juries were more commonly used for civil cases, the jury could be asked to decide whether a husband had exercised undue influence over his wife (though in that case, the jury did not answer the question).[100] In *McKenzie v. Royal Bank of Canada* (1934), the Privy Council affirmed that the spousal relationship was not one which automatically created a presumption of undue influence, adding:

> It may be true that in some cases it is easy for the wife to discharge the onus which lies on her as on everyone else outside the protected class to show that a particular contract was, in fact, procured by the undue influence of her husband.[101]

On the facts, the wife had not proven that this was a relationship of influence because she 'obviously possessed and exercised a will of her own' and understood business conditions.[102] In 1939, Winder wrote that there was no reason why a wife should not be able to prove a *de facto* relationship of influence but there were no previous authorities in which a wife had successfully done so.[103] There is little sign of successful claims for undue influence as between spouses in the decades that followed. In *Edgar v. Edgar*, a woman's claim for undue influence concerning an agreement made when she was separating from her husband failed because there was no evidence that the husband had put pressure on her.[104] The 1980s saw an increased number of reported cases in which people alleged undue influence by family members, largely in borrowing or guarantee cases. Almost all of these claims failed, either because there was insufficient proof of influence[105] or because a third-party lender was unaware of the circumstances that affected a guarantor or borrower's consent.[106]

In *Etridge*, Lord Nicholls reaffirmed as current law that spouses may establish on the facts that their particular relationship is one in which one person has influence over the other.[107] The court will:

---

99 *Barclays Bank v. O'Brien*, above n. 12, 192.
100 *Howes v. Bishop*, above n. 74, 392.
101 *McKenzie v. Royal Bank of Canada* [1934] AC 468, 475.
102 Ibid., 475.
103 W.H.D. Winder, above n. 24, 103.
104 *Edgar v. Edgar* [1980] 1 WLR 1410.
105 *Midland Bank v. Shephard* [1988] 3 All ER 17.
106 *Midland Bank plc v. Perry* [1987] 5 WLUK 196.
107 *Royal Bank of Scotland plc v. Etridge (No. 2)*, above n. 17, para. 19.

> note, as a matter of fact, the opportunities for abuse which flow from a wife's confidence in her husband ... Where there is evidence that a husband has taken unfair advantage of his influence over his wife, or her confidence in him, 'it is not difficult for the wife to establish her title to relief'.[108]

Lord Nicholls points out that it is likely to be more challenging for spouses who have guaranteed loans to their partner to meet the second requirement that the transaction 'calls for explanation'.[109] The possibility of proving that a particular intimate relationship is one that is susceptible to influence (and passive advantage-taking) is central to the argument in this chapter.

## 2.6. WHEN IS AN INTIMATE RELATIONSHIP A RELATIONSHIP OF INFLUENCE?

Given the wide range of relationship dynamics possible within marriages, it is right that English law does not apply a blanket presumption of influence to all marriages. It is appropriate to require people in intimate relationships – such as fiancés and spouses – to demonstrate on the facts that theirs is a relationship in which they are in some way vulnerable to exploitation.[110] However, the law must choose how to define and identify relationships of influence in intimate relationship scenarios. If we define 'relationship of influence' too narrowly, we will deny relief to some people who are at risk of being taken advantage of.

First, personal trust may not be the basis of vulnerability. It is not universally true that spouses have full confidence in each other. People may agree to the wishes of their loved ones without trusting the other to succeed in business, for instance, or to reciprocate their concern.[111] Ridge challenges the 'trust and confidence' rationale for the *Yerkey v. Jones* special equity.[112] In the *Garcia* case, the wife did not consent because she had confidence in her husband; her reasons included pressure from him and her desire to preserve her marriage.[113] Even where a spouse 'entrusts' their partner with decision-making power, they may not subjectively trust them. In light of the wide diversity of relationships, Ridge considers that 'generally, imbalance of power and constraints on free choice are more significant factors justifying relief'.[114] Consequently, she

---

108 Ibid., para. 19.
109 Ibid., para. 28.
110 *Zamet v. Hyman*, above n. 82, 1446; *Barclays Bank v. O'Brien*, above n. 12, 190.
111 Cf. M. Chen-Wishart, above n. 58, 253.
112 P. Ridge, 'High Hopes: The meaning and merits of unconscionability as the rationale for the High Court's decision in Garcia v National Australia Bank Ltd' (2000) *National Law Review* 8.
113 Ibid., para. 25.
114 Ibid., para. 33.

suggests that we need a more inclusive explanation than 'trust and confidence' for why spousal guarantors can merit protection. The potential for exploitation does not require trust between partners.[115]

### *2.6.1. Deferring to a Partner in Financial Matters*

Trust is frequently understood in spouse cases as specifically meaning entrusting the conduct of financial affairs to the other person. This originates in the 'fiduciary' cases involving advisers who were not family members. In *Barclays Bank v. O'Brien*, Lord Browne-Wilkinson observed that many marital relationships justify a *de facto* presumption of influence because the wife 'placed trust and confidence in her husband in relation to her financial affairs'.[116] Lord Nicholls in *Etridge* affirms that proof 'that the complainant placed trust and confidence in the other party in relation to the management of the complainant's financial affairs' will count for the presumption of influence.[117] Parties seem to set out to frame their relationship in this light. The husband in *Barclays Bank v. Rivett* testified that he handed over his wages to his wife, who dealt with all financial matters.[118] Establishing that one person habitually defers completely to the other in financial matters is the easiest way to be confident of persuading the court that the relationship between the parties is one that raises a presumption of undue influence. As a litmus test, this is relatively easy to apply, without enquiring into the emotional nature of the parties' relationship.

Some cases suggest a narrow concentration on whether there is dependence in relation to *financial decisions*. The Privy Council decision in *Enal v. Singh* illustrates this tendency.[119] In that case, an elderly man was 'completely dependent' for his 'care and normal living activity' on his daughter and her son.[120] The reasoning focuses on whether there was 'a relationship of trust and confidence between them in relation to Mr Maharaj's financial and business affairs'.[121] However, there is no logical reason why, if presumed undue influence is to respond to relational vulnerability, we should not be interested in wider forms of dependence.

---

115 Ibid., para. 36.
116 *Barclays Bank v. O'Brien*, above n. 12, 190.
117 *Royal Bank of Scotland plc v. Etridge (No. 2)*, above n. 17, para. 14.
118 *Barclays Bank Plc v. Rivett* [1997] EWCA Civ. J0210-1; (1997) 29 HLR 893, 897; see also *Malik v. Malik* [2024] EWHC 69 para. 135.
119 *Enal v. Singh* [2022] UKPC 13.
120 Ibid., para. 31.
121 Ibid., para. 52.

### 2.6.2. *Dependence or Vulnerability*

Lewison J suggests in *Thompson v. Foy*[122] that the criterion of specifically financial trust was not intended to be exhaustive.[123] In *Malik v. Sheikh*,[124] an elderly woman transferred a share in her property to the person who lent money to her sons' business. Fancourt J found that her relationship with her sons raised a presumption of influence. Notably, he emphasised the donor's vulnerability:

> The principle is not confined to cases where trust and confidence is reposed, either financially or generally, but extends to cases where there is evidence of dependence or vulnerability.[125]

Other cases since *Etridge* seem to signal an expanding conception of 'dependence or vulnerability'.[126] In *Macklin v. Dowsett*, landlords were aware that a financial disparity made their tenant 'vulnerable to exploitation by them'.[127]

Focusing directly on vulnerability within the relationship, which may have many causes, is preferable to using traditional proxies such as whether a person delegates the handling of their financial matters to a family member. We see this most clearly in cases involving elderly parents. The reason for their vulnerability to exploitation is not predominantly that they defer in financial matters. Many cases portray older parents who are vulnerable because they are dependent on their children in their day-to-day lives.[128] Their affection and desire to support their adult children may also contribute. Similarly, as behaviours within marriages evolve over time, it is less likely that many spouses and cohabitees will testify that they let their partners handle all money matters. Ridge observes that only a subset of marriages, such as the one in *Aboody*, involve wives who have no real choice but to entrust their husbands with financial management.[129] In *Barclays Bank v. O'Brien*, the rationale of financial deference sits side-by-side with a distinct rationale, based on sexual and emotional ties. The law should recognise the other factors that make one person vulnerable to influence in these relationships.

---

122 *Thompson v. Foy* [2009] EWHC 1076 (Ch.).
123 Ibid., para. 100.
124 *Malik v. Sheikh*, above n. 18.
125 Ibid., para. 50.
126 *Chin v. Chin*, above n. 40, para. 128.
127 *Macklin v. Dowsett*, above n. 18.
128 *Sollis v. Leyshon*, above n. 41; *Malik v. Sheikh*, above n. 18.
129 *Bank of Credit and Commerce International SA v. Aboody* [1990] 1 QB 923; [1992] 4 All ER 955.

## 2.7. GENDER AND INFLUENCE WITHIN INTIMATE RELATIONSHIPS

Much of the case law, and the scholarship on emotionally transmitted debt, reveals a clear gendered dimension to influence within intimate relationships.[130] This is hardly surprising, considering that women have frequently been economically dependent on their husbands until recent decades. We might expect that the changing status of women in society and their increased participation in the labour market has created a more equal sharing of power within family relationships. From this perspective, one might question not only the need for but also the appropriateness of a doctrine that seems to aim to protect wives from being dominated by their husbands. This critique would be salient if presumed undue influence reflected outdated assumptions about the subservience or economic dependence of women.

However, empirical evidence suggests that notwithstanding changes in the status of women in society and within marriages, there are still imbalances in power within relationships to which the law might appropriately respond, and that these frequently remain gendered. Empirical research suggests that fewer men offer guarantees for their wives' businesses.[131] It seems that men and women are exposed to differing degrees to the various factors that may make them accede to a partner's demands.[132] Fehlberg observed a contrast between the female and male sureties whom she interviewed. While the women were constrained by a 'complex web of economic and social factors', the men were largely affected primarily by their 'emotional commitment within the relationship'.[133]

Furthermore, despite significant changes affecting the respective roles of men and women, many marriages remain, for 'many and varied reasons, marked by disparities of economic and other power between the parties'.[134] Sociological evidence over the past half century has shown that husbands commonly make the major financial decisions within marriages.[135] Early explanations suggested that this was due to the spouses' relative financial contributions (the 'resource theory' of power).[136] One might therefore expect that, as women have attained a more equal position in the labour market, this

130 M. Donnelly, 'Hidden in Plain Sight? Gender in the Irish Financial Crisis' in L. Black and P. Dunne (eds.), *Law and Gender in Modern Ireland: Critique and Reform*, Hart Publishing, Oxford 2019.

131 B. Fehlberg, above n. 36, 320.

132 O. Gan, 'Spousal Agreements and Patriarchal Bargains: A Wife's Guarantee of Her Husband's Business Debts' (2022) 18 *European Review of Contract Law* 175, 195.

133 B. Fehlberg, above n. 36, 334.

134 *Garcia v. National Australia Bank Ltd.*, above n. 96, para. 20.

135 B. Fehlberg, above n. 36, 322.

136 R. Blood and D.M. Wolfe, *Husbands and Wives*, New York Free Press, New York 1960.

inequality within marriages might have decreased. However, evidence suggests that increases in women's education and earnings have not translated fully into the power to make financial decisions within families.[137] Scholars suggest that this may reflect gender norms, with women choosing not to subvert these norms by taking on greater decision-making power. This is consistent with Fehlberg's empirical work with wives who had acted as sureties. They described themselves as having less financial power than their partners.[138] This reinforces the importance of both paying attention to the specifics of each relationship and perceiving the wider forms that relational influence can take. Imbalances in the power to make financial decisions in relationships are likely to remain relevant, even though it is less likely in general that one partner will abdicate all financial decision-making to the other.

## 2.8. THE 'CALLS FOR EXPLANATION' REQUIREMENT: THE EXPLICABILITY OF GIFTS TO LOVED ONES

Once a person pleading undue influence shows that theirs is a relationship of influence, the second requirement to trigger the presumption of undue influence is that the transaction must be excessive and not explicable by ordinary motives.[139] The size of the gift may indicate 'that something may be amiss'.[140] It matters whether a transaction is 'seriously and inexplicably detrimental' to the weaker party.[141] Lord Nicholls in *Etridge* observes that the criterion of excess is a necessary filter to limit the application of presumed undue influence. It would be absurd for the law to catch every festive or birthday gift between family members.[142] The usual test for determining whether the transaction is sufficiently imbalanced is articulated by Lindley LJ in *Allcard*; that is, whether

> the gift is so large as not to be reasonably accounted for on the ground of friendship, relationship, charity or other *ordinary motives* on which ordinary men act, [in which case] the burden is upon the donee to support the gift (emphasis added).[143]

---

137 C. Vogler, C. Lyonette, and R. Wiggins, 'Money, Power and Spending Decisions in Intimate Relationships' (2008) 56 *Sociological Review* 117; M. Klesment and J. Van Bavel, 'Women's Relative Resources and Couples' Gender Balance in Financial Decision-Making' (2022) 38 *European Sociological Review* 739.

138 B. Fehlberg, above n. 36, 324.

139 *Rhodes v. Bate*, above n. 52; *Re Craig*, above n. 31.

140 *Royal Bank of Scotland plc v. Etridge (No. 2)*, above n. 17, para. 24; *Malik v. Sheikh*, above n. 18, para. 45.

141 Ibid., para. 45.

142 *Royal Bank of Scotland plc v. Etridge (No. 2)*, above n. 17, para. 24.

143 *Allcard v. Skinner*, above n. 22, 185.

We can only draw a line between transactions that are 'normal' and 'abnormal' in the context of a designated relationship by referring, implicitly or explicitly, to societal norms. Bigwood explains that the concept of exploitation is necessarily 'contextually contingent ... relative to the social institution, formal or informal, that is the context of the relationship or encounter between the parties involved'.[144] Buried within the enquiry as to whether a transaction 'calls for explanation' is the question of how much our society and legal system considers it appropriate for one person to sacrifice their individual interests within each type of relationship. The answer will vary across cultures and time.

Case law indicates that 'calls for explanation' is not a binary test. The more detrimental the transaction, the stronger evidence it is considered to provide of the existence of influence. 'Calls for explanation' has been interpreted in post-*Etridge* case law in a way that seems to make it a high threshold to meet so as to raise a presumption of undue influence: the question is 'whether a transaction is explicable in terms other than undue influence'.[145] To assess this, 'it must be necessary to look at it in its context and to see what its general nature was and what it was trying to achieve for the parties'.[146]

### *2.8.1. Understanding 'Calls for Explanation' as an Indicator of Advantage-Taking?*

Contemporary case law often presents 'calls for explanation' as evidence of *influence*. The greater the imbalance, the stronger the evidence it offers of the existence of influence. In *Malik v. Sheikh*, Fancourt J says: 'the more disadvantageous and inexplicable the transaction the more easily a relationship of influence will be established to exist'.[147] This analysis is apt for (hidden) pressure cases, where the presumption enables the court to infer that coercion may have occurred, even though it has not directly been proven. It translates less well to intimate relationship cases that involve passive exploitation of relational vulnerability. The existence of influence in a relationship is not the mischief which the doctrine seeks to prevent. Rather, the problem is *taking advantage* of that influence. We should therefore understand the explicability of the transaction as signalling possible advantage-taking, whether in the form of pressure or disregard for the other person's interests. It makes sense to understand the size of the gift or the imbalance of the transaction as a sign that the transaction itself is objectionable in that, due to its extent or imbalance,

---

144 R. Bigwood, 'Kakavas v Crown Melbourne Ltd – Still Curbing Unconscionability: Kakavas in the High Court of Australia' (2013) 37(2) *Melbourne University Law Review* 463, 485–86.

145 *Turkey v. Awadh* [2005] EWCA Civ. 382, para. 32.

146 Ibid., para. 32.

147 *Malik v. Sheikh*, above n. 18, para. 45.

merely accepting the benefit will constitute advantage-taking (unless the recipient proves that it was a free and informed decision by the giver).

### 2.8.2. *The 'Explicability' of Gifts in Personal Relationships*

The explicability criterion raises possible complications in relation to gifts to family members, where generosity is to be expected. The *Allcard* formulation expressly excludes gifts that can reasonably be accounted for due to the relationship between the parties. This comes back to the point that Lord Nicholls expressed in *Etridge*: it is entirely normal and not objectionable that people should give generous gifts to those for whom they care.[148] Cases such as *Turkey v. Awadh* show another way in which the familial context can make it harder to show that a transaction calls for explanation.[149] Where family members make a deal together, the fact that they do not investigate the precise benefits that will accrue to each of them is not sufficient in itself to trigger the presumption of influence.[150] This acknowledges that people are not purely motivated by financial self-interest within families. The resulting risk is that exceedingly generous gifts or improvident transactions within intimate relationships would *not* generally trigger the presumption of influence.

Davies J in *Malik v. Malik* considered that the mother who transferred shares to her sons was partly motivated by her assessment of the family interest and her own interest.[151] It was designed to protect the family business and prosperity from risks posed by the donor's estranged husband. We might frame this application of the criterion of ordinary motives as testing whether the transfer is sufficiently consistent with the donor's own self-interest not to warrant interference. On this reading, ordinary motives correspond to motives that are not excessively self-sacrificing. The law sees that people in families act from a mixture of individual self-interest and the collective interests of the family or other members, and it chooses to intervene only if a transaction meets some threshold of excessive subordination of the individual's self-interest. Other cases, such as *Malik v. Sheik*, suggest that the courts *do* draw a line, whereby excessive self-sacrifice satisfies the test of 'calls for explanation'. An elderly woman transferred half of the beneficial interest in her two properties to the creditor of her sons' business. This was held to 'certainly' and 'strongly' call for explanation.[152] She was 'potentially significantly disadvantaged by the

148 *Royal Bank of Scotland plc v. Etridge (No. 2)*, above n. 17, para. 24.
149 *Turkey v. Awadh*, above n. 145, para. 32.
150 Ibid., para. 41.
151 *Malik v. Malik*, above n. 118, para. 135.
152 Ibid., paras. 41, 46.

transaction', as the protection of her own interests would then depend on her sons.[153]

In the context of caring relationships, the law must understand this criterion of 'ordinary motives on which ordinary men act' in a way which takes into account that people will be more generous within caring relationships; and yet which does *not* deprive people in those most intimate relationships of the law's protection. This implies an external, objective criterion of reasonableness. The court must determine that certain transactions are *excessively* generous or imbalanced. This assessment can only draw on societal norms: what degree of imbalance or self-sacrifice do we consider crosses a line so as to signal a potential instance of exploitation? This aligns with what we see in the case law. The size of the gift is generally measured according to an implicit scale of how generous we expect people to be within a relationship of the sort that exists between the parties.

### *2.8.3. Shared Interests in Families: A Complicating Factor for Guarantees*

There is another confounding factor when we apply the criterion of self-interest to family relationships. Acting in the interests of a loved one might be readily explicable, for financial reasons as well as affective reasons. This was Lord Nicholls' view in *Etridge*. Given that spouses' finances are interconnected, 'a wife's affection and self-interest run hand-in-hand' when she guarantees a loan to her husband's business.[154] This is why the House of Lords repudiated the 'manifest disadvantage' test[155] in *Etridge*, reverting to the language of explicability drawn from *Allcard* in the nineteenth century.[156] *Etridge* indicates that usually a wife's guarantee for a loan to her husband will not satisfy the requirement of calling for explanation, though in some cases it may.[157]

Fehlberg questions the assumption that a wife will benefit from a loan to her husband's business. The wife will only benefit if the business succeeds and the couple stay together.[158] Even where businesses succeed, there is evidence that profits are commonly reinvested rather than withdrawn for the owner's family.[159] It is reasonable to conclude that whether or not the surety is likely to benefit from giving the guarantee will depend on the circumstances. If the business is likely to fail, or the husband will not share profits with the wife, then the guarantee should meet the criterion of calling for explanation.

---

153 Ibid., para. 40.

154 *Royal Bank of Scotland plc v. Etridge (No. 2)*, above n. 17, para. 28; B. Fehlberg, above n. 36, 321; M. Chen-Wishart, above n. 58, 258–259.

155 *National Westminster Bank plc v. Morgan*, above n. 51.

156 *Royal Bank of Scotland plc v. Etridge (No. 2)*, above n. 17, para. 29.

157 Ibid., paras. 30–31.

158 B. Fehlberg, above n. 36, 321.

159 Ibid., 326.

## 3. SELF-SACRIFICE, POWER AND EXPLOITATION IN INTIMATE RELATIONSHIPS

The object of this chapter is to argue that the law ought to recognise the potential for exploitation that arises from one person's willingness to subordinate their own interests within a relationship. People can be extremely generous towards those they care for, especially in romantic relationships. Several cases involve people giving houses as gifts.[160] The internalised motivation to prioritise the interests of a loved one over one's own interests can, if it is not reciprocated, create an asymmetry of which the other person can take advantage. When the other person *does* exploit this power imbalance, the law should respond using the doctrine of presumed undue influence.

Judges in the modern leading cases have acknowledged the existence of this concern for the other person within close relationships. Lord Browne-Wilkinson seems to refer to this form of undue influence in *Barclays Bank v. O'Brien*, when he says:

> the sexual and emotional ties between the parties provide a ready weapon for undue influence: a wife's true wishes can easily be overborne because of her fear of destroying or damaging the wider relationship between her and her husband if she opposes his wishes.[161]

Similarly, in *Etridge*, Lord Nicholls refers to the 'emotional interdependence which normally characterises a marriage relationship'.[162] In *Barclays Bank plc v. Rivett*,[163] Buckley J adopted this reasoning as 'capable of applying to a husband as well as to a wife'.[164]

The analysis in the following sections elaborates on the connection between strong emotional ties in close personal relationships and the risk of undue influence. Recognising this source of influence as salient does not mean invalidating all gifts between people in intimate relationships. It remains a matter for partners or family members to show that their specific relationship is one in which this feature is a marked one. The scale of the transaction and its effect on the giver will, as always, be a signifier as to whether the theoretical risk of a mismatch in motivations creating potential for advantage-taking has actually occurred in this instance. Crucially, the 'calls for explanation' limb of the test for presumed undue influence will ensure that only excessive gifts

160 *Louth v. Diprose*, above n. 43; *Re Craig*, above n. 31.

161 *Barclays Bank v. O'Brien*, above n. 12, 190–191; see also *Louth v. Diprose*, n. 43 above, (1993) 67 ALJR 95, 99.

162 *Royal Bank of Scotland plc v. Etridge (No. 2)*, above n. 17, para. 36.

163 *Barclays Bank plc v. Rivett*, above n. 118.

164 Ibid., 190–191.

(or imbalanced transactions), which significantly diverge from societal norms governing interactions in close relationships, will be invalidated.

## 3.1. THE SUBORDINATION OF ONE'S OWN INTERESTS IN CLOSE PERSONAL RELATIONSHIPS

It is commonplace that people act altruistically to benefit those individuals for whom they care deeply. Having consideration for the interests of the other person is the hallmark of loving relationships. Recall the motivations of Mrs. Stuart in *Bank of Montreal v. Stuart*. She was willing to stake everything she owned to support her husband's failing business, in order to help him and to relieve his distress.[165] Maugham J's reasoning for protecting engaged women seems to express this idea that the vulnerable party does not attend to her financial self-interest: 'she does not interest herself in her future pecuniary position as between herself and her husband'.[166] She is not keeping score.

There are a range of reasons why people commonly act to promote the interests of those who are closest to them. Some are psychological explanations.[167] People may be motivated by pure affection, a sense of moral duty, dependence, or some element of pressure.[168] Some mix of these reasons is likely, as illustrated by sureties who explain that they were motivated both by pressure and by love.[169] Commonly, people may have economic as well as affective motivations for acceding to a partner's demands.[170] The Australian decision of *Thorne v. Kennedy* applied the doctrine of unconscionable conduct to a harsh pre-nuptial agreement. Thampapillai criticises the trial judge's narrative as a simplistic, stereotyped portrayal of an vulnerable young woman and calculating older man.[171] He suggests that by ignoring Ms. Thorne's capacity to make rational decisions informed by her own economic self-interest, the judge presents 'a reductionist characterisation of a complex person'.[172] We should not gloss over the complex and diverse reasons why people consent to their partners' wishes. This chapter argues for a fuller recognition of that complexity. The law does not currently respond sufficiently directly to an important and common reason why people might subordinate their own financial self-interest to the needs of

---

165 *Bank of Montreal v. Stuart*, above n. 1, 137.

166 *In re Lloyds Bank Ltd.*, above n. 92, 302.

167 P. Blau, *Exchange and Power in Social Life*, Wiley, New York 1964, pp. 35–36.

168 See e.g. *UCB Corporate Services v. Williams* [2002] EWCA Civ. 555, para. 32.

169 B. Fehlberg, above n. 36, 332.

170 D. Thampapillai, 'Archetypes of Age and Romance: Unconscionable Conduct and the High Court in *Thorne v Kennedy*' (2018) *University of Queensland Law Journal* 299, 307; B. Fehlberg, above n. 36, 321.

171 D. Thampapillai, above n. 170, 313.

172 Ibid., 313.

their intimates. The extent to which this reason will operate will always depend on the specifics of the relationship. In any case, the specific reason why an individual is prepared to prioritise the other person's interests is not central to the analysis of how it gives rise to advantage-taking.

The essential point is the importance of recognising the affective reason, which can be present even in cases where there is neither material dependence nor external pressure. It is a source of vulnerability that we will not perceive unless we identify it. It is also important for constructing a legal response that the impediment to the person pursuing their own self-interest in this context is not that they are ill-informed, nor that they lack the capacity to make decisions in their own interests. The person who is acting altruistically is choosing freely, and consistently with their own choices and values, but those choices are shaped by their understanding of the other person's interests. The reason why they need protection is that they do not treat the interaction as one in which it is appropriate to pursue their financial self-interest. This internalised motivation to prioritise the interests of a loved one is a source of vulnerability that does not depend on economic dependence, deference in financial matters or specific personal sources of vulnerability such as physical or mental infirmity, cultural values or language constraints. The person who is vulnerable to being taken advantage of within their personal relationship need not be 'vulnerable' in any other sphere of decision-making. This vulnerability is entirely context-specific. When the case law focuses on the need for evidence of these other sources of vulnerability, it risks being underinclusive: failing to see a real source of relational vulnerability that may have been exploited in a particular instance.

There is a potentially gendered dimension to people's propensity to subordinate their interests to those of loved ones. There is evidence that men and women behave differently in family relationships, with women more likely in general to favour a collective interest over their individual interest.[173] Some studies suggest that women tend more than men to identify themselves in terms of their relationship to others, and to judge themselves by 'a standard of relationship, an ethic of nurturance, responsibility, and care'.[174] Baron explains how this 'perceived social role of helping and supporting their loved ones' can cause women to take on obligations that they know are disadvantageous.[175] She comments: 'These women are clearly not the self-seeking maximisers of self-interest assumed by contract law'.[176] If so, this might leave 'women particularly vulnerable to exploitation'.[177] It follows that legal recognition of the potential

[173] C. Gilligan, *In a Different Voice: Psychological Theory and Women's Development*, Harvard University Press, Cambridge MA 1982, p. 159.
[174] Ibid.
[175] P. Baron, above n. 8, 27.
[176] Ibid., 27.
[177] A. Wertheimer, *Exploitation*, Princeton University Press, Princeton NJ 1996, p. 260.

for exploitation that arises from one person abstaining from pursuing their self-interest may be more important to protect women than men (in the aggregate) from a source of relational vulnerability that women seem more frequently to experience.

## 3.2. POWER AND THE POTENTIAL FOR EXPLOITATION OF THIS MOTIVATION

This phenomenon of *other-focused* motivations for decision-making in relationships creates power imbalances and the potential for exploitation. This is so, even though the motivation to do what one's loved ones want arises without any pressure at all emanating from the other person. This constraining internal pressure 'can sometimes be exerted without anything being said at all'.[178] Hedlund characterises gift-giving in a religious context as an 'emotional necessity'.[179] For people who believe it is necessary to give such donations, not offering them would have a psychological cost. The *internalised* pressure or constraint that results from being in a close intimate relationship is conceptually distinct from the imposition of pressure by another person.

Nonetheless, this source of vulnerability creates the conditions for passive advantage-taking, to which presumed undue influence may appropriately respond. Lukes makes several observations about power which capture the power that a person can have over their partner due to the partner's willingness to prioritise their interests. First, the use of power does not require us to overcome the other person's will. One way in which we may exercise power over another is 'by influencing, shaping or determining' what the other person *wants*.[180] Second, the use of power can be unconscious rather than intentional. 'Inactive' power can arise from a person's status, rather than from their actions. This applies where one person defers to another.[181] Thus, influencing a loved one's priorities – simply by being the object of their affection – is itself a manifestation of power.

---

178 J.L. Cummins, above n. 15, 64.

179 R. Hedlund, 'Undue Influence and the Religious Cases that Shaped the Law' (2016) 5 *Oxford Journal of Law and Religion* 298, 313.

180 S. Lukes, *Power: A Radical View* 2nd ed., Palgrave MacMillan, London 2005, p. 27.

181 Ibid., 78.

One person's renunciation of pursuing their self-interest is the key condition that creates the potential to exploit them.[182] Chen-Wishart identifies this risk.[183] When a person

> does not consciously self-protect, she 'lets her guard down', believing that the defendant will safeguard her interests in the transaction, and her decisions will be coloured by a concern to maintain or develop her relationship with the defendant.[184]

The danger is that the two parties may be playing by different rules. This analysis fits with existing conceptions of exploitation. Goodin conceptualises 'taking unfair advantage' as 'availing oneself of strategic opportunities which are denied to one under the rules and ethos of the game at hand'.[185] It follows that 'sharp practice' which may be acceptable in an arm's-length commercial context 'would be deeply exploitative in affectionate contexts (between friends or lovers)'.[186] This is because people in these intimate relationships understand the nature of the relationship to be something other than the self-interested, adversarial pursuit of gain. It is specifically and paradigmatically exploitative 'to strive for narrow, egoistic advantage over friends and lovers, who have renounced any such pursuit of advantage over you'.[187]

Similarly, Bigwood identifies the elements of an interpersonal exploitation claim as involving both exploitable circumstances and the act of exploitation.[188] Using Bigwood's language, the willingness of one person to forgo their individual self-interest confers 'interpersonal bargaining power' on the other. This gives the advantaged person an opportunity to shape the bargain in a way that furthers their interests, at the expense of the other.[189] If one person's subordination of their own interests because of the relationship leads to a transaction that seems excessive and not explicable by reference to societal norms, that will signal that the other person has in fact taken advantage of the disparity in power. The doctrinal requirement that a transaction 'calls for explanation' thus serves as an indicator that the person benefiting from the transaction has taken unfair advantage of the relational imbalance.

---

182 T. Logar, 'Exploitation as Wrongful Use: Beyond Taking Advantage of Vulnerabilities' (2010) 25 *Acta Analytica* 329, 340.

183 M. Chen-Wishart, above n. 58, 243.

184 Ibid., 253.

185 R. Goodin, 'Exploiting a Situation and Exploiting a Person' in A. Reeve (ed.), *Modern Theories of Exploitation*, Sage, London 1987, 183.

186 Ibid., 183.

187 Ibid., 185.

188 R. Bigwood, above n. 144, 487.

189 Ibid., 488.

## 3.3. UNCONSCIONABILITY AND ADVANTAGE-TAKING IN INTIMATE RELATIONSHIPS

This analysis shows why it is appropriate for equity to respond to the risk of exploitation that may arise from the mismatch of motivations in personal relationships. Using the language of equity, it is 'unconscionable' for a person to take advantage of the fact that the person with whom they are dealing is not maximising their own self-interest due to the relationship between them. When you are in a relationship of this sort, in which the other person will take account of your interests, you come under a moral duty to reciprocate. This makes it unconscionable not to attend also to the wellbeing of that person and, by failing to do so, to profit unduly from their deference to your interests.[190] It breaches the social norms about how we interact with family members and loved ones. This recalls Chen-Wishart's relational explanation of presumed undue influence. It also picks up on the 'fiduciary' reasoning in the case law.

There is plenty of support in judicial *dicta* for this view that equity responds to a form of shabby conduct that consists of taking full advantage of the vulnerability, confidence or altruism of the other person. In the expectant heir case of *Aylesford v. Morris* (1873), Lord Selborne said that 'fraud' in that context meant 'an unconscientious use of the power arising out of these circumstances and conditions'.[191] Bowen LJ in *Allcard* describes presumed undue influence as, 'a fetter placed upon the conscience of the recipient of the gift, and one which arises out of public policy and fair play'.[192]

In *Etridge*, Lord Nicholls' speech frames influence in a way that can reach the willingness of people in intimate relationships to prioritise the interest of the other over their own:

> The relationship between two individuals may be such that, without more, *one of them is disposed to agree a course of action proposed by the other.* Typically this occurs when one person places trust in another ... *and the latter betrays this trust by preferring his own interests* (emphasis added).[193]

Lord Nicholls' second sentence applies more broadly than to cases of financial deference. The idea of trust and betrayal of trust by preferring one's own interests applies equally where one person is acting in an other-focused way due to an intimate relationship. In *Hammond v. Osborn*, Nourse LJ rejected the argument that claimants would have to prove that the defendant preferred their

---

190 P.J. Millett, 'Equity's Place in the Law of Commerce' (1998) 114 *Law Quarterly Review* 214, 219.

191 *Earl of Aylesford v. Morris* (1872–73) LR 8 Ch. App. 484, 490–491.

192 *Allcard v. Skinner*, above n. 22, 189–190.

193 *Royal Bank of Scotland plc v. Etridge (No. 2)*, above n. 17, para. 9.

own interests and acted unfairly.[194] Rather, he said, once the presumption was raised and not rebutted, we could characterise the conduct of the recipient as having 'preferred his own interests and ... not behaved fairly to the donor'.[195] Blatant disregard for the person's own interests would meet the threshold. In *Bank of Montreal v. Stuart*, Lord Macnaghten commented that '[n]o man in his senses with any regard to the interest of Mrs. Stuart' could have encouraged her to give the guarantee.[196] This picks up on the sense that it can be inappropriate in certain relationships of trust and deep affection to exercise the power to take advantage of the other person by simply pursuing one's own interests. The pursuit of self-interest that is paradigmatic in most of contract law is objectionable in deeply trusting relationships.

## 3.4. WHICH DOCTRINE: PRESUMED UNDUE INFLUENCE OR UNCONSCIONABLE BARGAINS?

This identification of mere passive exploitation as unconscionable raises the possibility that another private law doctrine may be the more appropriate tool to respond to this mischief. This alternative tool is the doctrine of unconscionability or unconscionable bargains. The close connections between the doctrines of undue influence and unconscionability are highlighted in the scholarly literature that discusses whether and how they might be combined.[197] English law has a very narrow doctrine of unconscionable bargains.[198] In contrast, other common law jurisdictions, such as Australia and Canada, have developed more expansive doctrines of unconscionability.[199]

Australian law uses the doctrine of unconscionability rather than presumed undue influence to respond to the relational vulnerability that arises from family relationships.[200] In *Commercial Bank of Australia Ltd. v. Amadio*,[201] Mason J explains that unconscionability responds where: 'the will of the innocent party, even if independent and voluntary, is the result of the disadvantageous position in which he is placed and of the other party unconscientiously taking advantage of that position'.

194 *Hammond v. Osborn*, above n. 52, para. 31.

195 Ibid., para. 31.

196 *Bank of Montreal v. Stuart*, above n. 1, 138.

197 See D. Capper, 'Undue Influence and Unconscionability: a Rationalisation' (1998) 114 *Law Quarterly Review* 479.

198 See G. Spark, *Vitiation of Contracts: International Contractual Principles and English Law*, Cambridge University Press, Cambridge 2013, 284.

199 *Commercial Bank of Australia Ltd. v. Amadio* [1983] HCA 14; (1983) 151 CLR 447; *Uber Technologies Inc. v. Heller* 2020 SCC 16; [2020] 2 SCR 118.

200 *Commercial Bank of Australia Ltd. v. Amadio*, above n. 199.

201 Ibid.

This explanation fits neatly with the justification advanced in this chapter for providing a protective remedy. The reason for equitable intervention is not that the person has not properly consented, but rather that it is not appropriate for the other person to take advantage of their disadvantage. Employing the doctrine of unconscionable bargains would sidestep one obstacle to using presumed undue influence, which is that undue influence seems currently to focus on external pressure, rather than internalised constraints.

Importantly, the narrow doctrine of unconscionable bargains in English law does not provide a promising starting point for adapting this doctrine to address the vulnerability that exists in intimate relationships. The doctrine would have to expand radically in order to accommodate these relational vulnerability cases. In any case, there is a principled reason why presumed undue influence might be more apposite than unconscionability, even if we had a broader doctrine of unconscionability. The core of presumed undue influence is relational pressure. The exploitation at issue in this chapter is entirely relational. The pre-existing personal relationship between the parties is the source of one party's preparedness to sacrifice their own interests in favour of that other person's interests. The unconscionable conduct of the beneficiary of this generosity lies in taking advantage by pursuing their naked self-interest; this is only unconscionable in the context of the relationship because it is inconsistent with the norms of conduct in such intimate relationships.

This marks a difference from so-called spiritual influence cases, in which the relevant relationship is with a religious leader. Ridge argues that the religious belief cases might better have been decided on the basis of unconscionable conduct than undue influence. Unconscionability may be a better fit for spiritual influence cases than for intimate relationship cases, even though both of these involve exploitation of a person's internal commitments, because the vulnerability in the relationship cases is relational in a way that the vulnerability in spirituality cases may not be. In spiritual influence cases, it may seem artificial to focus on the relationship between a donor and a single religious leader in order to establish a relationship of influence. In the intimate relationship cases, the relationship between the two people truly is the source of the vulnerability.

Lastly, there is a risk that appealing to unconscionable bargains might result in the application of too high a standard of active oppressive conduct. Some claims might not succeed because there was no active advantage-taking.[202] There is some doubt based on recent case law whether the Australian doctrine of unconscionable conduct requires 'proof of a predatory state of mind', not just 'indifference to, the best interests of the other party' to find unconscionable

[202] D. Thampapillai, above n. 170, 300.

conduct.[203] A person who takes advantage of a partner or family member's willingness to subordinate their own self-interest is passively exploiting that person. Presumed undue influence, which offers protection from passive advantage-taking, is the most appropriate tool to address the particular risk of advantage-taking in close personal relationships that this chapter considers.

## 3.5. CAN UNDUE INFLUENCE ACCOMMODATE INTERNALISED NORMS

A possible objection to protecting people from their own consenting self-sacrifice is that undue influence should respond to external pressure, not a person's own choices. We are generally held responsible for our choices, whatever mix of psychological factors and norms inform them. This concern is heightened if we consider, as *Etridge* suggests, that presumed undue influence cases are always just undue influence cases in the end.[204] Moreover, there is an express focus in important case law on the need for influence to have an external source, rather than a person's own motivations. Lindley LJ in *Allcard* emphasises that undue influence responds to influence exerted by another person, not to a person's own enthusiasms:

> The undue influence which Courts of Equity endeavour to defeat is the undue influence of one person over another; not the influence of enthusiasm on the enthusiast who is carried away by it, unless indeed such enthusiasm is itself the result of external undue influence.[205]

There are several potential difficulties in treating an internalised desire to prioritise the other person or the relationship as a basis for undue influence. First, it may be the donor's genuine own desire to favour their loved one, not a choice that they consider imposed upon them. Second, this is an internal enthusiasm, which might be hard to distinguish from the ordinary case of poor judgement, for which the law holds us responsible. Third, the person who benefits from the transaction is not responsible for the internal norms or commitments that lead the other person to prioritise them. The most we might say is that they are the source of the influence in that they are the person for whom the donor feels this sense of attachment.

---

203 *Kakavas v. Crown Melbourne Limited* [2013] HCA 25, para. 161; (2013) 250 CLR 392; cf. D. Thampapillai, above n. 170, 311.

204 *Royal Bank of Scotland plc v. Etridge (No. 2)*, above n. 17, para. 93.

205 *Allcard v. Skinner*, above n. 22, 183.

Ward LJ in *Drew v. Daniel*[206] differentiates between external influences and a person's own authentic preferences: 'There is no undue influence unless the donor if she were free and informed could say "This is not my wish but I must do it"'.[207] On its face, this definition of influence seems to exclude a person's own internalised motivations that prompt them to sacrifice their own interests out of concern for another. If you asked Mrs. Stuart why she agreed to risk everything she owned to guarantee her husband's liabilities, she would no doubt answer that it was indeed her 'wish' to do so. The desire to support and assist the people we care deeply about is undoubtedly a genuine and authentically-held preference.

However, the case law on spiritual influence clearly establishes that a person's own genuine beliefs and value commitments can give rise to a claim in presumed undue influence. Even in *Allcard* itself, the court was willing to apply the doctrine to a woman who acted from her own spiritual convictions. Lindley LJ overcame this obstacle by observing that a person's own thinking may have been subtly moulded by the influence of another. This answer will not apply in every case. In cases where there is an identifiable spiritual leader, we might attribute to them a key role in having shaped a person's religious commitments, but this is not always the case. Ridge identifies cases where it seemed to be primarily the person's own religious convictions and enthusiasm rather than a relationship with a specific religious advisor that motivated a transaction (*Hartigan v. ISKCON*[208] and *Tufton v. Sperni*[209]).[210] Despite judicial rhetoric that the law does not protect people from their own foolish decisions, the 'extreme improvidence' of the transaction in *Hartigan* spurred the court to intervene. Ridge concludes that 'the assertion that the courts do not undo unwise bargains is not convincing in the religious faith context':[211] the law does not require that subtle influence from another person have moulded the belief system that causes the transaction.

In any case, it seems unproductive to seek to attribute a person's propensity to act altruistically towards loved ones as between a purely internal psychological source and external influences. Each person's thoughts, values and preferences are what they are, shaped as they have been by all sorts of influences, subtle and overt. There is no meaningful sense in which we can say that certain of my beliefs are genuinely mine whereas others have been inculcated by other people. Nor is it necessary to do this in order to justify relieving somebody from the transaction on the ground of undue influence.

---

206 *Drew v. Daniel* [2005] EWCA Civ. 507.
207 Ibid., para. 36.
208 *Hartigan v. International Society for Krishna Consciousness Inc.* [2002] NSWSC 810.
209 *Tufton v. Sperni* [1952] 2 TLR 516 (PC).
210 P. Ridge, above n. 72.
211 Ibid., 83.

Presumed undue influence operates to protect people from exploitation, regardless of their consent and regardless of whether the other person in the relationship has caused that influence. If we take overt pressure as our model, we might be tempted to assume that an overborne will,[212] caused by the actions of the other party, is necessary for undue influence. However, presumed undue influence does not require these two elements. The fact that I have chosen to prioritise the interests of a loved one, with full consent arising from my authentically-held values, is not an obstacle to offering relief in undue influence. This is because presumed undue influence is not predicated on the quality of my consent. In *Etridge*, Lord Nicholls noted the wide range of forms that undue influence can take. He said that the doctrine should apply, 'whenever the consent thus procured *ought not fairly to be treated* as the expression of a person's free will' (emphasis added).[213] The point is not that the person did not consent: they did. It is that holding them to that consent permits their exploitation by a person who is not playing by the same rules.

The essence of presumed undue influence is taking advantage of a vulnerability that exists due to the relationship between two people. What my 'enthusiasm' – whether religious or interpersonal[214] – does is to create the potential to take advantage of me. My willingness to subordinate my own material interests makes me vulnerable to exploitation. The law of presumed undue influence may legitimately protect people whose choices are underpinned by these specific forms of internalised conviction. They are distinguishable from the person's 'own folly' as a specific source of vulnerability that affects their choices in limited contexts. There is a material difference between a person taking advantage of (i) their romantic partner's willingness to act altruistically towards them, and (ii) their partner's generally poor judgement. It also follows that we do not need to hold the recipient of the gift responsible in any sense for the influence. The recipient's responsibility is for taking advantage of the relational influence, not for creating it. This analysis is consistent with Farwell J's reasoning in *Powell v. Powell*, which takes a strict approach to gifts made by children under parental pressure. Farwell J said that the advising solicitor's duty

> is to protect the donor against himself, and not merely against the personal influence of the donee, in the particular transaction. The necessity for the protection arises in great measure from the natural bent of mind and will resulting from the relation (e.g.) of parent and child during the impressionable period of youth.[215]

---

212 *Drew v. Daniel*, above n. 206, para. 36.

213 *Royal Bank of Scotland plc v. Etridge (No. 2)*, above n. 17, para. 7.

214 *Louth v. Diprose*, above n. 43.

215 *Powell v. Powell* [1900] 1 Ch. 243, 247.

## 3.6. OTHER RELATIONSHIPS WHERE SELF-SACRIFICE MIGHT CREATE VULNERABILTY

### *3.6.1. Emotional Connection in Parent-Child and Other Familial Relationships*

The type of relational vulnerability that this chapter identifies may sometimes apply in certain other close familial relationships, beyond romantic or domestic partners. The law does not treat 'sexual relationships as standing in some special category of their own so far as undue influence is concerned'.[216] In suitable cases, purely emotional ties themselves might create a sufficient relationship of potential influence. The way the law on undue influence is structured allows us to ask about the features of the specific relationship between the parties.

The relationship between parents and their adult children or guardians and their wards was an early category of relationship to be recognised as prompting a presumption of influence by the parent over the child.[217] *In Turner v. Collins*, Lord Hatherley said that parental authority is rooted not in 'terror and coercion, but kindness and affection'.[218] In *Lancashire Loans Ltd v. Black*, Lawrence LJ highlighted the emotional connection between mothers and daughters, calling it 'undoubtedly one of the greatest intimacy and confidence'.[219] The Court of Appeal held that the presumption that parents have influence over their children did not necessarily come to an end at the moment that the child married and moved out. It would depend in each case on the circumstances of the individual relationship between parent and adult child. This is the right approach to take to whether the emotional connection is sufficiently strong in any personal or familial relationship to raise a presumption of influence.

Many modern cases conversely involve parents benefiting their adult children, for instance by giving guarantees.[220] For as long as the law characterises the relationship which can raise the presumption of influence as one of *dependence*, it will miss an important reason why parents might feel constrained to give their property to their adult children. Language such as 'ascendancy' or 'dependence' seems not to fit, unless we understand that the influence the child has is largely attributable to their parent's internalised commitment to promoting the child's interests. In *Watt v. State Bank of New South Wales*, the judges said the parents' vulnerability:

> stems from their love of their children. Their desire to help and protect them, to advance their interests, to maintain a close relationship, to avoid causing

216 *Royal Bank of Scotland plc v. Etridge (No. 2)*, above n. 17, para. 82.

217 See e.g. *Archer v. Hudson* (1844) 7 Beavan 551; *Hoghton v. Hoghton*, above n. 70.

218 *Turner v. Collins* (1871) LR 7 Ch. App. 329, 339, 340.

219 *Lancashire Loans Ltd v. Black* [1934] 1 KB 380, 411.

220 E.g. *Lloyds Bank v. Bundy* [1974] 3 WLR 501; *Coldunell Limited v. Gallon* [1986] QB 1184.

> disappointment, hurt or distress, to maintain the relationship may all make it difficult to say no.[221]

Similarly, the judgment in *Janesland Holdings Pty. Ltd. v. Simon* notes that:

> In many cases the parents are well aware of the improvidence of their decision but have agreed, however reluctantly, to proceed with the transaction because of their affection for their children, a perception that a refusal might be damaging to their relationship with them, and/or a conviction that they deserve the chance to make good.[222]

Baron suggests that there is a societal expectation that men may be willing to deprioritise their own interests 'where the good of their children is concerned'.[223] A 'societal obligation to provide for one's dependants'[224] informs case law on spiritual gifts and was influential in *Huguenin v. Baseley*. This internalised commitment to assist one's children is not necessarily switched off when they become adults. The extent to which a parent might continue to feel an imperative to prioritise their adult children's needs will undoubtedly vary widely. It follows that it should be possible for parents to cite this form of relational vulnerability, provided they can show that their relationship with their child is sufficiently close.

It is less likely that the courts will protect people in other family relationships without proof of specific vulnerability. In *Irvani v. Irvani*, Buxton LJ rejected a claim for undue influence between a man, who was vulnerable due to drug addiction, and his brother and sister.[225] He stated: 'Family loyalty, at least other than between husband and disadvantaged wife; business partnership; or impecuniosity; have never been seen as founding such a defence; nor should they, save perhaps in the most extreme case'.[226] It may be that the 'family loyalty' between siblings is typically less likely to lead to self-sacrificing decisions than that which frequently exists between parents and children or between romantic partners.

### *3.6.2. Analogous Case of Cultural Norms of Obedience*

Kapai draws attention to an analogous situation, in which people knowingly accede to acts that they know are not in their interests because they are compelled by internalised cultural norms. She argues that the law is currently

221 *Watt v. State Bank of New South Wales* [2003] ACTCA 7, 20.
222 *Janesland Holdings Pty Ltd v. Simon & Others*, above n. 16, para. 79.
223 P. Baron, above n. 8, 25.
224 P. Ridge, above n. 72.
225 *Irvani v. Irvani* [2000] 1 Lloyd's Rep. 412.
226 Ibid., para. 166.

insensitive to cultural norms which require people to obey others in a hierarchical family structure.[227] *Barclays Bank plc v. Coleman*, one of the joined cases in *Etridge*, concerned a Hassidic Jewish couple. The House of Lords was satisfied that, in light of cultural norms, this was factually a relationship of 'complete trust and confidence'.[228]

Using an inapposite label runs the risk of leading us astray when we need to determine whether a relationship is factually one of influence or not. Kapai argues that, by inquiring into 'trust and confidence' instead of the operative duty to obey, the courts fail to protect people from cultures with strong norms of obedience to authority. In addition, judges fail to perceive that people might be capable and independent in their professional lives, yet still compelled to obey authority figures in their personal lives. By recognising that the internalised imperative to conform to another person's wishes creates scope for exploitation, to which presumed undue influence should respond, the law could offer a remedy in these cases too.

## 4. CONCLUSION

The object of this chapter has been to bring to light a mechanism whereby a mode of decision-making that is commonplace within people's closest personal relationships creates a risk of passive exploitation. It often happens within intimate or familial relationships that one person may prioritise the interests of the other. If the beneficiary of that concern does not reciprocate with equal concern for the first person's interests, the mismatch in motivations produces a real risk of advantage-taking. The transaction may be conspicuously imbalanced as a direct result of this mismatch. Passive advantage-taking of this sort is unconscionable and provides a sufficient justification for us to apply the doctrine of presumed undue influence. The common law's usual premise that contracts result from the interaction of two hard-nosed actors, each defending their own interests, does not apply here. Applying the ordinary common law rules to uphold the bargain would simultaneously do an injustice to the person who acts on an internalised ethic of caring for another and enable the other person to exploit that natural drive. It follows that it is appropriate for the equitable doctrine to prevent this exploitation and to protect the giver from a transaction that meets a threshold of clear substantive unfairness that departs significantly from societal norms.

---

227 P. Kapai, 'Multiple Influences: Courting Culture in the Doctrine of Undue Influence' in P. Kapai (ed.), *Reciprocity in Contract*, University of Hong Kong, Hong Kong 2010, https://ssrn.com/abstract=1701638 (accessed 16.07.2025).

228 *Royal Bank of Scotland plc v. Etridge (No. 2)*, above n. 17, paras. 130, 283, 290.

In order to protect the person who suffers adverse material consequences from adopting an altruistic orientation within the context of their relationship, the legal system should expressly recognise this distinct source of relational vulnerability and the mechanism by which it can lead to exploitation. This does not require us to adapt the legal rules significantly. People seeking to avail themselves of the doctrine of presumed undue influence will still need to show that their individual relationship is one that is sufficiently close for this form of 'influence' to exist, involving subordination of one person's self-interest in the relationship. The only change required to the law will be for the courts to apply the test to identify *relationships of influence* in a way that recognises that affective influence and concomitant vulnerability do not require financial dependence or more general vulnerabilities. This form of vulnerability can ordinarily arise within the closest relationships, regardless of the independence or status that a person otherwise enjoys.

There is no need to fear that taking the step of recognising this form of vulnerability in intimate and familial relationships will lead to an explosion of successful undue influence claims or jeopardise the security of transactions. This is because the second requirement needed to raise the presumption, relating to the explicability of the transaction, acts as a filter and control. Even where the relationship is such that one party is disposed to subordinate their interests to those of the person for whom they care, it is only when the substance of the transaction diverges notably from societal norms for a relationship of that kind that the evidence will indicate that the person who benefits has taken undue advantage of their power in the relationship. The established criterion of whether a transaction is readily explicable permits the courts to differentiate between ordinary or even generous gifts that fall within accepted norms, and sacrifices that are so detrimental to the giver that the recipient's acceptance indicates passive exploitation.

# CHAPTER 4

# CONTRACT AND POWER IN THE AGE OF AI: ALGORITHMIC DISCRIMINATION AND FUNDAMENTAL RIGHTS IMPACT ASSESSMENTS

Aurelia Colombi Ciacchi, Greta Berardi and Alma-Cristina Onaie



## 1. INTRODUCTION

Powerful public or private parties often take decisions through algorithms. Not rarely, these decisions have the (mostly unintended) effect of directly or indirectly discriminating against certain groups of persons. Around this relatively recent societal problem – algorithmic discrimination – a new discourse in legal science is now developing.[1]

Many algorithms are not 'intelligent' enough to qualify as AI.[2] The term 'algorithmic discrimination' in this chapter refers to the use of algorithms independently of whether they form part of AI systems.

Two grounds of algorithmic discrimination seem to be the most frequent in practice: sex or gender on the one hand, and race or ethnic background on the other.[3] In EU law, the right not to be discriminated against on the ground of sex, race, colour, ethnic or social origin, genetic features, language, religion or belief, political or any other opinion, membership of a national minority, property, birth, disability, age or sexual orientation, is a fundamental right enshrined in Article 21(1) of the Charter of Fundamental Rights of the EU ('the Charter'). The terms 'discrimination' and 'discriminatory' in the present chapter refer to any of the grounds listed in Article 21(1) of the Charter.

This chapter begins by addressing some examples of algorithmic discrimination in contractual relationships (section 2.). Then it focuses on a specific instrument aiming at preventing algorithmic discrimination and other risks for fundamental rights related to the use of algorithms or AI

---

1 See, among others, J. Kleinberg et al., 'Discrimination in the Age of Algorithms' (2018) 10 *Journal of Legal Analysis* 113; F.J. Zuiderveen Borgesius, *Discrimination, artificial intelligence, and algorithmic decision-making*, Council of Europe, Directorate General of Democracy, 2018: https://rm.coe.int/discrimination-artificial-intelligence-and-algorithmic-decisionmaking/1680925d73 (accessed 17.03.2018); R. Xenidis and L. Senden, 'EU non-discrimination law in the era of artificial intelligence: Mapping the challenges of algorithmic discrimination' in U. Bernitz et al. (eds.), *General Principles of EU law and the EU Digital Order*, Kluwer Law International, Alphen aan den Rijn 2020, p. 157; F.J. Zuiderveen Borgesius, 'Strengthening Legal Protection against Discrimination by Algorithms and Artificial Intelligence' (2020) *The International Journal of Human Rights*, available at SSRN: https://ssrn.com/abstract=3561441 (accessed 16.03.2025); L. Grozdanovski, 'In search of effectiveness and fairness in proving algorithmic discrimination in EU law' (2021) 58(1) *Common Market Law Review* 99–136; A. Circiumaru, 'Futureproofing EU Law – The Case of Algorithm Discrimination' (30.07.2021), available at SSRN: https://ssrn.com/abstract=3953627 or http://dx.doi.org/10.2139/ssrn.3953627 (accessed 16.03.2025).

2 For a brief explanation of the difference between AI and algorithm see K. Ismail, 'AI vs Algorithms: What's the Difference?', *CMSWire*, Information Management, 26 October 2018, https://www.cmswire.com/information-management/ai-vs-algorithms-whats-the-difference/ (accessed 14.03.2025): 'An algorithm is a set of instructions – a preset, rigid, coded recipe that gets executed when it encounters a trigger. AI on the other hand – which is an extremely broad term covering a myriad of AI specializations and subsets – is a group of algorithms that can modify its algorithms and create new algorithms in response to learned inputs and data as opposed to relying solely on the inputs it was designed to recognize as triggers. This ability to change, adapt and grow based on new data, is described as "intelligence"'. For a more detailed explanation of the differences between rule-based algorithms and machine-learning algorithms see J. Gerards and R. Xenidis, *Algorithmic discrimination in Europe: Challenges and opportunities for gender equality and non-discrimination law*, European Commission, Directorate-General for Justice and Consumers, Publications Office, 2021, https://data.europa.eu/doi/10.2838/544956 (accessed 14.03.2025), 32–36.

3 See J. Gerards and R. Xenidis, *Algorithmic discrimination in Europe*, above n. 2.

systems: fundamental rights impact assessments. The first impact assessment model considered in this chapter (section 3.) is a national model: the Fundamental Rights and Algorithms Impact Assessment (FRAIA), developed in the Netherlands a few years ago to prevent violations of fundamental rights through algorithms.

The second model addressed in this chapter (section 4.) is the fundamental rights impact assessment prescribed by Article 27 of the EU AI Act. The AI Act requires not only public bodies but also several categories of private actors to conduct an FRIA prior to the use of a high-risk AI system. The AI Act is arguably designed to apply primarily in the private sector.[4] However, one of the models that mainly inspired the FRIA is the Dutch FRAIA, designed to apply to public authorities.

This chapter's concluding section (section 5.) questions the capability of these and similar fundamental rights impact assessment systems to prevent algorithmic discrimination by powerful contract parties in the EU. Finally, it highlights some lessons that the old discourse on fundamental rights obligations of private contractual actors could learn from the new discourse on fundamental rights impact assessments under the AI Act.

## 2. EXAMPLES OF ALGORITHMIC DISCRIMINATION IN PRIVATE CONTRACTUAL RELATIONSHIPS

Reported cases of algorithmic discrimination in private contractual relationships in the EU Member States[5] mainly concern three areas: (2.1) employment and platform work, (2.2) banking and insurance,[6] and (2.3) targeted advertising, price setting, and retail.

4 G. Barrachina Navarro and A. Boix Palop, 'The applicability of the Artificial Intelligence Act to the field of public administration and public services and special features regarding compliance: Special attention to Annex III and administrative action and particularities of compliance', in L. Cotino Hueso and D.-U. Galetta (eds.), *The European Union Artificial Intelligence Act. A Systematic Commentary*, Editoriale Scientifica, Napoli 2025, pp. 365–386.

5 See J. Gerard and R. Xenidis, *Algorithmic discrimination in Europe*, above n. 2, 83 et seq.

6 On discrimination connected to the use of algorithms in the financial sector, see *inter alia* A. Morse and K. Pence, 'Technological Innovation and Discrimination in Household Finance', in R. Rau, R. Wardro and L. Zingales (eds.), *The Palgrave Handbook of Technological Finance*, Springer Nature, London 2021, pp. 783–808; N. Remolina, 'The Role of Financial Regulators in the Governance of Algorithmic Credit Scoring', SMU Centre for AI & Data Governance Research Paper No. 2/2022, https://ssrn.com/abstract=4057986 (accessed 14.03.2025).

## 2.1. EMPLOYMENT AND PLATFORM WORK

In the area of employment, under EU law, the prohibition of *direct* discrimination on the grounds of ethnic origin,[7] gender,[8] religion or belief, disability, age or sexual orientation applies in both vertical and horizontal relationships.[9] By contrast, *indirect* discrimination on grounds of religion or belief, disability, age or sexual orientation can be justified if the restriction pursues a legitimate aim and if the means used for achieving the specific aim are both appropriate and necessary.[10] Scholars have observed that the protection against discrimination in employment matters under EU law tends to be stricter than the protection against discrimination in other types of legal relationships. This is due to the nature of employment contracts, where the relationship between employer and employee can arguably be compared to the one between the state and the individual on account of an imbalance of power between the parties and thus requires greater individual protections.[11]

However, notwithstanding all national and EU non-discrimination law instruments,[12] algorithmic discrimination in employment matters[13] occurs in different stages of the employment process covering the candidate sourcing,[14]

[7] Council Directive 2000/43/EC of 29 June 2000 implementing the principle of equal treatment between persons irrespective of racial or ethnic origin [2000] *OJ* L180/22.

[8] Directive 2006/54/EC of the European Parliament and of the Council of 5 July 2006 on the implementation of the principle of equal opportunities and equal treatment of men and women in matters of employment and occupation (recast) [2006] *OJ* L204/23.

[9] Council Directive 2000/78/EC of 27 November 2000 establishing a general framework for equal treatment in employment and occupation [2000] *OJ* L303/16.

[10] Ibid., Article 2(2)(i).

[11] K. Lutman, 'Artificial Intelligence and the prohibition of discrimination in the EU: A private law perspective' in A. Završnik and K. Simončič (eds.), *Artificial Intelligence, Social Harms and Human Rights. Critical Criminological Perspectives,* Palgrave Macmillan, Cham 2023, p. 83.

[12] For a brief *tour d'horizon* of EU non-discrimination law see S. Ganty and K. de Vries, 'Non-discrimination in EU social security law: Exploring safeguards against gender and racial discrimination' (1 December 2023) CEU Democracy Institute Working Papers No. 20, 2023, available at https://ssrn.com/abstract=4650622 or http://dx.doi.org/10.2139/ssrn.4650622 (accessed 16.03.2025).

[13] For a comparative overview see C. Hiessl, 'Jurisprudence of National Courts in Europe on Algorithmic Management at the Workplace' (2023) Report for the European Centre of Expertise in the Field of Labour Law, Employment and Labour Market Policies, 4 https://papers.ssrn.com/sol3/papers.cfm?abstract_id=3982735 (accessed 16.03.2025), with further references.

[14] K. Lutman, above n. 11, p. 86.

the selection procedure[15] as well as in conditions granting pay[16] and promotion.[17] Algorithmic discrimination affects platform workers too. For example, recent studies showed that female platform workers often receive lower pay than their male counterparts.[18]

Back in 2020, the Italian *Tribunale di Bologna*[19] found that the reputational ranking algorithm employed by the delivery platform Deliveroo was indirectly discriminatory to the detriment of female workers. The algorithm was used to give riders access to a system for booking and cancelling working shifts. The decision of which riders to prioritise was automated according to the measure of the riders' 'reliability' and 'participation'. This measure, however, was determined without any consideration of legally protected reasons for absence from work such as care duties (still performed mainly by women), illness, disability, personal beliefs, or strike actions. By treating all cancellations of work shifts without distinction, the algorithm limited female riders' work opportunities in an unfair and discriminatory way.[20]

In the Member States' legal systems, the status and legal protection of platform workers vary considerably.[21] Some countries, such as France and Greece, have improved the regulatory protection of those workers while reaffirming their status as independent professionals. In contrast, in other countries, such as Spain, platform workers are increasingly re-classified as employees.[22] The same result has been achieved in the Netherlands through case law. The Dutch Supreme Court judgment *Deliveroo Netherlands BV*,[23]

---

15 Ibid., p. 87. See also C. Carter, 'Why the algorithmic recruiter discriminates: The causal challenges of data-driven discrimination' (2024) 31(3) *Maastricht Journal of European and Comparative Law* 333–359, https://doi.org/10.1177/1023263X241248474 (accessed 16.03.2025) with further references; and L. Grozdanovski, above n. 1.

16 See J. Gerard and R. Xenidis, *Algorithmic discrimination in Europe*, above n. 2, p. 55.

17 K. Lutman, above n. 11, p. 87.

18 M. Kullmann-Klocke, 'Platform Work, Algorithmic Decision-Making, and EU Gender Equality Law' (2018) 34(1) *International Journal of Comparative Labour Law and Industrial Relations* 1, 2 et seq. with further references.

19 Tribunale di Bologna, ordinanza no. 2949/2019, 31 December 2020.

20 For a comment on this case see R. Xenidis, 'When Computers Say No: Towards a Legal Response to Algorithmic Discrimination in Europe' in B. Brożek, P. Przemyslaw and O. Kanevskaia (eds.), *Research Handbook on Law and Technology*, Edward Elgar Publishing, Cheltenham 2024, pp. 222–234.

21 C. Hiessl, 'Case Law on the Classification of Platform Workers: Cross-European Comparative Analysis and Tentative Conclusions' (12 March 2024), Forthcoming, *Comparative Labour Law & Policy Journal*, Available at: https://ssrn.com/abstract=3839603 or http://dx.doi.org/10.2139/ssrn.3839603 (accessed 16.03.2025).

22 O. Guinea, E. Sisto and O. du Roy, 'Regulating the Working Conditions of Platform Work: What Can We Learn from EU Member States?' *European Centre for International Political Economy (ECIPE)*, January 2024, https://ecipe.org/publications/regulating-the-working-conditions-of-platform-work/ (accessed 15.03.2025).

23 Dutch Supreme Court (Hoge Raad), *Deliveroo Netherlands BV v. Federation of Dutch Trade Unions* ECLI:NL:HR:2023:443.

although not directly addressing issues of algorithmic discrimination, is an important case defining the status of platform workers. Deliveroo operated on the basis of 'assignment agreements' rather than employment contracts.[24] Following a complaint submitted by the Dutch trade union FNV, the Dutch Supreme Court had to determine whether Deliveroo workers qualified as 'employees'.[25] The Court held that an agreement could be classified as an employment contract based on factors such as the nature and duration of the work, as well as the worker's degree of control over the work and working hours.[26] The Court concluded that the agreements concluded by Deliveroo with its workers could undoubtedly be classified as employment contracts.[27]

The new EU Directive 2024/2831 on improving working conditions in platform work[28] sets minimum standards of workers' protection: first and foremost is a legal presumption of employment, to be triggered when facts indicating control and direction are found. These facts will be determined according to national law and collective agreements, while taking into account EU case law. Platform workers, their representatives or national authorities may invoke this legal presumption and claim they are misclassified. It is up to the digital platform to prove that there is no employment relationship.[29] Moreover, one of the main objectives of the new Directive is to protect workers in the context of algorithmic management. The Directive bans the use of automated monitoring or decision-making systems for the processing of certain types of personal data of persons performing platform work, such as biometric data or information about their emotional or psychological state. Human oversight and evaluation are also guaranteed as regards automated decisions, including the right to have those decisions explained and reviewed. Workers must be duly informed about the use of automated monitoring and decision-making systems regarding their recruitment, their working conditions and their earnings, among other things.[30]

---

24 Ibid., para. 2(2)(ii).

25 Ibid., para. 2.3.

26 Ibid., para. 3.2.5.

27 Ibid., para. 3.4. For a comment on this judgment see C. Hiessl, above n. 21. See also De Brauw Blackstone Westbroek, 'Dutch Supreme Court delivers landmark decision: Deliveroo riders are employees' (De Brauw Blackstone Westbroek, 24.03.2023) https://www.debrauw.com/articles/dutch-supreme-court-delivers-landmark-decision-deliveroo-riders-are-employees (accessed 16.03.2025).

28 Directive (EU) 2024/283 of the European Parliament and of the Council of 23 October 2024 on improving working conditions in platform work [2024] *OJ* L2831.

29 Council of the EU, Press release 11.03.2024, 'Platform workers: Council confirms agreement on new rules to improve their working conditions', https://www.consilium.europa.eu/en/press/press-releases/2024/03/11/platform-workers-council-confirms-agreement-on-new-rules-to-improve-their-working-conditions/ (accessed 15.03.2025).

30 Ibid.

However, anti-discrimination experts have criticised the Directive as 'gender blind' and inattentive to the intersectional aspects of algorithmic management.[31]

## 2.2. BANKING AND INSURANCE

Banking and insurance are other significant areas where AI systems or algorithms are employed. The use of AI benefits these sectors in multiple ways. For example, AI allows for easier targeting of customers[32] and thus enhances market efficiency by accurately predicting the ability of a customer to repay bank loans, ensuring both improved risk assessment for financial institutions and greater creditworthiness verification for borrowers. However, algorithms and AI can also produce discriminatory effects. In the context of banking, two main forms of discrimination have been identified: price discrimination and access discrimination.[33]

The *SCHUFA* judgment of the CJEU[34] can be viewed as a landmark decision in banking, highlighting the risks associated with automated decision-making and its implications for transparency and fairness.[35] SCHUFA is a private company providing its partners with information about the creditworthiness of third parties based on a scoring system assessing the probability of their future repayment of loans.[36] Following a refusal to grant a loan to the applicant, based on the score calculated by the SCHUFA system, the applicant requested to have access to her personal data and that SCHUFA erase incorrect information.[37] SCHUFA only gave the applicant her score; however, it refused to disclose in

31 N. Kambouri, 'A gender critique of the new directive on platform work from the perspective of feminised and racialised labour' (2024) 10(2) *Labour & Law Issues* 55 et seq.

32 E. Baffour et al., 'Transforming banking: Examining the role of AI technology innovation in boosting banks financial performance' (2024) 96 *International Review of Financial Analysis* 103700, pp. 1, 2.

33 G. Alper, 'Contract law revisited: Algorithmic pricing and the notion of contractual fairness' (2022) 47 *Computer Law & Security Review* Article 105741, pp. 1, 2, https://colab.ws/articles/10.1016%2Fj.clsr.2022.105741 (accessed 15.03.2025).

34 Case C-634/21, *OQ v. Land Hessen(intervener SCHUFA Holding AG)* 7 December 2023, ECLI:EU:C:2023:957 (*'SCHUFA Holding')*.

35 For a comment on this judgment see E. Falletti, 'Credit Scoring Under Scrutiny by the Court of Justice of the European Union: Brief Remarks on the "SCHUFA Decision"' (14.02.2024). Available at: https://ssrn.com/abstract=4726282 or http://dx.doi.org/10.2139/ssrn.4726282 (accessed 16.03.2025), with further references. See also L. Flórez Rojas, I. Varošanec, L. Haitsma, L. Ardenghi, I. Emanuilov, G. Stoyanova, A. Tsvetkova, T. Nowak, A. Onaie, and L.-D. Bularca, 'Public decision-making using AI systems' in A. Colombi Ciacchi, L. Lane, T. Nowak, and L. Flórez Rojas (eds.), *AI and Public Administration: The (legal) limits of algorithmic governance*, JuLIA Handbook, 2024 (publication funded by the EU Justice Programme), pp. 83, 87–89 with further references.

36 *SCHUFA Holding*, above n. 34, para. 14.

37 Ibid., para. 15.

a detailed manner the methods employed to calculate such scores.[38] Following the domestic proceedings, the CJEU had to determine whether the system used by SCHUFA constituted 'automated individual decision-making' under Article 22(1) of the General Data Protection Regulation (GDPR).[39] Article 22 GDPR prohibits an individual from being subject to a decision based solely on automated processing unless it is justified.[40] According to the CJEU, for an act to fall within the scope of Article 22(1) GDPR three cumulative conditions must be met:

> first that there must be a 'decision', secondly, that that decision must be 'based solely on automated processing, including profiling', and, thirdly, that it must produce 'legal effects concerning [the interested party]' or 'similarly significantly [affect] him or her'.[41]

By 'decision' the Court means 'not only acts which produce legal effects concerning the person at issue but also acts which similarly significantly affect him or her'.[42] Hence the first condition was met. The second condition was also met, as SCHUFA did accept or reject applications for loans solely based on the risks calculated by its system.[43] As for the third condition, the Court agreed that the standard was met, as the score-based system leading to an acceptance or a refusal of a loan was sufficiently capable of producing a 'legal effect' or affecting the individual concerned 'similarly significantly'.[44] The Court then concluded that the SCHUFA system was to be regarded as 'automated individual decision-making' under Article 22(1) GDPR.[45] The automated system employed by SCHUFA was in fact the driving factor in determining the outcome of a loan application.

The *SCHUFA* case is a landmark judgment because it establishes that any agency using an automated system for individual decision-making is subject to Article 22 GDPR if the decision of the system is the determining factor in an outcome that has legal effects or similarly significant consequences.[46] This

---

38 Ibid., para. 16.

39 Ibid., para. 40.

40 Regulation (EU) 2016/679 of the European Parliament and of the Council of 27 April 2016 on the protection of natural persons with regard to the processing of personal data and on the free movement of such data, and repealing Directive 95/46/EC (General Data Protection Regulation) [2016] *OJ* L119/1.

41 *SCHUFA Holding*, above n. 34, para. 43.

42 Ibid., para. 44.

43 Ibid., para. 47.

44 Ibid., para. 48.

45 Ibid., para. 73.

46 E. Erskine-Fox and S. Dunne, 'SCHUFA case: CJEU rules on scope of article 22' (*TLT*, 05.08.2024) https://www.tlt.com/insights-and-events/insight/schufa-case-cjeu-rules-on-scope-of-article-22/ (accessed 13.02.2025).

will entail that agencies are now going to be more selective of their systems and will ensure that they do not employ solely automated means, therefore ensuring greater accountability.

However, one might question the extent to which the post-*SCHUFA* improvements in the use of automated decision-making in the credit sector will prevent price discrimination and access discrimination on grounds of gender, racial and ethnic background, disability, or other grounds listed in Article 21(1) of the Charter. A problem is that algorithmic discrimination in the credit and insurance sectors mostly takes the form of indirect discrimination. This is, for example, the case when an algorithmic credit scoring system uses predictors such as income or employment history, which are prima facie neutral towards protected groups, but still have a disadvantageous impact on women.[47]

## 2.3. TARGETED ADVERTISING, PRICE SETTING, AND RETAIL

The use of algorithms or AI in providing goods and services can raise significant concerns under EU non-discrimination law, as algorithmic decision-making may result in discriminatory practices and restrict access to certain products based on gender, ethnic background, etc. Algorithmic discrimination in the provision of goods and services mainly manifests itself through discriminatory advertising and discriminatory pricing.[48] For example, discriminatory advertising could occur when preferences on a shopping website are used as a proxy to indicate to a system the gender of the consumer and tailor products based on correlations between gender and product purchases even where gender itself is not the main criterion used by the system.

Article 3(1) of EU Directive 2004/113/EC prohibits gender discrimination in the provision of 'goods and services' in both the public and private sectors.[49] Similarly, Article 3(1)(h) of the Racial Equality Directive prohibits discrimination on account of ethnic or racial origin in the provision of goods and services.[50] However, the prohibition on gender discrimination does not extend to media activity and advertisements.[51] While the 2004 Directive explicitly covers a prohibition on gender discrimination, it does not address different protected grounds, and therefore price discrimination in private relationships based on a protected ground other than gender would escape

---

47 R. Xenidis, above n. 20, section 2.2.

48 K. Lutman, above n. 11, pp. 89–92.

49 Council Directive 2004/113/EC of 13 December 2004 implementing the principle of equal treatment between men and women in the access to and supply of goods and services [2004] *OJ* L373/37.

50 Council Directive 2000/43/EC of 29 June 2000 implementing the principle of equal treatment between persons irrespective of racial or ethnic origin [2004] *OJ* L180/22.

51 Council Directive 2004/113/EC, above n. 49, Article 3(3).

the scope of protection.[52] This means that an algorithmic system that would exclude, for example, persons above a certain age or with a certain religious affiliation from accessing given services or from purchasing certain goods would not, in principle, be contrary to EU secondary anti-discrimination law as it stands.[53]

Data protection law may provide, at least indirectly, some protection against algorithmic discrimination.[54] For example, in the case of *Meta Platforms Inc and Others v. Bundeskartellamt*, the CJEU was called to rule on whether Meta's data collection policies were in breach of Article 9 GDPR, which prohibits the processing of special categories of personal data. The Court also examined several other claims related to competition law and data protection.[55] One of the main issues in the dispute was the data collection method employed by Facebook: Facebook is financed through online advertisements that are tailored to individual users on the platform and this can be enabled by the data the user agrees to share when accepting the terms and conditions upon signing-up on the platform.[56] Facebook, through its terms and conditions, processes not only the data the user agrees to share but also the data 'off-Facebook' which is data collected following the visit to third-party apps that are linked to Facebook through programming.[57] The Higher Regional Court of Dusseldorf submitted several questions, including:

> If an internet user merely visits websites or apps to which the criteria of Article 9(1) of the GDPR relate, such as flirting apps, gay dating sites … or also enters information into them … and [an] undertaking, such as [Meta Platforms Ireland], uses interfaces integrated into those websites and apps … to collect data about those visits to the websites and apps and the information entered by the user, and links those data with the data from the user's Facebook.com account and uses them, does this collection and/or linking and/or use involve the processing of sensitive data for the purpose of that provision?'[58]

By its second sub-question the Court asked:

> does visiting those websites or apps and/or entering information and/or clicking or tapping on the buttons integrated into them by a provider … constitute manifestly

[52] K. Lutman, above n. 11, p. 92.

[53] R. Xenidis, above n. 19, section 3.1.

[54] F.J. Zuiderveen Borgesius, *Discrimination, artificial intelligence, and algorithmic decision-making*, above n. 1, section IV.3.

[55] Case C-252/21, *Meta Platforms Inc and Others v Bundeskartellamt* 04.07.2023, ECLI:EU:C:2023:537.

[56] Ibid., paras. 27–28.

[57] Ibid., para. 28.

[58] Ibid., para. 35.

making the data about the visits themselves and/or the information entered by the user public within the meaning of Article 9(2)(e) of the GDPR?[59]

According to the Court, for a derogation from Article 9(1) GDPR, it must be established that the data subject 'intended, explicitly and by a clear affirmative action, to make the personal data in question accessible to the general public'.[60] Merely visiting a website does not mean that the data subject consents to its data being made public.[61] Similarly, 'liking' or 'sharing' cannot be considered as a willingness of the user to make their personal data public; however, this is not so when the user can 'explicitly make a choice' based on preference settings.[62] This case on the one hand shows how data protection law and in particular Article 9 GDPR, can shield individuals from their sensitive data being processed without their consent. In this connection Article 9 GDPR could be applied also in the context of algorithmic pricing and advertised targeting, as AI systems rely on access to personal data to enable customisation. Therefore, Article 9 GDPR could prevent algorithms from engaging in discriminatory practices by restricting the processing of sensitive personal data when individuals have not given their explicit consent.[63] On the other hand Article 9 GDPR shows its limitations against targeted advertisements and algorithmic pricing for two main reasons. Firstly, under Article 9 GDPR the list of sensitive data does not cover every protected ground addressed by the anti-discrimination directives.[64] Such limited scope therefore entails that Article 9 will not be applicable when data about age or disability is being processed.[65] Secondly, consent plays an important role under Article 9(2)(a) GDPR, and therefore if an individual 'explicitly consents'[66] to their data being processed then they cannot rely on the protections afforded by paragraph 1.[67] This derogation can be especially problematic when individuals do not read the terms and conditions and proceed to consent to their personal data being processed.

---

59 Ibid.
60 Ibid., para. 77.
61 Ibid., para. 84.
62 Ibid., para. 85.
63 L. Drechsler and J.C.B. Sanchez, 'The Price Is (Not) Right: Data Protecton and Discriminaton in the Age of Pricing Algorithms' (2018) 9(3) *EJLT (European Journal Law & Technology)* 1, 9.
64 Article 9 GDPR covers data revealing racial or ethnic origin, political opinions, religious or philosophical beliefs, or trade union membership, and the processing of genetic data or biometric data.
65 L. Drechsler and J.C.B. Sanchez, above n. 63, p. 9.
66 Ibid., p. 9.
67 Ibid., p. 9.

# 3. THE FRAIA: A NATIONAL MODEL OF FUNDAMENTAL RIGHTS AND ALGORITHMS IMPACT ASSESSMENT

## 3.1. THE BACKGROUND: THREE ALGORITHMIC DISCRIMINATION SCANDALS IN THE NETHERLANDS

During the last few years, three algorithmic discrimination scandals came to light in the Netherlands. In all three of them the perpetrators were public bodies. The first and perhaps most famous scandal led to the resignation of the 'Rutte III' government in January 2021: the so-called *Toeslagenaffaire*, known internationally as the 'childcare benefit scandal'.[68] The tax administration (*Belastingdienst*) used algorithms to detect possible tax fraud by beneficiaries of childcare benefits. These algorithms clearly had discriminatory effects against persons with an immigration background. In its report about this Dutch scandal, Amnesty International speaks of 'xenophobic machines'.[69]

The second scandal was the SyRI case, which led to the much-discussed judgment *NJCM and FNV v. The State of the Netherlands* by the Hague District Court ('SyRI judgment').[70] The Risk Indication system known as 'SyRI' was a legal instrument introduced by the Dutch government aimed at helping local authorities to detect fraud tied to social benefits allowances or taxes in specific neighbourhoods.[71] The system, through a complex method of data

68 See L. Haitsma and M. Bouwmeester, 'Learning from control deficits in the childcare benefits scandal. A plea for multi-level analysis in law and policy research' (2023) 44(3) *Recht der Werkelijkheid* 57 with further references; L. Haitsma, 'The Murky Waters of Algorithmic Profiling Examining discrimination in the digitalized enforcement of social security policy' (2023) 44(2) *Recht der Werkelijkheid* 61 with further references; S. Ranchordás and Y. Schuurmans, 'Outsourcing the Welfare State: The Role of Private Actors in Welfare Fraud Investigations' (2020) 7(1) *European Journal of Comparative Law and Governance* 5, 11 et seq. See also L. Haitsma, L. Ardenghi, B. Ancuceanu, I. Varošanec and L. Flórez Rojas, 'Algorithmic Design' in A. Colombi Ciacchi, L. Lane, T. Nowak, and L. Flórez Rojas (eds.), *AI and Public Administration: The (legal) limits of algorithmic governance*', JuLIA Handbook, 2024 (publication funded by the EU Justice Programme), p. 32.

69 See the 2021 Amnesty International report 'Xenophobic machines: Discrimination through unregulated use of algorithms in the Dutch childcare benefits scandal', https://www.amnesty.org/en/documents/eur35/4686/2021/en/ (accessed 16.03.2025).

70 Hague District Court, *NJCM and FNV v. The State of the Netherlands* 06.03.2020, ECLI:NL:RBDHA:2020:865. For a comment see, among others, A. Meuwese, 'Regulating Algorithmic Decision-making One Case at the Time: a Note on the Dutch "SyRI" Judgment' (2020) 1 *European Review of Digital Administration & Law (ERDAL)* 209. See also A. Rachovitsa and N. Johann, 'The Human Rights Implications of the Use of AI in the Digital Welfare State: Lessons Learned from the Dutch SyRI Case' (2022) 22(2) *Human Rights Law Review* 1; S. Ranchordás and Y. Schuurmans, above n. 68, 6 et seq. See also L. Haitsma, L. Ardenghi, B. Ancuceanu, I. Varošanec and L. Flórez Rojas, 'Algorithmic Design', above n. 68, pp. 29–30.

71 Hague District Court, *NJCM and FNV v. The State of the Netherlands*, above n. 70, para. 3.1.

collection, known as 'black box'[72] identified natural or legal persons who might have been at risk of committing fraud and flagged such individuals to local authorities as 'worthy of investigation'.[73] One of the main issues analysed by the Court was whether the system interfered with the right to private and family life as enshrined in Article 8 of the European Convention of Human Rights (ECHR). The Court found that SyRI inadvertently reinforced existing biases by disproportionately flagging individuals with a lower socio-economic status or with an immigration background, as it was primarily deployed in 'problematic neighbourhoods'.[74] As a result, SyRI could produce discriminatory outcomes by targeting in a disproportionate manner individuals from lower-income areas.[75] In this connection the Court recalled that 'the right to respect for private life in the context of data processing concerns the right to equal treatment in equal cases, and the right to protection against discrimination, stereotyping and stigmatization'.[76]

This judgment successfully addressed the need for accountable and transparent AI systems. Transparency obligations under the GDPR ensure that data subjects are informed about their data being processed by an automated system.[77] To this end AI systems must be trustworthy. According to the High-Level Expert Group on AI appointed by the European Commission (AI HLEG), in order to be trustworthy an AI system must be fair and transparent both in substantive and procedural terms.[78]

However, transparency alone cannot guarantee the prevention of discrimination. Some scholars have criticised the SyRI judgment for having overlooked the discriminatory impacts caused by the automated system in relation to the right to social security which, similarly to the right to privacy, involves both transparency and non-discrimination.[79] Given the difficulty of

---

[72] Algorithm Watch, 'How Dutch activists got an invasive fraud detection algorithm banned' (*AlgorithmWatch*, 06.04.2020) https://algorithmwatch.org/en/syri-netherlands-algorithm/ (accessed 16.03.2025).

[73] Hague District Court, *NJCM and FNV v The State of the Netherlands*, above n. 70, para. 3.2.

[74] Ibid., para. 6.93.

[75] Ibid. The human rights and poverty-related aspects of the SyRI case were highlighted in the 'Brief by the United Nations Special Rapporteur on extreme poverty and human rights as *Amicus Curiae* in the case of NJCM c.s./De Staat der Nederlanden (SyRI) before the District Court of The Hague (case number: C/09/550982/HA ZA 18/388)', www.ohchr.org/Documents/Issues/Poverty/Amicusfinalversionsigned.pdf (accessed 17.03.2025). For a comment see, among others, A. Rachovitsa and N. Johann, above n. 70, 12.

[76] Ibid., para. 6.24.

[77] Articles 12–23 GDPR.

[78] AI HLEG, 'Ethics guidelines for trustworthy AI' (2019), https://digital-strategy.ec.europa.eu/en/library/ethics-guidelines-trustworthy-ai (accessed 12.02.2025), 12.

[79] I. Leijten, 'The Dutch SyRI Case: Some thoughts on indivisible interferences and the status of social rights' (IACL-AIDC Blog, 19.05.2020) https://blog-iacl-aidc.org/social-rights/2020/5/19/the-dutch-syri-case-some-thoughts-on-indivisible-interferences-and-the-status-of-social-rights (accessed 16.03.2025).

assessing the discriminatory impacts of the system because of the transparency gaps the system presented, the Court excluded from its analysis the right to social security thus failing to set a significant precedent in this sphere too.[80]

The third Dutch algorithmic discrimination scandal was the DUO case, which in some respects was similar to the SyRI case. The Education Executive Agency (*Dienst Uitvoering Onderwijs*, DUO) developed a risk-based system aimed at detecting fraud in student benefits.[81] According to a report published by Amnesty International,[82] the systems identified 'high-risk' students based on a two-fold test: firstly, an algorithm assigned to students a risk score; and secondly an employee from DUO would visit the domicile of the student based on the assigned risk score.[83] The main criteria used to determine the risk score were: age, education level and geographical distance from the residence of parents – which, however, resulted in targeting individuals from ethnic minorities in a disproportionate and unfair manner.[84] According to Amnesty International, while the system did not directly use criteria such as 'race', 'colour' or 'ethnicity'[85] to determine the risk score, its reliance on criteria relating to geographical location effectively constituted a proxy for ethnicity, resulting in unfair targeting.[86]

Few months ago, after an investigation, the Dutch Data Protection Authority concluded that DUO's algorithmic decision-making to assess fraud was discriminatory and unlawful, since there was no objective justification for the criteria used to determine the risk score.[87]

---

80 Ibid.

81 NL Times, 'Government to refund over 10,000 students over discriminatory DUO fraud checks' *NL Times* (12.11.2024), https://nltimes.nl/2024/11/12/government-refund-10000-students-discriminatory-duo-fraud-checks (accessed 08.02.2025).

82 Amnesty International, 'Netherlands: Profiled without protection: Students in the Netherlands hit by discriminatory fraud detection system' (20.11.2024) https://www.amnesty.org/en/documents/eur35/8794/2024/en/ (accessed 08.02.2025), p. 17.

83 Ibid.

84 NL Times, 'Government to refund over 10,000 students over discriminatory DUO fraud checks' *NL Times* (12.11.2024), https://nltimes.nl/2024/11/12/government-refund-10000-students-discriminatory-duo-fraud-checks (accessed 17.03.2025).

85 Amnesty International, 'Netherlands: Profiled without protection: Students in the Netherlands hit by discriminatory fraud detection system', above n. 82, p. 28.

86 Ibid., p. 29. See also S. de Heer, 'A Scandal on AI in Administration, Again. Fortifying Fundamental Rights in the Age of AI', *Verfassungsblog*, 25 July 2023, https://verfassungsblog.de/a-scandal-on-ai-in-administration-again/ (accessed 17.03.2025); L. Lane, L. Haitsma, T. Nowak, T. De Mari Casareto dal Verme, E. Marchesini, R. Carbone, S. Ranise, O. Davidsson and S. Molinari, 'Introduction to the Handbook' in A. Colombi Ciacchi, L. Lane, T. Nowak, and L. Flórez Rojas (eds.), *AI and Public Administration: The (legal) limits of algorithmic governance*', above n. 68, p. 15.

87 Dutch Data Protection Authority (*Autoriteitpersoonsgegevens*, AP), 'DUO's approach to fraud found to be discriminatory and illegal', 11.11.2024, https://www.autoriteitpersoonsgegevens.nl/en/current/duos-approach-to-fraud-found-to-be-discriminatory-and-illegal (accessed 17.03.2025).

After the above-mentioned algorithmic discrimination scandals, to prevent future cases of violations of fundamental rights through algorithms, the Dutch Government entrusted an interdisciplinary group of scientists from Utrecht University[88] with the task of drafting an impact assessment model. The product of their joint work, the 'Fundamental Rights and Algorithms Impact Assessment' (FRAIA), was published in 2022 by the Ministry of Interior and Kingdom Relations as a non-binding 'discussion and decision-making tool for government organisations'.[89]

## 3.2. THE FRAIA: FUNCTION, STRUCTURE, AND CONTENT

The FRAIA provides a systematic approach to assessing potential risks associated with algorithmic processes whilst ensuring compliance with fundamental rights. It serves as a platform to foster interdisciplinary discussions among those overseeing the creation or implementation of algorithmic systems, and it helps organisations to identify risks to human rights in using algorithms and take measures to address them. Consequently, it acts as a preventive tool, ensuring that organisations refrain from deploying algorithms that might have unclear or detrimental effects on fundamental rights.[90]

The framework of the FRAIA is divided into four main parts. The first three parts address the decision-making, whilst the last part revolves around more specific questions concerning fundamental rights. Each of these four parts is built following a structured approach and contains detailed questions aimed at ensuring that all the relevant points are addressed, and that the required stakeholders are included when addressing the potential concerns surrounding the use of algorithmic deployment.[91]

---

88 Janneke Gerards (Professor of Fundamental Rights in Europe), Mirko Tobias Schäfer (Associate Professor of AI, Data & Society), Iris Muis (Knowledge Valorisation Officer, expert on responsible AI and digital ethics), and Arthur Vankan (ICON – Media and Performance Studies).

89 J. Gerards, M.T. Schäfer, I. Muis, and A. Vankan, 'Fundamental Rights and Algorithms Impact Assessment (FRAIA)' (March 2022) Rijksoverheid.nl, https://www.government.nl/documents/reports/2021/07/31/impact-assessment-fundamental-rights-and-algorithms (accessed 19.03.2025). For the definition of the FRAIA as a 'discussion and decision-making tool for government organisations' see p. 2.

90 Ibid. The FRAIA has already been applied in pilot projects run by Dutch administrative agencies in cooperation with scientists. It was used for example in a combined Thrustworthy AI and fundamental rights assessment of a deep learning algorithm used by the province of Friesland. See M. Boonstra et al., 'Lessons Learned in Performing a Thrustworthy AI and Fundamental Rights Assessment' (2024) *IACAPAP ArXiv*, https://www.researchgate.net/publication/380814210_Lessons_Learned_in_Performing_a_Trustworthy_AI_and_Fundamental_Rights_Assessment (accessed 6 October 2025).

91 L. Haitsma, L. Ardenghi, B. Ancuceanu, I. Varošanec and L. Flórez Rojas, 'Algorithmic Design', above n. 68, p. 38.

### 3.2.1. Part 1: Why?

This first part of the FRAIA focuses on the intention behind using an algorithm. The impact assessment analysis in this part highlights the underlying motives and the intended effects of the use of an algorithm. To be able to address this subject in the most precise manner, the FRAIA provides five subtopics that guide this analysis.[92]

The first one, 'Reason and problem definition' (1.1), handles two aspects. On one hand, it focuses on reflecting on the actual reason behind the deployment of an algorithm: what problem should the intended use of the algorithm solve? On the other hand, this subtopic aims to find an answer to the question of why it is desirable to use an algorithm, knowing that other non-digital tools may be available to tackle the same problem.[93]

Building on this problem definition, the second subtopic that requires analysis (1.2 'Objective') is the objective that the use of the algorithm needs to achieve. This objective needs to be defined as concretely and specifically as possible, and in the case of several objectives, they must be ranked from the main objectives to the secondary objectives.[94]

The third subtopic 'Public values' (1.3), requires specific identification of the values that give rise to the development and use of the algorithm. Examples of public values are 'equality, respect for personal autonomy, solidarity, liberty, security, responsibility, sustainability, legal security, distributive justice, respect for vulnerable groups, participation, and efficient use of resources'. A curious detail: here the FRAIA specifies that the protection of fundamental rights (such as personal data protection, freedom of expression, the right of access to information, and the right to due process) 'may rank among the public values'. One may question why the verb 'may' is used: does this perhaps imply that a government organisation may pick and choose whether or not to include fundamental rights in its specification of the public values at the first stage of this impact assessment?

Anyway, here the FRAIA addresses the problem of conflicting public values:

> When multiple public values prompt the use of the algorithm, it is useful to reflect on the relative weight of these values. Which values are most important? What are the harms if the values cannot be (fully) realised by the algorithm?

If public values conflict as a result of using the algorithm, the FRAIA recognises that a comparative assessment must be made between them and a balancing exercise needs to be conducted, but this should happen in Part 4 of the impact

92 FRAIA, above n. 89, pp. 6–21.
93 Ibid., pp. 9–10.
94 Ibid., pp. 11–12.

assessment. In Part 1 the organisation should only point out the tension. The objective of identifying the various values at this first stage of the impact assessment only serves consciousness-raising and awareness purposes.[95]

Once the public values are set out, the fourth subtopic of Part 1, 'Legal basis' (1.4), aims at

> finding out whether there is a legal basis that explicitly and clearly allows for the use of an algorithm and renders this use sufficiently foreseeable. If an algorithm is expected to affect people's lives or freedom, and particularly if fundamental rights are expected to be affected, there must be a legal basis for its use.[96]

Here the FRAIA refers in particular to the specific requirements that apply on the basis of the European Convention on Human Rights in the case of fundamental rights infringements, two of which are particularly important for the use of algorithms: Firstly, the infringements of fundamental rights must be sufficiently foreseeable. This means that the legal basis must be defined sufficiently clearly for citizens and legal entities to know where they stand and, where necessary, to gear their actions to the expected outcomes. Secondly, the legal basis must provide appropriate guarantees against arbitrariness. This means, among other things, that there must be sufficient transparency about the decisions to be made, and that sufficient opportunities for legal protection must be in place.[97]

The fifth subtopic, 'Stakeholders and responsibilities' (1.5), focuses on the importance of a clear division of responsibilities and safeguarding the (various levels of) responsibilities within the process surrounding the use of an algorithm. This requires sound decision-making structures and organisational embedding of the algorithm.[98]

### *3.2.2. Part 2: What?*

After the Part 1 assessment of why an algorithm will be used and how the organisation will safeguard public values and interests, the FRAIA addresses the 'What' question: namely, the shape of the algorithm. Part 2 is divided into two sections: one concerning the *input* of the algorithm – meaning the data or digitally recorded details to be used – and one concerning the algorithm itself – meaning the *throughput* of the project.

The first section (2A) addresses four subtopics: 'Assessment: Algorithm type' (2A.1), 'Data sources and quality' (2A.2), 'Bias/assumptions in the

95 Ibid., pp. 13–15.
96 Ibid., p. 16.
97 Ibid., pp. 16–17.
98 Ibid., pp. 18–21.

data' (2A.3), and 'Security' (2A.4). Once the organisation has identified the type of algorithm, the next issue that needs to be scrutinised when examining the *input* of the algorithm is, of course, the data sources and the quality of the data. Here the FRAIA refers to the widely known 'garbage in = garbage out' principle. The organisation should identify possible assumptions and biases embedded in the data – such as representation bias – and how to correct, overcome or mitigate their influences on the algorithm's output. The organisation should also address the security of data from possible attacks, unauthorised access, etc. and take sufficient and adequate preventive measures.[99]

The questions contained in the second section (2B) centre on the algorithm itself. The first subtopic (2B.1) addresses the algorithm type – highlighting the importance of differentiating between a non-self-learning algorithm (in which humans specify the rubric the computer must observe) and a self-learning algorithm (in which the machine itself is finding patterns in the data). The organisation needs to explain the rationale behind choosing a specific type of algorithm over another algorithm or alternative non-algorithmic tools.[100]

The second subtopic (2B.2) is the ownership and control of the algorithm. When a government organisation chooses to have an algorithm developed by a third party, a clear arrangement concerning its ownership and management needs to be established. The organisation using the algorithm developed by the third party must itself also be able to explain how the algorithm operates.[101]

The third subtopic (2B.3) is algorithmic accuracy, which must be assessed based on specific evaluation criteria, determining whether the algorithm is suitable for its intended use. The testing process examines its performance, identifying error rates such as false positives and false negatives, while also considering the validity of the underlying assumptions in indicator selection and weighting. To mitigate potential biases, various corrective measures, including alternative sampling strategies and feature modifications, may need to be implemented.[102]

The fourth subtopic (2B.4) is transparency and explainability. It is essential to determine whether the algorithm's purpose, functioning, and data sources are clear, as well as to identify the internal and external groups for whom its operation will be made transparent and how this will be achieved. Additionally, the algorithm must be explainable to the relevant target groups, and its functioning should be communicated understandably. With respect to this issue, the concept of a 'black box' is often mentioned; this term is used to indicate completely non-transparent algorithms, where only the input

---

99 Ibid., pp. 24–32.
100 Ibid., pp. 34–36.
101 Ibid., p. 37.
102 Ibid., pp. 38–42.

and output are visible, while the internal processes remain unknown – an undesirable situation.[103]

### *3.2.3. Part 3: How?*

The third part of the FRAIA covers seven subtopics revolving around the implementation and the use of the algorithm concerned. In fact, an algorithm as such does not have undesired effects: they are caused by the implementation, use, or application of the algorithm, by the context in which the algorithm is used, or by the decisions and measures that are linked to the output of the algorithm.[104]

The first subtopic ('Decisions based on algorithmic output', 3.1) discusses which (types of) decisions may be based on the algorithmic output. They may be various types of decisions, such as administrative decisions in individual cases, policy measures, or decisions about the use of public resources. A central question here is whether, given the output the algorithm will generate, the algorithm can meet the organisation's expectations, considering the reasons, objectives, and public values identified in Part 1. When the algorithm is used in a different context from the one for which it has been developed or trained (for example, in a neighbourhood where the population structure or other relevant data clearly deviates from the training data), this may result in incorrect or biased output.[105] With regard to decisions based on algorithmic output, the FRAIA stresses the importance of 'safeguarding good governance and good administration', including civic participation and legal protection.[106]

The second subtopic ('The role of humans in the decision', 3.2) revolves around the following questions:

> What role do humans play in decision-making on the basis of the algorithmic output? How are they empowered to make decisions responsibly on the basis of the algorithmic output?
>
> Is there sufficient qualified staff in place to manage, review and adjust the algorithm, if needed, and will there be in future?[107]

---

[103] Ibid., pp. 43–46.
[104] Ibid., p. 47.
[105] Ibid., p. 49.
[106] Ibid., p. 50.
[107] Ibid., p. 51.

The third subtopic, 'Effects of the algorithm' (3.3), addresses four central questions:

> What will be the effects of using the algorithm for citizens and how will the 'human measure' be considered when making decisions based on the algorithm?
> What are the risks of stigmatisation, discrimination or otherwise harmful or adverse effects on citizens? How will these be combated or mitigated?
> How will the expected effects contribute to solving the problem that prompted the development/deployment of the algorithm ... and to achieving the proposed objectives?
> How do the expected effects relate to the public values being served ...? How are risks of undermining certain values handled?[108]

The fourth subtopic, 'Procedures' (3.4), concerns decision-making procedures and accountability mechanisms. It includes questions such as:

> How are the various relevant actors (administratively and politically accountable persons, and citizens) engaged in decision-making?

and

> How is it being safeguarded that these procedures meet the requirements of good governance, good administration and – where necessary – legal protection.[109]

When determining the algorithm's performance, contextual factors play a vital role. Therefore, the fifth subtopic is 'Context' (3.5). Contextual factors that need to be taken into account are time (When will the algorithm will be used and for how long?) and area (Where will the algorithm be used? In a specific geographical area? Does the algorithm concern a certain group of persons or cases?). A central question here is whether the algorithm can still be used if contextual factors change, or if it is used in another context than the one for which it was developed. Indeed, if the algorithm is applied in a different context than intended or trained for, discrepancies may lead to biased or inaccurate results.[110]

The sixth subtopic is 'Communication' (3.6) about the algorithm's use, which is essential to maintaining public trust and transparency. A central question here concerns the degree of openness with which the organisation can communicate the operation of the algorithm in the light of the objectives and context of its deployment.[111]

---

108 Ibid., pp. 53–55.
109 Ibid., pp. 56–57.
110 Ibid., pp. 58–59.
111 Ibid., pp. 60–61.

The seventh subtopic is 'Evaluation, auditing and safeguarding' (3.7). Both internal and external processes are essential for evaluating, auditing, and safeguarding the use of an algorithm. Internally, it is important, *inter alia*, to determine how often the algorithm should be assessed, whether qualified staff are in place, and if future-proofing measures exist. Externally, mechanisms for auditing and supervision should be established, ensuring that sufficient information is available for oversight.[112]

### *3.2.4. Part 4: Fundamental Rights*

The 'fundamental rights roadmap' in the FRAIA consists of seven steps, designed to assess the impact of algorithms on fundamental rights:[113]

The first step examines whether any fundamental rights are affected by the algorithm that is to be used.[114] To this purpose, Annex I of the FRAIA lists 31 fundamental rights grouped in four clusters (1. rights related to the person, 2. freedom rights, 3. equality rights, and 4. procedural rights).[115] Which fundamental rights are affected depends on the nature and objective of the algorithm. However, two fundamental rights are most likely to be affected: the right to protection of personal data, and the right to equal treatment.[116] As for the latter, the FRAIA explicitly states:

> Most algorithms result in some form of unequal treatment. This is inherent to the categorisation and profiling for with [*sic*] many algorithms are being used, and to the fact that many data sets are biased, in the sense that they reflect stereotypes existing in society or historical patterns of structural discrimination.[117]

The second step requires identification of the specific legal provisions and standards applicable to the infringement of the fundamental right(s) in question. Here the FRAIA requires i.a. to pay special attention to the equal treatment legislation and the legislation regarding protection of personal data.[118]

The third step evaluates how seriously a fundamental right is affected by the algorithm. It distinguishes among three grades of seriousness, labelled with

112 Ibid., pp. 63–65.
113 Ibid., p. 67.
114 Ibid., p. 69.
115 Ibid., pp. 85–95.
116 Ibid., p. 70.
117 Ibid., p. 70.
118 Ibid., pp. 71–73.

three colours – red, yellow, and green – which correspond to three grades of required justification in decision-making:

a. Serious interference, thus compelling reasons required as justification (red);
b. Medium-serious interference, thus due diligence required (yellow); and
c. Less serious interference, thus no special due diligence required (green).[119]

The FRAIA admits that no objectively and unequivocally right answer can be given to the question of whether an interference is serious, medium-serious, or less serious. It stresses that it is important to 'discuss this issue in a well-considered and open manner and to explain comprehensibly why you have opted for red, yellow, or green'.[120]

The fourth, fifth, sixth, and seventh steps evaluate the necessity, subsidiarity, and proportionality of the use of the algorithm with respect to the objectives pursued by it. The organisation needs to assess first these objectives, then whether the algorithm is a suitable means to realise them, and finally whether the algorithm's use is necessary to achieve these objectives, ensuring that no less intrusive alternatives exist. The suitability of an algorithm is an empirical question, requiring a realistic assessment of its potential benefits, such as cost reduction or efficiency gains, compared to the development and auditing costs. It also involves evaluating whether the algorithm can accurately predict outcomes, as unreliable algorithms with many false positives or negatives may pose significant problems. Generally, an algorithm is deemed problematic and not suitable if it lacks efficacy and threatens an important fundamental right (red or yellow code). With respect to necessity, the principle of using the 'best available techniques' applies; if alternative tools or measures can achieve the same objectives while causing less harm to fundamental rights, they should be prioritised. Finally, in the last step, the FRAIA requires the objectives to be weighed against the potential rights infringement to determine whether the impact remains proportionate and justified. Whilst no hard rules exist for balancing these factors, the more serious the fundamental rights infringement, the more significant the social objectives must be.[121]

To assist the readers of this chapter, a flowchart inspired by the FRAIA has been included below.

119 Ibid., p. 74.
120 Ibid., p. 75.
121 Ibid., pp. 76–80.

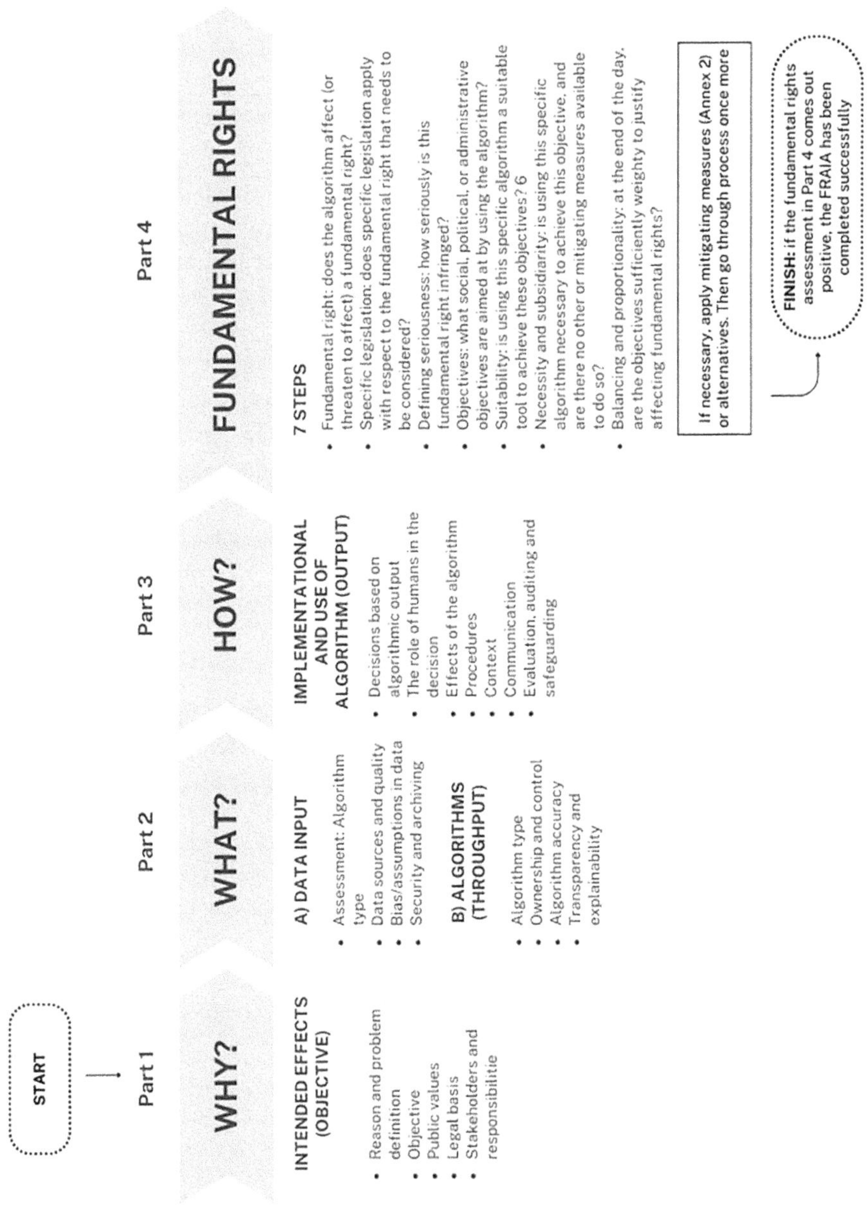


Flowchart of the FRAIA process. By Alma-Cristina Onaie

## 4. FUNDAMENTAL RIGHTS IMPACT ASSESSMENTS UNDER THE AI ACT: THE FRIA

The Dutch FRAIA of 2022 most likely inspired the European Parliament's amendments of 2023 to the AI Act proposal.[122] While neither the Commission's proposal of April 2021, nor the Council's general approach of 2022 contained any provision on fundamental rights impact assessments, such a provision *was* included in the European Parliament's amendments of June 2023,[123] which then, with some modifications, shaped the content of Article 27 of the AI Act as it was jointly adopted by Parliament and Council in 2024.[124]

Article 27 of the AI Act explicitly obliges deployers[125] of high-risk AI systems to conduct a fundamental rights impact assessment (FRIA). These high-risk systems are referred to in Article 6(2) and are listed in Annex III of the AI Act, which covers areas such as education, employment, access to public services, and law enforcement.[126]

Article 27 of the AI Act obligates not only public actors, but also three categories of private actors that deploy high-risk AI systems, to conduct fundamental rights impact assessments:

(1) private actors that provide public services,
(2) deployers of high-risk AI systems referred to in point 5(b) of Annex III, i.e. credit institutions that intend to use AI systems to evaluate the creditworthiness of natural persons or establish their credit score, and

---

122 Proposal for a Regulation of the European Parliament and of the Council laying down harmonised rules on artificial intelligence (Artificial Intelligence Act) and amending certain Union legislative acts, COM(2021) 206 final.

123 Amendments adopted by the European Parliament on 14 June 2023 on the proposal for a regulation of the European Parliament and of the Council on laying down harmonised rules on artificial intelligence (Artificial Intelligence Act) and amending certain Union legislative acts (COM(2021)0206 – C9-0146/2021 – 2021/0106(COD)). See H. Waem, J. Dauzier and M. Demircan, 'Fundamental Rights Impact Assessments under the EU AI Act: Who, what and how?', 07.03.2024, *Technology's Legal Edge*, https://www.technologyslegaledge.com/2024/03/fundamental-rights-impact-assessments-under-the-eu-ai-act-who-what-and-how/ (accessed 21.03.2025).

124 Regulation (EU) 2024/1689 of the European Parliament and of the Council of 13 June 2024 laying down harmonised rules on artificial intelligence and amending Regulations (EC) 300/2008, (EU) 167/2013, (EU) 168/2013, (EU) 2018/858, (EU) 2018/1139 and (EU) 2019/2144 and Directives 2014/90/EU, (EU) 2016/797 and (EU) 2020/1828 (Artificial Intelligence Act), *OJ* L 2024/1689.

125 Under Article 3(4) of the AI Act, a deployer is defined as a 'natural or legal person, public authority, agency, or other body using an AI system under its authority except where the AI system is used in the course of a personal non-professional activity'.

126 European Commission, 'Artificial Intelligence – Questions and Answers' (*European* Commission, 01.08.2024), https://ec.europa.eu/commission/presscorner/detail/en/qanda_21_1683 (accessed 21.03.2025).

(3) deployers of high-risk AI systems referred to in point 5(c) of Annex III, i.e. insurance providers that intend to use AI systems for risk assessment and pricing in relation to natural persons in the case of life and health insurance.

Concerning the first category, whilst the EU AI Act does not *per se* contain a strict definition of the term 'public services', Recital 96 offers examples of sectors where private entities may perform such functions, namely: education, healthcare, social services, housing, and the administration of justice. In this regard an argument could be made that the use of such a broad term – public service – may hint at a legislative intent for expansive application, to any private developer whose AI system has a tangible effect on public interests.

As to the second and third categories, the deployers of certain high-risk AI systems referred to in points 5(b) and (c) of Annex III of the EU AI Act encompass

> (b) AI systems intended to be used to evaluate the creditworthiness of natural persons or establish their credit score, with the exception of AI systems used for the purpose of detecting financial fraud; [and]
>
> (c) AI systems intended to be used for risk assessment and pricing in relation to natural persons in the case of life and health insurance.[127]

One thing that needs to be pointed out is that the FRIA is only a risk assessment. Its purpose is to assess the potential impact of high-risk AI systems on fundamental rights, instead of eliminating risk, thus focusing on risk management rather than risk elimination.[128] Therefore, the FRIA follows an *ex-ante* approach: The deployer should conduct the FRIA prior to putting the system into service and ensure that fundamental rights concerns are identified and addressed *before* the technology becomes operational.[129]

With respect to the methodology required when conducting an FRIA, the AI Act does not prescribe a specific approach. Article 27(5) of the AI Act delegates the responsibility of developing a standardised FRIA template for use across the EU to the AI Office,[130] likely in the form of a structured questionnaire, which aims to simplify the process for deployers while reducing administrative burdens. The AI Office has yet to develop such a questionnaire.

---

127 Regulation (EU) 2024/1689, above n. 124, Annex III (b),(c), and Recital 58.

128 T. Ajoodha and J. Browne, 'Fundamental Rights Impact Assessments: What are they? How do they work?' (CEDPO, January 2025) https://cedpo.eu/wp-content/uploads/CEDPO-micro-insight-paper-fundamental-rights-impact-assessments.pdf (accessed 21.03.2025).

129 A. Mantelero, 'The Fundamental Rights Impact Assessment (FRIA) in the AI Act: Roots, legal obligations and key elements for a model templat' (2024) 54 *Computer Law and Security Review* 106020; Regulation (EU) 2024/1689, above n. 124, Recital 96.

130 The AI Office is a new EU regulatory body established by the European Commission in its Decision of 24 January 2024: C(2024) 390 final.

The AI Act does not specify a time frame within which to fulfil this particular task. Therefore, one may argue that the general deadline of 2 August 2026 set in Article 113 of the AI Act applies.[131]

Article 27(1) outlines several key aspects that must be assessed irrespective of how the assessment is carried out. These aspects are outlined in the following table:

| | |
|---|---|
| Deployment context and intended purpose | (a) a description of the deployer's processes in which the high-risk AI system will be used in line with its intended purpose; |
| Operational duration and usage frequency | (b) a description of the period of time within which, and the frequency with which, each high-risk AI system is intended to be used; |
| Affected natural persons and groups | (c) the categories of natural persons and groups likely to be affected by its use in the specific context; |
| Specific risks of harm | (d) the specific risks of harm likely to have an impact on the categories of natural persons or groups of persons identified pursuant to point (c) of this paragraph, taking into account the information given by the provider pursuant to Article 13; |
| Human oversight measures | (e) a description of the implementation of human oversight measures, according to the instructions for use; |
| Risk mitigation measures | (f) the measures to be taken in the case of the materialisation of those risks, including the arrangements for internal governance and complaint mechanisms. |

## 5. CONCLUDING REMARKS

Almost 20 years ago, long before the mainstreaming of legal research on artificial intelligence in Europe, Gunther Teubner published the famous *Modern Law Review* article 'The Anonymous Matrix'.[132] This article advocated direct human rights obligations for private (transnational) actors. Teubner was one of the very few courageous scholars who first pleaded for the direct horizontal effect of fundamental rights at a time when the prevalent opinion in Germany and in some other European countries still denied it.

---

[131] EU Artificial Intelligence Act, 'The AI Act: Responsibilities of the European Commission (AI Office)' (*EU Artificial Intelligence Act*, 22.08.2024), https://artificialintelligenceact.eu/responsibilities-of-european-commission-ai-office/ (accessed 21.03.2025).

[132] G. Teubner, 'The Anonymous Matrix: Human Rights Violations by "Private" Transnational Actors' (2006) 69 *Modern Law Review (MLR)* 327.

In 2018, the Court of Justice of the European Union (CJEU) in the *Egenberger* case[133] decided that the prohibition of discrimination under Article 21(1) of the Charter directly applies not only in relationships between public authorities and individuals, but also in relationships between individuals.[134] A few months after the *Egenberger* judgment, the CJEU specified in the joined cases *Bauer and Brossonn* that the formulation of Article 51 of the Charter does not preclude direct obligations for individuals originating from mandatory and unconditional Charter provisions.[135] By 'individuals', the CJEU means any private parties, including the largest private multinational corporations. Therefore, if a contractual relationship falls within the scope of application of EU law,[136] the prohibition of discrimination under Article 21(1) of the Charter directly creates obligations for all contract parties.

Nowadays, after the *Egenberger* and *Bauer and Brossonn* judgments, the direct horizontal effect of EU fundamental rights in contract law is a matter of fact. Within the scope of application of EU law, it is now undisputed that at least Article 21(1) and Article 31(2) of the Charter directly bind private employers.[137]

However, some scholars may still argue that the Charter (and fundamental rights generally) only have direct horizontal effect in the somehow special field of labour law, given the lack of CJEU decisions on the direct horizontal effect of fundamental rights in other types of contractual relationships. The present chapter defends the opposite opinion. In our view, the CJEU case law since *Egenberger* and *Bauer and Brossonn* is to be interpreted in the sense that any Charter provision that is mandatory and unconditional and suitable content-wise to operate in the private sector, directly creates obligations for both public

133 Case C-414/16, *Vera Egenberger v. Evangelisches Werk für Diakonie und Entwicklung eV* 17.04.2018, ECLI:EU:C:2018:257.

134 For a comment on *Egenberger* see A. Colombi Ciacchi, 'The Direct Horizontal Effect of EU Fundamental Rights' (2019) 15(2) *European Constitutional Law Review* 294 https://doi.org/10.1017/S1574019619000154 (accessed 14.03.2025).

135 Joined cases *Stadt Wuppertal v. Maria Elisabeth Bauer* (C-569/16), *Volker Willmeroth v. Martina Broßonn* (C-570/16) ECLI:EU:C:2018:871. For a comment on *Bauer* and *Brossonn* see E. Frantziou, '(Most of) the Charter of Fundamental Rights is Horizontally Applicable: ECJ 6 November 2018, Joined Cases C-569/16 and C-570/16, Bauer et al' (2019) 15(2) *European Constitutional Law Review* 303–323, https://doi.org/10.1017/s1574019619000166 (accessed 14.03.2025).

136 The Charter's scope of application at the national level is limited to areas where the implementation of EU law takes place: see Article 51 of the Charter.

137 E. Muir, 'The Horizontal Effects of Charter Rights Given Expression to in EU Legislation, from Mangold to Bauer' (2019) 12(2) *REALaw* (*Review of European Administrative Law*) 185, https://www.uitgeverijparis.nl/nl/reader/206691/1001472463#auteurvoetnootnummer1001471363 (accessed 06.03.2024).

and private actors in potentially every type of contractual relationship that is regulated by an EU legal act.[138]

Article 27 of the AI Act arguably provides an additional confirmation of the direct binding force of EU fundamental rights on private contract parties in many areas beyond labour law. These are, at least, those areas where private actors must conduct fundamental rights impact assessments if they deploy AI systems, namely: (1) private actors that provide public services, (2) credit institutions that intend to use AI systems to evaluate the creditworthiness of natural persons or establish their credit score, and (3) insurance providers that intend to use AI systems for risk assessment and pricing in relation to natural persons in the case of life and health insurance.[139]

From the abovementioned observations this chapter deduces that the AI Act, together with the direct horizontal effect of Article 21(1) of the Charter, allows the limited capability of EU anti-discrimination Directives to tackle algorithmic discrimination to be at least partly overcome.[140]

However, not all algorithmic biases amount to discrimination under EU law. A structural limit of both EU and national anti-discrimination law is that while direct discrimination cannot be justified in principle, indirect discrimination comes with an open-ended justification regime. A prima facie indirectly discriminatory provision, criterion or practice can be objectively justified provided that it serves a legitimate aim and the means of achieving that aim are appropriate and necessary.[141]

Moreover, only very few cases of discrimination in contractual relationships reach the courts, and when they do so, it is often too late. Therefore, the prevention of discrimination becomes essential. Both the Dutch FRAIA and the EU FRIA are very interesting instruments of prevention of fundamental rights violations, including the fundamental right not to be discriminated against on grounds of gender, age, race, etc. While the FRAIA is an impact assessment model specifically designed for public bodies,[142] the FRIA is supposed to apply also to private organisations that use high-risk AI systems.[143]

---

[138] A. Colombi Ciacchi, 'The Direct Horizontal Effect of EU Fundamental Rights', above n. 134.

[139] See Article 27 AI Act and section 4 of this chapter.

[140] On the limits of EU anti-discrimination law with regard to algorithmic discrimination see R. Xenidis, above n. 20, section 2.2.

[141] Ibid.

[142] Governmental organisations are the main target of the FRAIA: see https://www.government.nl/documents/reports/2021/07/31/impact-assessment-fundamental-rights-and-algorithms; J. Gerards, M.T. Schäfer, A. Vankan and I. Muis, above n. 89, p. 2.

[143] See section 4 of this chapter. However, the AI Act remains an instrument based more on public law than on private law, because it primarily sets market-entry requirements rather than introducing rights for private parties that correspond to obligations of other private parties. See K. Henckel, 'Issues of conflicting laws – a closer look at the EU's approach to artificial intelligence' (2023) (2) *Nederlands Internationaal Privaatrecht (NIPR)* 199, 205.

However, although impact assessment models like the FRAIA and the FRIA might help in mitigating algorithmic discrimination, their effectiveness in practice may be questioned, since they leave a huge margin of discretion to the organisation that uses the algorithm. Therefore, the role of the courts in combating violations of national and EU anti-discrimination law by powerful public and private actors, including through the direct horizontal effect of Article 21(1) of the Charter if necessary, remains crucial.

# CHAPTER 5

# TECHNOLOGICAL POWER, PLANNED OBSOLESCENCE AND CONTRACTUAL REMEDIES

Francesco MEZZANOTTE*



## 1. INTRODUCTION

There are several factors that can lead to premature obsolescence of products, and their analysis has over time has been the preserve of scientific fields such as

* Full Professor of Private Law, Roma Tre University, Department of Law, francesco.mezzanotte@uniroma3.it.

economics,[1] marketing and business organisation,[2] sociology[3] and psychology of consumption.[4]

In more recent years, the phenomenon has also been widely investigated in its juridical aspects. Among the various possible causes of premature obsolescence (psychological, technical, economical, etc.),[5] the legal debate seems to be mainly centred on those of a material/operational nature, pointing to the premature breakdown, or reduction of performance, of a product, intentionally engineered by its own maker through the design of its hardware or software components. This is particularly evident if one focuses attention on the most recent legislative interventions enacted at EU level within the Circular Economy Package, where planned obsolescence (hereinafter 'p.o.') is presented as a form of *de facto* power available to technology holders, capable of artificially reducing the lifespan of manufactured goods in order to trigger their early replacement.[6]

After introducing the EU measures oriented towards the legislative governance of p.o. practices, this chapter questions why contract law does not seem to have been perceived as the most appropriate tool in this line of regulatory intervention. Despite some criticisms raised on the point during the legislative process, this choice appears justifiable in light of an overall

---

1 J. Bulow, 'An Economic Theory of Planned Obsolescence' (1986) 101 *The Quarterly Journal of Economics* 729; M. Chun-Hui, 'Planned obsolescence and monopoly undersupply' (2011) 23 *Information Economics and Policy* 51.

2 B.L. Bayus, 'Accelerating the durable replacement cycle with marketing mix variables' (1988) 5 *Journal of Product Innovation Management* 216; A. Utaka, 'Planned Obsolescence and Marketing Strategy' (2000) 21 *Managerial and Decision Economics* 339.

3 G. Slides, *Made to Break: Technology and Obsolescence in America*, Harvard University Press, Cambridge MA 2006; S. Latouche, *Bon pour la casse. Les déraisons de l'obsolescence programmée*, Les liens qui libèrent, Paris 2012.

4 R. Grewal, R. Mehta and F. Kardes, 'The Timing of Repeat Purchase of Consumer Durable Goods: The Role of Functional Bases of Consumer Attitudes' (2004) 41 *Journal of Marketing Research* 101; M. Cleveland, M. Kalamas and M. Laroche, 'Shades of Green: Linking Environmental Locus of Control and Pro-environmental Behaviors' (2005) 22 *Journal of Consumer Marketing* 198.

5 For an effective survey of the different possible types of premature obsolescence, see J. Valant, *Planned obsolescence: Exploring the issue*, European Parliamentary Research Service May 2016, pp. 2–3; A. Michel, *Premature Obsolescence: In Search of an Improved Legal Framework*, DPhil thesis, Université Catholique de Louvain, 2022, pp. 1–2.

6 On the role of factual powers in private law relationships, see C.M. Bianca, *Le autorità private*, Jovene, Naples 1977. In recent years, the topic has been the subject of renewed attention in the European legal debate: see among others F. Möslein (eds.), *Private Macht*, Mohr Siebeck, Tübingen 2016; P. Sirena and A. Zoppini (eds.), *I poteri privati e il diritto della regolazione. A quarant'anni da 'Le autorità private' di C.M. Bianca*, TrE-Press, Rome 2018; K. Barker, S. Degeling, K. Fairweather and R. Grantham (eds.), *Private Law and Power*, Hart Publishing, Oxford and Portland OR 2019; and for an effective synthesis, M. Renner, 'Private Power' in S. Grundmann, H.-W. Micklitz and M. Renner (eds.), *New Private Law Theory. A Pluralist Approach*, Cambridge University Press, Cambridge 2021, p. 248.

re-examination of the proper tools for power-regulation, consistent with the objectives of the circular economy and sustainable development.

In this respect, a categorisation of available legislative measures is proposed, distinguishing rationales of 'market governance' ('power *in* market') and of 'market containment' ('power *and* market'): it is suggested that the challenges posed by p.o. to the circular economy can be more pertinently framed within the latter logic.

## 2. P.O. IN THE EU PACKAGE ON CIRCULAR ECONOMY: LITTLE CONFIDENCE IN CONTRACT GOVERNANCE?

The marked environmental impact of p.o. practices has been object of direct or indirect regulation in a series of measures formally adopted by the European legislator in 2024. Looking at these interventions, it can be seen that, notwithstanding the widespread academic convictions that EU (consumer) contract law could broaden its goals from those of market regulation, to those of promotion of more responsible environmental behaviours,[7] the ordinary tools of contractual governance (i.e. governance *'of'/'by means' of* contract law) have remained substantially unexploited in the sustainable development campaign against p.o.[8]

---

7 In this sense, explicitly, A. De Franceschi, 'Planned Obsolescence challenging the Effectiveness of Consumer Law and the Achievement of a Sustainable Economy' (2018) *Journal of European Consumer and Market Law (EuCML)* 217, 221; on the topic, see also V. Mak and E. Terryn, 'Circular Economy and Consumer Protection: The Consumer as a Citizen and the Limits of Empowerment Through Consumer Law' (2020) 43 *Journal of Consumer Policy* 227.

8 Reference is made to the regulatory strategies depicted by S. Grundmann, F. Möslein and K. Riesenhuber, 'Contract Governance. Dimensions in Law & Interdisciplinary Research' in S. Grundmann, F. Möslein and K. Riesenhuber (eds.), *Contract Governance. Dimensions in Law & Interdisciplinary Research*, Oxford University Press, Oxford 2015, pp. 3, 42, where the authors describe, *inter alia*, 'governance of contract law' (i.e. procedural and substantive guidelines for designing contract law) and 'governance by means of contract law' (i.e. contract law pursuing regulatory goals, steering individual behaviour).

## 2.1. THE ECODESIGN FOR SUSTAINABLE PRODUCTS REGULATION

The absence of explicit references to contractual safeguards is not surprising in the context of Regulation 2024/1781 (Ecodesign for Sustainable Products Regulation, ESPR),[9] which mainly operates with an *ex ante* approach based on mandatory measures of regulation by design, imposed on the supply side of the market, meant to be progressively applied to all products traded in the EU, including those sold online.[10]

According to this piece of legislation,

> premature obsolescence means a product design feature or subsequent action or omission resulting in the product becoming non-functional or performing less well without such changes of functionality or performance being the result of normal wear and tear' [Article 2, point (21)].

On the premise that p.o. practices 'have an overall negative impact on the environment, in the form of increased waste and use of energy and materials' (Recital 7), ESPR aims at reducing this through specific product requirements, considered necessary to contribute to sustainable consumption. To this task, after listing as 'product parameters' a series of relevant fabrication aspects that have crucial environmental impact,[11] the Regulation applies them to ensure

> that products do not become prematurely obsolete, for reasons that include design choices by manufacturers, the use of components which are significantly less robust than other components, the impeded disassembly of key components, unavailable repair information or spare parts, software that no longer works once an operating system is updated or software updates that are not provided [ESPR, Article 5, paragraph 2].

---

9 Regulation (EU) 2024/1781 of the European Parliament and of the Council of 13 June 2024 establishing a framework for the setting of ecodesign requirements for sustainable products, amending Directive (EU) 2020/1828 and Regulation (EU) 2023/1542 and repealing Directive 2009/125/EC, [2024] *OJ* L 2024/1781 (ESPR).

10 On the ambitious scope of this line of intervention, cf. S. Becher and A.-L. Sibony, 'Confronting Product Obsolescence' (2021) 27 *Columbia Journal of European Law* 97, 144–145.

11 ESPR, Art. 5, para. 1: 'In order to address environmental impacts and based on the product parameters referred to in Annex I, the ecodesign requirements in the delegated acts adopted pursuant to Article 4 shall be such as to improve the following product aspects ("product aspects") where those product aspects are relevant to the product group concerned: (a) durability; (b) reliability; (c) reusability; (d) upgradability; (e) repairability; (f) the possibility of maintenance and refurbishment; (g) the presence of substances of concern; (h) energy use and energy efficiency; (i) water use and water efficiency; (j) resource use and resource efficiency; (k) recycled content; (l) the possibility of remanufacturing; (m) recyclability; (n) the possibility of the recovery of materials; (o) environmental impacts, including carbon footprint and environmental footprint; (p) expected generation of waste'.

## 2.2. THE EMPOWERING CONSUMER DIRECTIVE

With Directive (EU) 2024/825 (Empowering Consumers Directive, ECD),[12] the European Legislator has amended existing rules on pre-contractual information laid down in the Consumer Rights Directive (CRD),[13] as well as the legal discipline of unfair practices under the Unfair Commercial Practices Directive (UCPD).[14]

On the one hand, new rules supplement the information obligations relevant under the CRD by adding that products must bear: (i) a harmonised notice reminding consumers of the legal guarantee as well as possible differences under national law, and (ii) a harmonised label identifying goods covered by a commercial guarantee of durability with a duration longer than two years. Both the notice and the label shall be easily recognisable and understandable for consumers and easy to use and reproduce for traders.[15]

At the same time, the ECD extends the series of blacklisted practices relevant under the UCPD, in particular prohibiting

> planned early obsolescence practices, understood as a commercial policy involving deliberately planning or designing a product with a limited lifespan so that it prematurely becomes obsolete or non-functional after a certain period or after a predetermined intensity of use [Recital 16].[16]

---

12 Directive (EU) 2024/825 of the European Parliament and of the Council of 28 February 2024 amending Directives 2005/29/EC and 2011/83/EU as regards empowering consumers for the green transition through better protection against unfair practices and through better information, [2024] *OJ* L 2024/825 (ECD).

13 Directive 2011/83/EU of the European Parliament and of the Council of 25 October 2011 on consumer rights, amending Council Directive 93/13/EEC and Directive 1999/44/EC of the European Parliament and of the Council and repealing Council Directive 85/577/EEC and Directive 97/7/EC of the European Parliament and of the Council, [2011] *OJ* L 304 (CRD).

14 Directive 2005/29/EC of the European Parliament and of the Council of 11 May 2005 concerning unfair business-to-consumer commercial practices in the internal market and amending Council Directive 84/450/EEC, Directives 97/7/EC, 98/27/EC and 2002/65/EC of the European Parliament and of the Council and Regulation (EC) No. 2006/2004 of the European Parliament and of the Council, [2005] *OJ* L 149 (UCPD).

15 See in particular ECD, Art. 2(5) inserting Art. 22a into the CRD.

16 In connection to these premises, the Annex of the ECD (para. 4) adds to the Annex of the UCPD the following blacklisted practices: '23d. Withholding information from the consumer about the fact that a software update will negatively impact the functioning of goods with digital elements or the use of digital content or digital services. 23e. Presenting a software update as necessary when it only enhances functionality features. 23f. Any commercial communication in relation to a good containing a feature introduced to limit its durability despite information on the feature and its effects on the durability of the good being available to the trader. 23g. Falsely claiming that under normal conditions of use a good has a certain durability in terms of usage time or intensity. 23h. Presenting a good as allowing repair when it does not. 23i. Inducing the consumer to replace or replenish the consumables of a good earlier than necessary for technical reasons. 23j. Withholding

The operation of this line of intervention at a level other than that proper of the contractual relationship is made explicit by Recital 19 of the ECD, where it is stressed that the new prohibition

> complements and does not affect the remedies available to consumers in the event of a lack of conformity under Directive (EU) 2019/771. The use of features limiting the durability of the goods should be distinguished from manufacturing practices using materials or processes of general low quality resulting in limited durability of the goods. Lack of conformity of a good resulting from the use of low quality materials or processes should continue to be governed by the rules on the conformity of goods set out in Directive (EU) 2019/771.

## 2.3. THE RIGHT TO REPAIR DIRECTIVE

Building on this last remark, it is appropriate to conclude this brief survey with a focus on the contents of Directive (EU) 2024/1799 (Right to Repair Directive, RRD).[17] This piece of legislation is characterised by a double soul: on the one hand, it sets out rules on mandatory or incentivised repair services, respectively to be offered – beyond the legal guarantee period due under the sale contract – by producers and/or independent professionals; and at a different level, RRD amends the provisions of Directive (EU) 2019/771 (Sale of Goods Directive, SGD),[18] with the specific aim of adding a further green touch to the protections offered by that legislative measure.[19]

The former line of intervention widens the solutions granted by the original version of the SGD, which appeared very rarely concerned with maintenance and repair of goods outside the legal guarantee period of contractual nature. The new rules require manufacturers to offer repair options even after the two-year legal guarantee, and promotes the entrance to the market for third-party repairers willing to offer the same kind of services, with the ultimate aim of

information concerning the impairment of the functionality of a good when consumables, spare parts or accessories not supplied by the original producer are used, or falsely claiming that such impairment will happen'.

17 Directive (EU) 2024/1799 of the European Parliament and of the Council of 13 June 2024 on common rules promoting the repair of goods and amending Regulation (EU) 2017/2394 and Directives (EU) 2019/771 and (EU) 2020/1828, [2024] *OJ* L, 2024/1799 (RRD).

18 Directive (EU) 2019/771 of the European Parliament and of the Council of 20 May 2019 on certain aspects concerning contracts for the sale of goods, amending Regulation (EU) 2017/2394 and Directive 2009/22/EC, and repealing Directive 1999/44/EC, [2019] *OJ* L 136.

19 See, during the legislative procedure that has eventually brought to the RRD, E.-M. Kieninger, 'Recht auf Reparatur ('Right to Repair') und Europäisches Vertragsrecht' in (2020) (2) *Zeitschrift für Europäisches Privatrecht* 264.

'allowing consumers to seek affordable repair from the repair service provider of their choice'.[20]

Requiring repairs beyond the two-year period is crucial for addressing defects in goods that remain usable but have developed issues, preventing them from being prematurely discarded due to a lack of repair options.[21] Outside the seller's legal guarantee, repairs may be provided at no cost or for a fee, allowing manufacturers to cover labour and spare parts expenses.[22] In this regard, the RRD stipulates that repair costs must be reasonable and should not intentionally discourage consumers from taking advantage of the manufacturer's repair obligations. The original manufacturer is also required to supply spare parts and tools at reasonable prices, ensuring that third parties can offer repair services without barriers. Furthermore, manufacturers are prohibited from denying repairs solely because a third party previously fixed the item, as well as from implementing contractual terms, hardware, or software measures that hinder repairability.[23] Repairers are to provide consumers with essential information on their repair services, and in order to enhance competition – facilitating the consumer's free choice to decide by whom to have goods repaired and to help identify and choose suitable repair services – repairers should be able to use on a voluntary basis the standardised European Repair Information Form, provided in Annex I of the RRD.[24]

Although these new rules represent significant progress in the promotion of more sustainable consumption habits, it must be observed that from the perspective of the overarching objectives of circular economy they also show key limitations, connected to their relatively narrow scope of application. Indeed, it must be considered not only that the provisions of the RRD are relevant only for a defined series of products, coinciding with goods subject

---

20 RRD, Recital 3.

21 RRD, Recital 15 is clear in describing the repair as a service that operates beyond the remedies of the contractual relationship of sale: 'Directive (EU) 2019/771 imposes an obligation on sellers to repair goods in the event of a lack of conformity which existed at the time that the goods were delivered and which becomes apparent within the liability period. Where that obligation does not apply, a large number of defective, but otherwise viable, goods are prematurely discarded. In order to encourage consumers to have goods repaired in such situations, this Directive should impose an obligation on manufacturers to repair upon the consumer's request goods to which repairability requirements imposed by Union legal acts apply, since they are the addressees of those repairability requirements'.

22 RRD, Art. 5, para. 2(a).

23 RRD, Art. 5, paras. 6, 7.

24 RRD, Recital 12 and Art. 4.

to reparability requirements under EU law,[25] but also that the Directive is completely silent as to goods negotiated in B2C transactions.[26]

Looking at the second line of intervention of the RRD, which introduces amendments to the text of the SGD, it seems possible to confirm the presence of that 'light-touch' approach, already considered by several commentators, as a key feature of the 2019 legislation.[27]

With particular regard to the topic of the present analysis, this evaluation could be shared by observing that the SGD, although introducing durability among the requirements of conformity of consumer goods,[28] did not specifically tackle p.o. practices, which, as frequently observed, differ from the durability issue *per se* as they imply intention on behalf of the producer.[29] The same conclusion can be confirmed today, even considering the more recent modifications brought to the SGD by the RRD,[30] which, among other measures, has explicitly inserted 'repairability' within the notion of durability, but still lacks provisions on fraudulent behaviour by the seller and/or producer.[31]

---

25 In more detail, this list encompass: household washing machines and household washer-dryers (Commission Regulation (EU) 2019/2023); household dishwashers (Commission Regulation (EU) 2019/2022); refrigerating appliances (Commission Regulation (EU) 2019/2019); electronic displays (Commission Regulation (EU) 2019/2021); welding equipment (Commission Regulation (EU) 2019/1784); vacuum cleaners (Commission Regulation (EU) No. 666/2013); servers and data storage products (Commission Regulation (EU) 2019/424); mobile phones, cordless phones and slate tablets (Commission Regulation (EU) 2023/1670); household tumble dryers (Commission Regulation (EU) 2023/2533); goods incorporating light means of transport batteries (Regulation (EU) 2023/1542 of the European Parliament and of the Council).

26 On this point, see below, section 4.

27 See, in particular, explicitly, E. Van Gool and A. Michel, 'The New Consumer Sales Directive 2019/771 and Sustainable Consumption: A Critical Analysis' (2021) *EuCML* 136.

28 According to SGD, Art. 2, para. 13 '"durability" means the ability of the goods to maintain their required functions and performance through normal use'. On this point, with analysis extended to obsolescence of digital goods, see R. Barceló Compte, 'From Conformity to Sustainability: Understanding the Implications of Digital Content Modifications under Directives 2019/770 and 771' (2024) 24 *Global Jurist* 25, 46.

29 Y.M. Atamer and S. Grundmann, 'Sales Law in Transformation. Sustainability, Digitalisation, Servitisation' in S. Grundmann and Y.M. Atamer (eds.), *European Sales Law. Challenges in the 21st Century*, Intersentia, Cambridge, Antwerp and Chicago 2023, pp. 1, 13 et seq.; M. Feleppa, 'European Sales Law in the 21st Century' (2022) *Roma Tre Law Review* 167, 170.

30 For the remark that in the digital and in the green sector, consumer and market law is subject to rapid obsolescence see A. De Franceschi, 'The Sustainability of Consumer and Market Law: Green Claims, Greenwashing and the Right to Repair' (2023) *EuCML* 45, 48.

31 RRD, Art. 16, para. 1.

# 3. SUGGESTED (CONSUMER) CONTRACTUAL STRATEGIES AGAINST P.O.

With particular regard to the regulatory campaign concerning p.o., while several commentators have evaluated the legislative outcome of the Circular Economy Package (and in particular the interventions of the RRD) as a 'missed opportunity',[32] my impression is that the main amendments to the EU legislation that have been advocated as possible contractual constraints on p.o. practices unveil serious risks of scant effectiveness, especially if intended as means to pursue to the superior goals of sustainable development.

To justify this conclusion, I now review the main changes proposed in recent years by European *doctrine*.

## 3.1. EXTENSION OF THE LIABILITY PERIOD

In the academic discussion that has accompanied the legislative process of revision of the SGD, the extension of the liability period for non-conformity of goods has been the first and most direct measure suggested to control p.o. practices through contractual regulation. While the current EU legislative limit (two years) does not match the average lifespan of several manufactured products, the proposed reform would have aligned the durability requirement with a remedy capable of making it enforceable, not only to the benefit of the buyer, but of the environmental sustainability as a whole.[33]

Although this proposal has not been implemented with the RRD, Member States are still free to set different liability periods, longer than the one provided for in the SGD.[34] In this regard, the main operational issues that have been discussed concern: (i) the individuation of the proper normative level of intervention (legislative? regulatory? soft law?); and (ii) the scope of the extension of the liability period (one fixed, longer period? differentiated periods, standardised according to different classes of goods? fully differentiated

[32] See in particular S. Augenhofer, Y.M. Atamer, K. Południak Gierz and R. Küter, *European Commission's Proposal for a Directive on Common Rules Promoting the Repair of Goods. Feedback of the European Law Institute*, European Law Institute, Vienna 2023, p. 20.

[33] B. Keirsbilck, E. Terryn, A. Michel and I. Alogna, *Sustainable Consumption and Consumer Protection Legislation How Can Sustainable Consumption and Longer Lifetime of Products be Promoted through Consumer Protection Legislation?*, European Parliament, Policy Department for Economic, Scientific and Quality of Life Policies, Directorate-General for Internal Policies, 2020, pp. 20–21.

[34] SGD, Art. 10, para. 3: 'Member States may maintain or introduce longer time limits than those referred to in paragraphs 1 and 2'.

periods, depending on a case-by-case appreciation of the individual product's expected lifespan?).[35]

In this context, several observations can be made.

First of all, in light of the acquisitions coming from other scientific fields (e.g. engineers, software developers, etc.), the analysis of these alternative solutions raises doubts about the actual possibility of rigidly setting the '*proper* lifespan' of a (class of) products (e.g., given the fact that goods do not operate *in a vacuum*, but rather have a consumption that largely depends, in both quantitative and qualitative terms, on the evolution, technical and economic, of the highly interconnected contexts in which they are embedded).[36]

Leaving these technical considerations aside, in the specific context of sale-remedies, the formal extension of the liability period does not seem capable of producing effective results if not coupled with a corresponding extension of legal presumption of the existence of the defect (of durability) at the time of delivery, currently limited at one year by Article 11, paragraph 1, SGD, and at the maximum extendable up to two years after delivery at the discretion of the Member States (Article 11, paragraph 2, SGD).[37]

In practical terms, this means that even imagining the possibility of triggering the liability for non-conformity beyond the time limit set by the SGD (i.e. up to the longer period potentially ensured by the national legislators, as per Article 10, paragraph 3, SGD), consumers could not rely on the presumption of non-conformity, and would have to specifically prove the existence of the defect at the time of delivery. From the perspective of the buyer of goods allegedly manufactured with a p.o. practice, the extreme difficulty of providing the proof of such a durability defect, to be discussed in front of a court perhaps several years after the conclusion of the contract, is evident, and clearly capable of undermining the effectiveness of the overall proposal.

## 3.2. THE SCOPE OF THE BURDEN OF PROOF PENDING ON THE CONSUMER

The discussion over the temporal extension of the liability could appear pointless if one accepts that in the presence of fraudulent behaviour (as in the case of the p.o. practices relevant in the EU legislative framework) the seller

[35] For a discussion of these policy options, see E. Van Gool and A. Michel, above n. 27, pp. 141 et seq.

[36] See already Y.C. Lee and W.T. Chen, *Manufacturing Challenges in Electronic Packaging*, Spinger Science + Business Media, Dordrecht 1998; and with particular regard to the interconnected ('unbundled') digital environment, cf. G. Wagner, 'Robot Liability' in S. Lohsse, R. Schulze and D. Staudenmayer (eds.), *Liability for Artificial Intelligence and the Internet of Things*, Nomos, Baden-Baden 2019, pp. 27, 47.

[37] Y.M. Atamer and S. Grundmann, above n. 29, p. 35.

could not rely on the limitation period.[38] Indeed, this conclusion is shared in the legal systems of several Member States, and in the international context it is formalised in United Nations Convention on Contracts for the International Sale of Goods (CISG, Article 40).[39]

Even in this scenario, however, the burden of proof lying on the consumer appears problematic, since he/she must demonstrate not the simple lack of conformity, but the elements from which an intentional p.o. practice can be inferred.

The case law that has developed so far perfectly shows the difficulty of providing this kind of proof, even when the interested party is not a private consumer, but a public authority. A paradigmatic example in this respect is offered by one of the first judicial disputes concerning p.o. practices, litigated in the Italian legal system between 2018 and 2023. On 25 September 2018, the Italian Competition Authority (ICA) imposed fines on both Apple and Samsung in two separate rulings for engaging in unfair commercial practices related to software updates that significantly affected the performance of specific mobile phone models. The two companies were fined €10 million and €5 million, respectively.[40] These decisions quickly attracted global attention, for their clear connection with issues of p.o., in the wider debate on sustainable economy policies to be implemented in Europe.[41] However, in the subsequent appeal proceedings, the Italian Supreme Administrative Court annulled the sanctions imposed on the companies: the revision of both the first hearing decisions has been expressly justified, in two separate judgments, precisely on the basis of the lack of proof of an intentional p.o. practice affecting the operative systems of the products under analysis.[42]

In addition to the above (and to make things even more difficult for the consumer), it must be noted that in the structure of the SGD, consistently with the contractual nature of the remedy, liability for defective products can be invoked only against the seller, and not directly against the manufacturer.[43]

---

38 S. Augenhofer, Y.M. Atamer, K. Południak Gierz and R. Küter, above n. 32, p. 20; M. D'Onofrio, *Il difetto di durabilità del bene*, E.S.I., Naples 2023, pp. 63 et seq.

39 CISG, Art. 40: 'The seller is not entitled to rely on the provisions of articles 38 and 39 if the lack of conformity relates to facts of which he knew or could not have been unaware and which he did not disclose to the buyer'.

40 See Italian Competition Authority, 25.9.2018, PS11039, *Apple*, http://www.agcm.it/dotcmsdoc/allegati-news/PS11039_scorr_sanzDich_rett_va.pdf (accessed 27.2.2025); See Italian Competition Authority, 25.9.2018, PS11039, *Samsung*, http://www.agcm.it/dotcmsdoc/allegati-news/PS11009_scorr_sanz_omi_dichrett.pdf (accessed 27.2.2025).

41 See, for a discussion of the two cases, in the light of the debate on sustainability measures to be enacted at EU level, A. De Franceschi, above n. 7, 217.

42 Italian Supreme Administrative Court (*Consiglio di Stato*), VI, sez. VI, 13.1.2023 n. 448, *Apple*; VI, 09.06.2023, n. 6006, *Samsung*.

43 See, also from a *de jure condendo* perspective, J.-S. Borghetti, 'Direct Liability for Non-Conformity: It is Worth Pushing the Case?' in S. Grundmann and Y.M. Atamer (eds.), above n. 29, pp. 249 et seq.

## 3.3. THE SEARCH FOR EFFECTIVE REMEDIES

Even assuming that all the conditions triggering liability are met, one may eventually question whether the remedies that can then be invoked are effective in safeguarding the issues of sustainability and environmental protection that a regulation on p.o. should be expected to protect.

Looking at the hierarchy of measures provided for by the SGD in cases of defects of conformity (Article 13, pararaph 2), it is clear that from an environmental perspective, the repair option should be favoured over replacement[44] (at least when the latter activity implies the delivery of a new product).[45] Even though this conclusion appears explicit in the Recital 48 of the SGD,[46] the original legislative text did not seem to leave room for a clear order of remedies that could be imposed on the parties to the sale contract.

A stricter preference for the restorative remedy was envisaged in an early proposal of the RRD, which would have integrated Article 13, paragraph 2, SGD with the clarification that 'where the costs for replacement are equal to or greater than the costs for repair, the seller shall repair the goods in order to bring those goods in conformity'.[47]

This proposal has been criticised in academia, on the ground that it would have essentially delegated the whole implementation of the conformity obligation to the seller, on the basis of a costs-argument that the consumer would not have been able to observe, verify or challenge. The proposal seemed thus to convey a limitation of the existing guarantee for the buyer, with a substantial shift from a 'right to repair' to an 'obligation to accept repair'.[48]

---

44 C. Dalhammar, E. Maitre-Ekern, J.L. Richter, B. Puentes Cociňa and L. Milios, 'What is Right to Repair (R2r) and How Can It be Realised through Legal Interventions?' in S. Grundmann and Y.M. Atamer (eds.), above n. 29, pp. 165 et seq.; E. Terryn, 'A Right to Repair? Towards Sustainable Remedies in Consumer Law' in B. Keirsbilck and E. Terryn (eds.), *Consumer Protection in a Circular Economy*, Intersentia, Cambridge-Antwerp-Chicago 2019, pp. 127 et seq.

45 For a comparison, in light of sustainability goals, of the remedies of repair and replacement with refurbished, or second-hand, goods, see B.M. Loos, 'Furthering Sustainability by Developing Specific Provisions for the Sale of Secondhand Goods: Rubbish or Recycling?' in S. Grundmann and Y.M. Atamer (eds.), above n. 29, pp. 135, 140 et seq.; V. Mak and E. Terryn, above n. 7, p. 236.

46 SGD, Recital 48: 'As regards bringing goods into conformity, consumers should enjoy a choice between repair or replacement. Enabling consumers to require repair should encourage sustainable consumption and could contribute to greater durability of products'.

47 European Commission, Proposal for a Directive of the European Parliament and of the Council on common rules promoting the repair of goods and amending Regulation (EU) 2017/2394, Directives (EU) 2019/771 and (EU) 2020/1828, Brussels, 22.3.2023, COM(2023) 155 final 2023/0083 (COD).

48 Explicitly, S. Augenhofer, Y.M. Atamer, K. Południak Gierz and R. Küter, above n. 32, p. 12.

The final version of the RRD intervenes in the SGD in a much softer way: (i) with an extension of the liability period by 12 months (only), granted once, for consumers who opt for repair (Article 16, paragraph 2(a), RRD); (ii) with the specification that sellers 'may provide' the consumer with replacement goods, including refurbished goods, free of charge during the period needed for repair (Article 16, paragraph 4, RRD).

To adopt a Latin motto, one may conclude: '*parturient montes, nascetur ridiculus mus*'. Gently incentivising the consumer towards repair certainly militates in favour of a 'greener' sales law.[49] At the same time, if aimed at regulating p.o. practices in the light of the higher goals of sustainable development, the effective impact associated with these suggested reforms or interpretations of such an important piece of (consumer) contract law appears highly questionable.[50]

## 4. 'POWER *IN* MARKET' VS. 'POWER *AND* MARKET': TWO ALTERNATIVE REGULATORY STRATEGIES

The shortcomings inherent in the contract-governance strategies discussed so far suggest that looking at the regulation of technological power from a broader perspective would be beneficial. In particular, if one focuses on the different role that can be attributed to power in the framework of market relations and, more generally, in the economic institutions of society, it is possible to distinguish between two different models of legal control.

A first model ('Power *in* market') moves from the recognition of structural concentrations of power capable of affecting the relations among individuals and institutions in an *existing* market, and proposes *second-order* lines of intervention resulting in legal arrangements aimed at preventing or correcting inefficient, harmful, or disruptive effects on society.

Existing EU contract (and consumer) law clearly falls into this model, understood as an 'integrated view of regulation and private law in market transactions':[51] a body of rules whose ultimate rationale is centred on the logic of the (EU) internal market, aimed at fostering the full exercise of the fundamental economic freedoms dictated by the Treaties, enforced beyond

[49] As a general reference, see M. Niva and P. Timonen, 'The Role of Consumers in Product-oriented Environmental Policy: Can the Consumer be the Driving Force for Environmental Improvements?' (2001) 25 *International Journal of Consumer Studies* 331.

[50] Recently, on the limitations of consumer law as a tool to advance sustainable development, F. Pflücke, 'The Limits of Consumer Law in Pursuing Sustainability' in J. Nowag (eds.), *Research Handbook on Sustainability and Competition Law*, Edward Elgar, Cheltenham 2024, pp. 302 et seq.

[51] See S. Grundmann, F. Möslein, K. Riesenhuber, above n. 8, p. 22.

the legal boarders of individual Member States according to the spirit of the European Economic Constitution.[52]

While these features are certainly consistent with the structure and nature of EU private law (also in light of its historical origins), one has also to consider that in an era of pervasive private (technological) power, contemporary legal systems are increasingly faced with a different and more general issue: the definition of the objective scope of the market domain.[53]

Within this framework ('Power *and* market') the legal intervention takes upon itself the *first-order* decision on what is within and what is (should be) outside of the market logic, marking the border of the policy choices that cannot be left to the private economic powers, regardless of the more specific rules which govern their activities.[54]

Although this type of intervention is generally ascribed to pure public law, it seems possible to trace back to it interesting pieces of the most recent European regulation of a private nature as well. Relevant examples can be drawn from significant traits of the recent EU digital package, with particular regard to those control techniques that operate more by imposing *ex-ante* behavioural duties on power-holders (designed to reduce risks or to promote transparency) than by allocating counter-rights (or remedies) to power-subordinates.

One may consider, as an effective illustration, the list of Prohibited Artificial Intelligence Practices contained in the Artificial Intelligence Act (AI Act), which is aimed at preventing the misuse of AI as a tool for manipulative, exploitative and social control practices.[55] The list includes, among others, techniques deploying subliminal, manipulative, or deceptive techniques to distort behaviour and impair informed decision-making, causing significant harm; exploiting vulnerabilities related to age, disability, or socio-economic circumstances to distort behaviour, causing significant harm; and evaluating or

---

52 E.-J. Mestmäcker, 'European Economic Constitution' in J. Basedow et al. (eds.), *The Max Planck Encyclopedia of European Private Law*, Oxford University Press, Oxford 2012, pp. 588 et seq.; W. Sauter, 'The Economic Constitution of the European Union' (1998) 4 *Columbia Journal of European Law* 27 et seq.

53 See G. Resta, 'In search of the "Europeanness" of European Private Law' in H.-W. Micklitz and G. Vettori (eds.), *What is European in European private law? Che cosa c'è di europeo nel diritto privato europeo?*, Giuffrè, Milan 2022, pp. 273, 294, referring to the model of embedded/disembedded economy proposed by K. Polanyi, 'The Economy as Instituted Process' in K. Polanyi, C.M. Arensberg and H.W. Pearson (eds.), *Trade and Market in the Early Empires: Economies in History and Theory*, The Free Press, New York 1957, p. 243.

54 Cf. H.-W. Micklitz, 'The transformative politics of European private law' in P.F. Kjaer (ed.), *The Law of Political Economy Transformation in the Function of Law*, Cambridge University Press, Cambridge 2020, pp. 205, 227.

55 The list is set forth in Chapter II, Art. 5(1) of Regulation (EU) 2024/1689 of the European Parliament and of the Council of 13 June 2024 laying down harmonised rules on artificial intelligence and amending Regulations (EC) No. 300/2008, (EU) No. 167/2013, (EU) No. 168/2013, (EU) 2018/858, (EU) 2018/1139 and (EU) 2019/2144 and Directives 2014/90/EU, (EU) 2016/797 and (EU) 2020/1828, [2024] *OJ* L 2024/1689.

classifying individuals or groups based on social behaviour or personal traits, causing unfavourable treatment of those people ('social scoring').[56]

Another example of this regulatory technique can be found in the Digital Services Act ('DSA'),[57] which provides a targeted set of uniform rules in order to safeguard and improve not only the functioning of the internal market but also the safety and predictability of online environment. In this framework, DSA can be regarded as oriented toward cooperation between platforms and public authorities, requiring empowerment and accountability of the providers while allocating them relevant 'public' tasks on the condition of accepting specific rules and procedures. Reference can be made to obligations like that of designating a point of contact to communicate directly with the authorities (Article 11), making available any information on any restrictions that they impose in relation to the use of their service (Article 14), putting mechanisms in place to allow any individual or entity to notify them of the presence on their service of specific items of information that the individual or entity considers to be illegal content (Article 16), and many other obligations related to transparency, mitigation of risks and compliance.[58]

But what is of greater interest here is the distinction between the various 'intermediary services', namely 'Mere Conduit', 'Caching' and 'Hosting' services, given that only the latter category is authorised by the DSA for data storage.[59] This implies: (i) that data intermediation services are distinguished from other data-related services (e.g. data analysis); and that (ii) the DSA prevents intermediaries from differentiating their services, creating added value from the circulation of data, also for users. Hence, the strict measures imposed by the DSA could result in an effective constraint on the development of data services providers.

---

56 See E.J. Kindt and C. Jasserand, 'Chapter II. Prohibited AI Practices' in C. Pehlivan, N. Forgó and P. Valcke (eds.), *The EU Artificial Intelligence (AI) Act: A Commentary*, Kluwer Law International, Alphen aan Den Rijn 2025.

57 Regulation (EU) 2022/2065 of The European Parliament and of The Council of 19 October 2022 on a Single Market for Digital Services and amending Directive 2000/31/EC, [2022] *OJ* L 277.

58 F. Wilman, S.L. Kaleda and P.J. Loewenthal, *The EU Digital Services Act. A Commentary*, Oxford University Press, Oxford 2024, pp. 20 et seq.

59 Definitions of 'Mere conduit', 'Caching' and 'Hosting' service are set forth in Art. 3(g) of Regulation (EU) 2022/2065. Specifically, 'mere conduit' service consists of 'the transmission in a communication network of information provided by a recipient of the service, or the provision of access to a communication network'; 'caching' service consists of 'the transmission in a communication network of information provided by a recipient of the service, involving the automatic, intermediate and temporary storage of that information, performed for the sole purpose of making more efficient the information's onward transmission to other recipients upon their request'; and 'hosting' service, consists of 'the storage of information provided by, and at the request of, a recipient of the service'.

This model of *ex-ante* regulation is not necessarily a negative factor. On the contrary, in the definition of the scope of a market, it may be perceived as an opportunity for growth, especially for small and medium-sized companies keen to establish themselves as reliable players within the data economy.

Returning to the main topic of this chapter, it can be argued that the inadequacies of the contractual governance of p.o. detected above may depend – more so than on intrinsic flaws of the proposed reforms and interpretive strategies – on the wider scale of intervention that the legal system must consider when confronted with pivotal regulatory objectives such as those raised by circular economy and sustainable development.[60]

Consumer/Contract laws (and their remedies) are intrinsically connected to the apical acceptance of the market dynamic, whose rationale inevitably fosters consumption as a key factor for economic growth.[61] From this point of view, paradoxically, p.o. seems to make perfect sense, appearing as a natural companion to a society based on a free-market economy.[62]

It is probably no coincidence that, as is well known, the first formalisation of the term ('planned obsolescence') derives from the study by Bernard London, dating back to 1932, where it was suggested as a policy measure to be implemented during a phase of economic depression (in particular, with a 'lease of life' for manufactured products, imposed though legislative intervention in order to incentivise and to artificially feed 'the wheels of industry').[63]

By remaining confined to the 'Power *in* market' logic, the regulatory tools at the disposal of the policy-maker tend to coincide with those mechanisms that constitute the 'legal infrastructure of capitalism',[64] and that have historically recognised (or even directly granted) powers, to the controllers of production

---

60 J. Eyckmans, 'Circular Economy, An Economist's Perspective' in B. Keirsbilck and E. Terryn (eds.), above n. 44, p. 36.

61 It is here sufficient to recall that, according to J.A. Schumpeter, *Capitalism, Socialism, and Democracy*, Harper & Bros, New York 1942, 'creative destruction' – i.e. the incessant product and process innovation mechanism by which new production units replace outdated ones – is to be considered 'the essential fact about capitalism'.

62 A. Fishman, N. Gandal and O. Shy, 'Planned obsolescence as an engine of technological progress' (1993) 141 *Journal of Industrial Economics* 361.

63 B. London, *Ending the Depression through Planned Obsolescence*, Project Gutenberg, originally self-published, New York 1932, p. 6: 'New products would constantly be pouring forth from the factories and marketplaces, to take the place of the obsolete, and the wheels of industry would be kept going and employment regularized and assured for the masses'.

64 See T. Frankel, 'The Legal Infrastructure of Markets: The Role of Contract and Property Law' (1993) 73 *Boston University Law Review* 389, and more recently, K. Pistor, *The Code of Capital. How the Law Creates Wealth and Inequality*, Princeton University Press, Princeton NJ and Oxford 2019, p. 21: 'Capital is coded in law, and more specifically, in institutions of private law, including property, collateral, trust, corporate, bankruptcy law, and contract law'.

means, over the functionality of their products.[65] In more detail, the common features of 'liberal' private law institutions, such as contracts, property and intellectual property have traditionally offered support to the recognition of the idea that certain apical choices concerning the use of resources (and their cycles of exploitation) are proper to the economic arena (according to the demand and supply rationale), preventing either government or public authorities from interfering with the outcome produced by the exercise of parties' autonomy and (at least implicitly) powers.[66]

Paradoxically, this is further demonstrated if one looks at the inner logic of what is commonly regarded as the judicial case from which the debate on the need for a legal intervention constraining p.o. began.[67] Reference is obviously made to the so-called *Phoebus Cartel*, an anti-competitive alliance concluded in the early twentieth century between the largest electricity market companies operating in America and Europe, based on a strategic shortening of the lifespan of lightbulbs, in a way that reduced their durability and induced consumers to replace the product early.[68] Although the sanctioned practice described here clearly relates to the subject of p.o., it has been effectively observed that the Phoebus litigation mainly focused on collusion between the operators rather than the deliberate reduction of product durability, as anti-competitive practices addressed by competition law do not encompass those aimed at controlling product lifespan. This is confirmed by the banal observation that if a lightbulb manufacturer, perhaps an oligopolist in the market, had opted to reduce the longevity of its products on its own, this action would not have fallen under the scrutiny of antitrust authorities.[69]

All this highlights the peculiarities of the current debate on p.o. in the European context. The premises on which the most recent EU legal policies rely can be found in objectives that are exogenous to the domain of market economy ('Market *and* power'), being instead understandable (only) in light of the different logic of sustainable development,[70] where practices of intensive production and consumption are the cause of extremely relevant

---

65 For a recent critical analysis, U. Mattei and A. Quarta, *The Turning Point in Private Law. Ecology, Technology and the Commons*, Edward Elgar Publishing, Cheltenham 2018, pp. 11, 87.

66 See K. Pistor, above n. 64, p. 137 on the analysis of 'Private Property versus Sovereignty'.

67 L.A. Di Matteo and S. Wrbka, 'Planned Obsolescence and Consumer Protection: The Unregulated Extended Warranty and Service Contract Industry' (2019) 28 *Cornell Journal of Law and Public Policy* 483.

68 See M. Krajewski, 'The Great Lightbulb Conspiracy' (2014) 51 *IEEE Spectrum* 56, https://spectrum.ieee.org/the-great-lightbulb-conspiracy.

69 P.-E. Moyse, 'The Uneasy Case of Programmed Obsolescence' (2020) 71 *University of New Brunswick Law Journal* 61, 86: 'Programmed obsolescence was not the immediate cause of action in the 1949 litigation case. Collusion was'.

70 See K. Van Acker, 'Technology for the Circular Economy: A New Paradigm for the Way We Use Resources' in B. Keirsbilck and E. Terryn (eds.), above n. 44, p. 31.

environmental (p.o. as a source of waste)[71] and even social (p.o. as a potential source of individuals' indebtedness) concerns.[72]

From this perspective, the issue of p.o. shows radically deeper implications, and its regulatory goal – if it is to be taken seriously – forces the shift from a 'market governance' to a 'market containment' approach.[73]

Put simply: is it (still) permissible to delegate to the (technological) power of market actors the choice of what is the proper lifespan of goods, and thence of the business cycle that guides their production, exploitation and substitution? If one answers in the negative, it becomes clear how contract, and the regulation of its remedies, cannot be the instrument for pursuing this model of intervention. Regulation of private power can smoothly transit through contract law as long as the governance strategy is aimed at correcting the market failures in which the act of autonomy is embedded (especially with the rejection of the implicit premise of neutral market competitiveness, proper to liberal private law). In a regulatory environment in which instances of protection of non-economic interests and values take on preponderant weight, it appears no longer possible to remain anchored to the same paradigm.

Although deserving of more in-depth study than that conducted in this chapter, some of the lines of intervention on p.o. that have been recently implemented at EU level can coherently be framed within this change of perspective.

The most immediate evidence of such an evolved regulatory strategy can be drawn from the strong sustainability approach implemented by the new ESPR rules:[74] imposing a renewed series of product parameters, consistent with the goals of the circular economy, as mandatory condition for good to be traded in the EU is not only evidence of a meritorious holistic method, which appropriately follows regulation at every stage of a product's life cycle. In fact, what is most interesting here is that this type of measure ends up creating an 'entry requirement' capable of radically re-shaping the scope of the market

---

71 Pioneering in this sense is V. Packard, *The Waste Makers*, Longmans, London 1960, p. 34: 'In some cases the consumers have no choice but to be waste makers because of the way products are sold to them', https://www.soilandhealth.org/wp-content/uploads/0303critic/030320wastemakers/wastemakers.pdf (accessed 26.02.2025); see also P. Calcott and M. Walls, 'Waste, Recycling, and Design for Environment: Roles for Markets and Policy Instruments' (2005) 27 *Resource and Energy Economics* 287.

72 See European Economic and Social Committee, *Towards more sustainable consumption: industrial product lifetimes and restoring trust through consumer information*, Resolution CCMI/112-EESC-2013-1904, adopted on 17.10.2013, https://www.eesc.europa.eu/en/our-work/opinions-information-reports/opinions/towards-more-sustainable-consumption-industrial-product-lifetimes-and-restoring-trust-through-consumer-information (accessed 26.02.2025).

73 See G. Resta, above n. 53, pp. 296 et seq.

74 See above, section 2.1.

domain, with a public power taking over the selection of the type of goods and services on offer from commercial operators.[75]

On closer inspection, a similar type of intervention can be detected in the imposition and promotion of repair services by market actors, as required by the RRD.[76] Decoupling the right to repair from the horizontal commercial relationship between seller and buyer, bound by the privity of contract, and guaranteeing it through the planned mandatory availability of repair services represents further evidence of a legislative policy evidently inspired by a first-order choice in favour of sustainable consumption that is not delegated to market forces, but is made upstream of their concrete organisation and operation. Precisely because it is disconnected from the individual contractual relationship, the call for an expansion of this intervention measure must therefore be fully endorsed: not only with a revisitation that will hopefully lead over time to it encompassing an increasing number of products, but above all with the extension of its scope of application beyond consumer contracts, to also include goods traded in B2B relationships.[77]

## 5. CONCLUSION

Beyond its pre-juridical technicalities, and even beyond the details of the most recent definition of its legislative notion, the topic of p.o. appears extremely relevant because of its ability to take to extremes certain issues that (although probably in more nuanced terms) may be found underlying the entire debate surrounding sustainable development policies.

From the perspective of p.o. governance, it is easy to grasp the substantial continuity of the issues underlying questions that only apparently operate on different levels, formally ranging from pure horizontal (private) to plain vertical (public) poles: (i) how to grant a buyer the right to a 'durable' good; (ii) where to draw the line between durability, 'proper' lifespan of products and entrepreneurial innovation; and, (iii) is it still possible to foster market freedoms when sustainability dictates their restriction?

---

75 On this point, see M. Feleppa, 'Improving the Regulation of Planned Obsolescence: Comparing the EU and Australian Responses from an End-User Perspective', DPhil thesis, Roma Tre University and University of Technology Sydney, 2025, p. 142.

76 See above, section 2.3.

77 See explicitly S. Augenhofer, *European Commission's Public Consultation on Sustainable Consumption of Goods – Promoting Repair and Reuse. Response of the European Law Institute*, European Law Institute, Vienna 2022, p. 15: 'For the goal of sustainability to be reached, it is imperative that the right to repair – as well as other means which foster sustainability – are also strengthened in B2B contracts. Here it is up to national legislators to act. However, a proposal by the EC for B2C relations could serve as a model for national amendments. In order to provide legal certainty for businesses, it would also be preferable if there were no differences between B2B and B2C rules'.

In a recent article on the relationship between consumer protection and circular economy, Micklitz suggests that the claim to reconcile these two elements, leaving the former essentially unchanged, may resemble an attempt to square the circle. Hence his question: 'Is the circular economy setting an end to consumer [contract] law, at least to the consumer [contract] law as it stands after 50 years?'.[78]

My impression is that not all acquisitions of the 'traditional' EU private regulatory law are necessarily destined to be disruptively revised. One must, however, accept their radical unsuitability to resolve issues that, on closer inspection, do not concern market governance profiles, but instead call for (or imply) a policy of market containment.

The legal control of private power is not necessarily internal to the logic of the economic institutions. Depending on the political decisions of rule-makers, the regulatory choice may well impose the demarcation of spheres of justice shielded from commercialisation, demonstrating an ambition to build a European society valid *beyond* its market organisation.

[78] H.-W. Micklitz, 'Squaring the Circle? Reconciling Consumer Law and the Circular Economy' (2019) 8(6) *EuCML* 229, 237.

# CHAPTER 6

# CONTRACTING WITH NATURE: EMPOWERING NONHUMAN INTERESTS IN NEGOTIATIONS

Felix Aiwanger



'You cannot negotiate with nature' is a phrase quite frequently used in debates on political and legal instruments to fight climate change. Thereby, it is meant that nature will not align to human interests, but can rather exist independently from humankind and would most probably even thrive in a better state without humankind. In the following, however, I want to explore whether negotiations and contracts resulting from such negotiations may nevertheless serve as tools to conceive ways in which humans align their interests and their power to their coexistence with nature and other species.

Contract negotiations allow us and even force us to better understand another person's needs and to factor them into the decisions we make. Economically speaking, contracts are a means to internalise external effects, i.e. effects of one's decisions that would operate to the detriment of someone else.

By 'someone else', economic literature traditionally refers to other humans and their individual, supposedly self-serving interests:[1] The famous example used by *Ronald Coase* in his seminal article 'The Problem of Social Cost' is that of a farmer and a cattle-raiser, whose straying cattle destroy the farmer's crops.[2] According to Coase, bargaining between the farmer and the cattle-raiser leads to an optimal allocation of the affected resources as long as transaction costs are ignored. Through payments of money, each party is able to communicate its interests to the other party and to incentivise the other party to take into account the value of the external interests. Leaving other flaws of this theory aside,[3] its outcomes crucially depend on who counts as a party to be included in the bargaining process. Tellingly, in the Coasean example, it is the farmer and the cattle-raiser negotiating a mutually profitable contract, but not the cattle raised or the plants grown by the farmer, let alone other elements of nature that may be affected by these human activities.

Nowadays, the notion of nature as the subject of rights does not sound absurd anymore, has been evolving in the legal discourse[4] and is tested in practice by some jurisdictions.[5] While Christopher Stone aimed at compensating damage done to nature through tort law,[6] current debates centre around constitutional perspectives.[7] In this vein, Article 71(1) of the Ecuadorian Constitution grants nature rather general rights, like the right to recognition of its existence, its maintenance and its functions. On the other hand, the status as a legal person conferred to the Whanganui river in New Zealand pursuant to Section 14(1) of the Te Awa Tupua (Whanganui River Claims Settlement) Act 2017 is

1 Cf. A.C. Pigou, *The Economics of Welfare*, Macmillan, London 1920, p. 151.

2 R.H. Coase, 'The Problem of Social Cost' (1960) 3 *The Journal of Law and Economics* 1, 2 et seq.

3 See, for instance, M. Kelman, 'Consumption Theory, Production Theory, and Ideology in the Coase Theorem' (1979) 52 *Southern California Law Review* 669, 678 et seq.

4 For an overview, see J.M. Angstadt and M. Hourdequin, 'Taking Stock of the Rights of Nature' in D.P. Corrigan and M. Oksanen (eds.), *Rights of Nature: A Re-Examination*, Routledge, London and New York 2021, pp. 14, 15 et seq.; A. Putzer, T. Lambooy, R. Jeurissen and E. Kim, 'Putting the rights of nature on the map. A quantitative analysis of rights of nature initiatives across the world' (2022) 18 *Journal of Maps* 89, 90 et seq.

5 Ley de Derechos de la Madre Tierra, Law No. 071 of 21.12.2010 (Bolivia); Arts. 71, 72 Constitución de la República del Ecuador; *Salim v. State of Uttarakhand and others*, Writ Petition (PIL) 126/2014 (High Court of Uttarakhand, India, 20.03.2017, not final); § 14(1) Te Awa Tupua (Whanganui River Claims Settlement) Act 2017 (New Zealand); Ley para el reconocimiento de personalidad jurídica a la laguna del Mar Menor y su Cuenca, Law 19/2022 of 30.09.2022 (Spain).

6 C.D. Stone, 'Should Trees Have Standing? – Toward Legal Rights for Natural Objects' (1972) 45 *Southern California Law Review* 450, 473 et seq.

7 See, e.g., K. Sanders, '"Beyond Human Ownership"? Property, Power and Legal Personality for Nature in Aotearoa New Zealand' (2018) 30 *Journal of Environmental Law* 207, 231 et seq.; A. Fischer-Lescano, 'Natur als Rechtsperson – Konstellationen der Stellvertretung im Recht' (2018) (4) *Zeitschrift für Umweltrecht* 205, 213 et seq.; J. Kersten, *Das ökologische Grundgesetz*, C.H. Beck, Munich 2022, pp. 100 et seq.

understood as enabling the river, *inter alia*, to conclude contracts.[8] However, no more light has been shed on this aspect so far. Therefore, I would like to draw an initial sketch of how the model of contract law could be applied to our interaction with nature. I will proceed in three parts: identifying the potential parties to contracts with nature (Section 1.); outlining the possible content of contracts with nature and the potential contract types (Section 2.); and evaluating the suitability of the contractual model in light of alternative designs (Section 3.).

## 1. CONTRACTING PARTIES

Whether nature or elements of nature can[9] or should[10] hold rights, is not the concern of this chapter. I will thus start from the premise that we recognise nature as capable of holding rights, albeit the following deliberations may rebound on those preliminary questions by showing potential consequences of such capacity to hold rights.

### 1.1. NATURE AS A CONTRACTING PARTY

Due to its very hybrid[11] and diffuse character, a lot of different views, interests and ideas can be projected onto nature. To operationalise it as a contracting party, we have to specify which concrete physical phenomena are affected. The discourse on rights of nature sometimes speaks of 'nature' as a whole.[12] It is questionable whether this refers to a purely imagined construct of thought – as in the case of corporations as legal entities – or whether there is a physical reference point – be it the earth as a planet or even the whole universe as one

---

8 E.L. O'Donnell and J. Talbot-Jones, 'Creating legal rights for rivers: lessons from Australia, New Zealand, and India' (2018) 23(1) *Ecology and Society* 7 https://doi.org/10.5751/ES-09854-230107 (accessed 30.11.2024); V. Kurki, 'Can Nature Hold Rights? It's Not as Easy as You Think' (2022) 11 *Transnational Environmental Law* 525, 539 (at fn. 54).

9 See V. Kurki, above n. 8.

10 See N. Pain and R. Pepper, 'Can Personhood Protect the Environment? Affording Legal Rights to Nature' (2021) 45 *Fordham International Law Journal* 315, 375 et seq.; A. Fischer-Lescano, above n. 7, 206; N. Büscher, 'Soll es Rechte der Natur geben? Naturethisch-rechtsphilosophischer Essay zu der Frage, ob der Natur der Status als Rechtssubjekt zukommen sollte' (2024) 46 *Natur und Recht* 165.

11 Cf. A. Gutmann, *Hybride Rechtssubjektivität. Die Rechte der „Natur oder Pacha Mama" in der ecuadorianischen Verfassung von 2008*, Nomos, Baden-Baden 2021, pp. 103 et seq.

12 For example, LG Erfurt 02.08.2024, KlimR 2024, 286, 287 et seq.; N. Büscher, above n. 10; see also J. Mührel, 'Welche Natur? Zur Spezifizierung des Trägers der Rechte der Natur im Globalen Norden' (2022) (9) *Zeitschrift für Umweltrecht* 464, 466.

unity. This organicistic macro-perspective can be contrasted with a perspective that builds on the smallest elements of nature, such as micro-organisms. A practical standpoint, however, commends an intermediate perspective, which proceeds from phenomena on the human scale. To avoid any unintended anthropocentrism, however, we have to remain aware of the merely practical reasons for choosing this perspective.

From the intermediate perspective, we can distinguish three groups of natural entities: (1) living or biotic nature, such as animals, plants or other living organisms; (2) non-living or abiotic nature, such as rivers, landscapes, mountains and their components; (3) ecosystems as combinations of living and non-living nature. National and European legislation on the protection of nature combines elements from some or all of the three groups to define nature or the natural environment[13] and includes the interactions or relations between the groups in the definition.[14] These relations can roughly be described in the following way: animals, plants and other living organisms use particular landscapes, rivers, mountains and other non-living parts of nature as their habitat, with specific combinations of the living and the non-living forming ecosystems. Translated to the legal realm, primarily the living elements of nature as holders of legally relevant interests may qualify as contracting parties, whereas the other elements may serve to bundle similar interests of these parties:[15] For example, a river as the subject of rights[16] or as a contracting party would not refer to the non-living elements, like water or stones, within the river, but rather define in geographic terms an ecosystem, which in turn stands for the multitude of animals and plants inhabiting the ecosystem and for their individual interests. A shared interest in the integrity of the ecosystem may thus be allocated to 'the river' as an abbreviation for the aforementioned conceptual steps. To organise such bundling of aligned interests under the umbrella of a unified legal subject, the contractual structures of corporate law could provide guidance. Their concrete application, however, lies beyond the scope of this chapter.

13 Cf. Art. L110-1(I), Art. L411-1A(I) Environmental Code (France); Art. 5 No. 20 Nature Protection Act (Poland); Art. 3 Biodiversity and Natural Heritage Act (Spain); Reg. 2(1) Conservation (Natural Habitats, &c.) Regulations 1994 (UK).

14 See § 7(1) No. 2 of the German Nature Protection Act; Cour d'appel de Paris 30.03.2010, No. 08/02278.

15 Cf. J. MühREL, above n. 12, 470.

16 See, e.g., R. Göksu, 'Can a River be Considered a Legal Person? Investigating the Possibility for the Atrato River' (2022) 108 *Archiv für Rechts- und Sozialphilosophie* 82, 90 et seq.; C. Clark, N. Emmanouil, J. Page and A. Pelizzon, 'Can You Hear the Rivers Sing? Legal Personhood, Ontology, and the Nitty-Gritty of Governance' (2018) 45 *Ecology Law Quarterly* 787.

## 1.2. THE OTHER PARTY

On the other side of a contract with nature is usually a conventional human party, whose interests are potentially conflicting with the interests of nature, as they require an interference with nature. These interests might be allocated to human individuals or human collectives in the forms known to corporate law. Strictly speaking, humans are, of course, part of nature, too, but their interests and their position of power stand in such a stark contrast to the vulnerable rest of nature that separate legal roles are appropriate. On the other hand, domesticated animals and plants should not be excluded from nature, since they are at least as vulnerable and as exposed to human influence as the rest of nature.[17]

Apart from contracts between nature and humans, contracts between different elements of nature may be conceivable too. However, for such internal conflicts, nature has its own set of rules, which only humans have withdrawn from. Though these rules are not fully accessible from the external perspective of humans, they bear a closer connection to internal conflicts of nature than human-made law. This is why their applicability to conflicts within nature should be respected in principle. If, however, a conflict is influenced by human activities in a given case, human efforts to coordinate between elements of nature can indeed be reconstructed as a contract. Examples would include arrangements between so-called invasive species – which have been introduced by humans – and the native species threatened by them, or between endangered species like wolves and livestock threatened by them while being used for human purposes.

## 1.3. REPRESENTATION OF NATURE

Since neither nature nor natural elements are able to communicate their interests and to make an offer or to accept one, they need to be represented by someone else equipped with these abilities. Who may act as a representative of nature in the negotiation and conclusion of a contract?

In a first attempt, we can distinguish between private and public representatives. The conventional public authorities, however, are subject to a conflict of interest, as they are obliged to accommodate all affected interests in their decisions instead of advocating particular interests. Moreover, they are

---

[17] With regard to domesticated animals see A. Peters, 'Rights of Nature Include Rights of Domesticated Animals' in P.B. Donath, A. Heger, M. Malkmus and O. Bayrak (eds.), *Der Schutz des Individuums durch das Recht – Festschrift für Rainer Hofmann zum 70. Geburtstag*, Springer, Berlin and Heidelberg 2023, pp. 15, 25 et seq.

exposed to political pressures.[18] State commissioners or ombudspersons with a special mandate to represent particular interests – such as nature protection commissioners or animal protection commissioners[19] – may be suitable as representatives under the condition that organisational and procedural safeguards for their exclusive accountability towards the represented interests are in place.

Private representatives would first have to be appointed, e.g. by a court, and the execution of their tasks according to the interests of nature would have to be supervised, in a manner comparable to the role of trustees or guardians managing the affairs of minors or disabled adults.[20] An alternative model is displayed in Article 71 (2) of the Ecuadorian constitution and Article 38(1) of the Ecuadorian Código Orgánico General de Procesos, which allow any private individual to step in as representative of nature in a given case. Similarly, Article 1248 of the French Civil Code allows any person with an interest in the action to claim damages for ecological harm done to nature. With this mode of representation, the representative's qualification can only be reviewed as part of the case's merits in a subsequent proceeding. Although it is not uncommon in the law that the power of representation is pending,[21] the contract partner in these scenarios has options to ascertain the position of her counterpart. The lack of such options in our case contradicts the need for legal certainty, being of particular relevance in contractual relationships.

In lieu of one individual, a collective entity or committee may act as the representative body for nature in contract negotiations. Suitable for this task would be non-governmental organisations that have committed themselves to the interests of nature in their statutes. To a certain extent, this model is traceable in Article 9(2) of the Aarhus Convention[22] and the legislation implementing it. Alternatively, a committee could be specially installed for the purpose of representing nature, being composed of private or state players. Partly staffed with state players, partly with members of the indigenous community, the commission *Te Pou Tupua* acts as legal representative of the Whanganui river in New Zealand pursuant to Section 18(2) of the Te Awa Tupua (Whanganui River Claims Settlement) Act 2017. Spanish legislation granting personhood to the lagoon Mar Menor takes a twofold approach: the so-called *Comité de Representantes*, one of three bodies permanently representing the lagoon is

18 C.D. Stone, above n. 6, 472 et seq.; J. Leimbacher, *Die Rechte der Natur*, Helbing & Lichtenhahn, Basel and Frankfurt am Main 1988, pp. 415 et seq.

19 Such commissioners are enshrined for example in § 41 Animal Protection Act (Austria); § 43 State Nature Protection Act of Schleswig-Holstein (Germany).

20 Guardianship was ordered for the rivers Ganges und Yamuna in *Salim v. State of Uttarakhand and others*, above n. 5, para. 19.

21 See, e.g., § 170 of the German Civil Code.

22 Convention on Access to Information, Public Participation in Decision-making and Access to Justice in Environmental Matters of 25.06.1998, 2161 United Nations Treaty Series 447.

composed of civil servants and members of the community neighbouring the lagoon, as laid down in Article 3(1) of the Spanish *Ley para el reconocimiento de personalidad jurídica a la laguna del Mar Menor y su Cuenca*. Additionally, Article 6 of this Act authorises any natural or juristic person to invoke the rights of the lagoon in an administrative or court proceeding.

With regard to the scope of representation, individual or collective representatives can have broad competences, like a guardian has for certain spheres of life, or their competence can be limited to a specific instance, comparable to that of a *next friend* or *guardian at litem* for a child or to a nature protection organisation in representative action proceedings. For the purposes of a particular case, the task of incorporating interests of nature into contract negotiations could also be entrusted to a human bystander, whose own interests coincide with the interests of nature and are affected likewise. The pre-existing motivation of such a bystander to take action could be utilised for the sake of nature. If, for example, a landowner already has a selfish interest to proceed against nuisance coming from neighbouring property, it would strengthen her legal position to assert the thereby infringed interests of natural elements on top of her own interests.[23] Such an additional representation of natural interests has been granted by a German Regional Court to the buyer of a car who was claiming damages due to a defeat device manipulating diesel emissions.[24] The Court based what it called '*Schutzverstärkung*' (enhancement of protection) on the EU Charter of Fundamental Rights without further integrating the concept into existing legal doctrine.

At this point, I will only hint at the potential of artificial intelligence as a mouthpiece of nature. Feeding an artificial intelligence with data regarding the interests of natural elements may enable machines to communicate contractual agreements, just as artificial intelligence is used for corporate decision-making.[25] Doubts remain, however, regarding the still necessary, but less transparent human influence on the selection of data used to train an artificial intelligence for articulating interests of nature. Furthermore, the utterances produced in this way would need to be reviewed and occasionally revised by humans.

---

23 J. Leimbacher, above n. 18, p. 416.

24 LG Erfurt 02.08.2024, KlimR 2024, 286, 287 et seq.; 17.10.2024, ZUR 2024, 684, 685 et seqq.

25 F. Möslein, 'Robots in the boardroom: artificial intelligence and corporate law' in W. Barfield and U. Pagallo (eds.), *Research Handbook on the Law of Artificial Intelligence*, Edward Elgar, Cheltenham and Northampton MA 2018, p. 649.

## 2. TYPES AND CONTENT OF CONTRACTS WITH NATURE

The possible content of a contract with nature depends on the legal positions held by nature, which hence can be acquired or alienated by nature. The presupposed recognition of nature or its elements as subjects of rights does not answer the question of *which* rights are held by one of these subjects. Rather, certain rights would initially have to be allocated to them, reflecting the interests that justify their recognition as legal subjects in the first place. Independent from the details of this initial allocation, we can discern three levels of transactions the parties of a contract with nature can agree upon.

### 2.1. INALIENABLE RIGHTS

The first level entails a certain minimum protection that cannot be disposed of and therefore is inalienable. It stands beyond the scope of private autonomy and freedom of contract so that it cannot validly be made the object of a contract. If nevertheless a contract disposing of this minimum protection is concluded, it is null and void due to its violation of public policy.

In the case of humans, rights that cannot be alienated by way of a contract concern their fundamental interests in bodily, mental, and also economic integrity. Typically, the fundamentals of human activities are inalienable, whereas particular manifestations, parts or products of these activities may be traded with. For instance, it is widely considered impossible to sell body parts[26] or personality rights[27] as such,[28] but the temporary manpower or right to use emanations of one's personality may indeed be sold. These taboos can be explained in two ways: Such alienations might offend moral views of the general public; or it might be inferred that the alienating party would never voluntarily have agreed to give up her fundamental protections so that the contract is deemed to have been entered into under undue influence. Thereby, we paradoxically protect the autonomy of the concerned party by depriving it of the autonomy to dispose of the protection.

Applying these principles to contracts with nature, rights to the functionality of ecosystems, to the fulfilment of their existential requirements and to the bodily and mental integrity of the living beings inhabiting them could be

---

26 R. Andorno, 'Buying and Selling Organs: Issues of Commodification, Exploitation and Human Dignity' (2017) 1(2) *Journal of Trafficking and Human Exploitation* 119, 120 et seq.

27 M.J. Radin, 'Market-Inalienability' (1987) 100 *Harvard Law Review* 1849, 1892 et seq. with reference to Kant and Hegel.

28 G. Resta, 'Personal Identity and European Contract Law' (2022) 18(3) *European Review of Contract Law* 205, 209 et seq.

assigned to this first level of protection.[29] Along these lines, section 43(2) of the Te Awa Tupua (Whanganui River Claims Settlement) Act 2017 of New Zealand only allows the river's representatives to grant rights to use the river for a maximum term of 35 years, but not to sell the respective land. How can such limitations be justified when dealing with nature and not with human parties? Invoking public morals would require the rather unlikely shift away from the traditional anthropocentric focus on humans as bearers of fundamental interests to an ecocentric perspective. But the doubts with regard to the voluntary motivation behind an alienation of fundamental protections are even stronger if done by nature: as nature can only conclude contracts through human representatives (see section 1.3. above), the risk of a contract that does not adhere to the interests of nature is higher than in the case of a party concluding a contract by herself. Technically speaking, rights which we still regard as alienable by humans under the caveat of personal participation in the contract conclusion, prove inalienable if belonging to nature.

## 2.2. ALIENATION OF NATURE

The second level of contractual protection entails rights that are initially allocated to nature and that its representatives can validly dispose of in contracts. To acquire such a right, the other party to the contract – mostly a human party (see above section 1.2.) – has to deliver a performance in return, reflecting the value accorded to the right by nature. While gratuitous transactions are also conceivable, their relevance for contracts with nature is negligible due to transactions of gratuitous character usually being associated with close personal relationships.

The object of a contract with nature may firstly be the alienation of rights which allow the other party to interfere with nature and which can be conceptualised as property rights.[30] Existing rules for the protection of natural habitats allocate rights to use certain areas to the animals and plants living there, be it in terms of conservation areas, national parks or biotopes. Transparency in respect of these allocations is achieved by recording them in publicly available registers, such as the Natura 2000 network pursuant to Article 3 of the Habitats Directive of 1992. To acquire property rights to these areas, a human party could offer to pay an amount of money to a fund or trust managed for the benefit of the natural elements involved. In the case

29 Cf. with regard to absolute protection against irreparable damages C.D. Stone, above n. 6, 485 et seq.

30 K. Bradshaw, *Wildlife as Property Owners: A New Conception of Animal Rights*, University of Chicago Press, Chicago IL and London 2020, pp. 57 et seq.; T. Wesche, *Die Rechte der Natur. Vom nachhaltigen Eigentum*, Suhrkamp, Berlin 2023, pp. 163 et seq.

of a permanent transfer, the respective contract would be classified as a sales contract, and in the case of a temporary transfer, as a lease contract. Instead of monetary payment, the other party could also offer to perform measures for the protection of the affected parts of nature that she would otherwise not be obliged to perform, introducing elements of a service contract. In the fashion of a barter contract, a human purchaser could herself transfer property rights to nature in exchange for the property rights transferred to her. Monetary as well as non-monetary obligations borne by the human party can be agreed upon not only to the benefit of the same natural element that is party to the contract, but also to the benefit of other, independent elements of nature, resulting in a contract for the benefit of a third party.

Services rendered to humans by natural elements without human influence may constitute another object of contracts with nature – so-called ecosystem services like the storage of carbon in forests, the pollination of plants or the prevention of flooding by wetlands or beaver dams.[31] An older study has estimated the monetary value of such services at 16 to 54 trillion US dollars (averaging 33 trillion) per year.[32] A common classification distinguishes between provisioning, regulating and cultural ecosystem services. The latter encompass not only the recreational value of nature, but any intangible benefits,[33] including the commercial use of depictions from nature.[34] It has already been discussed and even practised that the beneficiaries of ecosystem services undertake to pay an amount of money in return. So far, however, it is not nature that is considered their contracting partner and provider of the services, but humans, e.g. landowners, who promote the functioning of the respective ecosystem or at least do not interfere with it.[35] They cannot count as representatives of nature, since they may (and usually do) use eventual profits for themselves and do not have to administer them for the benefit of nature. What is more, the remuneration for not interfering with nature is based on the premise that they have corresponding *rights* to interfere. Under this premise, nature would first have to acquire these rights (cf. below section 2.3.) from them and could in return transfer the right to remuneration from the beneficiaries of ecosystem services by way of assignment. Thus, even if we follow the reasoning behind

31 As to the variety of ecosystem services see the contributions in G.C. Daily (ed.), *Nature's Services. Societal Dependence on Natural Ecosystems*, Island Press, Washington, DC 1997, pp. 71 et seq.

32 R. Costanza et al., 'The value of the world's ecosystem services and natural capital' (1997) 387 *Nature* 253, 259.

33 O. Bastian, K. Grunewald and R.-U. Syrbe, 'Classification of ES' in K. Grunewald and O. Bastian (eds.), *Ecosystem Services: Concept, Methods and Case Studies*, Springer, Berlin and Heidelberg 2013, pp. 48 et seq.

34 K. Bradshaw, above n. 30, p. 92.

35 R. Brouwer, 'Payments for ecosystem services' in M. Potschin, R. Haines-Young, R. Fish and R.K. Turner (eds.), *Routledge Handbook of Ecosystem Services*, Routledge, London and New York 2016, pp. 548 et seq.

the human-to-human transactions, it turns out that a contractual relationship between nature and the beneficiary of ecosystem services helps to explain the results. What may be striking is that the services are rendered to the beneficiary independently from the conclusion of a contract. Yet, without a contract the beneficiary is to be deemed unjustly enriched at the expense of nature and, being aware of the lack of a contractual basis, may incur strict liability for restitution of this enrichment.

## 2.3. ACQUISITION OF NATURE

The third level of contractual protection entails potential transactions with nature by which nature acquires rights that originally are not allocated to it. To do so, nature has to offer something in return to the other party, flowing from the rights that are allocated to nature in the first place. Such consideration may also consist in the payment of money, with the representatives of nature being able to use for this purpose the funds allocated to nature and resulting from alienations of nature, gratuitous donations to nature or statutory liability towards nature, e.g. by virtue of tort law. If the consideration does not consist in the payment of money, but in the transfer of property rights or services by nature, we are dealing with the same barter-like transactions that we have already encountered from an inverse perspective (above section 2.2.).

Against this background, the acquisitive activities of nature can be targeted at the supply of habitats or the conditions of living in these habitats. As far as this requires human actions or omissions, they can form the content of service contracts with humans who are in the position to conduct the respective activities. Such contracts may feature elements of patient contracts, especially if they relate to the medical treatment of wild animals and in a certain sense also if other natural elements or ecosystems are to be restored ('recovered') to an intact state by specifically trained personnel. Existing provisions on patient contracts, however, are tailored to human patients and thus not applicable, but may serve as a conceptual parallel for the possible content of recovery contracts with nature, such as duties of disclosure and documentation.

A particular form of services for nature consists in the management of its affairs through representation outwards and organisation inwards. The obligations underlying the function of representative of nature may also be based on a contract. For this, there just has to be at least one representative who has been appointed by statute, by the authorities or by a court and who can appoint further persons as representatives or managers through the conclusion of contracts with them. Such contracts may take the form of employment contracts or consultancy contracts and provide for different obligations, for instance depending on whether the services owed rather relate to the management of assets or to the ascertainment of the interests of nature from environmental scientists, on whose expertise representatives of nature may have to draw from time to time.

Apart from contracts for services, the supply of habitats might also require contracts over certain items, especially parcels of land. Thus, it would be conceivable to acquire land on behalf of nature against payment of money from funds administered for nature in order to use this land for the reintroduction of a rare species. Moreover, the acquisition of items can serve not only to directly fulfil the interests of nature, but also to invest capital for the benefit of nature. Instead of first having to establish a foundation or trust for the sake of advancing the interests of nature and to then invest the foundation's or trust's funds in valuable assets or securities, representatives of nature could simply conclude contracts with an investment purpose by virtue of their mandate.

## 3. CRITICAL APPRAISAL OF THE MODEL

Standards for contracts with nature could be set either by states and their national legislation or, independently from state regulation, by private actors concluding contracts with the relevant content, complying with these contracts, and resolving disputes without the involvement of a state.[36] The familiar mechanisms for contract formation and performance could be applied and adjusted to the specific circumstances of contracts with nature. For example, the interpretation of such contracts would require rules on how to determine something like the intent of nature, and *force majeure* and other changes of the natural circumstances would play a bigger role compared to the average human-to-human contract.

While the contractualisation of nature protection appears to be feasible in principle, it has to be questioned in how far the approach yields better legal results than other regimes. Therefore, in the following sections, I would like to assess the contractual model, examine possible objections and explore what the contractual model can accomplish beyond a purely intellectual exercise. As a reference point, I start from the existing, state-operated machinery of nature protection law.

---

36 Cf. J. Basedow, 'The State's Private Law and the Economy. Commercial Law as an Amalgam of Public and Private Rule-Making' in N. Jansen and R. Michaels (eds.), *Beyond the State. Rethinking Private Law*, Mohr Siebeck, Tübingen 2008, pp. 281, 287 et seq.

## 3.1. ALTERNATIVE: PUBLIC ENFORCEMENT OF NATURE PROTECTION LAW

The current law of Western industrialised nations is based on an instrumental concept of nature, with its exploitation for human purposes being administered by state bodies. Within this framework, we already encounter elements of the contractual model outlined above. For example, the '*Eingriffsregelung*' (intervention rule) of German nature protection law prohibits at its first level 'avoidable harm to nature and countryside' (§ 15(1) Federal Nature Protection Act) and thereby establishes a non-negotiable minimum protection (cf. above section 2.1.). At its second level, the rule imposes an obligation to take in-kind compensation or substitution measures in a broader sense for unavoidable harm (§ 15(2) Federal Nature Protection Act). This remedy is reminiscent of the barter-like contracts for the benefit of the affected nature or third-party natural elements that we encountered above (cf. section 2.2.). The opportunity to acquire in a way the right to interfere with nature against payment of money is eventually provided by § 15(6) Federal Nature Protection Act in cases of unavoidable, non-compensable and non-substitutable harm, subject to a balancing of interests. In sum, the intervention rule proves rather rigid, frames harm done to nature as a regrettable, but mostly inevitable, side-effect of projects for the sake of human interests that should not be called into question and in practice concentrates on compensation and substitution measures.[37]

A structurally similar, but more flexible approach can be found in the French provisions on the liability for ecological damage. Article 1252 of the Civil Code enables a court to make orders for the prevention of damage. Pursuant to Article 1247 of the Civil Code, if damage incurred is not negligible, it has to be remediated, primarily in kind under Article 1249(1) Civil Code and subsidiarily by the payment of damages under Article 1249(2) Civil Code and penalties under Article 1250 Civil Code. The protection of environmental interests and obligations to compensate for damage can also be made the subject of contracts according to Article L132-3 of the French Environmental Code. Such contracts may be concluded between landowners on one side and public authorities or private organisations committed to environmental protection on the other side. A very similar function is fulfilled by conservation easements created for governmental bodies or charitable organisations,[38] which have become quite popular in the United States due to associated tax benefits.[39] In contrast,

---

[37] See, e.g., for Germany M. Gellermann, '§ 15 BNatSchG' in R. v. Landmann and G. Rohmer (eds.), *Umweltrecht*, vol. 2, 104th update, C.H. Beck, Munich 2024, para. 47.

[38] See, as a model law, the Uniform Conservation Easement Act.

[39] J.L. Olmsted, 'Conservation Easements: New Perspectives in an Evolving World' (2011) 74 *Law and Contemporary Problems*.

contractual solutions under the German Nature Protection Law have so far been confined to contracts with a state party on one side,[40] although § 3(3) of the Federal Nature Protection Act would allow for a different interpretation and gives precedence to contractual agreements over public enforcement. If nature is accepted as a legal subject, these provisions could serve as a gateway for contracts with nature. State actors, on the other hand, are always bound by a wide array of interests (cf. section 1.3.) and, hence, are not able to adequately incorporate the interests of nature in negotiations, which are considered under the premise that each party aims at maximising the interests it represents.

## 3.2. ENFORCEMENT DEFICITS IN THE PROTECTION OF NATURE BY THE AUTHORITIES

In addition to the shortcomings regarding representation of nature, state-driven environmental law inherently suffers from enforcement deficits, which may at least be mitigated by a contractual model. These deficits stem from various features of public enforcement: the wide range of possible cases requires highly complex and confusing rules, whose application demands efforts that can barely be expended in a typical case. Their lack of transparency diminishes the rules' acceptance by their addressees, whereas contractual clauses can be tailored to the concrete case and increase the willingness to comply with them due to their creation in a cooperative process.[41]

The high degree of effort required not only in the application of the law, but also in the gathering of the necessary information on the affected interests of nature with the help of experts[42] makes environmental law highly susceptible to the phenomenon of 'regulatory capture' by representatives of the respective counter-interests, whose proposed legal reasoning and offered information may readily be adopted by the authorities.[43] This holds all the more true, as those with interests in interfering with nature are financially strong, well-organised, homogenous groups, while nature itself is not even able to participate in proceedings and its representatives are in a worse financial and organisational

---

[40] E. Rehbinder, 'Vertragsnaturschutz – Erscheinungsformen, Rechtsprobleme, ökologische Wirkungen' (2000) *Deutsches Verwaltungsblatt* 859, 862; C. Windstosser, *Vertragsnaturschutz – Ein Verwaltungsinstrument mit ungewisser Zukunft?*, Duncker & Humblot, Berlin 2008, pp. 71 et seq.

[41] M. Kloepfer and W. Durner, *Umweltschutzrecht*, 3rd ed., C.H. Beck, Munich 2020, p. 73.

[42] U. Ramsauer, 'Allgemeines Umweltverwaltungsrecht' in H.-J. Koch, E. Hofmann and M. Reese (eds.), *Handbuch Umweltrecht*, 6th ed., C.H. Beck, Munich 2024, pp. 145, 182 et seq.

[43] For the United States see J. Mintz, 'Has Industry Captured the EPA? Appraising Marver Bernstein's Captive Agency Theory after Fifty Years' (2005) 17(1) *Fordham Environmental Law Review* 1, 23 et seq.

position.[44] Counterbalancing this asymmetry, the contractual model provides nature with legal positions that allow specialised and motivated representatives to get for their clients the most out of negotiations, to scrutinise or obtain by themselves the information on the circumstances in question, and to ensure compliance with the terms agreed upon.

## 3.3. TRANSACTION COSTS IN THE CONTRACTUAL MODEL

Putting effort into negotiations, gathering information and monitoring the performance of a contract bring about transaction costs in the context of each individual contract relationship. At first glance, bundling these expenses through the state-run enforcement machinery appears to reduce these costs, and may therefore be viewed not as more effective (above section 3.2.), but nevertheless as more efficient from a macroeconomic perspective. The wide diffusion of state competences in environmental law,[45] however, raises serious doubts as to whether considerable economies of scale can be achieved. Linking and coordinating administrative authorities usually proves a cumbersome endeavour. In contrast, private actors representing similar interests in contract negotiations have tried-and-tested mechanisms on hand to develop common standards, be it in the form of model agreements or standard terms and conditions, which are adopted and refined and can even establish private sets of norms across national borders. The remaining private transaction costs incurred in the interests of nature and thus in the public interest could be subsidised with public funds.

## 3.4. COMMERCIALISATION OF NATURE?

Turning the protection of nature into the object of a contract may very well give rise to the critique that it may foster an image of nature as a replaceable commodity and thereby curtail respect for the intrinsic value of nature.[46] Due to their unique features and their complex embedding in ecosystems, elements of nature can neither be replaced nor weighed in monetary terms.[47] This is why attempts to advocate for granting nature rights normally aim at

---

44 Cf. G.J. Stigler, 'The theory of economic regulation' (1971) 2(1) *The Bell Journal of Economics and Management Science* 3, 12 et seq.

45 See, e.g., for Germany, U. Ramsauer, above n. 42, p. 183.

46 Cf. M. Gellermann, above n. 37, para. 2: 'sale of indulgences'.

47 B. Hoops, 'What If the Black Forest Owned Itself? A Constitutional Property Law Perspective on Rights of Nature' (2022) 11 *Transnational Environmental Law* 475, 497.

its decommodification.[48] Yet, these maxims and goals do not contradict the contractual model presented here. In this model, nature is precisely no longer the object of discretionary human powers, but as a subject is itself in charge of its interests, for which its representatives may demand sums of money that render harmful actions unprofitable and thus promote a shift to more considerate alternatives. In that way, contract law translates the interests of nature into the language of economic calculation. Certainly, one may criticise the pervasive role of this language for human behaviour, but it simply has to be faced as the language in which negotiations over the interests of nature are conducted, for example if nature protection organisations waive their claim rights against payment of money from opposing companies.[49]

## 4. INSTEAD OF A CONCLUSION

In contrast to the conventional public enforcement of nature protection, private contracts with nature would enable more flexible solutions, as the particular case may require. By involving the other party in negotiations, contracts may also lead to a higher acceptance of the outcome. Furthermore, contractual solutions are neutral in the sense that none of the parties is affiliated with a political body that may be subject to political pressure. Most importantly, however, through a contract, nature could be viewed as an equal partner to interact with and not as a resource to be exploited.

Contracts with nature could shift the anthropocentric discourse of traditional nature protection law and instigate new discourses. Beyond the abstract classification of nature as a legal subject, it is contractual relations that create links between otherwise isolated legal subjects and that fills their rights with life. Instead of a conclusion, this may mark a tentative starting point for future negotiations on how the law can and should frame our interaction with nature. You cannot negotiate with nature. But you cannot negotiate without nature, either.

48 A. Acosta, 'Living Well: ideas for reinventing the future' (2017) 38 *Third World Quarterly* 2600, 2610.

49 M. Biederbeck, A. Neubacher and G. Traufetter, 'Geld oder Klage' (2013) 13 *Der Spiegel* 44.

# CHAPTER 7
# NO-CONTRACT LAW AND POWER

Tom HICK*



## 1. INTRODUCTION[1]

While consideration of the importance of power relations for contract law, and inversely, the importance of contract law for power relations, gains traction, the *absence* of a contract and power remain largely ignored. To accentuate the juxtaposition, one could say that, while contract law and power

* Tom Hick is Senior Research Fellow at the Max Planck Institute for comparative and international private law in Hamburg. This article is based on a part of his doctoral dissertation, *A European Structure for 'No-Contract Law' in the 21st Century*, written at the KU Leuven. Part of the dissertation has been published as T. HICK, *Liability for Failed Contract Negotiations – A Comparative, Structural, and Historical Analysis*, New York, Routledge, 2025.

is a topic, *no*-contract law and power appears to be a non-topic. Indeed, the incidence of power relations on broken-off contract negotiations or a refusal to accept an offer appear largely absent from legal scrutiny within the law of obligations. It is true that this lack of attention for power relations within the general law of obligations must be complemented with certain corrections at the level of competition law (abuse of dominant position, abuse of relative power positions) and specific obligations to contract (water and energy supply, postal services, *et cetera*). Yet, these corrections are limited in scope and leave a considerable number of cases untouched, without there being a good reason for this distinction from the perspective of the law of obligations; hence the question about *no-contract law and power.*

Take a recent and mediatised *fait divers*: price negotiations between supermarket chain Carrefour and PepsiCo fail. The reason Carrefour gives for this failure are the high prices that PepsiCo asks; PepsiCo in turn states that it broke-off negotiations because they were unable to reach an agreement with Carrefour.[1] For PepsiCo, losing access to a supermarket chain such as Carrefour certainly is an unfortunate event, but, at least in the short run, one they can afford. Otherwise, they would likely have adapted their prices in order to get a contract with Carrefour. Given how important Carrefour is to selling food-products, suppliers of such products seem to be exposed to a choice of giving in or losing access to a market. The smaller the supplier of such food-products is, the more this dynamic will be detrimental, particularly to suppliers active merely on a national or local level. Farmers, in their recent protests in several EU Member States, have blamed these negotiation dynamics as part of the issues that make their work so difficult (impossible?) today.

So, given the socio-economic importance of the phenomenon of no-contract and power relations, I suggest addressing the issue. For that purpose, it will first be necessary to substantiate my claim that the influence on and interrelation between no-contract law and power is largely ignored. This will be done by first discussing no-contract law and power as it stands (section 2.) and how within that context the corrections to no-contract law and power are not comprehensive (section 3.). Then, I suggest a blue-print for no-contract law and power (section 4.). Finally, a conclusion to sum the argumentation up and provide an outlook (section 5.).

The chapter is set at a rather high level of abstraction; to make its implications more palpable, I will rely on examples stemming from Belgian, French, and German law. Citations will be translated into English in the main text; the original language version will be provided in footnotes.

1 L. Van Driessche, 'Litige sur les prix avec Carrefour: PepsiCo s'attribue l'initiative', *L'Echo*, https://www.lecho.be/entreprises/grande-distribution/litige-sur-les-prix-avec-carrefour-pepsico-s-attribue-l-initiative/10517990.html (accessed 25.02.2024).

# 2. NO-CONTRACT LAW AND POWER AS IT STANDS

## 2.1. NO-CONTRACT LAW

Before addressing the question of no-contract law and power, the question of no-contract law first must be addressed. That is because no-contract law is not self-evident. Contract law, that is, the set of rules governing the (valid) formation, performance, and termination of contracts, *is*. No-contract law, being the set of rules governing the absence of a contract, however, is not perceived as a body of law. I suspect that to be due to the fact that legally speaking, the absence of a contract is not an issue. Indeed, based on freedom of contract – being the freedom to contract, to decide with whom to contract, decide on what to contract, or quite simply not to contract (freedom from contract) – the absence of a contract is a perfectly acceptable outcome. Hence, the no-contract scenario *a priori* does not call for any legal intervention. Parties to negotiations are free to break-off negotiations or refuse to accept an offer submitted to them.

This entails a specific risk-allocation, namely that *the loss lies where it falls*. Indeed, given that the no-contract scenario is lawful, each party will have to accept the loss it suffers. This understanding must of course be nuanced in the sense that national legal systems do provide for liability that can arise during contract negotiations and allows losses to be re-allocated. Generally, this liability is called pre-contractual liability or *culpa in contrahendo*. For historical reasons and comparative purposes,[2] I find it more concise to speak of liability for contract negotiations.

Roughly speaking, liability for contract negotiations enables assessment of the conduct of parties in the negotiation process and compensation for the pure economic loss that parties may suffer due to the failure to conclude a contract. Thereby, depending on the conduct that negotiators adopt, the risk can be (partially) re-allocated. On top of this general liability for contract negotiations, some legal systems do also provide, under some circumstances, for different variations on obligations to contract. Often, they relate, more or less articulately, to a notion of legitimate expectations.[3] Under Dutch law,

---

2 The *culpa in contrahendo*, literally and historically, designates a fault in contracting. That is a different set of cases than is dealt with in no-contract law. 'Pre'-contractual liability seems to presuppose something about the legal basis of liability for contract negotiations in as far as it locates it before the conclusion of the contract. From a comparative perspective, however, pre-contractual liability is not always extra-contractual. What is more, once negotiation agreements are concluded in the negotiation process, the terminology of 'pre-contractual' becomes unuseful, as a negotiation agreement would be a pre-contractual contract. Hence the choice of liability for contract negotiations.

3 See on this notion I. Zuloaga, *Reliance in the Breaking Off of Contractual Negotiations*, Intersentia, Cambridge 2019.

since the *Plas Bouwonderneming BV v. gemeente Valburg* decision of the Hoge Raad,[4] it is recognised that parties can no longer be free not to contract if 'this would be unacceptable on the basis of the other party's legitimate expectation that the agreement will be concluded or in view of the other circumstances of the case'. Essentially, this means that parties no longer were free to exercise their freedom from contract and thus *had to* contract (obligation to contract).[5] The recent reform of Belgian contract law also provides for some form of an

---

4 HR 18.06.1982, *NJ* 1983, 723 (11), ECLI:NL:HR:1982:AG4405, paras. 3.4–3.5: 'It cannot be excluded that negotiations on an agreement have reached such a stage that the very breaking-off of those negotiations under the given circumstances must be regarded as contrary to good faith, since the parties were entitled to expect that any contract would in any case result from the negotiations. In such a situation, there may also be room for an obligation to compensate for lost profit.... An obligation to do so [to reimburse costs incurred in the context of the preliminary negotiations] might even exist if the negotiations had not yet reached a stage where the municipality in good faith could no longer break off those negotiations, but had already reached a stage where it would not have been free to do so in the given circumstances without bearing the costs incurred by Plas in whole or in part'.
Original text [Dutch]: '*Niet uitgesloten is dat onderhandelingen over een overeenkomst in een zodanig stadium zijn gekomen dat het afbreken zelf van die onderhandelingen onder de gegeven omstandigheden als in strijd met de goede trouw moet worden geacht, omdat pp. over en weer mochten vertrouwen dat enigerlei contract in ieder geval uit de onderhandelingen zou resulteren. In zo een situatie kan er ook plaats zijn voor een verplichting tot vergoeding van gederfde winst. ...*
*Een verplichting daartoe [tot vergoeding van in het kader van de voorafgaande onderhandelingen gemaakte kosten] zou zelfs kunnen bestaan, als de onderhandelingen nog niet in een zodanig stadium zouden zijn geraakt dat de gemeente te goeder trouw die onderhandelingen niet meer had mogen afbreken, maar reeds wel in een stadium dat zulk afbreken haar in de gegeven omstandigheden niet meer zou hebben vrijgestaan zonder de door Plas gemaakte kosten geheel of gedeeltelijk voor haar rekening te nemen*'.
Confirmed in HR 12.08.2005, ECLI:NL:HR:2005:AT7337 (*Centraal Bureau Bouwtoezicht BV v. JPO Projecten BV*), para. 3.6: 'The criterion for assessing the obligation to pay compensation in the event of the cessation of negotiations is that each of the negotiating parties – who are obliged to allow their conduct to be influenced by each other's legitimate interests – is free to break off negotiations, unless this would be unacceptable on the basis of the other party's legitimate expectation that the agreement will be concluded or in view of the other circumstances of the case'.
Original text [Dutch]: '*als maatstaf voor de beoordeling van de schadevergoedingsplicht bij afgebroken onderhandelingen heeft te gelden dat ieder van de onderhandelende partijen – die verplicht zijn hun gedrag mede door elkaars gerechtvaardigde belangen te laten bepalen – vrij is de onderhandelingen af te breken, tenzij dit op grond van het gerechtvaardigd vertrouwen van de wederpartij in het totstandkomen van de overeenkomst of in verband met de andere omstandigheden van het geval onaanvaardbaar zou zijn*'.

5 The court 'orders Papagayo to enter into a rental agreement with Watersports concerning the diving school within two months of service of this judgment, in accordance with the provisions as included in the agreement submitted as exhibit 8 to the statement of reply ..., under threat of a penalty payment of NAf 1,500 for each day or part of a day that Papagayo remains in default, with a maximum of NAf 150,000'; GiEA Curaçao 11.12.2017, ECLI:NL:OGEAC:2017:186, para. 5.2. Free translation. Original text [Dutch]: Het Gerechtshof '*veroordeelt Papagayo om binnen twee maanden na betekening van dit vonnis een huurovereenkomst ter zake de duikschool met Watersports aan te gaan, conform de bepalingen*

obligation to contract in Article 5.17, second paragraph, second sentence Belgian Civil Code:

> If a legitimate expectation has been created that the contract would have been concluded without any doubt, this liability may include compensation for the loss of the expected net benefits from the contract not concluded.[6]

French law, quite explicitly so, discards any form of an obligation to contract in Article 1112, second paragraph, French Civil Code:

> In case of fault committed during the negotiations, the reparation of the resulting loss is not calculated so as to compensate for the loss of benefits which were expected from the contract that was not concluded.[7]

Indeed, by stating that compensation for anticipated benefits under the expected contract cannot be recovered, it should be clear that no corresponding obligation to contract exists.

Such obligations to contract, however, are perceived as a very exceptional and questionable encroachment upon the freedom of contract of the parties under such an obligation. Franz Bydlinski pointedly formulated this understanding: 'The obligation to contract does not merely restrict freedom of contract; it virtually negates it'.[8] Yet, as Jan Busche has shown in *Privataunotnomie und Kontrahierungszwang*,[9] such an understanding of freedom of contract is insufficient, as it only looks at the freedom of contract of the individual who's freedom from contract is limited, while overlooking the freedom to conclude a contract of the counter-party:

> Insofar as it is said that there is an antinomy between the idea of freedom of contract rooted in the [Bürgerliches Gesetzbuch] BGB and the institution of the obligation

*zoals opgenomen in de overeenkomst overgelegd als productie 8 bij conclusie van antwoord ..., een en ander op straffe van een dwangsom van NAf 1.500 voor iedere dag of gedeelte van een dag dat Papagayo hiermee in gebreke blijft, met een maximum van NAf 150.000*'.

6 Original text [French]: '*Lorsque la confiance légitime que le contrat serait sans aucun doute conclu a été suscitée, elle peut impliquer la réparation de la perte des avantages nets attendus du contrat non conclu.*' / [Dutch] '*Wanneer het rechtmatig vertrouwen is gewekt dat het contract zonder enige twijfel gesloten zal worden, kan deze het herstel van het verlies van de verwachte netto-voordelen uit het niet gesloten contract inhouden*'.

7 Original text [French]: '*En cas de faute commise dans les négociations, la réparation du préjudice qui en résulte ne peut avoir pour objet de compenser ni la perte des avantages attendus du contrat non conclu, ni la perte de chance d'obtenir ces avantages*'.

8 F. Bydlinski, 'Zu den dogmatischen Grundfragen des Kontrahierungszwanges' (1980) 180 no. 1/2 *Archiv für die civilistische Praxis (AcP)* 1, 4. Free translation. Original text [German]: '*Der Kontrahierungszwang beschränkt aber nicht bloß die Vertragsfreiheit; er negiert sie geradezu*'. In the same sense, see I.S.J. Houben, *Contractdwang*, Kluwer, Deventer 2005, p. 1.

9 J. Busche, *Privatautonomie und Kontrahierungszwang*, Mohr Siebeck, Tübingen 1999.

> to contract, this thesis cannot be substantiated by the present study, at least insofar as it concerns the consideration of the general obligation to contract. The contrary assumption of an insoluble contradiction between freedom of contract and coercion to contract corresponds to the view of liberalism at the end of the 19th century, in which the individual was only ever understood as the holder of legal positions. It was not recognised that the coexistence of individuals under a legal system also gives rise to immanent bonds of freedom rights or even duties towards other holders of rights. Rather, these were only ever seen as encroachments of public law into private law, from which the catchphrase 'socialisation of private law' quickly developed. This obscured the fact that the root of the general obligation to contract is to be found in private law and not in public law. It was overlooked that the principle of freedom of contract only follows the principle of private autonomy without fully reflecting it in legal reality. Freedom of contract does not mean freedom from all obligations in the sense of an isolated coexistence of individualistic freedom rights but is only conceivable with regard to the integration of the individual into the social network with other individuals. This bond concretises the legal institution of the general obligation to contract. It therefore does not have an antinomic character, but rather reinforces the freedom-securing character of the contract law system.[10]

To be able to maintain such an individualistic understanding of freedom of – and specifically freedom *from* contract – within the general law of obligations of (at least) Western private law systems, less individualistic understandings of freedom of contract needed to be applied by way of correction. That is what can be observed specifically in the context of supplying essential goods/ services (below, section 2.2.) and competition law (below, section 2.3.). There,

10 J. Busche, *Privatautonomie und Kontrahierungszwang*, Mohr Siebeck, Tübingen 1999, pp. 238–239 (citations omitted). Free translation. Original text [German]: '*Soweit also gesagt wird, es bestehe eine Antinomie zwischen dem im BGB verwurzelten Gedanken der Vertragsfreiheit und dem Institut des Kontrahierungszwangs, so läßt sich diese These durch die hiesige Untersuchung jedenfalls insoweit nicht erhärten, als es um die Betrachtung des allgemeinen Kontrahierungszwangs geht. Die gegenteilige Annahme eines unlösbaren Widerspruchs zwischen Vertragsfreiheit und Kontrahierungszwang entspricht der Sichtweise des Liberalismus ausgangs des 19. Jahrhunderts, in der das Individuum immer nur als Inhaber von Rechtsstellungen begriffen wurde. Nicht gesehen wurde, daß aus dem Zusammenleben der Individuen unter einer Rechtsordnung auch immanente Bindungen der Freiheitsrechte oder sogar Pflichten gegenüber anderen Trägern von Rechten entstehen. Diese wurden vielmehr immer nur als Übergriffe des öffentlichen Rechts in das Privatrecht aufgefaßt, woraus sich schnell das Schlag- wort von der „Sozialisierung des Privatrechts" entwickelte. Damit wurde der Blick darauf verstellt, daß die Wurzel des allgemeinen Kontrahierungszwangs im Privatrecht und nicht im öffentlichen Recht zu suchen ist. Übersehen wurde, daß der Grundsatz der Vertragsfreiheit nur dem Prinzip der Privatautonomie folgt, ohne es vollends in der Rechtswirklichkeit abzubilden. Vertragsfreiheit bedeutet nicht das Freisein von sämtlichen Bindungen im Sinne eines isolierten Nebeneinander individualistischer Freiheitsrechte, sondern ist nur denkbar im Hinblick auf die Einbindung des Individuums in den Sozialverbund mit anderen Individuen. Diese Bindung konkretisiert das Rechtsinstitut des allgemeinen Kontrahierungszwangs. Es hat damit keinen antinomischen Charakter, sondern verstärkt den freiheitssichernden Charakter der Vertragsrechtsordnung*'.

the freedom of and from contract appears to be limitable where another party is in some form of *dependence*. This creates a dynamic of a liberal starting point which leads to socio-economically intolerable and unsustainable consequences, hence calling for corrections. Let us now briefly look at these corrections.

## 2.2. SPECIFIC OBLIGATIONS TO CONTRACT

Some goods and/or services are considered to be essential for individuals, typically – and without being exhaustive – water and electricity provision, postal services and telecommunication, public transport, and certain compulsory insurances. Since parties depend on these goods and/or services, the providers of these goods and/or services are under an obligation to contract.[11] The underlying ratio and the understanding of freedom of contract, in these cases, thus is that freedom of contract is limited by the *needs* of individuals. It is because in a contemporary society, individuals are considered to be dependent on these goods and/or services that the providers thereof have to provide them under certain defined conditions. A critical reading could be given of what are considered to be needs in contemporary society, but that is not the point here. Instead, I want to highlight the fact that in the field of these specific statutory obligations to contract, a different understanding of freedom of contract seems to prevail.

## 2.3. ABUSE OF (RELATIVE) MARKET POWER

This same idea of freedom of contract as limited by the dependence of others also seems to underlie much of competition law. The prohibition of abuse of market power, a commonplace both at the EU and national level, provides a remedy in cases of a refusal to contract where a party depends on that contract. In the *Bronner* case,[12] the ECJ was confronted with a prejudicial question concerning a case in which the editor of a small daily newspaper (Oscar Bronner) was denied a contract for home deliveries of his newspaper with the distribution service of a much bigger publisher (*Mediaprint*). The ECJ formulated three[13] conditions for an abuse of dominant position in case of a refusal to provide a service:

---

11 I.S.J. Houben, *Contractdwang*, Kluwer, Deventer 2005 provides an extensive analysis of these specific obligations to contract under Dutch law; J. Busche, *Privatautonomie und Kontrahierungszwang*, Mohr Siebeck, Tübingen 1999, pp. 301–643 does so under German law.

12 Case C-7/97, *Oscar Bronner GmbH & Co. KG v. Mediaprint Zeitungs- und Zeitschriftenverlag GmbH & Co. KG and others* [1998] ECR I-07791.

13 N. Petit, *Droit Européen de la Concurrence*, LGDJ, Paris 2020, para. 1183, p. 468.

> in order to plead the existence of an abuse within the meaning of Article 86 [now 102] of the Treaty in a situation such as that which forms the subject-matter of the first question, not only that the refusal of the service comprised in home delivery be likely to eliminate all competition in the daily newspaper market on the part of the person requesting the service and that such refusal be incapable of being objectively justified, but also that the service in itself be indispensable to carrying on that person's business, inasmuch as there is no actual or potential substitute in existence for that home-delivery scheme'.[14]

Thus the three conditions formulated by the ECJ are

(i) that the refusal of service 'be likely to eliminate all competition in the daily newspaper market on the part of the person requesting the service';
(ii) 'that such refusal be incapable of being objectively justified'; and that
(iii) 'the service in itself be indispensable to carrying on that person's business, inasmuch as there is no actual or potential substitute in existence for that home-delivery scheme'.

The last condition formulated by the ECJ clearly refers to a requirement of dependence.

Given how limitative/restrictive the first condition of claiming an abuse of an *absolute* power position – 'likely to eliminate all competition in the daily newspaper market on the part of the person requesting the service' – is, prohibitions of *relative* market power exist at the national level. A relative power position denotes a situation in which an undertaking is not (necessarily) dominant on a given market but is in a situation of dominance in *relation to* another undertaking (hence *relative*):

> On the other hand, economic dominance is not necessarily related to the size of market shares, but to the relative power of a company over its partners that makes them vulnerable; it reflects a strong bargaining power of one company over another, which does not require a dominant position in a whole market.[15]

[14] Case C-7/97, *Oscar Bronner GmbH & Co. KG v. Mediaprint Zeitungs- und Zeitschriftenverlag GmbH & Co. KG and others* [1998] ECR I-07791, 7831, para. 41, ECJ, 26.11.1998.

[15] Opinion n° 15-A-06 of 31.03.2015 *relatif au rapprochement des centrales d'achat et de référencement dans le secteur de la grande distribution*, para. 993. Free translation. Original text [French]: '*En revanche, la domination économique n'est pas forcément liée à l'importance des parts de marché, mais à la puissance relative d'une entreprise sur ses partenaires qui les rend vulnérables; elle reflète un pouvoir fort de négociation d'une entreprise sur une autre, qui ne nécessite pas une position dominante sur l'ensemble d'un marché*' (Autorité de la concurrence – Competition Authority).

Under German law, such a prohibition was enacted as early as 1957 (entry into force on 1 January 1958) (§ 20 Gesetz gegen Wettbewerbsbeschränkungen (GWB)). It extends the prohibition of abuse of an absolute power position to

> undertakings and associations of undertakings to the extent that other undertakings as suppliers or purchasers of a certain type of goods or commercial services are dependent on them in such a way that sufficient and reasonable possibilities for switching to third parties do not exist and there is a significant imbalance between the power of such undertakings or associations of undertakings and the countervailing power of other undertakings (relative market power).[16]

The French legislator enacted a comparable prohibition in 1986 (Article L. 420-2, second paragraph *Code de commerce*) in which 'the abuse by an undertaking or a group of undertakings of the state of economic dependence in which customer or supplier finds itself is also prohibited, where it is likely to affect the functioning or structure of competition'. Examples of such an abuse are 'refusals to sell, tying, discriminatory practices as referred to in Articles L. 442-1 to L. 442-3 or range agreements'.[17] The Belgian legislator followed in 2019 (Article IV.2/1, second paragraph Code of Economic Law) by providing that

> It is prohibited for one or more undertakings to abuse a position of economic dependence in which one or more undertakings find themselves in relation to it or them, where competition is likely to be affected on the Belgian market concerned or a substantial part thereof.

The following may be considered abusive practice:

1° the refusal of a sale, purchase or other transaction conditions;
2° the direct or indirect imposition of purchase or sale prices or other unfair transaction conditions;

---

16 Translation from Gesetze im Internet, https://www.gesetze-im-internet.de/englisch_gwb/englisch_gwb.html#p0100.
Original text [German]: '*Unternehmen und Vereinigungen von Unternehmen, soweit von ihnen andere Unternehmen als Anbieter oder Nachfrager einer bestimmten Art von Waren oder gewerblichen Leistungen in der Weise abhängig sind, dass ausreichende und zumutbare Möglichkeiten, auf dritte Unternehmen auszuweichen, nicht bestehen und ein deutliches Ungleichgewicht zur Gegenmacht der anderen Unternehmen besteht (relative Marktmacht)*'.

17 'The abuse by an undertaking or a group of undertakings of the state of economic dependence of a customer or supplier is also prohibited, where it is likely to affect the functioning or structure of competition. Such abuses may in particular consist of refusals to sell, tying, discriminatory practices as referred to in Articles L. 442-1 to L. 442-3 or range agreements'.
Original text {French]: '*Est en outre prohibée, dès lors qu'elle est susceptible d'affecter le fonctionnement ou la structure de la concurrence, l'exploitation abusive par une entreprise ou un groupe d'entreprises de l'état de dépendance économique dans lequel se trouve à son égard une entreprise cliente ou fournisseur. Ces abus peuvent notamment consister en refus de vente, en ventes liées, en pratiques discriminatoires visées aux articles L. 442-1 à L. 442-3 ou en accords de gamme*'.

3° the limitation of production, outlets or technical development to the detriment of consumers;
4° applying unequal conditions to equivalent services with regard to economic partners, thereby placing them at a competitive disadvantage;
5° making the conclusion of contracts conditional on the acceptance by economic partners of additional services which, by their nature or according to commercial practice, have no connection with the subject of these contracts'.[18]

Though the structure and conditions of application of these provisions differ to some extent, they are all built around an abuse of a situation of dependence in a situation of *relative* power imbalance (as opposed to an abuse of an absolute power position).

## 2.4. NO-CONTRACT LAW AND POWER

While under the general law of obligations a rather individualistic understanding of freedom of contract prevails, a more social or welfarist understanding of freedom of contract appears to underly specific statutory obligations to contract and within competition law. Indeed, in these cases the understanding of freedom of contract appears to be one limited by the needs

---

[18] Free translation. Original text [French]: '*Est interdit le fait pour une ou plusieurs entreprises d'exploiter de façon abusive une position de dépendance économique dans laquelle se trouvent une ou plusieurs entreprises à son ou à leur égard, dès lors que la concurrence est susceptible d'en être affectée sur le marché belge concerné ou une partie substantielle de celui-ci.*
*Peut être considérée comme une pratique abusive: 1° le refus d'une vente, d'un achat ou d'autres conditions de transaction; 2° l'imposition de façon directe ou indirecte des prix d'achat ou de vente ou d'autres conditions de transaction non équitables; 3° la limitation de la production, des débouchés ou du développement technique au préjudice des consommateurs; 4° le fait d'appliquer à l'égard de partenaires économiques des conditions inégales à des prestations équivalentes, en leur infligeant de ce fait un désavantage dans la concurrence; 5° le fait de subordonner la conclusion de contrats à l'acceptation, par les partenaires économiques, de prestations supplémentaires, qui, par leur nature ou selon les usages commerciaux, n'ont pas de lien avec l'objet de ces contrats*'.
Original text [Dutch]: '*Het is verboden in hoofde van één of meer ondernemingen misbruik te maken van een positie van economische afhankelijkheid waarin één of meerdere ondernemingen zich bevindt, waardoor de mededinging kan worden aangetast op de betrokken Belgische markt of op een wezenlijk deel daarvan.*
*Er kan sprake zijn van misbruik bij: 1° het weigeren van een verkoop, een aankoop of van andere transactievoorwaarden; 2° het rechtstreeks of zijdelings opleggen van onbillijke aan- of verkoopprijzen of van andere onbillijke contractuele voorwaarden; 3° het beperken van de productie, de afzet of de technische ontwikkeling ten nadele van de verbruikers; 4° het toepassen ten opzichte van economische partners van ongelijke voorwaarden bij gelijkwaardige prestaties, hun daarmede nadeel berokkenend bij de mededinging; 5° het feit dat het sluiten van overeenkomsten afhankelijk wordt gesteld van het aanvaarden door de economische partners van bijkomende prestaties, die naar hun aard of volgens het handelsgebruik geen verband houden met het onderwerp van deze overeenkomsten*'.

of the counter-party – independently of the question of how these needs will be defined. Put differently: where a party is dependent on a given contract (party A), this warrants a limitation of the freedom from contract of the party upon which the other is dependent (party B).

The dissonance between the two understandings of freedom of and from contract results in a dynamic in which the individualistic understanding of freedom of contract is corrected in specific instances. Though plausible, such a dynamic also begs the question as to whether it is desirable to maintain such a rule-exception (or rule-correction, if you will) regulatory approach. It may seem more sensible to rely on a less pronounced individualistic understanding of freedom of contract under general no-contract law and prefer a more social or welfarist one instead. This should predictably allow the tension of the rule-correction dynamic to be overcome or at least lessened. From the angle of the materialisation of freedom of contract, Jan Busche has argued for such a less individualistic and more social or welfarist understanding of freedom of contract. He argues that the freedom of contract of the one party should be limited by the freedom of contract of the other:

> Freedom to conclude a contract and the obligation to contract – conceived in their fullest form – are to a certain extent the antipodes in a contract law system. However, a contract law system cannot be constructed solely according to one or the other. A contract law system based solely on the model of freedom of contract is doomed to failure because it ignores the fact that the conclusion of a contract is inherently bound by freedom. Those who can insist on their freedom to establish a contract under all circumstances and in this way make use of the freedom from contract, paralyse contract law and strip it of its actual function, which lies in the bringing together of two- or more-sided interests and thus in the possibility of all-sided, legally recognised self-determination. One party's freedom to establish a contract is always also the other party's freedom to establish a contract.[19]

His argument is convincing. All the more so, as this individualistic approach to *no*-contract law appears outdated. Indeed, this understanding appears

---

19 J. Busche, *Privatautonomie und Kontrahierungszwang*, Mohr Siebeck, Tübingen 1999, pp. 644–645. Free translation. Original text [German]: '*Vertragsbegründungsfreiheit und Kontrahierungszwang – in vollkommener Ausprägung gedacht – stellen gewissermaßen die Antipoden in einem Vertragsrechtssystem dar. Dabei kann ein Vertragsrechtssystem weder allein nach dem einen noch nach dem anderen Bauplan errichtet werden. Ein nur dem Leitbild der Vertragsbegründungsfreiheit folgendes Vertragsrechtssystem ist zum Scheitern verurteilt, weil es außer Acht läßt, daß bereits dem Vertragsschluß eine Freiheitsbindung immanent ist. Wer unter allen Umständen auf seiner Vertragsbegründungsfreiheit beharren kann und auf diese Weise von der Freiheit Gebrauch macht, Verträge nicht abschließen zu müssen, lähmt das Vertragsrecht und entkleidet es seiner eigentlichen Funktion, die in der Zusammenführung zwei- oder mehrseitiger Interessen und damit in der Möglichkeit allseitiger, rechtlich anerkannter Selbstbestimmung liegt. Die Vertragsbegründungsfreiheit der einen Seite ist immer auch die Vertragsbegründungsfreiheit der Gegenseite*'.

almost anachronistic when compared to contemporary contract law where a strong tendency towards a more social or welfarist starting point is perceptible. While, historically, contract law remained *relatively*[20] liberal and insensitive to power relations, a more social or welfarist understanding of contract law has traditionally been relegated to pronouncedly protective fields of the law. Those fields are consumer protection law, labour law, *et cetera*. Yet, with the recent recodification movements of the French and Belgian law of obligations, doctrines that aim at ironing out undesirable *consequences* of unequal bargaining positions have been codified: Article 1143 French Civil Code[21] provides for economic duress ('*violence économique*') as one of the possible defects in consent. The Belgian Article 5.37 Belgian Civil Code codifies the abuse of circumstances ('*abus de circonstances*'/'*misbruik van omstandigheden*').[22] Though technically somewhat differing, both doctrines allow a contract that is considered grossly unbalanced to be adapted, provided that this unbalance between parties' rights and obligations follows from an excessive imbalance of bargaining power.

---

Yet Busche bases an obligation to contract on the very idea or institution of the contract. As freedom of contract is based on the pre-supposition that both parties are free, it must – to be sensibly applied – also provide the means to have both parties being free to contract. Hence, in some cases – in order to re-establish freedom of contract – an obligation to contract must be re-applied.

20 It is important to stress this relative stand. Within contract law, more social tendencies did already exist, such as, for instance, the surge of duties to act in good faith.

21 'There is also duress where one contracting party exploits the other's state of dependence and obtains an undertaking to which the latter would not have agreed in the absence of such constraint, and gains from it a manifestly excessive advantage'. Translation by https://www.trans-lex.org/601101/_/french-civil-code-2016/#head_11 (accessed 02.04.2024). Original text [French]: '*Il y a également violence lorsqu'une partie, abusant de l'état de dépendance dans lequel se trouve son cocontractant à son égard, obtient de lui un engagement qu'il n'aurait pas souscrit en l'absence d'une telle contrainte et en tire un avantage manifestement excessif*'.

22 'Art. 5.37. Abuse of circumstances
There is abuse of circumstances if, at the time of the conclusion of the contract, there exists a manifest imbalance between the performances as a result of the abuse by one of the parties of the circumstances linked to the other party's weak position.
In this case, the weaker party may claim the adaptation of its obligations by the court and, if the abuse is decisive, the relative nullity'. Unpublished translation by C. Boruki.
Original text [French] '*Art. 5.37. Abus de circonstances*
*Il y a abus de circonstances lorsque, lors de la conclusion du contrat, il existe un déséquilibre manifeste entre les prestations par suite de l'abus par l'une des parties de circonstances liées à la position de faiblesse de l'autre partie.*
*En ce cas, la victime peut prétendre à l'adaptation de ses obligations par le juge et, si l'abus est déterminant, à la nullité relative*'. /
[Dutch] '*Art. 5.37. Misbruik van omstandigheden*
*Er is misbruik van omstandigheden wanneer bij de contractsluiting een kennelijk onevenwicht bestaat tus- sen de prestaties als gevolg van het misbruik door de ene partij van omstandigheden die verbonden zijn aan de zwakke positie van de andere partij.*
*In dit geval kan de benadeelde aanspraak maken op de aanpassing van zijn verbintenissen door de rechter en, indien het misbruik doorslaggevend is, op de relatieve nietigheid*'.

In light of the foregoing, it is quite striking to see that such a process of alignment does not occur under no-contract law. All the more so, as the root of the unbalanced contract lies precisely in the negotiation process. It is there that unequal bargaining positions may lead to unbalanced contracts, or precisely to no contract at all. While the former now can be corrected, the latter can't. This furthermore contributes to maintaining the premises from which such unequal bargaining power stems, namely the credible threat of not contracting. This threat, if credible, provides party A with the position of saying: 'take it or leave it' on whatever conditions party A defines, leaving party B with no realistic alternative but to accept a very disadvantageous offer. As Horst Eidenmüller tellingly illustrates this dynamic:

> Two lorry drivers speeding towards each other on a narrow road: Whoever swerves loses. Suddenly, one of them rolls down the side window, pulls out his steering wheel and throws it out of the window for the other to see. Now only the other driver can avoid it, and that is exactly what is intended. Similar stipulations on certain agreement positions often play a major role in contract negotiations: 'final', limited offers are submitted, for example, and the bidder is away and therefore no longer available for further negotiations.[23]

This act of 'pulling out the steering wheel and throwing it out of the window' in contract negotiations, is the threat of not contracting. The possibility and credibility of this threat relies on the freedom from contract and ensuing lawfulness of not contracting. So, the liberal understanding of freedom of and, specifically, from contract provides the background against which imbalanced bargaining positions are created and exacerbated. Those, then, either lead to (un)balanced contracts which – and this seems to be accepted practice in contemporary contract law systems – can be corrected where considered necessary, or to the absence of a contract, which cannot specifically be scrutinised in light of the existing power relations. This rule-correction approach in no-contract law, though creating an unfortunate dissonance, could be functioning provided that the corrections to it were sufficiently comprehensive. Yet, that does not appear to be the case, as I will now discuss.

---

[23] H. Eidenmüller, 'Druckmittel in Vertragsverhandlungen' in R. Zimmermann (ed.), *Störung der Willensbildung bei Vertragsschluss*, Mohr Siebeck, Tübingen 2007, p. 108. Free translation. Original text [German]: '*zwei Lastwagenfahrer, die auf einer schmalen Straße aufeinander zu rasen: Wer ausweicht, verliert. Plötzlich kurbelt der eine die Seitenscheibe herunter, reißt sein Steuerrad heraus und wirft es – für den anderen sichtbar – aus dem Fenster. Jetzt kann nur dieser noch ausweichen, und genau das ist beabsichtigt. Ähnliche Festlegungen auf bestimmte Einigungspositionen spielen aus in Vertragsverhandelungen häufig eine große Rolle: Es werden etwa ‚letzte', befristete Angebote abgegeben, und der Anbieter ist verreist und deshalb für weitere Verhandlungen nicht mehr erreichbar*'.

# 3. THE REGULATORY GAP IN NO-CONTRACT LAW AND POWER

## 3.1. THE COMPETITION LAW GAP

Competition law, one could say, aims at regulating competition. This leads to two logical, yet, from our perspective, problematic consequences.

*First*, competition law can only be triggered to the extent that regulation of competition in general is considered necessary. The recent Belgian prohibition of abuse of a relative power position illustrates this aptly. For its application, the claimant must prove the (i) existence of a situation of economic dependence, (ii) an abuse of that situation of dependence, and (iii) *an impact on competition*.[24] Indeed, after the adoption of the Belgian prohibition of abuse of relative power position and based on the French experience,[25] Wouter Devroe was sceptical about the insertion of such a criterion of impact on competition.[26] At first, Belgian courts did not apply it;[27] more recent decisions, however, did.[28] Anyhow, from a competition law perspective, the restriction of the scope of application is understandable. Yet, it leaves out a considerable number of cases in which the difference in bargaining power leads to the absence of a contract.

---

24 W. Devroe, 'Hoofdstuk 3. Modernisering van Belgisch mededingingsrecht en invoering van een verbod op misbruik van economische afhankelijkheid' in *Nieuw economisch recht in b2b-relaties*, Intersentia, Mortsel 2020, para. 83, pp. 85–86; I. Claeys and T. Tanghe, 'De b2b-wet van 4 april 2019: bescherming van ondernemingen tegen onrechtmatige bedingen, misbruik van economische afhankelijkheid en oneerlijke marktpraktijken (Deel 2)' (2019) 83(10) *Rechtskundig Weekblad (RW)* 363, 365, para. 8.

25 Under French law, it has been regarded as yet another hindering element to a useful application of the prohibition (F. Puel and V. Rebeyrotte, 'Abus de puissance contractuelle et pratique anticoncurentielle' (2015) *AJ Contrats d'affaires* 499, para. 1.1.1.) Some have spoken about a 'sterile application of the prohibition', leading to few applications of the norm (see A. Decocq and G. Decocq, *Droit de la concurrence*, LGDJ, Paris 2021, p. 402, para. 296; E. Claudel, 'L'abus de dépendance économique: un sphinx renaissant de ses cendres? (commentaire de l'article 1143 nouveau du code civil et de la proposition de loi visant à mieux définir l'abus de dépendance économique)' (2016) *Revue trimestrielle de droit commercial et de droit économique (RTD Com.)* 460, 463.

26 W. Devroe, 'Hoofdstuk 3. Modernisering van Belgisch mededingingsrecht en invoering van een verbod op misbruik van economische afhankelijkheid' in *Nieuw economisch recht in b2b-relaties*, Intersentia, Mortsel 2020, p. 90, paras. 93–94.

27 Ent. Antwerp, 16.04.2021, *Limburgs Rechtsleven* 2022, (149), *TBH* 2021/5 (646), case note J. Stuyck; Ent. Gent, 28.10.2020, *Competitio* 2020/4 (369). See also the analysis in H. Burez, F. Tuytschaever, E. Wijckmans and F. Wijckmans, 'Hoofdstuk 9. Misbruik van een positie van economische afhankelijkheid' in *Mededingingsrecht*, LeA Uitgevers, Hoegaarden 2022, p. 247, para. 9.22. J. Stuyck, 'Ongewenste reflexwerking van het verbod van misbruik van economische machtspositie op de norm der eerlijke *handelsgebruiken*' (2021) (5) *Revue de Droit Commercial Belge – Tijdschrift voor Belgisch Handelsrecht* 654, para. 4.

28 Gent 04.04.2022, *Competitio* 2022/1, (36) p. 40, para. 8; Antwerp 20.10.2021, *Competitio* 2021/3 (285), p. 288, para. 6.

Take one of the early cases that have been brought under the Belgian prohibition of abuse of relative power position.[29] A small retailer and repairer of hunting guns claims damages for the termination of a concession contract against the producer of the hunting guns which he sells. By way of commercial retaliation, the producer refuses to further deliver guns to the small retailer. The court in that case considers that the refusal to sell guns to the retailer is a prohibited abuse of position of economic dependence and orders an injunction to continue delivering guns and gun-related products.[30] In that decision, the requirement of an impact on competition had not been applied and it is doubtful whether it would have been fulfilled. If the requirement had been duly applied, this situation could not have been legally remedied. Hence, the inherent limitation of competition law proves problematic from a law of obligations perspective which focuses on balancing individual interests rather than market structures in general.

*Second*, competition law *remedies* have a sanctioning character, considered necessary to regulate competition. Again, this seems sensible from a competition law perspective but much less so from a law of obligations perspective. It is, of course, true that victims of competition law infringements can also claim compensation for their individual harm. But again, that is limited to cases featuring an infringement of competition law in the first place and thus only available based on the – from a law of obligations perspective – arbitrary distinction of an impact on competition.

All in all, although the division between competition law and the law of obligations may lose some its sharpness, the dividing line still exists with the consequences just described for how no-contract law and power are covered.

## 3.2. THE SPECIFIC OBLIGATIONS TO CONTRACT GAP

The shortcoming of specific obligations to contract, again, very much is inherent in the fact that they are *specific* obligations to contract; that is, they do not cover every kind of situations in which it may be necessary/desirable to provide for an obligation to contract. The *Swiss Postal case* offers an interesting illustration of this issue.[31] At stake was the distribution of two leaflets by the Swiss Post which had just been privatised. The Swiss Post refused to deliver the leaflets as they feared that it would be detrimental to their reputation as the content of the leaflets criticised some farmers that would be among the addressees. Given the strategic position of the Swiss Post, alternative

29 Ent. Antwerp, 16.04.2021, *LiRe* 2022, (149).

30 Ent. Antwerp, 16.04.2021, *LiRe* 2022, (149), p. 156, para. 3.2.6.

31 Swiss. Fed. Trib., 07.05.2002, 4C.297/2001, BGE 129 III (35): *Die Schweizerische Post v. Verein gegen Tierfabriken* (Appeal).

means to have these leaflets distributed were lacking and none of the specific obligations to contract under which the Swiss Post was, could be invoked (the delivery request in question did not fall under the specific provision obliging the Swiss Post to deliver *magazines* as they were free *leaflets*). Hence, due to the specific scope of the obligation to distribute magazines, the Swiss Post was not statutorily obliged to distribute these leaflets. To resolve the issue, the Swiss Federal Tribunal decided that even absent such a specific obligation to contract, there still was a general obligation to contract under the law of obligations based on general duties of conduct: 'a duty to contract can also arise from general principles of private law such as the prohibition of immoral behaviour'.[32]

The existence of such an obligation to contract was dependent on four cumulative criteria: (i) offering products or services publicly; (ii) the goods or services are necessary in normal circumstances and need not be vital; (iii) the party in need cannot reasonably obtain the products or services elsewhere; and (iv) the seller cannot provide valid grounds for his refusal to contract.[33] Based on those four criteria, the Swiss Federal Tribunal found that an obligation to contract lay on the Swiss Post.

For want of a specific obligation to contract, the Swiss Federal Tribunal found a general obligation to contract within the law of obligations which was specifically based on dependence, or – as the Tribunal put it – '(ii) the goods or services are necessary in normal circumstances and need not be vital; (iii) the party in need cannot reasonably obtain the products or services elsewhere'.

## 3.3. NECESSITY OF NO-CONTRACT LAW AND POWER

It appears that the gap between the rule (individualistic freedom of contract) and the correction (welfarist freedom of contract) is not in a process of alignment and that this stands in pronounced contrast to what can be observed in contract law. This could be more acceptable if the corrections within competition law or specific obligations to contract were comprehensive; yet, they are not. In consequence, a small food processing company will have no remedies at its disposal where it faces the refusal to contract by a supermarket chain. This is not only problematic where the food processing company does not get the supply contract, but also to the extent that the mere threat of not contracting

---

32 Ibid., para. 6.3, p. 45. Free translation. Original text [German]: '*Vielmehr kann sich eine Kontrahierungspflicht auch aus allgemeinen Prinzipien des Privatrechtes wie dem Verbot sittenwidrigen Verhaltens ergeben*'.

33 Ibid., para. 6.3, pp. 45–46.

significantly diminishes its bargaining position – as is well documented in the case of the food supply chain.[34]

So, a no-contract law that deals with power imbalance appears to be necessary on two co-existing levels: *first* at an analytical level – providing the tools to analyse no-contract cases from a power-related perspective; and *secondly*, claim oriented – providing claims where the no-contract case results from an abuse of a situation of dependence. The first level follows the second; providing the second will thus also cover the first.

Based on the foregoing, I suggest a blueprint for a no-contract law that takes power imbalances into consideration, in the next section.

## 4. BLUEPRINT FOR A NO-CONTRACT LAW AND POWER

### 4.1. BI- OR MULTI-LATERAL FREEDOM OF CONTRACT

A no-contract law that is conceptually able to take the power dimension into account is one that is based on an understanding of freedom of contract as taking place in society and thus as limited by others' freedom of contract (welfarist understanding). In other words, freedom of contract is not conceived as that of an isolated individual that must be kept free from any kind of intervention (individualist understanding), but as an individual whose use of its freedom of – and specifically *from* – contract has repercussions for other individuals and their freedom of – and specifically *to* – contract. This means, that one person's the freedom from contract should potentially be subject to restrictions where it annihilates the freedom to contract of another.

---

34 'Agricultural producers … particularly vulnerable to UTPs [unfair trading practices] as they often lack bargaining power that would be equal to that of their downstream partners. Their alternatives in terms of getting their products to consumers are limited (this vulnerability is exacerbated where so called hold-up situations occur which may make alternatives virtually non-existing due to the perishability of a product)'. (Impact assessment of 12.04.2018, Initiative to improve the food supply chain (unfair trading practices), SWD (2018) 92 final, p. 9). These problems have been recognised not only at a European level but also worldwide. In 2016, the executive summary of the UNCTADs (United Nations Conference on Trade and Development) note on *Enforcement of competition policy in the retail sector: Competition issues in the food retail chain* stated that 'the creation of superstores and supermarkets has evolved into a process of concentration that has radically changed the relationship of forces between producers, manufacturers and retailers. … The asymmetry of power between providers and retailers has led to abusive and unfair practices difficult to counter through competition law, and this has led to the adoption of different regulatory measures to prevent and stop the market power of supermarkets from hindering competition and harming consumer welfare'.

## 4.2. DEPENDENCE

This understanding of freedom of contract translates into the understanding that the exercise of the freedom of contract could give rise to liability where the counterparty is in a situation of dependence. Precisely *when* an individual or undertaking is in such a situation of dependence is a difficult question. It can be answered in a more or less restrictive fashion. Realistically, no one single good answer exists, but it will constantly be re-negotiated and depends on political ambitions and preferences. In function thereof, the understanding of 'dependence' can be more or less effective for attaining that political ambition.

Two opposing tendencies can be singled out: either dependence concerns only minimal needs for subsistence, such as access to water, essential food, shelter, *et cetera*, or dependence extends to variants of a decent human life, such as access to electricity, education, internet, *et cetera*. Furthermore, being in a situation of dependence can either be understood in an *absolute* way, meaning that for all human beings the same standard of dependence applies, or in a *relative* way, meaning that what one is dependent on varies in relation to one's overall way of living.

The implications of opting for one or another approach are, of course, far reaching. If, for instance, dependence is considered to exist only in an absolute sense, based on the bare minimum for subsistence, well-off people likely will never be able to bring a claim; conversely, a relative understanding that is based on a decent standard of living may contribute to making well-off individuals better-off. But again, no single correct answer exists to this question, and it is only in function of a political ambition that the adequacy of choosing one or another approach may sensibly be evaluated.

Regardless of how exactly dependence will be understood, it should open the way to an obligation to contract – provided some additional conditions of application are fulfilled. In the *Swiss Postal case*, the Federal Tribunal decided that such an obligation to contract should only arise where offers are made to the public, and that no objective justification can be given for such a refusal to contract. In the competition law context, there must be some form of abuse of the situation of dependence. Let us now discuss these additional conditions leading to a liability claim. There are, of course, many ways of constructing such a general obligation to contract based on dependence, and I shall not discuss them in detail. Instead, I will stick to suggesting one possible blue-print for no-contract law and power while also showing the different levers one can use in designing such an obligation to contract.

## 4.3. WRONGFUL PRACTICE BASED ON DEPENDENCE: ABUSE

A situation of dependence alone, probably will not be considered sufficient to give rise to liability. The mere state of dependence of one party (party B) cannot be blamed on the other party upon which it is dependent (party A). As Western liability law systems tend to rely on some form of reprehensible conduct in order to give rise to liability, it seems implausible to rely on dependence alone to justify an obligation to contract. Hence, it seems sensible to add a requirement of some form of blameworthy conduct.[35] In that context, it will be *adopting conduct which that party would not have adopted absent the dependence of the counterparty* that could trigger liability. A common practice of supermarkets, for instance, is to consciously delay the beginning of price negotiations to exert greater pressure on sellers of food products and thereby force them to lower the prices they charge because they *must* sell – otherwise their products may perish. If these sellers of food products were not dependent upon the supermarket(s) for the sale of their food products, they would turn to other buyers, and the technique of artificial delay would not work. Hence, artificially delaying the start of negotiations is a practice which a supermarket can only afford because the seller of food products is in a situation of dependence.

Where the threat of not-contracting is used in a way which *that party would not have risked to absent the dependence of the counterparty*, this conduct could also trigger an obligation to contract.

I argue for an obligation to contract based on dependence and conduct that could only be risked due to the dependence; more shortly put, based on an abuse of dependence in a no-contract context. It would form the counterpart to an abuse of dependence in a concluded contract (abuse of circumstances) (above section 2.4.), such as enacted under Belgian law in Article 5.37 Belgian Civil Code. Another advantage is that it connects very well to already existing prohibitions of abuse of (relative) power positions under competition law and market practices law. This should allow for greater interoperability, cross-understanding and fertilisation between the law of obligations, competition law, and market practices law – a bridge which today often is too burdensome to cross, though of fundamental importance.

[35] Save, of course, for strict liability, but strict liability does not seem plausible to me in these cases.

## 4.4. OVERCOMING THE VOLUNTARISTIC STALEMATE: *OBLIEGENHEIT* TO CONTRACT

Yet, there remains a sizeable practical issue with an obligation to contract, namely a voluntaristic stalemate: if concluding a contract is conceived as a voluntaristic act, a forced contract appears internally inconsistent. Practice teaches us indeed that the implementation of such an obligation to contract, understood as parties *having* to reach an agreement, proves difficult. The Dutch Curaçaoan saga on forced contracting illustrates this aptly:[36] in essence, the operator of a beach, Papagayo, agrees in a letter of intent to grant a company a lease right to install a diving school in a building on that beach. In this company, Watersports, there are (simplified) two parties. Ultimately, Papagayo signs the lease agreement not with Watersports, but with one of the two parties privately. The other party demands compliance with the letter of intent. In 2017, the Court of First Instance in Curaçao rules as follows:

> 5.1. declares that Papagayo acted unlawfully vis-à-vis Watersports by entering into the rental agreement not in the name of Watersports but in the name of [defendant in the action under subsection 1] privately;
> 5.2. orders Papagayo to enter into a rental agreement with Watersports concerning the diving school within two months of service of this judgment, in accordance with the provisions as included in the agreement submitted as exhibit 8 to the statement of reply ..., under threat of a penalty payment of NAf 1,500 for each day or part of a day that Papagayo remains in default, with a maximum of NAf 150,000;[37]

On appeal, Papagayo disputes having acted unlawfully but the court does not accept this. On the contrary, the court finds that Papagayo failed to sufficiently take Watersports' interests into account and by 'deviating at the last minute from the line always followed – "breaking off negotiations" – acted unlawfully'.[38] However, the court is of the opinion that forcing parties to contract is not the

---

[36] This development is based on what I have written in T. Hick, 'Aansprakelijkheid voor afgebroken onderhandelingen in België en Nederland: Op koers voor toenadering' (2022) 29 *NTBR* 243, 254, para. 27.

[37] GiEA Curaçao 11.12.2017, ECLI:NL:OGEAC:2017:186, para. 5.1. Free translation. Original text [Dutch]: '*5.1. verklaart voor recht dat Papagayo onrechtmatig heeft gehandeld jegens Waterports door de huurovereenkomst niet op naam van Watersports af te sluiten maar op naam van [verweerder in conventie sub 1] privé;*
*5.2. veroordeelt Papagayo om binnen twee maanden na betekening van dit vonnis een huurovereenkomst ter zake de duikschool met Watersports aan te gaan, conform de bepalingen zoals opgenomen in de overeenkomst overgelegd als productie 8 bij conclusie van antwoord ..., een en ander op straffe van een dwangsom van NAf 1.500 voor iedere dag of gedeelte van een dag dat Papagayo hiermee in gebreke blijft, met een maximum van NAf 150.000*'.

[38] GHACMB, 15.11.2019, ECLI:NL:OGHACMB:2019:257, para. 2.4.4. Free translation. Original text [Dutch]: '*op het laatste moment afwijken van de steeds gevolgde lijn – het "afbreken van de onderhandelingen" – onrechtmatig' was.*

appropriate sanction, as the relationship between the parties has been largely disrupted and therefore 'will create more problems than solve them'.[39] Instead, the performance interest will have to be compensated. Compensation of the performance interest involves the need 'to determine the difference between the hypothetical situation that Watersports would have been in if the written lease had been put in its name and the actual situation as it existed when it was not'.[40] To determine this difference, a multitude of circumstances must be taken into account, such as the 'difficult relationship between the persons involved at Watersports and the likelihood that (further) conflicts would have arisen within Watersports, as well as whether Watersports, as Papagayo argues, can be blamed for its own fault'.[41]

The case is then referred to the *Hoge Raad*, on the grounds that the Common Court of Justice of Aruba, Curaçao, Sint Maarten and of Bonaire, Sint Eustatius and Saba allegedly went beyond the bounds of the law on appeal. Indeed, Papagayo had not asked the court to reform the contracting order, but to decide that it had not wrongfully broken-off negotiations. In this sense, the *Hoge Raad* decides that 'the court therefore is not free to substitute another form of compensation for the court's order that [Papagayo] enter into a rental agreement with Watersports'.[42] Be that as it may, this saga clearly shows how practically difficult the enforcement of an obligation to contract appears to be.

To escape this voluntaristic stalemate, I suggest working with an *Obliegenheit* to contract. Without going in detail into what an *Obliegenheit* is,[43] it consists of the following elements: once an abuse of dependence has been proven, parties are under an *Obliegenheit* to contract. That means that the party that abused its position of power (party A) must give best efforts and act constructively to

---

39 GHACMB, 15.11.2019, ECLI:NL:OGHACMB:2019:257, para. 2.6. Free translation. Original text [Dutch]: '*meer problemen zal creëren dan oplossen*'.

40 GHACMB, 15.11.2019, ECLI:NL:OGHACMB:2019:257, para. 2.7. Free translation. Original text [Dutch]: '*dan om het vaststellen van het verschil tussen de hypothetische situatie waarin Watersports zou hebben verkeerd wanneer de schriftelijke huurovereenkomst wel op haar naam zou zijn gesteld en de werkelijke toestand zoals die bestond toen dat niet was gebeurd*'.

41 GHACMB, 15.11.2019, ECLI:NL:OGHACMB:2019:257, para. 2.7. Free translation. Original text [Dutch]: '*moeizame verstandhouding tussen de bij Watersports betrokken personen en de kans dat het binnen Watersports tot (nadere) conflicten was gekomen, alsmede de vraag of Watersports, zoals Papagayo betoogt, eigen schuld kan worden verweten*'.

42 HR 11.06.2021, ECLI:NL:HR:2021:860, para. 3.2.3. Free translation. Original text [Dutch]: '*het hof daarom niet vrij om een andere vorm van schadevergoeding in de plaats te stellen voor de door het gerecht uitgesproken veroordeling van [Papagayo] om een huurovereenkomst met Watersports aan te gaan*'.

43 See B. Freleteau, *Devoir et incombance en matière contractuelle*, LGDJ, Paris 2017, p. 633; S. Hähnchen, *Obliegenheiten und Nebenpflichten. Eine Untersuchung dieser besonderen Verhaltensanforderungen im Privatversciherungsrecht und im allgemeinen Zivilrecht unter besonderer Berücksichtigung der Dogmengeschichte*, Mohr Siebeck, Tübingen 2010; T. Ehrensperger, *Strukturen und Verletzungen von Obliegenheiten im Schweizerischen Privatrecht (unter Ausschluss des Versicherungsrechts)*, University of Zurich, Zürich 2004.

reach an agreement. If it fails to do so, it loses its freedom from contract and thus must accept an offer made by the party that has been abused (party B). Of course, that offer need only be accepted if it is a reasonable offer.[44]

Proceeding in such a way offers the considerable advantage of leaving much space for party autonomy. Yet, it also sets incentives in such a way that the party that abused the other's dependence has an interest in working constructively towards finding an agreement. Otherwise, it could quite simply boycott the re-negotiations. Thereby, the previously imbalanced power relationship is recalibrated.

Such an *Obliegenheit* to contract gets really interesting in a context where the power imbalance is of such importance that no negotiations are possible at all (standardised contracting), and a simple take-it-or-leave-it scenario arises. Given its dependence, the dependent party has no choice but to take the offered contract or to have none at all. Provided this could be classified as an abuse of dependence – which is a real but open question – it could mean that parties then actually would have to negotiate and where party A would not act constructively, could have to accept a reasonable offer from party B. The potential to rebalance this unlimited number of unbalanced contract negotiations seems as promising as it might seem unsettling.

## 5. CONCLUSION

I started by claiming that in the slow but palpable process of increasingly taking power relations into account in contract law, the no-contract scenario is being overlooked. Hence, no-contract law and power does not seem to exist as a legal discipline, though it very much exists in daily practice. To substantiate this point, I first explained the existing framework of no-contract law and power; that is to say, the dynamic of rule-correction between the general law of obligations on the one hand and, on the other, specific obligations to contract and competition law. Looking at these three fields in conjunction proved that the underlying understanding of freedom from contract in the general law of obligations differs critically from the understanding prevailing in the field of specific obligations to contract or competition law. This dissonance, however, is not resolved comprehensively by these corrective fields of law, as they leave open considerable regulatory gaps. Hence, considering no-contract law and power is necessary.

---

44 In more detail in T. Hick, *Liability for Failed Contract Negotiations – A Comparative, Structural, and Historical Analysis*, New York, Routledge, 2025, chapter 8. Also briefly explained in T. Hick, 'The Coronacrisis and Its Impact on Creditors: Frustration of Purpose' (2022) 36 *European Review of Private Law* 389, 414–416.

To provide a blue-print for no-contract law and power, I based myself on the underlying assumption found in the context of specific obligations to contract and competition law, namely that in cases of dependence, legal intervention is warranted in order to counter the undesirable consequences that dependence can structurally have on individuals. This is expressed by a concept of freedom of contract which understands freedom of contract as limited by the needs of counterparties. As Jan Busche put it, '*Die Vertragsfreiheit ist eine auf Gegenseitigkeit verbürgte und damit immanent gebundene Freiheit*'.[45] Hence, when one party is dependent on the conclusion of a given contract, curtailing the freedom of contract of the party that refuses the dependent party a contract can be warranted. Dependence on its own, however, is unlikely to suffice to curtail one's freedom of contract, for the mere fact of dependence cannot be blamed upon the party in a position of power. Yet, such considerations of blameworthiness are still of great importance in Western private law systems. Hence, relying on an *abuse of dependence* seems like an approach which is both intuitively convincing and compatible with existing legal frameworks pertaining to no-contract law and power.

An obligation to contract based on an abuse of the counterparty's dependence on contract conclusion appears to be a suitable and necessary starting point for no-contract law and power. Yet, the *contradictio in terminis* of forcing a voluntaristic act via an obligation to contract appears both conceptually and practically speaking problematic. Hence, an alternative approach is needed which allows volition to be forced. I have argued and explained this and how an *Obliegenheit* to contract could do just that, namely by incentivising re-negotiations. So doing, parties maintain their private autonomy. If, however, the party under the *Obliegenheit* fails to live up to the required standard of care in re-negotiations, it loses its freedom from contract and with it, its freedom to refuse an offer made by the counterparty – provided the offer is reasonable. Then, it has to accept that offer. Thus, the reluctant negotiator is incentivised to cooperate.

---

45 J. Busche, *Privatautonomie und Kontrahierungszwang*, Mohr Siebeck, Tübingen 1999, p. 655. Free translation: 'Freedom of contract is a freedom guaranteed by reciprocity and thus intrinsically bound'.

# CHAPTER 8

# POWER IN LABOUR CONTRACT NEGOTIATIONS: THE RESTRICTION OF FREEDOM OF NEGOTIATION TO CLOSE THE GENDER PAY GAP

Stefanie JUNG*

## 1. INTRODUCTION[1]

Despite numerous efforts at the European and national levels, an unadjusted gender pay gap of 12 per cent is still evident within the EU.[2] With 14.2 per cent, England is even above the EU average.[3] Therefore, the proclaimed goal of the European Parliament in 2013 to close the gender pay gap by 2020 was evidently missed.[4] For this reason, the EU now wants to improve the existing legislation to effectively reduce the gender pay gap. As a result, the Directive on Pay Transparency[5] ('PT-Dir.') was adopted in May 2023. This Directive must be transposed into national laws by 7 June 2026[6] and will require significant regulatory action in the Member States, especially from Germany.[7] Compared

* Prof. Dr. iur. Stefanie Jung is Professor of Corporate Law at the Technical University of Munich, TUM School of Management (Heilbronn Campus). The author would like to thank Prof. Dr. iur. Peter Krebs (University of Siegen) for his valuable suggestions and advice in the preparation of this chapter and Melissa Dowse (Technical University of Munich) for her support with the translation. The author would also like to express her gratitude to all SECOLA participants for their helpful feedback.

1 The discussion of the new EU Directive on Pay Transparency is based on S. Jung, 'Der Einfluss der neuen europäischen Vorgaben zur Entgelttransparenz vor Beschäftigung auf Gehaltsverhandlungen' (2024) 41 *NZA (Neue Zeitschrift für Arbeitsrecht)* 18 et seq. and S. Jung, 'Die EU-Entgelttransparenz-Richtlinie: Eckpunkte und Umsetzungsspielräume' (2024) 77 *Recht der Arbeit* 89 et seq. No specific reference is made to the possible verbatim (translated) adoptions of text passages or further developed text passages taken from these articles.

2 12% in 2023, see Eurostat, Gender pay gap in unadjusted form by NACE Rev. 2 activity – structure of earnings survey methodology, 25.02.2025, https://ec.europa.eu/eurostat/databrowser/view/EARN_GR_GPGR2/default/table?lang=en (accessed 26.06.2025).

3 14.2% refers to the gender pay gap in 2023. In 2024, the gender pay gap decreased to 13.1%, see Office for National Statistics, Gender pay gap in the UK: 2024, 29.10.2024, https://www.ons.gov.uk/employmentandlabourmarket/peopleinwork/earningsandworkinghours/bulletins/genderpaygapintheuk/2024 (accessed 26.06.2025). Data for the EU in 2024 is not yet available.

4 European Parliament resolution 2013/2678(RSP) of 12 September 2013 on the application of the principle of equal pay for men and women for equal work or work of equal value, [2013] *OJ* C 93: The European Parliament 'calls on the Commission to support Member States in reducing the gender pay gap by at least five percentage points annually with the aim of eliminating the gender pay gap by 2020'.

5 Directive of the European Parliament and of the Council (EU) 2023/970 of 10 May 2023 to strengthen the application of the principle of equal pay for equal work or work of equal value between men and women through pay transparency and enforcement mechanisms [2023] *OJ* L 132 (PT-Dir.).

6 See also L. Marek and S. Sawodny, 'Neue Richtlinie der Europäischen Union zur Entgelttransparenz' (2023) 15 *Arbeitsrecht Aktuell* 397; S. Roloff in *Beck'scher Online-Kommentar Arbeitsrecht*, as of 01.06.2025, C.H. Beck, Munich, EntgTranspG Section 1 marginal n. 6.

7 There is a need for implementation, particularly of the pre-contractual requirements, as Germany does not yet have any corresponding regulations. However, the Directive also requires further adjustments to German law, e.g., for the right to information. See generally on the need for adaptation in Germany, e.g., R. Winter, 'Den Anforderungen der EU-Entgelttransparenzrichtlinie bald nachkommen – Die Zeit läuft' (2024) 41 *NZA* 8 et

to the latter, in France, the transposition of the Directive will entail smaller amendments,[8] given that the French legislator has already taken relatively far-reaching measures.[9] Likewise, in the UK, considerable regulatory efforts to reduce the gender pay gap were implemented with the Equality Act in 2010 (EqA 2010) and the Equality Act 2010 (Gender Pay Gap Information) Regulations dating back to 2017. Since then, however, the government has not committed itself to new, more far-reaching rules despite the considerable gender pay gap that still exists. Although the UK does not have to implement the requirements of the relevant EU Pay Transparency Directive, there are corresponding regulatory considerations at a political level.[10]

These recent regulatory efforts at the European level no longer focus solely on the period of employment but also cover the pre-employment period and, thus, particularly the salary negotiation phase. Prior to the Directive's regulations, there were no harmonised minimum standards governing the salary negotiation phase.[11] Until recently, most Member States also did not

---

seq.; J. Günther and M. Schiffelholz, 'Die Entgelttransparenzrichtlinie: Inhalte und Unterschiede zum Entgelttransparenzgesetz' (2023) 28 *Neue Zeitschrift für Arbeitsrecht Rechtsprechungs-Report* 568 et seq.

8 Art. L. 1221-6 C. trav. (Code du travail) stipulates, for example, that questions at the interview must be directly and necessarily related to the assessment of the applicant's professional suitability. However, the French legislator should clearly stipulate that questions about previous salary are prohibited, as this aspect has not yet been discussed despite the broad wording. Cf. e.g., F. Duquesne, *Droit du travail 2024*, 19th ed., Gualino, Paris 2024, marginal n. 214. Exceptions have so far been provided for regarding gender-neutral job advertisements (cf. Art. L. 1142-2 C. trav.), but the wording of the Directive does not permit this. Furthermore, France does not yet have any requirements for the mandatory indication of pay or pay range.

9 See G. Auzero, D. Baugard and E. Dockès, *Droit du travail 2024–2025*, 37th ed., Dalloz, Paris 2023, marginal n. 755, who assess the provisions as progressive and comprehensive, while P.-H. Antonmattei, *Droit du travail*, 3rd ed., LGDJ, Paris 2023, marginal n. 141, categorises the provisions as incomplete and confusing.

10 For example, the government has launched a pilot project in which the participating companies – as stipulated by the Directive – are providing salary information in job advertisements on a trial basis and waiving questions about previous salary. See UK Government, 'Government launches pay transparency pilot to break down barriers for women', 08.03.2022, https://www.gov.uk/government/news/government-launches-pay-transparency-pilot-to-break-down-barriers-for-women (accessed 26.06.2025). On the impact of the EU requirements on the UK, see also the law firm Clyde & Co. on its website, Clyde & Co, 'Pay Transparency: How are changes in the EU likely to impact UK employers now and in the future?', 24.11.2023, https://www.clydeco.com/en/insights/2023/11/how-are-changes-in-the-eu-likely-to-impact-uk-empl (accessed 26.06.2025).

11 Proposal for a Directive of the European Parliament and of the Council COM(2021) 93 final of 4 March 2021 to strengthen the application of the principle of equal pay for equal work or work of equal value between men and women through pay transparency and enforcement mechanisms (2021), p. 11 ('Commission's Proposal for a PT-Dir.').

stipulate such standards.[12] The EU is thus creating a whole new regulatory approach to reduce the gender pay gap (section 6. details this approach). This chapter analyses these newly introduced pre-contractual requirements of the EU Pay Transparency Directive, which are also being discussed to a similar extent at the UK level. However, this chapter does not cover the other measures for transparency and enforceability of claims during the employment phase.

The new idea of focusing on the salary negotiation phase is rooted in the salary differences that result from the pre-contractual phase and frequently manifest long-term differences in salary development.[13] Against this backdrop, this chapter will assess the impact of these new pre-contractual regulations on the negotiation dynamics between employers and applicants. In this regard, what will be explored particularly is the influence of these regulations on the balance of power between the parties. This allows for a prediction of the probable impact of those rules on the gender pay gap. Furthermore, the chapter also addresses possibilities to circumvent the regulations' set-up requirements and non-gender-related effects on the overall power distribution in negotiations. This is necessary, as only a comprehensive analysis can reveal the actual possible impact of the new directive. Moreover, the novel regulatory approach encompassing the negotiation phase will be put in the broader context of recent regulatory tendencies of the EU and national regulators, who have increasingly sought to achieve regulatory objectives by opting for the limitation of the freedom of negotiation over the freedom of contract.

## 2. *STATUS QUO* OF THE GENDER PAY GAP

As already mentioned, an unadjusted gender pay gap of 12 per cent is still evident within the EU.[14] In countries such as Germany and Austria, the

---

12 The European Commission states that so far, only four Member States have stipulated that salary information must be provided in the pre-contractual phase. Only Portugal is said to have a ban on asking questions about pre-salary. See European Commission, Commission Staff Working Document, Impact Assessment, SWD(2021) 41 final (2021), p. 41.

13 S. Napari, 'Gender differences in early-career wage growth' (2009) 16 *Labour Econ. (Labour Economics)* 140, 142, concerning Finnish employees, shows that a gender pay gap exists from the outset and then increases significantly within the first 10 years. J. Mazei, J. Hüffmeier, P.A. Freund, A.F. Stuhlmacher, L. Bilke and G. Hertel, 'A meta-analysis on gender differences in negotiation outcomes and their moderators' (2015) 141 *Psychological Bulletin* 85, 97 point out that this results from the fact that salary increases relate to the starting salary. On how gender differences in starting salaries result from different negotiation behaviours, see J. Säve-Söderbergh, 'Gender gaps in salary negotiations: Salary requests and starting salaries in the field' (2019) 161 *Journal of Economic Behavior & Organization* 35, 35 et seq.

14 12% in 2023, see Eurostat, above n. 2.

unadjusted gender pay gap even amounts to approximately 18 per cent.[15] By contrast, France ranks close to the EU average at 12.2 per cent.[16] Outside the EU, with 14.2 per cent, England has a bit higher unadjusted gender pay gap than France.[17] However, the unadjusted gender pay gap is generally even greater, particularly for higher earners who traditionally negotiate their salary.[18] Further, considerable differences are detectable for the various occupational fields.[19] For example, a particularly high gender pay gap occurs in the finance and insurance sector. According to Eurostat, the gender pay gap in this sector was 26.1 per cent in Germany and as high as 32.1 per cent in France in 2023.[20] The gender pay gap also depends heavily on age. The data from the EU shows that the pay gap is significantly smaller for young employees than for older employees.[21] This is because the gender pay gap increases over time, as salary increases usually relate to the current salary.[22]

In addition, over the last 10 years, the unadjusted gender pay gap in the EU has only been reduced by an average of 4 percentage points.[23] With a reduction of 4.5 percentage points, Germany ranks close to the EU average.[24] In France, a reduction of only 3.3 percentage points was achieved.[25] Remarkably, in the UK, in the same time period, the unadjusted gender pay gap was reduced more significantly (by 5.4 percentage points). That said, the unadjusted gender pay gap in England was, however, also well above the EU average 10 years

---

15 Germany (2023): 17.6%; Austria (2023): 18.3%, see Eurostat, above n. 2.

16 Eurostat, above n. 2.

17 14.2% refers to the gender pay gap in 2023. In 2024, the gender pay gap decreased to 13.1%, see Office for National Statistics, above n. 3. Data for the EU in 2024 is not yet available.

18 The UK puts the gender pay gap for the top 10% of earners at 14.9% for 2023, which increased to 15.5% in 2024. Office for National Statistics, above n. 3. Eurostat does not provide a corresponding analysis for the EU. More generally on this phenomenon, see N. Quadlin, T. Vanheuvelen and C.E. Ahearn, 'Higher education and high-wage gender inequality' (2023) 112 *Social Science Research* 102873; H. Mandel and A. Rotman, 'Revealing the Concealed Effect of Top Earnings on the Gender Gap in the Economic Value of Higher Education in the United States, 1980–2017' (2021) 58 *Demography* 551 et seq.

19 For the EU see Eurostat, above n. 2. For the UK see Office for National Statistics, above n. 3.

20 See Eurostat, above n. 2. In the UK, the gender pay gap for financial managers and directors was 28% in 2024. See Office for National Statistics, above n. 3.

21 In Germany, e.g., the gender pay gap in 2023 amounted to 8.4% for employees aged between 25 and 34 and to 26.3% for employees aged between 55 and 64. See Eurostat, above n. 2. Gender pay gap in unadjusted form by age – NACE Rev. 2 activity (B-S except O) – structure of earnings survey methodology, 21.02.2025, https://ec.europa.eu/eurostat/databrowser/view/earn_gr_gpgr2ag__custom_17396958/default/table?lang=en (accessed 26.06.2025). In the UK, the gender pay gap is also higher for older employees. See Office for National Statistics, above n. 3.

22 On this effect J. Mazei, J. Hüffmeier, P.A. Freund, A.F. Stuhlmacher, L. Bilke and G. Hertel, above n. 13, 97.

23 Eurostat puts the gender pay gap at 16% for 2013 (EU-27) and 12% for 2023. In 10 years, the gender pay gap has thus been reduced by 4 percentage points. See Eurostat, above n. 2.

24 From 22.1% in 2013 to 17.6% in 2023. See Eurostat, above n. 2.

25 From 15.5% in 2013 to 12.2% in 2023. See Eurostat, above n. 2.

ago.[26] Hence, despite the substantial reduction, the gap is still above average compared to the EU (and France in particular).

The reasons for the differences described and their respective significance are disputed. Yet, a considerable part of the gender pay gap is *not* attributable to the above-average proportion of women in low-paid jobs and[27] part-time work,[28] or the unequal division of domestic caring responsibilities[29].[30] The

---

26 In 2013, the gender pay gap in the UK was 19.8%, see Office for National Statistics, New Earnings Survey (NES) and Annual Survey of Hours and Earnings (ASHE): Gender Pay Gap Time Series, 29.10.2019, https://www.ons.gov.uk/file?uri=/employmentandlabourmarket/peopleinwork/earningsandworkinghours/adhocs/006331newearningssurveynesandannualsurveyofhoursandearningsashegenderpaygaptimeseries/002546.xls (accessed 26.06.2025), while the EU average was only 16%. In Germany, however, which is also well above the EU average, this has only led to a reduction of 4.5 percentage points in the last decade. See Eurostat, above n. 2.

27 On the low wage rate among female employees in the EU, see Statistisches Bundesamt, Niedriglohnquote in der Europäischen Union, 2024, https://www.destatis.de/Europa/DE/Thema/Bevoelkerung-Arbeit-Soziales/Arbeitsmarkt/Qualitaet-der-Arbeit/_dimension-2/niedriglohnquote.html (accessed 26.06.2025). In the UK see Office for National Statistics, Low-paid employees, high-paid employees and middle-paid employees broken down various characteristics, https://www.ons.gov.uk/visualisations/dvc2757/fig04/datadownload.xlsx (accessed 26.06.2025).

28 For the EU, see Eurostat, Full-time and part-time employment by sex, age and occupation (1,000), 12.06.2025, https://ec.europa.eu/eurostat/databrowser/view/lfsa_epgais__custom_11473519/default/table?lang=en (accessed 26.06.2025). For the UK, see Office for National Statistics, EMP01 SA: Full-time, part-time and temporary workers (seasonally adjusted), 10.06.2025, https://www.ons.gov.uk/employmentandlabourmarket/peopleinwork/employmentandemployeetypes/datasets/fulltimeparttimeandtemporaryworkersseasonallyadjustedemp01sa (accessed 26.06.2025).

29 Providing an overview for European countries, European Institute for Gender Equality, Gender Equality Index 2019: Work-life balance, https://eige.europa.eu/publications-resources/toolkits-guides/gender-equality-index-2019-report/informal-care-older-people-people-disabilities-and-long-term-care-services?language_content_entity=en (accessed 26.06.2025). On the distribution of unpaid domestic caring responsibilities, e.g., in Germany, see Bundesministerium für Familie, Senioren, Frauen und Jugend, 'Auf dem Weg zu Entgeltgleichheit von Frauen und Männern – Daten, Ursachen, Maßnahmen', July 2020, pp. 20 et seq., https://www.bmfsfj.de/resource/blob/159872/c10d77c1198719376488fb63e67514c5/auf-dem-weg-zur-entgeltgleichheit-von-frauen-und-maennern-deutsch-data.pdf (accessed 26.06.2025). For the distribution of domestic caring responsibilities in UK, see UK Government, Department for Work and Pensions, Family Resources Survey: financial year 2019 to 2020, 25.03.2021, https://www.gov.uk/government/statistics/family-resources-survey-financial-year-2019-to-2020/family-resources-survey-financial-year-2019-to-2020#:~:text=Seven%20per%20cent%20of%20UK,million%20versus%201.8%20 million%20males (accessed 26.06.2025).

30 Commission's Proposal for a PT-Dir., above n. 11, p. 3. See also D. Leythienne and P. Ronkowski, *A decomposition of the unadjusted gender pay gap using Structure of Earnings Survey data*, Publication Office of the European Union, Luxembourg 2018, p. 13. In the UK, the results are comparable, see Office for National Statistics, 'Understanding the gender pay gap in the UK', 17.01.2018, https://www.ons.gov.uk/employmentandlabourmarket/peopleinwork/earningsandworkinghours/articles/understandingthegenderpaygapintheuk/2018-01-17 (accessed 26.06.2025).

European Commission, for example, assumes that two-thirds of this gap cannot be explained by factors such as part-time work, etc.[31] In this respect, however, there are considerable differences between the countries. In Germany, for example, a relatively high proportion of the gender pay gap can be explained by such factors, while this proportion in England and France is considerably lower.[32] However, in conclusion, the EU law-maker is of the opinion that discrimination, too, affects women.[33] As for the UK, it is also assumed that a proportion of the gender pay gap is due to discrimination.[34]

## 3. THE CONCEPT OF THE PAY TRANSPARENCY DIRECTIVE[35]

Against this backdrop, the EU Pay Transparency Directive aims to achieve equal pay between men and women by way of 37 articles setting up minimum standards for the Member States (see Article 1 PT-Dir.). For this purpose, the European legislator has provided three central levers that will combat various functional deficits of the current legislative landscape. The first is pay transparency.[36] In particular, pay transparency in the course of the employment period should enable those workers supposedly affected by discrimination to identify unjustified unequal treatment. Moreover, pay transparency is supposed

---

[31] Commission's Proposal for a PT-Dir., above n. 11, p. 3.

[32] See D. Leythienne and P. Ronkowski, above n. 30, pp. 14 et seq.

[33] See e.g., Recital 15, sentence 3 PT-Dir. and European Commission, '2024 report on gender equality in the EU', Publications Office of the European Union, Luxembourg 2024, p. 31.

[34] E.g., UK Parliament, Women and Equalities Committee, Gender Pay Gap, 08.03.2016, https://publications.parliament.uk/pa/cm201516/cmselect/cmwomeq/584/584.pdf (accessed 26.06.2025) (especially with respect to older female employees).

[35] See on this S. Jung, 'Die EU-Entgelttransparenz-Richtlinie: Eckpunkte und Umsetzungsspielräume', above n. 1, 89 et seq.

[36] On the importance of pay transparency for equal pay in general, see M.P. Recalde and L. Vesterlund, 'Gender Differences in Negotiation: Can Interventions Reduce the Gap?' (2023) 15 *Annual Review of Economics* 633, 646 et seq., who provide an overview of the status of the discussion. It should be borne in mind that the effects vary depending on the type and form of transparency. Also providing an overview on pay information disclosure is M. Brown, A.J. Nyberg, I. Weller and S.D. Strizver, 'Pay Information Disclosure: Review and Recommendations for Research Spanning the Pay Secrecy–Pay Transparency Continuum' (2022) 48 *Journal of Management* 1661, 1661 et seq.; T. Husemann, 'Der Richtlinienvorschlag der Kommission zur Stärkung des Grundsatzes der Entgeltgleichheit' (2022) 15 *Europäische Zeitschrift für Arbeitsrecht* 166, 185, in the context of the Commission's Proposal for a PT-Dir., is critical of information and transparency as a means of combating pay discrimination. See M. Bennedsen, E. Simintzi, M. Tsoutsoura and D. Wolfenzon, 'Do Firms Respond to Gender Pay Gap Transparency?' (2022) 77 *The Journal of Finance* 2051, 2076 et seq. on the fact that transparency can also have an impact on the development of average wages.

to have preventive effects.[37] Article 6(1) PT-Dir. therefore stipulates that employers must disclose to their employees the respective (non-discriminatory) criteria used to determine their pay, the level of pay (i.e., gross annual pay and gross hourly pay[38]) as well as pay progression. Article 7 PT-Dir. determines a right to information for employees about their individual pay level compared to the average pay level.[39] Moreover, in the future, any contractual clauses that currently prevent employees from exchanging information about their salary situations[40] must also be declared inadmissible by the Member States (cf. Article 7(5) PT-Dir.).[41] This enables employees to obtain relevant information more easily through informal exchanges. According to Article 9 PT-Dir., employees will also receive information on the gender pay gap prevailing at their workplace.[42] Article 10 PT-Dir. further stipulates that both employers and employee representatives must, under certain circumstances, jointly carry out a pay assessment to correct and prevent unjustified and unaddressed salary differences. This provision, as such, is not a transparency regulation but rather establishes a monitoring and enforcement mechanism aimed at a cooperative elimination of existing barriers to equal pay. However, some of the requirements mentioned above allow for a nuanced approach by the Member States, differentiating the requirements depending on the employer's size (see, e.g., Article 6(2) PT-Dir., Article 9(2) to (5) PT-Dir.). The provisions are complemented by rules aimed at efficiently enforcing claims brought

---

37 Stating that pay secrecy facilitates pay discrimination and the persistence of the gender pay gap, M. Brown, A.J. Nyberg, I. Weller and S.D. Strizver, above n. 36, 1670 with further references.

38 Art. 3(1)(b) PT-Dir.

39 The provision explicitly refers to the pay level and not the pay. For the corresponding definitions, see Art. 3(1)(a) and (b) PT-Dir. For the formation of comparative groups concerning proof of equal or equivalent work, see Art. 19 PT-Dir.

40 Employees must, therefore, not be prevented from voluntarily sharing information about their salary with other employees. See also recital 44 sentence 3 PT-Dir.

41 Until now, pay secrecy has been enforced partly by contract and partly by cultural practices. Studies from the US show that employers continue to try to prevent employees from sharing this information. See S. Sun, J. Rosenfeld and P. Denice, 'On the Books, off the Record: Examining the Effectiveness of Pay Secrecy Laws in the U.S.' (March 2021) IWPR Policy Brief (Institute for Women's Policy Research Policy Brief), p. 5 https://www.iwpr.org/wp-content/uploads/2021/01/Pay-Secrecy-Policy-Brief-v4.pdf (accessed 26.06.2025). The provision is initially aimed at reducing the contractual hurdles. On possible positive effects of outlawing pay secrecy clauses (however, also differentiating according to educational level) see M. Kim, 'Pay Secrecy and the Gender Wage Gap in the United States' (2015) 54 *Industrial Relations: A Journal of Economy and Society* 648 et seq. Generally, on the effects of pay secrecy, see e.g., I. Burn and K. Kettler, 'The more you know, the better you're paid? Evidence from pay secrecy bans for managers' (2019) 59 *Labour Econ.* 92 et seq.; see also M. Baker, Y. Halberstam, K. Kroft, A. Mas and D. Messacar, 'Pay Transparency and the Gender Gap' (2023) 15 *American Economic Journal: Applied Economics* 157 et seq. on salary disclosure laws.

42 See also recital 38 sentences 1–3 PT-Dir. For comprehensive information on the reporting obligations, see R. Winter, above n. 7, 13 et seq.

forward by victims of discriminatory actions. Another key element of the new regulatory approach is thus improved enforcement. In this context, the legislator initially recognised the fundamental necessity of clarifying key terms, including 'pay' and 'work of equal value' (cf. Article 3(1)(a) and (g) PT-Dir.).[43] The third chapter of the Directive also contains further procedural requirements, including Article 14 PT-Dir., which aims to simplify employee access to justice.[44] Similarly, Article 15 PT-Dir. stipulates participation rights for qualified organisations and, particularly, equal treatment bodies for corresponding court proceedings. Besides 'other remedies' anchored in Article 17 PT-Dir.,[45] Article 16 PT-Dir. also establishes a right to compensation for victims of discrimination. The aim of simplified enforcement of claims for victims of discrimination is also facilitated through Articles 18 to 20 PT-Dir., which govern the burden of proof.

However, above all, what sets the novelty of the Directive's approach apart from all prior regulatory efforts is that the proposed rules do not merely aim to provide transparency for the period of the employment relationship but also set up requirements for the pre-contractual phase, where applicants initially negotiate their salary with the employer. Accordingly, the Directive now regulates the negotiation process, identifying it as a key factor to combat the gender pay gap. In this context, the Pay Transparency Directive provides three measures restricting the freedom of negotiation. First of all, the Directive stipulates that pay information must be provided prior to negotiation (Article 5(1) PT-Dir.). Second, employers are no longer allowed to inquire about the applicant's pay history details during job interviews (Article 5(2) PT-Dir.). The basic idea behind these two new rules is to reduce negotiation imbalances by lowering information asymmetries between the parties. Applicants on the one hand should be provided with more pay information and employers on the other hand should be restricted to gain certain information (outlawing questions about the pay history). Third, employers will be required to design the application procedures in a non-discriminatory manner. As the starting point of that process, job advertisements are to be formulated as gender-neutral (Article 5(3) PT-Dir.). The following comments focus on this novel approach to regulating the pre-contractual phase with the help of the three measures mentioned above.

---

43 Recital 16 sentence 3 PT-Dir. On these objectives also already the Commission's Proposal for a PT-Dir., above n. 11, p. 2. On the fundamental need for conceptual precision, see G. Thüsing in *Münchener Kommentar BGB*, vol. 1, 10th ed., C.H. Beck, Munich 2025, AGG Section 8 marginal nn. 52 et seq.; T. Husemann, above n. 36, 174 et seq. is generally critical of attempts to clarify the concept of equivalent work in the context of the Commission's Proposal for a PT-Dir.

44 Recital 46 sentence 1 PT-Dir., see also Commission's Proposal for a PT-Dir., above n. 11, p. 15.

45 See e.g., the injunction to cease and desist the violation (Art. 17(1)(a) PT-Dir.).

## 4. LIMITATION OF POSSIBLE EFFECTS

Before discussing the individual provisions concerning the pre-contractual phase in more detail below, the following section will explore the probable impact of the Directive's design on the gender pay gap. Therefore, the aim is to delineate the potential scope of the Directive, particularly regarding the pre-contractual requirements. In this context, it has to be borne in mind that the Pay Transparency Directive does not intend to eliminate or fully close the gender pay gap. The Directive merely strives to *reduce* the gender pay gap. The essential aim of these provisions is to reduce salary differences based on discrimination against, or different negotiating behaviour of, women. Accordingly, the Directive does not contain any measures that address alternative causes of pay differences (e.g., the above-average proportion of women in low-paid employment or the unequal division of care and caring responsibilities).[46] In detail, it remains controversial what proportion of the gender pay gap is due to discrimination or different negotiating behaviour.[47] The European Commission assumes that at least two-thirds of this gap cannot be explained by factors such as part-time work, etc.,[48] although there are considerable differences between the Member States in this respect.[49] However, this does not mean that discrimination and differences in negotiation behaviour *can* explain two-thirds of the gender pay gap. Rather, discrimination and differences in negotiation behaviour are merely two factors that may be able to explain a part of this proportion.[50] Furthermore, it has to be borne in mind that discrimination can also occur in the case of structural differences, e.g., concerning deciding what constitutes work of equal value.[51] As a result, however, only part of the gender pay gap can potentially be reduced by the EU Pay Transparency Directive. But even in this respect, the potential of the rules is subject to certain limitations. Certainly, the Directive takes on a more

46 The EU is also endeavouring to make progress in this respect with further measures. See on this European Commission, above n. 33, pp. 32 et seq.

47 In detail, see H. Trübenbach, *Neue Wege zur Entgeltgleichheit zwischen Frauen und Männern*, Duncker & Humblot, Berlin 2024, pp. 92 et seq.; on pp. 95 et seq. the author states, '*dass das genaue Entgeltdiskriminierungsausmaß in Deutschland unbekannt ist*' (translation: 'that the exact extent of pay discrimination in Germany is unknown'). See also C. Boll, J. Leppin, A. Rossen and A. Wolf, *Magnitude and Impact Factors of the Gender Pay Gap in EU Countries*, Publication Office of the European Union, Luxembourg 2016, p. 26, who state: 'Despite the considerable amount of empirical work, no clear picture on direction and significance of this effect has yet emerged'.

48 Commission's Proposal for a PT-Dir., above n. 11, p. 3.

49 D. Leythienne and P. Ronkowski, above n. 30, pp. 13 et seq. In the UK, the results are comparable: see Office for National Statistics, above n. 30.

50 In detail H. Trübenbach, above n. 47, pp. 90 et seq.

51 Cf. H. Trübenbach, above n. 47, pp. 92 et seq. Also stating that explicable differences (e.g., part-time work) could be explained by 'constraints applying more to women than men'; see also European Commission, above n. 33, p. 31.

comprehensive approach than before and, therefore, regulates both the pre-contractual and contractual phases. Concerning the pre-contractual phase, the employer's negotiation process with the employee about their salary is regulated. Yet, the new provisions regarding the negotiation process can only include the pre-contractual phase of *new* hires; negotiations on salary increases in the context of *existing* employment relationships will not be subjected to the new regulatory regime. One reason is that not all approaches – such as the ban on asking about salary history – can be applied to negotiations in existing employment relationships. This is because, for example, the employer would already know the salary history, which practically eliminates the functionality of a ban on inquiring about this information.[52] Moreover, the legislator probably assumed that the regulation of negotiations during the employment relationship would be superfluous due to the transparency requirements in place. Even if the latter point cannot necessarily be agreed with, studies suggest that the pre-contractual phase significantly influences the gender pay gap. This is based on the fact that pay differences occurring at this stage often cement long-term differences in the overall salary development of the employee.[53] It should also be noted that salary increases often relate to the starting salary (percentage increases, e.g., by five per cent). On this account, the gender pay gap that occurs at the start of employment increases over the course of the employment period.[54] However, even for new hires, the regulations cannot contribute to reducing the gender pay gap in every given constellation. This is because the regulations are heavily based on the assumption that salary is negotiated. However, studies show that a considerable proportion of job seekers *do not* actively discuss their salary with their employer. These individuals would, therefore, only benefit to a limited extent from the requirements set up by Article 5 PT-Dir.[55] This applies all the more to the numerous sectors that are subject to collective agreements, where any negotiation possibilities for employees are limited from the outset.[56] Whether applicants negotiate or are able to negotiate their salary also depends on various factors, including

---

52 However, consideration could have been given to whether alternative regulatory options might be available in such situations.

53 S. Napari, above n. 13, 142 shows, regarding Finnish employees, that a gender pay gap exists from the outset and then increases significantly within the first 10 years. On how gender differences in starting salaries result from different negotiating behaviour, see J. Säve-Söderbergh, above n. 13, 35 et seq.

54 J. Mazei, J. Hüffmeier, P.A. Freund, A.F. Stuhlmacher, L. Bilke and G. Hertel, above n. 13, 97.

55 However, such persons can also benefit from the Pay Transparency Directive, especially if a contract is concluded.

56 If a collective agreement is in force, the main issue in terms of salary is the pay scale and bonuses.

gender, risk appetite, and level of education.[57] Even given the situation that applicants actually negotiate their salary, this would not automatically imply that the applicable regulations will also contribute to closing the gender pay gap. Rather, the gender pay gap will only be reduced if women are to benefit more strongly than men from the proposed measures of the EU Pay Transparency Directive.[58] This remains to be analysed below for the individual regulations. Generally, studies conclude that women are more likely to accept the first salary offer instead of engaging in salary negotiations.[59] More recent studies, however, no longer confirm this assumption uniformly.[60] Anyway, a lower propensity to negotiate among women would prove problematic insofar as the introduced regulations could not achieve their desired effect. Instead, they could even generate advantages for men who take on salary negotiations. It would therefore be essential to the functioning design of the regulations that they not only regulate negotiations but also incentivise women to negotiate their starting salary with their employer. For the EU Pay Transparency Directive to be successful, it is also important that the Directive regulates the core areas of negotiation, which will be discussed below as well. It should also be borne in mind that the gender pay gap has so far been viewed purely in monetary terms. The regulations are, therefore, also not designed to reduce any existing differences that express themselves in non-monetary aspects, such as flexible working hours, work-from-home days, further training, or annual leave. In this respect, to date, there has also been a lack of systematically collected data that allows for relevant conclusions to be drawn on possible gender gaps in these aspects. Moreover, the Directive only sets a minimum standard; so, the actual effects will depend heavily on how the Member States transpose the provisions into national law.

---

57 See e.g., R.E. Hall and A.B. Krueger, 'Evidence on the Incidence of Wage Posting, Wage Bargaining, and On-the-Job Search' (2012) 4 *Am. Econ. J.: Macroecon. (American Economic Journal: Macroeconomics)* 56, 57 and 64; on gender differences, see also A. Leibbrandt and J.A. List, 'Do Women Avoid Salary Negotiations? Evidence from a Large-Scale Natural Field Experiment' (2015) 61 *Manag. Sci. (Management Science)* 2016 et seq. (gender differences); D.A. Small, M. Gelfand, L. Babcock and H. Gettman, 'Who goes to the bargaining table? The influence of gender and framing on the initiation of negotiation' (2007) 93 *J. Pers. Soc. Psychol. (Journal of Personality and Social Psychology)* 600 et seq. (gender differences in compensation in general); M. Marks and C. Harold, 'Who asks and who receives in salary negotiation' (2011) 32 *Journal of Organizational Behavior* 371, 380 et seq. (risk propensity). However, recent studies also indicate that women may not be less willing to enter into negotiations after all. See L.J. Kray, J.A. Kennedy and M. Lee, 'Now, Women Do Ask: A Call to Update Beliefs about the Gender Pay Gap' (2024) 10 *Academy of Management Discoveries* 7 et seq. (the authors even find that women reported negotiating their salary more often than men).

58 This chapter is not about the general debate on gender differences in salary negotiations.

59 C.L. Exley, M. Niederle and L. Vesterlund, 'Knowing When to Ask: The Cost of Leaning In' (2020) 128 *Journal of Political Economy* 816, 828 et seq.

60 See L.J. Kray, J.A. Kennedy and M. Lee, above n. 57, 7 et seq.

Overall, the Directive's potential scope of action is limited, particularly with regard to effective regulation of salary negotiations. Therefore, the Directive's design does not set out to completely eliminate the gender pay gap. Rather, it can only represent one measure paving the way to equal pay for men and women. With this in mind, the decisive factor in assessing the Directive's effectiveness is evaluating whether it is likely to achieve any tangible, i.e. quantifiable, progress concerning the gender pay gap despite its limited scope. After all, it is precisely this progress that would justify the additional restriction of freedom and increased bureaucracy that the Directive entails.

## 5. PAY TRANSPARENCY IN THE NEGOTIATION PHASE

### 5.1. ENTITLEMENT TO INFORMATION ON REMUNERATION

#### *5.1.1. Regulation*

Article 5(1)(a) PT-Dir. stipulates that the employer must inform the applicant of the initial pay (e.g., EUR 42,000) or its range (e.g., EUR 40,000 to 45,000).[61] Regarding a collective agreement applicable to the position, applicants must also receive the corresponding terms on the initial pay or the corresponding range (Article 5(1)(b) PT-Dir.). According to Article 3(1)(a) PT-Dir., 'pay' not only contains the 'ordinary basic or minimum wage or salary' but also 'any other consideration, whether in cash or in kind, which a worker receives directly or indirectly … in respect of his or her employment from his or her employer'. However, according to the Directive, the information must not be broken down accordingly. Rather, it can be concluded from the Directive that only a total amount is to be stated. Information on non-monetary aspects such as holidays, flexible working hours or possible work-from-home days does not have to be made available to job applicants before the job interview. The Directive, therefore, does not combat any existing discrimination about these aspects. At the same time, this definition also prevents non-monetary aspects from being granted as compensation for monetary inequalities (e.g., the option of waiving salary for more remote work). Article 5(1) sentence 2 PT-Dir. stipulates that the required information on initial pay can be provided to applicants 'in a manner such as to ensure an informed and transparent negotiation on pay, such as in a published job vacancy notice, prior to the job

[61] For information on specific starting salaries or ranges on the US labour market, see C. Stahle, 'Advertised US Salary Ranges Are Widening in Some Areas', 18.05.2023 https://www.hiringlab.org/2023/05/18/advertised-salary-ranges/ (accessed 26.06.2025).

interview or otherwise'.[62] The catch-all phrase 'otherwise'[63] not only grants discretion in the means of information dissemination but apparently also on the point in the time. However, as the information is intended to facilitate transparent wage negotiations, the provision should be interpreted so that the information is to be provided prior to debating the salary.[64] That means that the information could also be provided just before the negotiation. In this case, the rule would probably barely produce any effect. Yet, Member States have discretion in the transposition of this requirement. This allows individual Member States to stipulate a stricter rule, regulating, e.g., that the information must be included mandatorily in published job advertisements.

Whilst the wording of the Directive's text is ambiguous on the potentially restrictive effect of priorly received pay information regarding the salary range (e.g., EUR 40,000 to 45,000), recital 32 sentence 2 PT-Dir. clarifies that this 'transparency' should allow for 'an informed decision about the expected salary' but specifically not limit the parties' 'bargaining power'[65].[66] Although recital 32 PT-Dir. does not explicitly include the constellation of starting salaries (e.g., EUR 42,000), the same rationale must apply accordingly. As a result, in their negotiations, employers and employees can agree on a salary that deviates from the priorly indicated initial pay or named range. In practice, contrary to what the Pay Transparency Directive prescribes, employers may be tempted to tactically suggest that they are legally not permitted to make, or would have considerable difficulties making, an offer above the communicated range or specifically stated salary. Less informed employees could thus be deterred from

---

62 The other language versions formulate this accordingly. German: '*wie beispielsweise in einer veröffentlichten Stellenausschreibung, vor dem Vorstellungsgespräch oder auf andere Weise*'; French: '*par exemple dans un avis de vacance d'emploi publié, avant l'entretien d'embauche ou d'une autre manière*'; Italian: '*ad esempio in un avviso di posto vacante pubblicato, prima del colloquio di lavoro o altrimenti*'. The Spanish version, however, omits 'before the job interview' ('*por ejemplo, en el anuncio de la vacante que se publique o por otro medio*') and the Dutch version formulates it slightly differently (but without changing the content): '*voorafgaand aan het sollicitatiegesprek of anderszins, geïnformeerde en transparante onderhandelingen over de beloning worden gevoerd, bijvoorbeeld in een gepubliceerde vacature*'.

63 See also the other language versions, German: '*auf andere Weise*'; French: '*d'une autre manière*'; Spanish: '*por otro medio*'; Italian: '*altrimenti*'; Dutch: '*anderszins*'.

64 For more details on the problem of the timing of the provision of information, see S. Jung, 'Der Einfluss der neuen europäischen Vorgaben zur Entgelttransparenz vor Beschäftigung auf Gehaltsverhandlungen', above n. 1, 23 et seq.

65 Also in German, French and Italian, the recital speaks somewhat misleadingly of 'bargaining power'. The Dutch version speaks of 'negotiating position' ('*onderhandelingspositie*') and the Spanish version of negotiating ability or negotiating skill ('*capacidad de negociación*').

66 T. Husemann, above n. 36, 185, had feared this with respect to the Commission's Proposal for a PT-Dir.; cf. on this interpretation question also C. Rolfs and L. Lex, 'Die Entgelttransparenz-Richtlinie: Entgeltgleichheit zum Preis bürokratischer Überlastung?' (2023) 40 *NZA* 1353, 1355; J. Günther and M. Schiffelholz, above n. 7, 569. For possible restrictions due to the objective and gender-neutral criteria, see C. Rolfs and L. Lex, above n. 66, 1355 et seq.

attempting to negotiate. However, a clear transposition into national law and a corresponding information campaign should be able to contain this risk.

According to Article 5(1)(a) PT-Dir., the initial pay or the relevant range should be based on 'objective, gender-neutral criteria'. However, disclosing the respective criteria to applicants before the negotiations is not mandatory.[67] Rather, these criteria may only be disclosed to them after the establishment of an employment relationship unless Member States impose higher requirements within their discretionary rights in the Directive's transposition. The general lack of mandatory disclosure of these aspects grants employers leeway in their informational practices. Since the parties can settle on a salary deviating from the initially stated salary or range, the employer can, for example, state the payment of an initial salary, which assumes that the applicant merely fulfils the minimum requirements of the defined objective and gender-neutral criteria. The employer could, therefore, state the *minimum* wage for the position instead of the *usual* wage. If the applicant can then demonstrate qualifications exceeding these pre-defined minimum requirements, the employer has the option of making a better offer. For the applicant, in turn, it is more difficult to argue for a higher salary if they are not aware of the 'objective, gender-neutral criteria' beforehand and their relation to the stated initial pay or range. Likewise, employers also have a certain leeway in stating very wide ranges.[68] The resultant lack of specificity and transparency would wholly counteract the purpose of the provision. This is because the information provided would be stripped of its informative value for the applicants' decisions. However, extreme deviations of stated ranges from the actual remuneration practice of the particular employer could, for example, indicate a circumvention and thus a breach of the requirements for the mandatory disclosure or could be interpreted as going against Article 3(1)(a) PT-Dir. ('ordinary' wage). In their process of implementation into the national legal orders, Member States should consider further regulating the disclosure requirements of the salary ranges to be stated, so as to grant legal certainty.

Article 4(4) sentences 2 and 3 PT-Dir. regulate the meaning of 'objective, gender-neutral criteria'. These criteria should firstly not be based 'directly or indirectly on workers' sex'. Further, they encompass 'skills, effort, responsibility and working conditions, and, if appropriate, any other factors relevant to the specific job or position'.[69] In this regard, negotiation skills are also likely to

---

67 E.g., Art. 6(1) PT-Dir. states that 'Employers shall make (information (author's note)) easily accessible to their workers', while Art. 5 PT-Dir. is limited to regulations on 'pay transparency prior to employment', as can be seen from the title. Already S. Jung, 'Der Einfluss der neuen europäischen Vorgaben zur Entgelttransparenz vor Beschäftigung auf Gehaltsverhandlungen', above n. 1, 21.

68 On the ranges in relation to the US labour market, see C. Stahle, above n. 61.

69 Art. 4(4) sentence 3 PT-Dir.

be a possible criterion, as they can constitute a relevant competence for a job.[70] As the EU Pay Transparency Directive sets up a minimum standard, individual Member States (e.g., Germany[71]), however, would be free to exclude negotiation competencies as a skill on the basis that this might not be a gender-neutral criterion.[72]

Applying these 'objective, gender-neutral criteria' factually allows employers to make different offers to applicants for the same or equivalent work.[73] However, it remains questionable to what extent other factors may affect pay. One question arising could be whether an employer can lawfully counter an existing alternative offer from a competing company with a salary increase or a better salary offer.[74] The answer depends on whether alternative salary offers can be classified as an objective, gender-neutral criterion. In this regard, despite these alternative offers being neither directly nor indirectly related to gender, the definition in Article 4(4) sentence 3 PT-Dir. is narrow. The wording 'factors which are relevant to the specific job or position' would have to be understood broadly in order to categorise 'alternative offers' as an objective, gender-neutral criterion. At least from an economic point of view, the relevance can be confirmed, as competing offers are part of a functioning market based on supply and demand. Other framework conditions that are not rooted in the employee and do not relate to their specific job, such as the labour market situation and the company's financial situation, could also constitute borderline cases for the interpretative scope of Article 4(4) sentence 3 PT-Dir. Hence, at least at the Member State level, clear interpretative guidelines on the interpretation of the requirements should be provided.

---

70 However, the German Federal Labour Court does not consider a reference to negotiating skills to be sufficient to rebut the presumption of gender-based pay discrimination. Bundesarbeitsgericht – BAG (German Federal Labour Court) 16.02.2023, *NZA* 2023, 958, 964; see N. Oberthür, 'Das BAG als Motor zur Förderung der Entgeltgerechtigkeit' (2023) 76 *Neue Juristische Wochenschrift* 2754, 2756 et seq.; F. Temming, 'Zum Entgeltgleichheitsgrundsatz im Arbeitsrecht' (2023) 55 *Juristische Arbeitsblätter* 951, 954 et seq.; C. Rolfs and L. Lex, above n. 66, 1355 et seq.; C. Röhner, 'Equal Pay: EU-Richtlinie zur Lohntransparenz stärkt Entgeltgleichheit' (2023) 56 *Zeitschrift für Rechtspolitik* 145, 146.

71 Given the ruling of the German Federal Labour Court, the German law-maker might use this leeway.

72 See also S. Jung, 'Der Einfluss der neuen europäischen Vorgaben zur Entgelttransparenz vor Beschäftigung auf Gehaltsverhandlungen', above n. 1, 21.

73 See also recital 17 sentence 2 PT-Dir.; C. Rolfs and L. Lex, above n. 66, 1354 et seq. on ambiguities regarding criteria that can justify differences in pay.

74 Regarding the legal situation in Germany, the German Federal Labour Court has stated that a difficult labour market situation or difficulties in recruiting staff can be cited in order to rebut the presumption of disadvantageous pay, BAG 16.02.2023, *NZA* 2023, 958, 963 et seq.

### 5.1.2. *Influence on the Negotiation Dynamics and the Balance of Power*

The requirements for information on the initial pay or the relevant range and the regulation of 'objective, gender-neutral criteria' will significantly impact the parties' negotiation dynamics and balance of power. This also concurs with the provision's aim, which is to reduce information asymmetries between applicants and employers. Thereby, the legislator intends to strengthen the applicant's negotiating position and promote 'an informed and transparent negotiation on pay'[75] (cf. Article 5(1) sentence 2 PT-Dir.). Moreover, the requirements are supposed to increase the general inclination to enter into negotiations. Apart from the informative value for applicants, it should be borne in mind that the published information also enables companies to obtain knowledge on their competitors' paid salaries and salary ranges.[76]

In view of the influence on the negotiation dynamic, a distinction must be made as to whether the employer states a specific figure (e.g., EUR 42,000) or a possible pay range (a so-called 'range offer'[77]) (e.g., EUR 40,000 to 45,000). Mentioning a range could potentially positively affect applicants, especially women. This is based on the prevalent assumption that women, more likely than men, tend to accept the first salary offer over initiating salary negotiations.[78] In this respect, one study concluded that women are more likely to initiate negotiations if a salary range is stated than if no salary range is given.[79] Therefore, range offers could contribute to closing the gender pay gap. However, the current state of research on this aspect is not entirely clear and more recent studies even propose that women do not in fact tend to start negotiations less often than men.[80] Nonetheless, with negotiations generally leading to higher salaries,[81] it is important to encourage all applicants – but especially women – to negotiate their pay to close the gender pay gap. The aim,

---

75 The German and French language versions are worded slightly differently with regard to 'informed', but this does not result in a concrete difference. German: '*fundierte und transparente*', French: '*éclairée et transparente*', Spanish: '*informada y transparente*', Italian: '*informata e trasparente*', Dutch: '*geïnformeerde en transparante*'.

76 See Z. Cullen, 'Is Pay Transparency Good?' (2024) 38 *Journal of Economic Perspectives* 153, 170 with reference to a previously unpublished study by Zoe Cullen, Simon Jaeger, and Nina Roussille.

77 S. Jung and P. Krebs, *Die Vertragsverhandlung – Taktische, strategische und rechtliche Elemente*, Springer Gabler, Wiesbaden 2016, p. 52.

78 C.L. Exley, M. Niederle and L. Vesterlund, above n. 59, 828 et seq.

79 C.X. Chen, V. Fung and L. Laviers, 'Labor Market Participants' Reactions to Salary Range Disclosures' (2023), available at SSRN 4599573, pp. 24 et seq.

80 P.G. O'shea and D.F. Bush, 'Negotiation for Starting Salary: Antecedents and Outcomes Among Recent College Graduates' (2002) 16 *Journal of Business and Psychology* 365, 374; L.J. Kray, J.A. Kennedy and M. Lee, above n. 57, 7 et seq.

81 P.G. O'shea and D.F. Bush, above n. 80, 365 et seq.; M. Marks and C. Harold, above n. 57, 386 (who also address which negotiation strategies are successful).

however, is not to encourage women individually to engage in negotiations[82] but to create conditions that equally enable women generally to participate in negotiations. Mentioning a range indicates that there are negotiating opportunities, which could encourage women to negotiate[83] and achieve better results. In this respect, studies suggest that women tend to perform worse in negotiations if it is unclear whether there is room for negotiation.[84] Another study found that indicating relatively narrow salary ranges could prove particularly helpful for female applicants.[85] Further, studies also indicate that applicants are more likely to enter into negotiations if they are initially given the opportunity to express their salary expectations.[86] Member States could, therefore, go beyond the minimum requirements of the Directive and stipulate a mandatory inquiry of applicants' salary expectations as part of the application process.[87]

Women also negotiate better if they are aware of the bargaining range[88].[89] The indication of a range leads to more transparency, especially regarding the bargaining range from the employer's perspective. This could also contribute to reducing the gender pay gap. However, the specified range is not indicative of the actual 'zone of possible agreement' (ZOPA). Rather, employers can define the range to their advantage. The latter fact stresses the importance of applicants gathering salary information for comparable positions. Currently, this preparation is still within the applicant's realm of responsibilities. Employers do not have to provide this information.

Generally, it can be assumed that many applicants will accept the stated range as a possible negotiation zone.[90] Agreements outside this range will, therefore, become less likely – although they remain permissible. The remaining flexibility towards the upper range will probably only be explored by particularly risk-prone applicants. Also, in this regard, despite inconclusive studies, men are often considered to be more willing to take risks.[91] Therefore,

---

82 Such approaches are referred to as 'fixing-the-woman'. E.g., Recalde and Vesterlund warn against this. See M.P. Recalde and L. Vesterlund, above n. 36, 634 et seq.

83 C.X. Chen, V. Fung and L. Laviers, above n. 79, 3 et seq.

84 Cf. D.A. Small, M. Gelfand, L. Babcock and H. Gettman, above n. 57, 603 et seq. (esp. p. 606); A. Leibbrandt and J.A. List, above n. 57, 2017.

85 C.X. Chen, V. Fung and L. Laviers, above n. 79, 24 et seq.

86 P.G. O'shea and D.F. Bush, above n. 80, 374. The study does not investigate possible gender differences in this respect.

87 Critical on this regulatory option is O. Lobel, 'Knowledge Pays: Reversing Information Flows And The Future Of Pay Equity' (2020) 120 *Columbia Law Review* 547, 580.

88 It should be noted here that the salary range is not the same as the possible agreement zone.

89 J. Mazei, J. Hüffmeier, P.A Freund, A.F. Stuhlmacher, L. Bilke and G. Hertel, above n. 13, 97.

90 Cf. on the suggestive power of the range offer S. Jung and P. Krebs, above n. 77, p. 52.

91 It is a common belief that women are more risk-averse. However, studies show that distinctions must be made and that the studies conducted on that topic are not clear in this respect. Providing an overview on the state of research e.g., C.C. Eckel and P.J. Grossman,

they could draw greater benefits from possible deviations from the stated range than women. In contrast, women could be discouraged from doing the same because of fear of the so-called 'backlash effect'. The backlash effect indicates that women who do not behave in a gender-stereotypical manner in negotiations (e.g., those who negotiate brashly or overly confidently) must expect negative consequences from their negotiating partner.[92] Trying to negotiate a wage outside the given salary range could be perceived as aggressive and, therefore, not in line with gender stereotypes. However, literature also suggests that demands from women within the salary range mentioned could at least cause a lesser prominent backlash effect than would be the case if the range were not mentioned at all.[93] This reduced backlash effect could possibly encourage women to make higher demands within the stated salary range. This would be an important aspect to consider for regulatory purposes, as studies exhibit that women tend to make lower demands, ultimately contributing to their overall lower salaries.[94]

Conversely, specifying a concrete starting salary[95] could lead to an undesirable gender effect. Although the disclosure of the starting salary also increases transparency, it could also be interpreted by women in particular as a signal that there is no possibility of negotiation from the outset. Hence, women could understand a specific starting salary in the sense that the employer is also only prepared to pay the stated salary. This misconception could be more likely to deter women than men from negotiating their salary.[96] As negotiations generally lead to higher salaries,[97] this could have a negative effect on the

---

'Chapter 57 Differences in the Economic Decisions of Men and Women: Experimental Evidence' in C.R. Plott and V.L. Smith (eds.), *Handbook of Experimental Economics Results*, North-Holland, Amsterdam 2008, pp. 1061 et seq.; S. Maxfield, M. Shapiro, V. Gupta and S. Hass, 'Gender and risk: women, risk taking and risk aversion' (2010) 25 *Gender in Management: An International Journal* 586 et seq.; A. Filippin and P. Crosetto, 'A Reconsideration of Gender Differences in Risk Attitudes' (2016) 62 *Manag. Sci.* 3138.

92 Cf. instead of many L.A. Rudman, C.A. Moss-Racusin, J.E. Phelan and S. Nauts, 'Status incongruity and backlash effects: Defending the gender hierarchy motivates prejudice against female leaders' (2012) 48 *J. Exp. Soc. Psychol. (Journal of Experimental Social Psychology)* 165 et seq.; S. Faludi, *Backlash: The Undeclared War Against American Women*, Broadway Books, New York City 1991, passim.

93 J. Mazei, J. Hüffmeier, P.A. Freund, A.F. Stuhlmacher, L. Bilke and G. Hertel, above n. 13, 97 assume a lower backlash effect when women state that the demands relate to standard salaries.

94 J. Säve-Söderbergh, above n. 13, 35 et seq.

95 On possible negative consequences in general, see D.N. Nevická and E. Ladiverová, 'Is the right to equal pay for equal work or work of equal value distant reality or only utopia?' (2022) 12 *The Lawyer Quarterly* 282, 288.

96 On the effect that women tend to perform worse in negotiations if it is unclear whether there is room for negotiation, see D.A. Small, M. Gelfand, L. Babcock and H. Gettman, above n. 57, 603 et seq. (especially p. 606); A. Leibbrandt and J.A. List, above n. 57, 2017.

97 P.G. O'Shea and D.F. Bush, above n. 80, 365 et seq.; M. Marks and C. Harold, above n. 57, 386 (who also address which negotiation strategies are successful).

gender pay gap. To counteract this possible effect, the Member States could also require companies to state whether (or not) they are open to negotiating the pay further in the case of a specifically stated initial pay level as part of the implementation process.[98] This requirement would at least ensure the desired transparency for the scope of salary negotiation. For an even higher level of transparency, the requirement could also include the disclosure of willingness to negotiate on the salary range (and possibly also outside the stated range). In the event of a willingness to negotiate, the latter requirement, alongside the option to mandatorily inquire about the applicant's expectations, could increase the overall likelihood of salary negotiations, which particularly women could profit from.

From a tactical negotiation perspective, stating an initial pay level or its range primarily affects the otherwise existing information asymmetries between the applicant and the employer. Information asymmetries generally lead to negotiation imbalances.[99] The specific constellation of salary negotiations implies a typically weaker position of the applicant. This is due to the fact that employers usually know the job market well and are often able to accurately assess their BATNA (best alternative to a negotiated agreement).[100] This means employers are particularly good at estimating their chances of attracting another candidate[101] for a certain salary.[102] Based on their industry-specific knowledge, they can often also estimate the job applicant's alternatives quite well (i.e., the applicant's BATNA). In comparison, job applicants are comparatively less well-informed. Although applicants may be able to determine their own BATNA,[103] they generally face more difficulties in assessing the employer's alternatives,

[98] On the positive effects of indicating the possibility of negotiation, see A. Leibbrandt and J.A. List, above n. 57, 2016 et seq.

[99] Recital 32 sentence 1 PT-Dir.

[100] BATNA is a key concept in negotiation science, which R. Fisher, W.L. Ury and B. Patton in particular focused on in their book 'Getting to Yes' (R. Fisher, W.L. Ury and B. Patton, *Getting to Yes: Negotiating Agreement without Giving In*, revised ed., Penguin, London 2012, pp. 99 et seq.). J.F. Nash also emphasised the relevance of negotiation alternatives as early as 1950, J.F. Nash, 'The Bargaining Problem' (1950) 18 *Econometrica* 155 et seq.

[101] This does not apply to all situations. This may not be the case for SMEs that need to fill a management position, e.g., as they have little or no experience with such appointments.

[102] Conversely, the Bundesvereinigung der Deutschen Arbeitgeberverbände (Confederation of German Employers' Associations) fears that the regulation could be used to obtain sensitive salary information from competitor companies. Bundesvereinigung der Deutschen Arbeitgeberverbände, 'EU-Richtlinie zur Lohntransparenz ignoriert Ursachen, belastet Betriebe und leistet keinen Beitrag zur Entgeltgleichheit', 11.05.2021, p. 3, https://arbeitgeber.de/?s=EU-Richtlinie+zur+Lohntransparenz+ignoriert+Ursachen%2C+belastet+Betriebe+und+leistet+keinen+Beitrag+zur+Entgeltgleichheit (accessed 26.06.2025). Likewise, J. Günther and M. Schiffelholz, above n. 7, 569.

[103] An applicant's BATNA may consist of maintaining the existing employment contract with another employer or accepting an offer from another employer.

particularly the applicable salary ranges.[104] In some cases, employees may not even be able to evaluate their own chances of being offered another job with another employer (and the accordingly offered salary).[105] In this case, they do not even possess sufficient information about their BATNA. As a result, employers tend to have better information about the possible ZOPA (zone of possible agreement) than applicants. This gives way to the risk that employees, regardless of gender, will 'sell themselves short' due to the information asymmetry arising from a lack of information about the initial salary or its range. While the transparency regulation introduced does not directly overcome these information asymmetries, it guarantees a minimum standard for information that applicants will receive and can consequently draw relevant conclusions from. In this context, the information received on the initial pay or pay range could particularly benefit women.[106] This applies all the more, given studies proving that negotiation differences between the sexes occur particularly in ambiguous negotiation situations. Hence, improved provision of information can generally reduce this circumstance.[107]

It should be borne in mind, however, that by stating the starting salary or the respective range, the employer is now necessarily setting the 'anchor'[108] for the salary negotiation.[109] Whether it is an advantage or a disadvantage for applicants if they can set the first anchor is still debated.[110] To date, this exact question appears to have been insufficiently researched. Yet, studies indicate that applicants could potentially benefit from setting an anchor (here, making

---

[104] This is because the margins within the profession are often high. Cf. Statistisches Bundesamt, Press release no. 423, 27.10.2020, https://www.destatis.de/DE/Presse/Pressemitteilungen/2020/10/PD20_423_623.html (accessed 26.06.2025).

[105] Well-informed employers may even be better informed in this respect, as they will know, e.g, whether comparable employers are currently hiring.

[106] J. Mazei, J. Hüffmeier, P.A. Freund, A.F. Stuhlmacher, L. Bilke and G. Hertel, above n. 13, 97 could also be understood in this direction with respect to salary information in general.

[107] Cf. e.g., H.R. Bowles, L. Babcock and K.L. Mcginn, 'Constraints and triggers: Situational mechanics of gender in negotiation' (2005) 89 *J. Pers. Soc. Psychol.* 951, 957; W.H. Bylsma and B. Major, 'Two Routes to Eliminating Gender Differences in Personal Entitlement: Social Comparisons and Performance Evaluations' (1992) 16 *Psychology of Women Quarterly* 85, 93; I. Hernandez-Arenaz and N. Iriberri, 'Gender differences in alternating-offer bargaining: an experimental study' (2023) 26 *Experimental Economics* 879, 911.

[108] The anchor does not necessarily have to be the same as the first offer: e.g., if the employer names a range, this represents the anchor. The employer can then, e.g., make a concrete (first) offer with a particular applicant in mind.

[109] Without this requirement, it is not uncommon for an employer to first ask the applicant about their salary expectations, and the applicant will therefore set the 'anchor'.

[110] This depends on various factors. As a general rule, it should be borne in mind that anchors from applicants could have less of an effect than anchors from employers, as employers can presumably counteract them more effectively.

a first offer).[111] However, eliminating this anchor option could harm women less than men because studies indicate that men are more likely to utilise the anchor effect.[112] In any case, due to Article 5(1)(a) PT-Dir., the employer[113] can now take advantage of the so-called anchoring effect.[114] As a consequence of this effect, the job applicant's 'offer'[115] tends to be biased in the direction of the anchor stated by the employer. The anchoring effect will be particularly strong if the applicant is confronted with the information at a stage when they have not yet formed any precise ideas about their likely salary.[116] The latter would be applicable to constellations where the information is already included in the job advertisement.[117] In addition, the anchor is also likely to have a particularly strong effect on job starters and previously unemployed applicants. This is rooted in the lack of mental orientation with an existing salary for these applicant groups.[118] Hence, these individuals are more prone

---

111 See B. Major, V. Vanderslice and D.B. Mcfarlin, 'Effects of Pay Expected on Pay Received: The Confirmatory Nature of Initial Expectations' (1984) 14 *J. Appl. Soc. Psychol. (Journal of Applied Social Psychology)* 399, 399 et seq. (studying the impact of a job applicant's pay expectations on starting salary offers); T.J. Thorsteinson, 'Initiating Salary Discussions With an Extreme Request: Anchoring Effects on Initial Salary Offers' (2011) 41 *J. Appl. Soc. Psychol.* 1774, 1779 et seq. However, the studies were conducted with students. Furthermore, their findings are not based on field experiments, which is why their explanatory value is limited.

112 M. Conklin, R. Choupani and E. Doğdu, 'Is it Really a Man's World? Using Real-Life Negotiations to Reframe the Negotiation Gender Gap' (2023) 68 *Saint Louis University Law Journal* 145, 154, and 158.

113 On the positive aspects of anchoring, see e.g., A.D. Galinsky and T. Mussweiler, 'First offers as anchors: The role of perspective-taking and negotiator focus' (2001) 81 *J. Pers. Soc. Psychol.* 657, 665.

114 Cf. e.g., fundamentally on the anchoring effect B. Englich, T. Mussweiler and F. Strack, 'Playing Dice With Criminal Sentences: The Influence of Irrelevant Anchors on Experts' Judicial Decision Making' (2006) 32 *Personality and Social Psychology Bulletin* 188 et seq. On how high the anchor should be set, see Y. Maaravi and S. Segal, 'Reconsider what your MBA negotiation course taught you: The possible adverse effects of high salary requests' (2022) 139 *Journal of Vocational Behavior* 103803. On the risks of extreme anchors M. Schweinsberg, G. Ku, C.S. Wang and M.M. Pillutla, 'Starting high and ending with nothing: The role of anchors and power in negotiations' (2012) 48 *J. Exp. Soc. Psychol.* 226 et seq.

115 As already explained above in n. 108, the anchor is not to be equated with the first offer. The applicant's salary expectations can, e.g., represent the 'first offer', while the stated range would set an anchor. In any case, this offer will be influenced by the anchor set by the employer, in this case, the information about the salary range.

116 See R.M. Liebert, W.P. Smith, J.H. Hill and M. Keiffer, 'The effects of information and magnitude of initial offer on interpersonal negotiation' (1968) 4 *J. Exp. Soc. Psychol.* 431, 438 et seq. on the effects of limited information regarding initial offers (anchors).

117 For more information on when the employer must disclose the information, see section 5.1.1. above.

118 An existing employment relationship is the status quo and often also the applicant's BATNA. On the status quo as BATNA S. Jung and M. Matejek, 'Multidimensionalität von (Mediations-)Verhandlungen – Teil 1' (2021) 24 *Zeitschrift für Konfliktmanagement* 102, 103. On the fact that focusing on one's own goal can counteract the anchor effect, see A.D. Galinsky and T. Mussweiler, above n. 113, 666.

to be exposed to a strong anchoring effect.[119] However, the currently available evidence in studies does not suggest the existence of any major gender effects with respect to anchoring bias.[120] Since the parties can also agree on a different salary than the initially stated pay (see section 5.1.1. above), the employer can tactically use the starting salary for the purpose of a maximised anchoring effect. For example, stating a starting salary as an anchor can be based on the applicant merely fulfilling the minimum requirements of the respective objective and gender-neutral criteria. Setting the anchor this low initially works in favour of the employer, allowing for a higher salary offer in the course of the negotiation. This could have a particularly negative impact on women's salary negotiations.[121] The same applies to the range. If the range *de facto* spans from EUR 40,000 to EUR 50,000, the employer could only disclose the range partly (e.g., from EUR 40,000 to EUR 45,000). In this way, the employer can effectively use the anchoring effect and consequently avoid outcomes exceeding the factual range.[122] The permissible lack of transparency regarding the objective and gender-neutral criteria at the time of salary negotiations (see section 5.1.1.) contributes to the tactical use of salary information by employers. In this regard, employers, however, must still factor in the risk that this practice may result in qualified applicants not applying altogether or at least in some selection effects (see in more detail below).[123] However, with the Member States' discretion to

---

119 See R.M. Liebert, W.P. Smith, J.H. Hill and M. Keiffer, above n. 116, 439, for the fact that a poor information situation favours the anchor effect. On the effects of uncertainty, see L.A. Barron, 'Ask and you shall Receive? Gender Differences in Negotiators' Beliefs about Requests for a Higher Salary' (2003) 56 *Human Relations* 635, 645 et seq.

120 A. Caputo, 'Relevant information, personality traits and anchoring effect' (2014) 13 *International Journal of Management and Decision Making* 62, 70 et seq. concludes that women are less affected by the anchor effect, while A. Kudryavtsev and G. Cohen, 'Behavioral biases in economic and financial knowledge: Are they the same for men and women?' (2011) 1 *Advances in Management & Applied Economics* 15 et seq. find that women are more susceptible to the anchor effect. M. Beblo, D. Beninger and E. Markowsky, 'It's education, not gender: A research note on the determinants of an anchoring bias in experimental WTA elicitations' (2017) 1 *Journal of Behavioral Economics for Policy* 51, 51 et seq. in turn find gender to be less responsible for certain differences than gender-specific education and employment patterns (which ultimately lead to women being more subject to the effect). T. Yasseri and J. Reher, 'Fooled by facts: quantifying anchoring bias through a large-scale experiment' (2022) 5 *Journal of Computational Social Science* 1001, 1012 find no gender differences. Also C. Eroglu and K.L. Croxton, 'Biases in judgmental adjustments of statistical forecasts: The role of individual differences' (2010) 26 *International Journal of Forecasting* 116, 128.

121 J. Brandl, L. Yilmaz and B. Schönherr, 'Gender differences in pre-career salary estimations. A classroom experiment with job offers based on the pay transparency reform in Austria' (January 2021), available at SSRN 3796934 pp. 1 et seq.

122 Comparable elements, such as a company car, might not be mentioned and could rather be used as a 'bargaining chip'.

123 See references below. Cf. M. Belot, P. Kircher and P. Muller, 'How Wage Announcements Affect Job Search – A Field Experiment' (2022) 14 *Am. Econ. J.: Macroeconomics* 1, 22 (on savings of job postings). However, on the directed search theory in the labour market, the

set up more far-reaching obligations to disclose the objective, gender-neutral criteria (e.g., the publication of the criteria alongside the initial pay or the range), the tactical use of salary information can be reduced. As part of the implementation process of the Directive, the Member States also have the option of regulating the stated range. Nonetheless, there is no regulatory option available that could limit or offset the general disadvantage for applicants due to the anchoring effect. This negative consequence is rather the mirror image of the advantages gained by greater transparency. In this regard, the EU legislator probably assumed that the advantages of transparency would outweigh the disadvantages of the anchoring effect. Without drawing from concrete studies on this, the legislator's motives in this matter remain speculative.

In general, the effect of indicating the salary or the corresponding range will probably also depend on the specific time at which the applicant receives the information (for the flexibility on this aspect as granted by the Directive, see section 5.1.1. above). If the relevant information is already included in the job advertisement, which Member States have the discretion to establish as a mandatory practice, there is a high likelihood of effects on the applications for such positions.[124] In this context, one study indicates that women are more likely to be deterred from applications where a wide salary range is listed.[125] Smaller salary ranges, however, seem more likely to encourage women to apply than men.[126] This evidence suggests that the Member States should carefully design their requirements for employers to disclose these details and the determination of the range. Determining the range in detail will prove particularly important, considering evidence from studies on the situation in the US. Here, the results show that some companies specify particularly large ranges. The wide scope of these ranges considerably undermines the purpose of disclosing such information.[127]

If, however, the information is only disclosed immediately before the salary negotiation, the applicant can hardly process the information and consciously orientate their negotiation strategy accordingly. Therefore, this approach would also limit the effect of providing prior information.[128] The regulation could then most likely not contribute to closing the gender pay gap. Thus, Member

---

research situation is complex. In this respect, gender effects, too, have to be taken into account.

124 On this, see the references below. K.M. Kuhn, 'Ambiguity in advertised compensation: Recruiting implications of nominal compliance with pay transparency legislation' (2024) 109 *J. Appl. Psychol.* 599 et seq. also shows that employers who use wide ranges are rated as less trustworthy.

125 D. Bernard, J. Croom and B. Yang, 'The Joint Effect of Pay Range Disclosure Width and Gender on Job Applications' (2023), available at SSRN 4546369, pp. 1 et seq.

126 See C.X. Chen, V. Fung and L. Laviers, above n. 79, 20.

127 See C. Stahle, above n. 61.

128 See also European Commission, above n. 12, p. 40, which emphasises, however, that the information would at least still have a certain positive effect.

States can and should set higher requirements and, for example, require the disclosure of information at least two working days before the interview, which would ensure a bigger effect on the gender pay gap. On the downside, the latter option would prevent quick and spontaneous salary negotiations. Certain negative effects from the lack of spontaneity for employers and applicants can, therefore, not be ruled out and must be weighed against the advantages of reducing the gender pay gap.

## 5.2. PROHIBITION OF QUESTIONS REGARDING SALARY HISTORY

### *5.2.1. Regulation*

In addition to pay transparency in accordance with Article 5(1) PT-Dir., Article 5(2) PT-Dir. bans employers from enquiring about applicants' pay histories. This means employers are prohibited from asking applicants about their remuneration, including their current and previous employment. Hence, career starters cannot benefit from this provision. From the outset, the regulation will benefit people who have already gained experience in corresponding employment relationships.

In this respect, Article 5(2) PT-Dir. expressly prohibits only the questioning of applicants. The wording of the provision is, therefore, very narrow. However, recital 33 sentence 2 PT-Dir. clarifies that the term is to be understood more broadly. As a result, the rule is intended to cover all proactive attempts to obtain pay history information.[129] This broad understanding is central to the effectiveness of the provision. Otherwise, various options to circumvent the requirements would eliminate the provision's effectiveness. Thus, it is recommended that in the implementing provisions, Member States specify that all proactive attempts to obtain information are prohibited. This would leave no room for any interpretative doubts. Yet, the challenge will be to delineate the exact scope of 'proactive information gathering'.

However, according to the Directive, applicants remain free to use their previous salary as an argument in the negotiations.[130] Moreover, Article 5(2) PT-Dir. even allows the employer to inquire directly about the salary of

129 The result can be achieved either by interpretation or by analogy. See S. Jung, 'Der Einfluss der neuen europäischen Vorgaben zur Entgelttransparenz vor Beschäftigung auf Gehaltsverhandlungen', above n. 1, 23.

130 See also C. Rolfs and L. Lex, above n. 66, 1356; on the Commission's Proposal for a PT-Dir., see T. Husemann, above n. 36, 184. Studies indicate that applicants would certainly make use of this option. B. Cowgill, A. Agan and L.K. Gee, 'The Gender Disclosure Gap: Salary History Bans Unravel When Men Volunteer Their Income' (2024) 35 *Organization Science* 1571, 1581 et seq.

possible competing job offers because the wording of Article 5(2) PT-Dir. only refers to current or previous employment relationships but does not entail competing potential employment relationships.[131] According to the view expressed here, the salary history ban can also not be applied by analogy to inquiries about competing offers.[132] However, the Directive merely sets out a minimum standard (Article 1 PT-Dir.). Hence, once more, Member States could introduce a ban on questions regarding competing offers.

Irrespective of the interpretation and implementation of the legislation, attempts by employers to circumvent this requirement cannot be practically ruled out. In practice, employers can, for example, make an applicant a low offer within the specified salary range. From the applicant's reaction, the employer can potentially deduce whether the applicant's current salary is higher. This is because applicants who already earn more would usually bring this up in the negotiation on their own initiative to argue for a higher salary. This possibility of circumvention could only be ruled out entirely if Member States were also to prohibit applicants from using their previous salary as an argument in the negotiation.[133] Alternatively, the legislator could also introduce a 'right to lie' for applicants. In this way, applicants with a poor BATNA (in this case, the previous salary) would be allowed to deceive without fearing legal consequences. This would, in turn, reduce employers' ability to obtain reliable information.[134] Regarding the question of pregnancy, such provisions already exist. Consequently, employers are not allowed to ask about this personal matter.[135] Likewise, it is also legally recognised that women have a right to lie and, therefore, do not have to fear any legal consequences if they deceive a potential employer about this aspect.[136] However, that situation is not entirely

---

131 In this respect, an analogy also appears to be problematic, as the situations are not fully comparable.

132 See already S. Jung, 'Der Einfluss der neuen europäischen Vorgaben zur Entgelttransparenz vor Beschäftigung auf Gehaltsverhandlungen', above n. 1, 23.

133 On such dynamics, see also O. Lobel, above n. 87, 580.

134 One study suggests that applicants would also make use of this option. See S. Khanna, 'Salary History Bans and Wage Bargaining: Experimental Evidence' (2020) 65 *Labour Econ.* 101853.

135 For the case law of the European Court of Justice, see e.g., G. Thüsing in *Münchener Kommentar BGB*, vol. 1, 10th ed., C.H. Beck, Munich 2025, AGG Section 8 marginal nn. 23 et seq. On the legal situation in Germany, see e.g., C. Armbrüster in *Münchener Kommentar BGB*, vol. 1, 10th ed. C.H. Beck, Munich 2025, Section 123 marginal n. 49; A. Feuerborn in *NomosKommentar BGB*, vol 1, 4th ed., Nomos, Baden-Baden 2021, Section 123 marginal n. 56. Generally on the treatment of pregnant women under EU law, see C. Barnard, *EU Employment Law*, 4th ed., Oxford University Press, Oxford 2012, pp. 403 et seq.

136 On the legal situation in Germany, see e.g., M. Rehberg in *Beck Online-Großkommentar (BeckOGK) BGB*, as of 01.05.2025, C.H. Beck, Munich, Section 123 marginal nn. 31, 36; C. Armbrüster in *Münchener Kommentar BGB*, vol. 1, 10th ed., C.H. Beck, Munich 2025, Section 123 marginal nn. 19, 47; A. Feuerborn in *NomosKommentar BGB*, vol 1, 4th ed. Nomos, Baden-Baden 2021, Section 123 marginal n. 45.

comparable to the question about salary history. If the applicant lies about her pregnancy, there is practically no way for the employer to establish this. This is because requesting relevant documents or proof is socially unacceptable. Yet, it is quite common for employers to ask for current employment contracts during salary negotiations to check the stated previous salary. This circumstance makes it much easier to uncover a lie about previous salary if employers unlawfully request the relevant information. Should an applicant refuse to provide these documents, employers could draw conclusions regardless. At the same time, the right to lie does not mean that the applicant may go so far as to falsify documents.

It should also be noted that employers can sometimes estimate the salary very well without any active inquiry or presentation of documents. This applies at least to cases where they know the applicant's exact position and area of responsibility in a specific company. These details can still be lawfully obtained by employers, which limits the effect of the rule.

Furthermore, the Directive does not explicitly stipulate that pay history must not play a role in determining the applicant's salary. Indirectly, this could possibly result from the requirement that employers must create pay structures based on objective, gender-neutral criteria (Article 4(3) sentence 1 PT-Dir.). The applicant's pay history should not be considered if it is assumed that it does not constitute such a criterion.[137] If the ECJ does not confirm this interpretation, the Member States could, however, prescribe a corresponding requirement by way of their discretion in the Directive's transposition. In practice, however, there is a risk that once the employer gains knowledge of the previous salary, it will nevertheless be considered when determining salary. In this respect, employers could be tempted to achieve this outcome by strategically making use of their discretionary room regarding the pay assessment.

In conclusion, it can be stated that the effect of the prohibition of questions pursuant to Article 5(2) PT-Dir. will depend heavily on the interpretation of the provision and its implementation by the Member States. Irrespectively, it will probably not be possible to completely prevent the acquisition of information on applicants' salary history and the consequential influence of this information on remuneration in practice. However, Article 5(2) PT-Dir. could constitute a major step in this direction if it is implemented extensively.[138]

---

137 See S. Jung, 'Der Einfluss der neuen europäischen Vorgaben zur Entgelttransparenz vor Beschäftigung auf Gehaltsverhandlungen', above n. 1, 24.

138 On similar legislative efforts in the US, O. Lobel, above n. 87, 579 reflects: 'although these reforms have corrective potential, their ability to close the gender gap remains limited'. And on p. 580: 'Any meaningful reform that considers gender differences in negotiations, as well as gender biases that continue to plague salary structures, must do more than merely ban salary inquiries'.

### 5.2.2. *Influence on the Negotiation Dynamics and the Balance of Power*

The ban on questions described above has an impact on the negotiation dynamics and the balance of power. The rule aims to balance negotiations by preventing employers from obtaining pay history information, which means reducing transparency. The rule will affect the negotiation dynamics because the current employment relationship and salary often represent the applicant's BATNA.[139] This applies at least if the applicant can continue the existing contract and there is no more attractive offer from another employer available. Therefore, if the employer finds out the current salary or the competing offer, he can assess the applicant's negotiating position reasonably well. By knowing his own BATNA, he is also aware of any possible existing agreement zone (ZOPA).[140] Therefore, the employer can theoretically concentrate on claiming the largest possible share of the so-called 'negotiation pie'[141] for himself, even if, in practice, many other aspects also play a role (such as budgets, long-term employee satisfaction, etc.). However, it is much more difficult for the applicant to ascertain the employer's negotiating strength and the ZOPA. This lack of knowledge leads to a disadvantage for the applicant when negotiating with the employer.[142] Even information about a former employment relationship is relevant for the employer. This applies regardless of the fact that this information does not provide any concrete information about the applicant's BATNA.[143] However, it still operates as a signal from the labour market[144] and regularly gives the employer an indication of the applicant's expectations.[145] This negotiation situation perpetuates gender-specific pay gaps, as the gap already arises at the starting salary. The existing

139 If the applicant receives another offer, he or she even has the opportunity to renegotiate the salary of their current employment relationship, so that the situation can even improve over time from the applicant's point of view.

140 The ZOPA (zone of possible agreement) describes the zone in which the respective BATNAs overlap. See S. Jung and P. Krebs, *The Essentials of Contract Negotiation*, Springer, Cham 2019, p. 171.

141 The term 'negotiation pie' refers to the total value of the negotiation. In this respect, the ZOPA indicates the total negotiation value that can be achieved through an agreement. See S. Jung and P. Krebs, above n. 140, pp. 125 et seq. (on the term 'negotiation pie') and S. Jung and M. Matejek, above n. 118, 104.

142 See e.g. P.A. Bamberger and V. Alterman, 'Navigating the Practical Complexities of Pay Transparency: Implications for Employers and Public Policy' (2024) 56 *Compensation & Benefits Review* 37, 43 on information asymmetries.

143 O. Lobel, above n. 87, 571 et seq. assumes that the pay history will serve as an anchor for the employer and thereby harm women in negotiating their wages.

144 See also Z. Cullen, above n. 76: 'they may learn more about what a candidate could produce by seeing other firm wage offers'.

145 However, the signal is not easy to analyse. If the employee is dissatisfied with their current job, a merely comparable or slightly higher salary could prompt them to change jobs. In the case of a satisfied employee, the offer will probably have to be considerably higher due to the switching costs.

gap is perpetuated and cemented by referring to the initial pay level in future negotiations. Hence, by prohibiting questions on pay history, the Directive aims to counteract the 'perpetuation of the gender pay gap',[146] at least for cases when employees change organisations.[147] The underlying idea is that a more balanced negotiating position can only be achieved if the employer's ability to obtain information is restricted. Article 5(2) PT-Dir. accordingly aims to reduce transparency for the employer and thus ensures uncertainty about the BATNAs on both sides.[148] This is intended to reduce the employer's persistent negotiating advantage, which should benefit women in particular due to their often lower salary history. The option of simply refusing to provide information on previous salary is not a practicable alternative, as women receive lower offers if they refuse such a request for information from the employer.[149]

In contrast to the legal situation in some US States, the EU Pay Transparency Directive does not explicitly stipulate that previous salary may not play a role in determining salary (on this and on any implicit requirement, see already under section 5.2.1. above).[150] However, if a Member State were to implement the principle that the salary history may not be considered, this would weaken the option to state one's previous salary as a negotiating argument even more. Yet, its (potential) significance cannot be reduced to zero due to the discretionary scope of the employer. For employees, however, an essential tactic for obtaining a better salary would be practically eliminated in any case. In the worst case, the regulation could prevent the conclusion of employment contracts despite a possible agreement zone (ZOPA). This could be the case if the employer cannot make a better offer based on the high previous salary than he would make to a comparable applicant without the corresponding previous wage. This situation could occur more frequently with managers. This applicant group would then be particularly more likely to emigrate to other third countries outside the EU (e.g., Switzerland). Since, statistically speaking, men have higher salaries due to the gender pay gap, this could affect them more and thus contribute to a reduction in the gender pay gap. However, this effect would simply be 'bought' by the fact that actually sensible contracts would not be concluded. This may have negative economic

---

146 Recital 33 sentence 1 PT-Dir.

147 Within an organisation, employers possess this information and do not have to ask. The rule is therefore aimed at reducing the gender pay gap regarding intra-organisational job changes. See also M. Brown, A.J. Nyberg, I. Weller and S.D. Strizver, above n. 36, 1682.

148 M. Brown, A.J. Nyberg, I. Weller and S.D. Strizver, above n. 36, 1682 therefore fear a 'prisoner's dilemma'.

149 L. Frank, 'Why Banning Questions About Salary History May Not Improve Pay Equity', *Harvard Business Review* (05.09.2017), https://hbr.org/2017/09/why-banning-questions-about-salary-history-may-not-improve-pay-equity (accessed 26.06.2025). See also O. Lobel, above n. 87, 573.

150 Stressing the potential positive aspects of such provisions, O. Lobel, above n. 87, 580 et seq.

consequences. Even if this worst-case scenario does not materialise, it cannot be ruled out that the regulation could generally result in lower salaries being paid, as the BATNA argument for the applicant (but not for the employer) would be considerably weakened. However, it could also be the case that the regulation will at least effectively reduce the gender pay gap. A reduction of the gender pay gap could build on the fact that women will often have been paid a lower previous salary.[151] Hence, they could benefit disproportionately from the provision because the lower pay history makes it generally more challenging for them to use the BATNA argument as successfully as men do. At the same time, however, it is assumed that this advantage will come at the cost of disadvantages for high-performing women.[152]

Initial studies on salary history bans in the US[153] actually suggest that the ban on asking questions when hiring new employees could facilitate closing the gender pay gap.[154] According to some studies, employees with low wages (which disproportionately include women), in particular, are offered higher salaries if employers are unaware of their salary history.[155] However, it has not yet been clearly proven whether this result is 'bought' by lower wages overall. Some of the studies come to this conclusion,[156] while other studies, on the contrary, assume an overall wage increase.[157] That may also be due to the fact that the studies do not differentiate according to the specific legal situation in the individual US States. However, this seems crucial as the legal situation

---

151 This can be explained by the fact that the gender pay gap is already evident in the starting salary. S. Napari, above n. 13, 142, shows, for Finnish employees, that a gender pay gap exists from the outset.

152 J. Meli and J.C. Spindler, 'Salary History Bans and Gender Discrimination' (2019), available at SSRN 3361431 pp. 1 et seq. (on non-strategic companies).

153 Possible salary history bans in the US are regulated by the individual States. An overview of the legal situation can be found under HR DIVE, 'Salary history bans: A running list of states and localities that have outlawed pay history questions', 30.04.2025, https://www.hrdive.com/news/salary-history-ban-states-list/516662/ (accessed 26.06.2025). Providing an overview O. Lobel, above n. 87, 567 et seq.

154 For an overview, see US Department of Labor – Women's Bureau (Amy Dalrymple), 'Equal Pay in the United States: Salary History Bans', ISSUE Brief, March 2023, p. 4 https://masslawyersweekly.com/wp-content/blogs.dir/1/files/2023/05/DOL-salary-history-bans.pdf (accessed 26.06.2025); see also M.A. Barach and J.J. Horton, 'How Do Employers Use Compensation History? Evidence from a Field Experiment' (2021) 39 *Journal of Labor Economics* 193 et seq.; J. Davis, P. Ouimet and X. Wang, 'Hidden Performance: Salary History Bans and the Gender Pay Gap' (2022) 11 *The Review of Corporate Finance Studies* 511 et seq.

155 See e.g., M.A. Barach and J.J. Horton, above n. 154, 193 et seq.; see also J.E. Bessen, C. Meng and E. Denk, 'Perpetuating Inequality: What Salary History Bans Reveal About Wages' (June 2020), available at SSRN 3628729 p. 24.

156 J. Davis, P. Ouimet and X. Wang, above n. 154, 511 et seq.

157 J.E. Bessen, C. Meng and E. Denk, above n. 155, 19 et seq. (regarding job changers).

varies from State to State.[158] For example, some US States only stipulate a ban on questions, while others explicitly stipulate that such information may not be used to determine the salary.[159] With the help of these previous studies, it is therefore impossible to determine with certainty whether a ban on questions alone achieves these effects or whether an additional stipulation is required that prior salary may not be considered. In this context, however, one study points out that a question ban alone is unlikely to close the gender pay gap. Instead, the study suggests that this can only be achieved in conjunction with further regulatory efforts and, on top of it, a sensitisation of employers.[160] In addition to careful legal implementation, the Member States should, therefore, also ensure that the new requirements are communicated appropriately to achieve the desired effects. Moreover, it is unclear whether the initial positive results from the US can be transferred to the EU. In this respect, it could make a difference that the proportion of employment contracts governed by a collective agreement is higher in the EU than in the US.[161]

## 5.3. GENDER-NEUTRAL JOB ADVERTISEMENTS AND NON-DISCRIMINATORY RECRUITMENT PROCESS

### *5.3.1. Regulation*

Article 5(3) PT-Dir. requires the recruitment procedure to be conducted in a 'non-discriminatory manner'. Consequently, job advertisements must be formulated in a gender-neutral way, and gender-neutral job titles have to be chosen. Gender-neutral job titles are particularly relevant in countries such as Germany and France, where a distinction is made between masculine and

---

[158] Giving an overview, A. Cook, 'The New Jersey Ban on Salary History Questions: Closing the Gender Wage Gap One Question at a Time' (2019) 16 *Rutgers Journal of Law & Public Policy* 1, 9 et seq.

[159] In California, an applicant's prior salary may not be used to determine his or her salary for the new position, even if the applicant voluntarily provides the information. Cf. Art. 432.3(a) Labor Code. The provision does not comment on alternative offers from other employers.

[160] E.L. Sherman, R. Brands and G. Ku, 'Dropping Anchor: A Field Experiment Assessing a Salary History Ban with Archival Replication' (2023) 69 *Manag. Sci.* 2919 et seq.

[161] However, there are considerable differences between the Member States in the EU. See on collective bargaining coverage in the EU in 2018 European Commission, Commission Staff Working Document, Impact Assessment, SWD(2020) 245 final (2020), p. 12 (estimated collective bargaining coverage 56%). See also Statistisches Bundesamt, 'Tarifbindung in der Europäischen Union', 14.06.2023, https://www.destatis.de/Europa/DE/Thema/Bevoelkerung-Arbeit-Soziales/Arbeitsmarkt/Tarifbindung_EU.html (accessed 26.06.2025).

feminine nouns.[162] However, also for job advertisements in English,[163] gender-neutral job titles play a role in terms of gender-related personal pronouns and possessive articles referring to those job titles, respectively, the person supposed to work in such a position. The provision does not specify which 'gender-neutral'[164] formulations would be suitable. In a narrow sense, the formulations could only include gender-abstract nouns (such as '*Auszubildende*' or '*Fachkraft*' in German) and gender-neutral formulations (such as 'they'). According to the understanding given here, however, the requirement is to be understood more broadly and, therefore, permits all gender-sensitive formulations. The formulations commonly used and accepted in the individual Member States depend on the cultural context.[165] The requirement can consequently also be met, for example, by using both masculine and feminine forms (e.g., in German, '*Abteilungsleiter/Abteilungsleiterin*'[166] respectively '*Abteilungsleiter*in*'[167]). The generic masculine form supplemented by 'm/f/d'[168] is probably also permissible. Instead of referring to a job title (e.g., in German '*Abteilungsleiter*'), one can also refer to the activity (e.g., in German '*Abteilungsleitung*'), or the participle can be used in the plural (e.g., in German '*Mitarbeitende*'). In the latter case, the expression is neutralised (e.g., in German, also '*Studierende*'). Alternatively, neutral expressions (in German, e.g., '*Fachkraft*') can be chosen. In English, the use of the plural ('they') or formulations based on 'one' or 'you' proves helpful. France also recognises the neutral pronoun '*iel*'. As the Directive sets a minimum standard, the Member States can decide whether they want to permit the usage of all forms of gender-sensitive language or go beyond the minimum standard. In general, the Member States should also reflect upon English job titles (e.g., account manager) in job advertisements written in another language (e.g., French or German). English job titles are, per se, gender-neutral. In

162 German and French are so-called grammatical gender languages. See on this instead of many D. Stahlberg, F. Braun, L. Irmen and S. Sczesny, 'Representation of the Sexes in Language' in K. Fiedler (ed.), *Social Communication*, Psychology Press, New York 2007, pp. 163, 164 et seq.

163 English is a so-called natural gender language, i.e. its pronouns are mostly gender-neutral. See on this instead of many D. Stahlberg, F. Braun, L. Irmen and S. Sczesny, above n. 162, 165 et seq.

164 German: '*geschlechtsneutral*'; Spanish: '*neutros con respecto al género*'; Italian: '*neutri sotto il profilo del genere*'; Dutch: '*genderneutraal*'. Only the French wording appears to be broader ('*non sexistes*').

165 S. Demarmels, '"Gesucht: Assistentin oder Sekretär der Geschäftsleitung" – Gendersensitive Formulierungen in Stellenanzeigen aus der Perspektive der Textsorte' in M. Nielsen, K. Luttermann and M. Lévy-Tödter (eds.), *Stellenanzeigen als Instrument des Employer Branding in Europa – Interdisziplinäre und kontrastive Perspektiven*, Springer, Wiesbaden 2017, pp. 249, 265.

166 In French e.g., '*avocat/avocate*'.

167 In French e.g., '*musicien.ne*'.

168 The abbreviation stands for 'male/female/diverse'.

countries where the generic masculine is recognised, however, they may be interpreted using the generic masculine formulation.[169]

Whether the Directive's requirement to formulate job adverts in a gender-neutral way should be interpreted more broadly is still debatable. Research on the topic also focuses, for example, on the effects of using stereotypically masculine characteristics to describe a job (e.g., using terms such as 'decisive, aggressive, competitive, goal-orientated'[170]). Ultimately, the Directive does not intend to regulate the wording of job adverts to this detailed extent[171] and, therefore, gives employers more flexibility in this regard. The Member States are at liberty to stipulate more far-reaching requirements in this respect. However, from a regulatory perspective, it should be noted that such regulations would be extremely difficult to draft. After all, the effect of stereotypical formulations is highly dependent on the context. The Directive likewise does not stipulate that job advertisements must contain formulations such as 'Applications from women are expressly encouraged'. This seems sensible, given that research has shown such statements can be counterproductive.[172]

Furthermore, it remains open which specific requirements can be derived from the Directive's obligation of a non-discriminatory recruitment process. In this context, it is questionable, for example, whether gender-neutral language should also be used in job interviews. In this respect, Article 5(3) PT-Dir. could at least be understood in a way that requires job titles to be used in a gender-neutral manner in the application process, i.e., even beyond the job advertisement. This is because the provision mentions gender-neutral language for job titles separately and thus not solely in the context of job advertisements ('job vacancy notices and job titles'[173]). As the provision only covers the period before employment, this requirement does not apply to the employment relationship itself. However, Member States can also go beyond the Directive's minimum standard in this case.

---

169 Cf. F. Van Meurs, H. Korzilius, B. Planken and S. Fairley, 'The effect of English job titles in job advertisements on Dutch respondents' (2007) 26 *World Englishes* 189, 199 et seq. on the perception of English terms in the Netherlands.

170 See on the terminology S. Demarmels, above n. 165, p. 262.

171 This is also indicated by the recitals, which contain no reference in this direction.

172 This could be suggested by a study analysing equal employment opportunity statements in the US. A. Leibbrandt and J.A. List, 'Do Equal Employment Opportunity Statements Backfire? Evidence From a Natural Field Experiment on Job-Entry Decisions' (2018) *NBER (National Bureau of Economic Research)* Working Paper 25035 pp. 1, 2 et seq.

173 German: '*Stellenausschreibungen und Berufsbezeichnungen*'; French: '*les offres d'emploi et les dénominations de postes*'; Spanish: '*los anuncios de las vacantes de trabajo y las denominaciones de los puestos de trabajo*'; Italian: '*avvisi di posto vacante e i titoli professionali*'; Dutch: '*vacatures en functiebenamingen*'.

### 5.3.2. *Influence on the Negotiation Dynamics and the Balance of Power*

Article 5(3) PT-Dir. has to be viewed in the context of studies demonstrating that women generally feel less included when the generic masculine is used.[174] Accordingly, such studies imply that women's interest may be higher if the job advertisements are worded neutrally[175].[176] The chosen formulations may also affect their behaviour, which is why women tend to apply less frequently for jobs if the job profile is pre-designed for male applicants in terms of language.[177] Although this positive connection cannot be consistently verified in studies,[178] the regulation might hopefully increase the number of female applicants in professions where job advertisements were previously tailored to male applicants. Formulations depicting male bias are primarily found in male-dominated professions.[179] Since these areas generally offer higher salaries,[180]

---

174 D. Stahlberg and S. Sczesny, 'Effects of the generic use of the masculine pronoun and alternative forms of speech on the cognitive visibility of women' (2001) 52 *Psychologische Rundschau* 131, 134 et seq. (specifically on Germany); providing an overview on generics in job advertisements S. Demarmels, above n. 165, pp. 261 et seq.; providing a general overview on the empirical research on generics D. Stahlberg, F. Braun, L. Irmen and S. Sczesny, above n. 162, 171 et seq.; P. Gygax, U. Gabriel, O. Sarrasin, J. Oakhill and A. Garnham, 'Generically intended, but specifically interpreted: When beauticians, musicians, and mechanics are all men' (2008) 23 *Language and Cognitive Processes* 464 et seq. show that in German and French the generic masculine even overrides stereotype information (regarding French and German).

175 In this respect, studies are generally broader in scope and are not usually limited to gender-neutral job titles.

176 D. Gaucher, J. Friesen and A.C. Kay, 'Evidence that gendered wording in job advertisements exists and sustains gender inequality' (2011) 101 *J. Pers. Soc. Psychol.* 109, 116 et seq. demonstrate that the job appeal for women is higher when the job is described in more feminine terms. In contrast, L. Del Carpio and T. Fujiwara, 'Do Gender-Neutral Job Ads Promote Diversity? Experimental Evidence from Latin America's Tech Sector' (2023) *NBER* Working Paper 31314 p. 3 show that interest does not increase if the field in question is one in which women are very strongly underrepresented. In occupational fields in which women are relatively well represented, however, interest increases, according to the authors' findings.

177 S.L. Bem and D.J. Bem, 'Does Sex-biased Job Advertising "Aid and Abet" Sex Discrimination?' (1973) 3 *J. Appl. Soc. Psychol.* 6, 15. In more detail on the effects of using the generic masculine in job advertisements S. Demarmels, above n. 165, pp. 261 et seq.

178 Emphasising the limited effect of the linguistic format of job advertisements, S. Tang, X. Zhang, J. Cryan, M.J. Metzger, H. Zheng and B.Y. Zhao, 'Gender Bias in the Job Market: A Longitudinal Analysis' (2017) 1 *Proceedings of the ACM on Human-Computer Interaction* 1, 15. Likewise, E.J. Castilla and H.J. Rho, 'The Gendering of Job Postings in the Online Recruitment Process' (2023) 69 *Manag. Sci.* 6912, 6912 et seq. generally on gendered job postings.

179 Cf. D. Gaucher, J. Friesen and A.C. Kay, above n. 176, 113.

180 See European Commission, *Gender segregation in the labour market: root causes, implications and policy responses in the EU*, Publications Office of the European Union, Luxembourg 2009, passim. On occupational segregation in the UK, see UK Government, 'The Case for Change', July 2019, p. 2, https://assets.publishing.service.gov.uk/media/5d401e01e5274a4012298f4b/GEO_GEEE_Strategy_Problem_Analysis_Rev_2__1_.pdf (accessed 26.06.2025).

the gender pay gap could possibly be reduced by the provision. This would at least be the case if the higher number of female applicants were to lead to more female recruitment for a comparable wage.

In any case, the Member States should specify which formulations are specifically permitted for job titles when implementing the Directive. In this regard, studies confirm that not all job titles have the same effect.[181] However, the findings of studies vary considerably. For example, the results on the use of the generic masculine supplemented by 'm/f/d'[182] are ambiguous.[183] In the case of both terms (e.g., in German, '*Abteilungsleiter/Abteilungsleiterin*' or in French, '*avocat/avocate*'), one study demonstrated positive effects.[184] However, the same study concluded that the plural participle (in German '*Mitarbeitende*') and formulations with an asterisk (e.g., in German '*Mitarbeiter*innen*') were not perceived significantly more positively.[185] Yet, in France, a study investigated the impact of different formulations on the mental representations of gender and concluded that it generally leads to positive effects. Still, the results varied depending on whether the participants were asked about male-, neutral- or female-stereotyped professions.[186]

In general, the studies also indicate that various factors play a role in the wording of job adverts. For example, despite gender-neutral job titles,

---

181 A. Damelang and A. Rückel, 'Was hält Frauen von beruflichen Positionen fern? Ein faktorieller Survey zum Einfluss der Gestaltung einer Stellenausschreibung auf deren Attraktivitätseinschätzung' (2021) 73 *Kölner Zeitschrift für Soziologie und Sozialpsychologie* 109, 120 et seq.; L.K. Horvath and S. Sczesny, 'Reducing women's lack of fit with leadership positions? Effects of the wording of job advertisements' (2016) 25 *European Journal of Work and Organizational Psychology* 316 et seq. Generally providing an overview on the perception of different formulations D. Stahlberg, F. Braun, L. Irmen and S. Sczesny, above n. 162, 174 et seq.

182 The abbreviation stands for 'male/female/diverse'.

183 L.K. Horvath and S. Sczesny, above n. 181, 322 observe that women are considered less suitable for high-status positions when the generic masculine supplemented by 'm/f' is used. However, noting a significant positive effect, A. Damelang and A. Rückel, above n. 181, 120 et seq.

184 L.K. Horvath and S. Sczesny, above n. 181, 316 et seq. observe that women are considered similarly suitable for high-status positions than men when both terms are used. Generally providing an overview on the positive effects on cognitive inclusion regarding those formulations D. Stahlberg, F. Braun, L. Irmen and S. Sczesny, above n. 162, 174 et seq.

185 A. Damelang and A. Rückel, above n. 181, 121. In another study, D. Stahlberg and S. Sczesny, above n. 174, 136, however, came to the general conclusion that the use of the so-called 'Binnen-I' (in German: '*PolitikerInnen*') at least leads to a stronger mental inclusion of women. Generally providing an overview on the perception of different formulations, D. Stahlberg, F. Braun, L. Irmen and S. Sczesny, above n. 162, 177.

186 H. Xiao, B. Strickland and S. Peperkamp, 'How Fair is Gender-Fair Language? Insights from Gender Ratio Estimations in French' (2023) 42 *Journal of Language and Social Psychology* 82 et seq. Providing an overview on perceptions regarding formulations in English D. Stahlberg, F. Braun, L. Irmen and S. Sczesny, above n. 162, 174 et seq.

the wording can be male-dominated[187] and, therefore, disproportionately discourage women from applying.[188] Solely the requirement of Article 5(3) PT-Dir. to use gender-neutral job titles can consequently not fully neutralise the gender effects of job advertisements. Rather, the national legislator would have to set further requirements, such as measures to prevent the predominant use of stereotypically male characteristics to describe a position. However, if the legislator were to set such requirements, this could have an impact on the stated salary. Indeed, studies show that a lower salary is stated for job offers aimed at female applicants.[189] This is also likely to be reflected in the agreed salaries due to the anchoring effect.[190] A trade-off between reducing the gender pay gap and the general salary level could, therefore, also occur in this respect.

A study from Poland also concludes that female applicants who were presented with a female job title were assessed less favourably.[191] Hence, the use of gender-neutral job titles during the job interview could potentially also have adverse effects on women as long as discriminatory stereotypes still exist, despite the positive intention.

## 6. PAY TRANSPARENCY IN THE NEGOTIATION PHASE – A NEW REGULATORY APPROACH

The EU continuously strives to close the gender pay gap (see Article 119 Treaty establishing the European Economic Community (Treaty of Rome), now Article 157 TFEU and Directive 2006/54/EC and the Commission Recommendation of 7 March 2014).[192] To date, the focus has been placed on preventing discrimination by establishing the principle of equal pay for equal work or work of equal value (cf. Article 157 TFEU). Since 2014,

---

187 See e.g., D. Gaucher, J. Friesen and A.C. Kay, above n. 176, 109 et seq. or also M.P. Born and T.W. Taris, 'The Impact of the Wording of Employment Advertisements on Students' Inclination to Apply for a Job' (2010) 150 *The Journal of Social Psychology* 485 et seq. on subtle differences between traits and behaviour terms. Additionally analysing gender-associated terms A. Damelang and A. Rückel, above n. 181, 121 (although the results are not statistically significant).

188 At least recognising a significant effect on the attractiveness of the job advertisement A. Damelang and A. Rückel, above n. 181, 121.

189 S. Chaturvedi, K. Mahajan and Z. Siddique, 'Words Matter: Gender, Jobs and Applicant Behavior' (June 2021), Discussion Paper 21747, School of Economics, Bristol, available at SSRN 4730629 pp. 1 et seq.

190 For the anchor effect, see already above n. 114.

191 M. Formanowicz, S. Bedynska, A. Cisłak, F. Braun and S. Sczesny, 'Side effects of gender-fair language: How feminine job titles influence the evaluation of female applicants' (2013) 43 *European Journal of Social Psychology* 62 et seq.

192 For the development of the legal framework, see e.g., T. Husemann, above n. 36, 167 et seq.; A. Baumgärtner in *BeckOGK BGB*, as of 01.06.2025, C.H. Beck, Munich, AGG Section 5 marginal nn. 73 et seq.; more broadly also C. Langenfeld and R. Lehner

the European Commission has recommended that Member States achieve this goal, especially through greater transparency.[193] As a result, Germany introduced the Pay Transparency Act in 2017.[194] France[195] and the UK[196] also undertook regulatory efforts to realise the principle of equal pay for equal work and work of equal value. What these legal requirements have in common is that they are primarily aimed at the employment relationship, even though some pre-contractual aspects are covered as well.[197] The aim of equal pay is generally to be achieved through a mixture of transparency measures during the employment relationship and restrictions on the freedom of contract. The new EU Pay Transparency Directive initially pursues this approach further and expands the corresponding regulatory framework. For example, the Directive provides for standards for transparency during the employment relationship and prohibits contractual clauses that prevent the exchange of salary information. These instruments are complemented by procedural provisions which improve the enforceability of claims.

What is particularly noteworthy, however, is that the EU Pay Transparency Directive now also encompasses the pre-contractual period and thus chooses a novel regulatory approach. Article 5 PT-Dir. is designed to regulate the negotiation process. Also, in this respect, the provision is initially aimed

---

in E. Grabitz, M. Hilf and M. Nettesheim (eds.), *Recht der Europäischen Union*, 84th supplementary delivery January 2025, C.H. Beck, Munich, AEUV Art. 157 marginal nn. 5 et seq.

193 Commission Recommendation 2014/124/EU of 7 March 2014 on strengthening the principle of equal pay between men and women through transparency [2014] *OJ* L 69/112.

194 Entgelttransparenzgesetz, 30.06.2017, BGBl. I p. 2152.

195 In France, the Code du travail (C. trav.), in particular, contains corresponding provisions. In addition to a general prohibition of discrimination under labour law (Art. L. 1132-1 C. trav.), the principle of equal pay for equal work and work of equal value is also explicitly regulated in France (Art. L. 3221-2 C. trav.). Entrepreneurs in France should work towards closing the gender pay gap (Art. L. 1142-7 C. trav.). Cf. on these provisions e.g., F. Duquesne, above n. 8, passim; G. Auzero, D. Baugard and E. Dockès, above n. 9, passim.

196 The starting point for regulatory efforts in the UK is the Equal Pay Act 1970, which was initially adopted in the course of EU legislation and is now largely out of force. Cf. e.g., S.B. Lahuerta, P. Rejchrt and A. Patrick, 'The UK Pay Transparency Regulations: apparent transparency without accountability?' (2024) 44 *Legal Studies* 21, 22. Sections 39–83 EqA 2010 now contain general provisions to protect employees from discrimination. In this context, ss. 64–80 EqA 2010 are specifically aimed at regulating sex equality in the professional sphere. Finally, the Equality Act 2010 (Gender Pay Gap Information) Regulations (GPGIR) of 2017 concretise disclosure obligations.

197 According to Art. L. 1134-1 (1) C. trav. (Code du travail) applicants can, e.g., already sue for discrimination. Art. L. 1221-6 C. trav. also stipulates that questions at the job interview must be directly and necessarily related to the assessment of the applicant's professional suitability. Gender-neutral job offers have also already been made standard in France (Art. L. 1142-1 No. 1 C. trav.), unless it is a profession defined on a state list for which gender is relevant (Art. L. 1142-2 C. trav.). In the UK, applicants are also expressly treated as employees in s. 39 EqA 2010, thus covering the pre-contractual dimension at least to some extent. In Germany, question bans for employers, in particular, are being discussed regarding the pre-contractual phase.

at transparency and requires employers to provide the applicant with pay information prior to negotiation (Article 5(1) PT-Dir.). Conversely, by prohibiting questions about prior salary, the Directive also aims to limit employers' ability to obtain information that could lead to disparate pay (Article 5(2) PT-Dir.). In addition, a non-discriminatory application procedure is required, including gender-neutral job advertisements (Article 5(3) PT-Dir.). This is the first time the EU has comprehensively regulated the pre-contractual negotiation phase. In this way, the provisions restrict not only the freedom of contract but also the freedom of negotiation. To reduce the gender pay gap, the freedom of the parties to organise the negotiation process is being curtailed. Through a combination of restrictions on freedom of negotiation and freedom of contract, the EU legislator strives for pay equality between the sexes. The EU lawmaker realised that a focus merely on restrictions to the freedom of contract would not solve the problem.

This new regulatory approach aligns with the increasing tendency of the EU regulator to govern the negotiation phase. Particularly in situations where the options for further substantive regulation appear to be largely exhausted (at least politically), the EU legislator seems to be increasingly considering restricting the freedom of negotiation. This trend has been particularly noticeable in the last two decades. For example, special negotiations, such as those on corporate co-determination in the SE (Societas Europaea), are subject to special requirements. The SE was introduced at the European level in 2001, and the SE Directive[198] dedicates its Section II to the 'negotiating procedure' and regulates, among other things, the establishment of a negotiating body (Article 3 SE Directive) and the duration of negotiations (Article 5 SE Directive). The restrictions on the freedom of negotiation are combined with restrictions on the freedom of contract: Article 21 of the SE Directive, for example, contains provisions on the agreement's content on co-determination in the SE (Societas Europaea). Since 2019, Directive (EU) 2019/633[199] has also regulated specific negotiations on the sale of agricultural, fishery, and food products. Article 3 of the Directive (EU) 2019/633 prohibits certain unfair trading practices in this respect. Moreover, the Unfair Commercial Practices (UCP) Directive[200] contains numerous provisions relating to negotiating

198 Council Directive 2001/86/EC of 8 October 2001 supplementing the Statute for a European company with regard to the involvement of employees [2001] *OJ* L 294/22–32.

199 Directive of the European Parliament and of the Council (EU) 2019/633 of 17 April 2019 on unfair trading practices in business-to-business relationships in the agricultural and food supply chain [2019] *OJ* L 111/59–72.

200 Directive of the European Parliament and of the Council 2005/29/EC of 11 May 2005 concerning unfair business-to-consumer commercial practices in the internal market and amending Council Directive 84/450/EEC, Directives 97/7/EC, 98/27/EC and 2002/65/EC of the European Parliament and of the Council and Regulation (EC) No 2006/2004 of the European Parliament and of the Council [2005] *OJ* L 149/22–39.

behaviour in the B2C context (see, e.g., Article 5(4)(b) in conjunction with the black-list in the annex, 8, 9 UCP Directive (aggressive commercial practices) and Article 5(4) (a) in conjunction with the black list in the annex and Articles 6 and 7 UCP Directive (misleading commercial practices)).

In addition to the debate on the individual provisions of the Pay Transparency Directive concerning the pre-contractual negotiation phase, the EU's regulatory efforts and those of the UK legislator should be taken as an opportunity to generally reflect on the concept of freedom of negotiation. The concept is still unknown at the European level, and the idea has not been discussed in Germany either.[201] To date, even the term 'freedom of negotiation' has hardly been used in connection with private autonomy in German literature[202] or case law.[203] The situation in the UK appears to be comparable.[204] In contrast, in France, the concept of freedom of negotiation has even been taken up in law. Article 1112(1) sentence 1 French Civil Code explicitly establishes the freedom of negotiation, naming three different forms: '*L'initiative, le déroulement et la rupture des négociations précontractuelles sont libres*'.[205] This principle has been embedded in a subchapter on negotiations

201 See S. Jung, 'Die Verhandlungsfreiheit als Pendant zur Vertragsfreiheit' [to be published soon] *JuristenZeitung* on Germany. The author aims to close this gap and establish freedom of negotiation as a counterpart to freedom of contract.

202 See S. Jung, above n. 201. An exceptions to this are K. Bischoff, 'Vorvertragliche Verhandlungsinstrumente und ihre Wirkungen im deutschen und US-amerikanischen Recht' (2004) 103 *Zeitschrift für Vergleichende Rechtswissenschaft* 190, 192; and N. Nolte in F.J. Säcker and T. Körber (eds.), *TKG – TTDSG*, 4th ed., Fachmedien Recht und Wirtschaft, Frankfurt 2023, TKG Section 20 marginal n. 47. See also J. Köndgen, *Selbstbindung ohne Vertrag*, Mohr, Tübingen 1981, p. 161 (referring to this, e.g., G. Hölzle, *Verstrickung durch Desinformation*, Mohr Siebeck, Tübingen 2012, p. 28). Cf. also M. Seyderhelm, *Grundrechtsbindung Privater*, Nomos, Baden-Baden 2021, p. 66 with regard to the third-party effect of the principle of equality, whereby in this respect he probably refers to the freedom of contract.

203 Exceptionally, however, see e.g., BGH (German Federal Court) 24.09.2002, *NJW* 2003, 748, 751 as well as VG Weimar (Administrative Court Weimar) 03.06.2005, *BeckRS* 2005, 30026.

204 A search on Westlaw UK merely shows 10 results for the UK (using the search term 'freedom of negotiation'). Also in the literature, the topic is rarely discussed. The first three hits on Westlaw therefore do not deal with the legal situation in the UK, but with freedom of negotiation in France. An exception to this is, however, B.K. Chatterjee, 'The Legal Status of Pre-Contract Negotiations' (2011) 20 *The Commonwealth Lawyer* 35 et seq. See also J. Steyn, 'The role of good faith and fair dealing in contract law: a hair-shirt philosophy?' (1992) 58 *Arbitration* 51, 56 using at least the term.

205 Free translation: 'The initiative, the course and the termination of the pre-contractual negotiations are free'. Generally referring to the differences between *culpa in contrahendo* and Art. 1112 Code Civil, H.J. Sonnenberger, 'Die Reform des französischen Schuldvertragsrechts, des Regimes und des Beweises schuldrechtlicher Verbindlichkeiten durch Ordonnance Nr. 2016-131 vom 10.2.2016: Erster Teil, Quellen der Schuldverhältnisse' (2017) 25 *Zeitschrift für Europäisches Privatrecht* 6, 23 et seq.

since 2016[206],[207] which emphasises the importance that French law attaches to this phase. However, the discussion to date has focused strongly on the restriction of good faith in Article 1112(1) sentence 2 French Civil Code[208] and less on the freedom of negotiation,[209] which is why even in France, an in-depth debate about the concept is needed. The EU Pay Transparency Directive, in conjunction with Article 1112(1) sentence 2 French Civil Code, could be used as a starting point for an in-depth discussion of the concept of freedom of negotiation and its possible restrictions. Reflecting on the restrictions of the freedom of negotiation will be key, as such restrictions prove to have a significant impact on the balance of power between the negotiating parties and, therefore, have the potential to also significantly influence the eventual outcome of negotiations.

## 7. CRITICAL REFLECTION

The EU Pay Transparency Directive ultimately pursues an important goal: to reduce the perpetuating gender pay gap. However, whether the Directive can achieve its goal must be critically analysed. In this respect, it should first be noted that the Directive is limited in its scope. The Directive may only reduce the proportion of the gender pay gap that is based on discrimination or different negotiating behaviour. In terms of legal policy, the European Commission should, therefore, consider adopting regulations regarding further drivers of the gender pay gap in the future (e.g., the unequal distribution of care and caring responsibilities[210]). Within its sphere of influence, the effect of the Directive will largely depend on the respective transposition in the individual Member States. The minimum standard set by the EU will probably not be sufficient to significantly improve the gender pay gap. The lack of effectiveness is not attributable to the measures themselves. On the contrary, the chosen approaches, namely transparency, enforcement, and, in particular, the regulation of the negotiation process, appear quite promising in this respect.

---

206 Art. 2 Ordonnance n° 2016-131 of 10 February 2016. On the advantages of the explicit regulation of freedom of negotiation in the Code Civil, see A. Zouhal, 'Réforme du droit des obligations: les négociations précontractuelles' (2016) *Revue juridique de l'Ouest* 51, 53.

207 Sous-section 1: Les négociations (Articles 1112 à 1112-2) Code Civil.

208 Art. 1112(1) sentence 2 Code Civil: '*Ils doivent impérativement satisfaire aux exigences de la bonne foi*'. Translation: 'They must necessarily satisfy the requirements of good faith'. (translated with deepl.com). See, e.g., G. Chantepie and M. Latina, *Le nouveau droit des obligations*, 2nd ed., Dalloz, Paris 2018, marginal nn. 173 et seq.; Picod, JurisClasseur Code Civil, LexisNexis, Paris, as of 5.9.2024, Art. 1112-112-2, § 14 et seqq.

209 Brief descriptions can be found, e.g., in G. Chantepie and M. Latina, *Le nouveau droit des obligations*, 3rd ed., Dalloz, Paris 2024, marginal nn. 170 et seq.; Picod, JurisClasseur Code Civil, LexisNexis, Paris, as of 5.9.2024, Art. 1112-112-2, § 11 et seq.

210 Recital 15 sentence 2 PT-Dir.

This chapter focuses on the analysis of measures related to the negotiation process. In this respect, a reduction in the gender pay gap could be set up to fail, primarily based on the requirements being extremely susceptible to circumvention. This observation could especially apply to Member States that will opt for an exact transposition of the minimum standards. In this sense, the regulations would impose a significant (financial and bureaucratic) burden on companies whilst not fully realising the positive effects for female employees and applicants. For example, the German Pay Transparency Act shows that this underlying risk is real: the adopted German law has so far not revealed any positive effects in practice,[211] yet it causes considerable costs for companies.[212] A significant reduction in the gender pay gap would probably only be achieved if national legislators were to concretise at least the Directive's requirements and even surmount the minimum standards set up with stricter provisions. This could prove to be the only effective way to largely avoid circumvention. At the same time, this would constitute a considerable interference with private autonomy. Accordingly, the freedom of negotiation would be significantly restricted, particularly in the pre-contractual area. In this case, the positive effects that might be achieved with respect to the gender pay gap would have

[211] Bundesministerium für Familie, Senioren, Frauen und Jugend, 'Zweiter Bericht der Bundesregierung zur Wirksamkeit des Gesetzes zur Förderung der Entgelttransparenz zwischen Frauen und Männern sowie zum Stand der Umsetzung des Entgeltgleichheitsgebots in Betrieben mit weniger als 200 Beschäftigten', August 2023, passim, https://www.bmfsfj.de/resource/blob/229484/7c1deeee794163514c0221663af940d2/zweiter-bericht-entgelttransparenzgesetz-data.pdf (accessed 26.06.2025); Institut für Angewandte Wirtschaftsforschung, Evaluationsgutachten zum Entgelttransparenzgesetz gem. § 23 EntgTranspG, 2023, p. 14 et seq. (p. 22 et seq. according to BT-Drs. 20/8100), https://www.iaw.edu/abgeschlossene_iaw-gutachten.html?fjahr=1702335600&file=files/dokumente/ab%20Januar%202023/DB_DS_20_8100.pdf (accessed 26.06.2025); M.P. Recalde and L. Vesterlund, above n. 36, 649 with further references; see also A. Jochmann-Döll, C. Klenner and A. Scheele, 'Entgeltgleichheit im digitalen Wandel? Eine explorative Studie zu betrieblichen Prüfungen der Entgeltgleichheit von Frauen und Männern' (2022) Hans-Böckler-Stiftung Working Paper Forschungsförderung No. 244, p. 58; A. Peichl and J. Schricker, 'Entgelttransparenzgesetz gegen Lohndiskriminierung: Viel Aufwand, wenig Nutzen?' (2019) 72 *Ifo-Schnelldienst (Information und Forschung Schnelldienst)* 3 et seq.; H. Baumann, C. Klenner and T. Schmidt, 'Entgeltgleichheit von Frauen und Männern: Wie wird das Entgelttransparenzgesetz in Betrieben umgesetzt? Eine Auswertung der WSI-Betriebsrätebefragung 2018' (2019) 45 *Report des Wirtschafts- und Sozialwissenschaftliches Institut* 1 et seq.; cf. also D. Benkert, 'EU-Richtlinienentwurf zur Entgelttransparenz verabschiedet' (2023) 20 *Neue Juristische Wochenschrift-Spezial* 276; on the lack of effect at plant level also L. Göbel, I. Wller and A.J. Nyberg, 'How Employers and Employees React to Rising Pay Transparency Expectations: An Exploratory Study' (2020) *Academy of Management Proceedings*. Differing, however, is H. Von Platen, 'Das Entgelttransparenzgesetz: Wenig Aufwand. Viel Nutzen' (2019) 72 *Ifo-Schnelldienst* 8 et seq.

[212] Bundesvereinigung der Deutschen Arbeitgeberverbände (BDA), 'Karriere- und Erwerbschancen von Frauen verbessern', 27.02.2017, p. 14 et seq., https://arbeitgeber.de/wp-content/uploads/2021/01/BDA_Stellungnahme_Karriere_und_Erwerbschancen_von_Frauen_verbessern_Februar2017.pdf (accessed 26.06.2025). The BDA also warned against a tightening of the regulations in this regard (p. 2).

to be set against the impending negative consequences of these restrictions. The Member States will, therefore, face the challenge of finding a balanced solution. In this respect, the current status of research only provides limited guidance. In some cases, there are still gaps in the research (e.g., about gender-neutral language). For other aspects, the detailed regulatory options have not been fully researched (for example, the studies on salary history bans do not generally differentiate between the various detailed regulations). In addition, the studies refer to the situation in the US and not in the EU. The results are not necessarily fully applicable to the circumstances presented in the EU (see also the situation with salary history bans). In addition, the interplay between the regulations is extremely complex and has hardly been analysed to date. In some cases, there are also opposing effects (e.g., more transparency but a stronger anchoring effect). These factors inhibit a well-rounded assessment of the regulations' effectiveness in advance. In addition, the existing studies do not always allow clear conclusions to be drawn. Rather, they sometimes present diverging findings (e.g., about the tendency to negotiate salary). Moreover, the different methodologies complicate a proper evaluation of the results.[213]

Nevertheless, the Directive proves to have promising potential to significantly reduce the gender pay gap, provided that it is implemented carefully and in a balanced (i.e., stricter but not too strict) manner. The negative effects of such a restriction on the freedom of negotiation are not easily recognisable. According to the view expressed here, however, there is at least a chance that the advantages will outweigh the disadvantages resulting from the Directive's restriction of the freedom of negotiation. As this is an extremely sensitive area, the effects of the Directive should be carefully analysed. Germany has carried out such an assessment, e.g., for the German Pay Transparency Act.[214] Similar study approaches could explore whether the desired results are being achieved and draw close attention to any unintended 'side-effects'. This would give legislators the option of adapting the legislation accordingly.

[213] Some of the results are obtained by simulations, while others are based on real-world data. See also critically P.G. O'Shea and D.F. Bush, above n. 80, 368.

[214] Bundesministerium für Familie, Senioren, Frauen und Jugend, above n. 211, passim.

# CHAPTER 9

# EUROPEAN PRIVATE LAW AND INTERSECTIONALITY: THREE STRATEGIES*

Martijn W. Hesselink and Lyn KL Tjon Soei Len



* This contribution grew out of a discussion paper written originally for the seminar 'Intersectionality and private law Justice' taught by the authors in April 2023 at the European University Institute in Florence. It was presented at the SECOLA conference on 'Contract law and power' held on 14–15 June 2024 at University College London. We thank the participants in the conference as well as Aditi Bagchi, Daphné Budasz and Rutger Claassen for their fantastic comments on an earlier version.

## 1. INTRODUCTION

In recent decades, intersectionality has been taken up across a wide variety of geographical, disciplinary, and political contexts. One key role of intersectionality, as an analytic, is to expose the ways in which instances of multiple marginalisation across various intersecting vectors of social oppression (such as race, gender, class, and religion) are made invisible through law and through legal concepts that purport to contribute towards a more just society. Private law theorising tends to be celebratory of private law's relation to justice,[1] but most of these efforts do not engage with intersectionality, and either marginalise or disregard private law's role in creating and maintaining injustices along intersecting vectors of oppression. While intersectionality's relevance has been noted in the context of European private law ('EPL') scholarship,[2] this space is particularly slow to recognise its significance. The possibility of taking up intersectionality in this context arises alongside a slow shift in European self-perceptions that are firmly rooted in assertions of Europe's colourblind reality.[3] This shift is particularly delayed within the sphere of private law and its theory, given prevailing assumptions about private law's political neutrality.[4] In the relative absence of a political discourse on

1 Cf. A. Bagchi, 'Public justice and private consent' in H. Dagan and B.C. Zipursky (eds.), *Research Handbook on Private Law Theory*, ch. 4, Edward Elgar, Cheltenham 2020.

2 L.K.L. Tjon Soei Len, 'Progress towards what? On the need for an intersectional paradigm shift in European private law' (2022) 1(2) *European Law Open* 363; L.K.L. Tjon Soei Len, 'Justifying racial and gendered contract in Europe' (2022) 51(1) *Netherlands Journal of Legal Philosophy* 25; M.W. Hesselink, 'EU private law injustices' (2022) 41 *Yearbook of European Law* 83; M.W. Hesselink, 'The Power of Reasons in European Private Law' (2022) 51(1) *Netherlands Journal of Legal Philosophy* 58.

3 F. El-Tayeb, *European Others. Queering Ethnicity in Postnational Europe*, University of Minnesota Press, Minneapolis MN 2011; G. Wekker, *White Innocence*, Duke University Press, Durham NC 2016; L.K.L. Tjon Soei Len, 'On politics and feminist legal method in legal academia' in M. Bartl and J. Lawrence (eds.), *The Politics of European Legal Research*, Edward Elgar, Cheltenham 2022.

4 In other areas of law, intersectionality and critical legal analyses that centre on race, have had a longer and deeper engagement even though Continental Europe remains a difficult space in which to work on the linkage between law and racial power, see for instance M. Möschel, *Law, Lawyers and Race*, Routledge, New York 2014.

intersectionality in this predominantly white space, initial questions arise as to intersectionality's implications for European private law and the theorising of its relationship to (in)justice.

In this chapter we position intersectionality as pivotal to questions of private law's relation to justice. We identify three different strategies for taking up intersectionality in the space of European private law, which offer three distinct ways in which intersectionality's encounter with European private law could produce valuable knowledge and insights. We also caution as to how intersectionality is taken up in the European space of private law theorising and the risks of changed meaning. The chapter explores what intersectionality may do in the space of European private law and how it may recast (European) private law's role as a potential site to advance, or thwart, pursuits of justice. How might intersectionality be taken up in the European private law sphere and what sort of work is entailed in intersectionality's encounter with European private law? Centring this question, we offer insight into intersectionality's significance to recasting dominant understandings of private law's relation to (in)justice in the EU context, and into the various ways in which intersectionality can – and ought to – be made more central to European private law discourse.

After introducing intersectionality (section 2) and the context of European private law (section 3), we discuss three possible strategies in the subsequent three sections. First, we offer an immanent critique of influential liberal social justice and private law justice accounts of (European) private law. This critique shows that intersectionality ought to be central rather than marginal within contemporary dominant justice theories, even on their own terms (section 4). Then, shifting from ideal theory towards non-ideal theory, we proceed by showing how liberal justice could be occupied so as to contribute towards the reparation of historical and ongoing structural wrongs in the concrete contexts of interpersonal relationships governed by private law. In this context, we give concrete examples of what this might entail (section 5). Subsequently, we consider the possibility that private law is so structurally flawed that it is beyond repair and must be abolished, and suggest that the premise of private law abolition may be the most promising strategy for rethinking European private law in terms of intersectionality (section 6). Finally, we offer some concluding observations (section 7). Throughout the chapter, our focus will be mainly on the core field of contract law.

# 2. INTERSECTIONALITY

## 2.1. AN INTERSECTIONAL LENS

Intersectionality is a lens that renders visible how different vectors of social hierarchy intersect and mutually reinforce each other, thus shaping people's varying experiences of oppression and marginalisation. As Audre Lorde put it, 'there is no such thing as a single-issue struggle because we do not live single-issue lives'.[5] Kimberlé Crenshaw coined the term 'intersectionality' three decades ago as an intervention to and critique of the dominant paradigm of American antidiscrimination law.[6] In this context, intersectionality aimed to make legible experiences of Black women in a society characterised by structural racism and sexism, which were made invisible under legal analysis of discrimination. The naming of the concept of intersectionality occurred as a necessary response to the invisibility of multiple marginalisation within civil rights struggles for racial justice, and within feminist struggles for gender justice. Intersectionality thus serves to bring experiences of multiple marginalisation from the margins to the centre of political attention where they belong. While coined as a term three decades ago, intersectionality is rooted in a much longer history of collaborative and socially transformative Black feminist thought and movements that centres lived experiences of multiple marginalisation and oppression.[7]

## 2.2. INTERSECTIONALITY TRAVELS

Since its coinage, the concept has travelled to a wide range of contexts,[8] and has settled in the heart of feminist studies to call attention to the struggles of multiply marginalised persons who find themselves at the intersection of

---

5 A. Lorde, *Sister outsider*, Penguin Books, London 1984, p. 133.

6 K. Crenshaw, 'Demarginalizing the Intersection of Race and Sex: A Black Feminist Critique of Antidiscrimination Doctrine, Feminist Theory and Antiracist Politics' (1989) (1) *University of Chicago Legal Forum* 139.

7 G.T.A. Hull, P.B. Scott and B. Smith (eds.), *All the Women are White, All the Blacks are Men, But Some of Us Are Brave*, Feminist Press, New York 1981; bell hooks, *Feminist Theory from Margin to Center*, South End Press, Boston MA 1984; The Combahee River Collective, *The Combahee river collective statement*, Zilla Eisenstein (self-published) 1977; P.H. Collins, *Black Feminist Thought: Knowledge, Consciousness, and the Politics of Empowerment*, Unwin Hyman, Boston MA 1990.

8 For reflections on the various contexts of intersectionality, see K. Crenshaw, 'Postscript' in H. Lutz, L. Supik, and M.T. Herrera Vivar (eds.), *Framing Intersectionality: Debates on a Multi-Faceted Concept in Gender Studies*, Routledge, London 2012; E. Grabham et al. (eds.), *Intersectionality and Beyond: Law, Power and the Politics of Location*, Routledge, New York 2009.

several kinds of discrimination and marginalisation such as race, ethnicity, gender, class, and ability. It has travelled also geographically, because these forms of power and domination, and thus multiple marginalisation and oppression, are not specifically American phenomena.[9] On the contrary, they are also structural features of the European Union and its Member States. Therefore, as a lens, intersectionality is pertinent to all contemporary social contexts within the European Union, including contexts governed by European private law.

## 2.3. EXTRACTION, APPROPRIATION, AND COMMODIFICATION

As a preliminary note of caution, we want to highlight that with intersectionality's arrival in new spaces, like any concept, it is bound to be modified as it is picked up and contextualised.[10] Such modifications may be beneficial from the political and epistemic points of view of becoming an effective idea and creating knowledge, respectively. However, there are also real ethical, political, and epistemic risks when intersectionality enters predominantly white spaces. Intersectionality's rootedness in Black feminism is significant when addressing potential (unintentional) adaptations of the concept and ways of engagement within white spaces that are in fact undermining and counterproductive. Real ethical and political risks include extraction, appropriation, and commodification, which disconnect intersectionality from Black feminist social and political struggles and position it as an abstract intellectual analytic that functions – counterproductively – to benefit and sustain established hierarchies rather than to challenge and dismantle them.[11] Epistemic risks include alteration

9 Contrast French President Emmanuel Macron in his speech 'Fight against separatism – the Republic in action' (www.elysee.fr/emmanuel-macron/2020/10/02/fight-against-separatism-the-republic-in-action-speech-by-emmanuel-macron-president-of-the-republic-on-the-fight-against-separatism.en): 'Anglo-Saxon traditions based on a different history, which is not ours' and 'certain social science theories entirely imported from the United States, with their problems'.

10 The moral and ethical significance of modifications to intersectionality are reviewed, for instance, by J.C. Nash, 'A love letter from a critic, or notes on the intersectionality wars' in J.C. Nash, *Black Feminism Reimagined: After Intersectionality*, Duke University Press, Durham NC 2019, see ch. 1 for a critical reflection; see also K. Crenshaw, above n. 8.

11 See S. Bilge, 'Intersectionality Undone: Saving Intersectionality from Intersectionality Studies' (2013) 10(2) *Du Bois Review* 405; J.C. Nash, above n. 10. For similar risks concerning positionality statements made by white scholars (extraction, self-affirmation and self-legitimation, reinforcing hierarchies, re-centring whiteness), see J.K. Gani and R.M. Khan, 'Positionality Statements as a Function of Coloniality: Interrogating Reflexive Methodologies' (2024) 68(2) *International Studies Quarterly* sqae038.

of the concept.[12] These risks require specific attentiveness and critical reflection in the context of intersectionality's travel into the space of European private law.[13] In our attempt to identify strategies for taking up intersectionality in the space of European private law, we thus also raise caution. Intersectionality's encounter with European private law must be accompanied by questions such as: Who gets to take up intersectionality, and when and why? Who and what is allowed to travel where? Who are and can be at home in the European legal academy?[14] And, most importantly, what meaning and political purchase remains for intersectionality in the course of European private law theorising? The question of who and what is at stake in intersectional analyses must remain central when it travels into European private law discourse.

# 3. EUROPEAN PRIVATE LAW

## 3.1. PRIVATE LAW SUBJECTS

The lens of intersectionality can do important analytical work in European private law because relationships governed by private law have significant justice implications. Private law determines rights, obligations, and remedies between private persons. In doing so, it shapes and reshapes, produces, and reproduces, interpersonal relationships. Persons subject to private law – private law subjects – include both natural and legal persons. As a baseline, formal equality shapes private law's understanding of the person: in principle, every natural or legal person can be the holder of any private right, obligation, or remedy. However, contemporary private law's conception of persons also has certain substantive (or 'materialised') aspects. In other words, it considers relevant certain differences between the ways in which persons are situated within the relationships it governs. Yet, private law has been highly selective as to the material features of persons and relationships it chooses to consider. EU private law, in particular, differentiates only in terms of certain specifically defined categories of persons, such as 'consumer' and 'trader', which are legally

---

12 These risks should be given serious consideration, as concepts that raise concerns about racism can and do become 'non-performatives', as shown by Sara Ahmed in the case of 'diversity' within academic institutions. See S. Ahmed, *On Being Included: Racism and Diversity in Institutional Life*, Duke University Press, Durham NC 2012.

13 As authors and outsiders to Black feminist struggles, we are drawn to these concerns and their pertinence to this chapter in light of our own varying positions of power within and outside the European legal academy and our various engagements in scholarship at the intersection of European private law and social injustice. We believe that extraction, appropriation, commodification, and denaturation constitute epistemic injustices that require our own critical reflection, as a matter of reparative scholarship, in light of our positionalities and varying investments in this predominantly white space.

14 L.K.L. Tjon Soei Len, above n. 3.

constructed capacities in which persons are understood to have certain private rights, obligations, and remedies.[15]

### 3.2. COLOUR BLIND MATERIALISATION

This type of twentieth-century European private law 'materialisation' is still structurally blind towards the specific ways in which multiply marginalised persons come to private law relationships. Conversely, this also means that private law comes in a very specific way to persons. It presents itself as neutral but corresponds, amongst other things, to gender- and racially-dominant and privileged experiences. Apart from very few exceptions, private law is structurally blind towards forms of oppression and marginalisation that are structurally present in our society. Insofar as private law is neutral towards such forms of oppression and marginalisation, it reproduces and reinforces them. And to that same extent, the present-day private law person is still shaped through white, patriarchal, heteronormative, cisgender, and ableist perspectives, assumptions, values, and beliefs.

The contemporary private law understanding of the person is thus no longer formal; that is, no longer categorically blind towards substantive inequalities. Yet, it is materialised in a specific way, where selective accounts of power imbalances (unequal bargaining power) and other 'weaknesses' are considered.[16] The specific materialisation of European private law in fact codes, organises, naturalises, and reproduces power to the advantage of those in more privileged positions. By taking the experiences of those who are privileged (e.g., racially, gendered etc.) as general and universal, and therefore as the norm and standard for neutrality, some experiences of multiply marginalised persons are treated as somehow more specific, exceptional, and therefore less appropriate for informing the interpretation of generally applicable rules. As a result, the experiences of multiply marginalised persons can become illegible through

---

15 See e.g. Directive 2011/83/EU of the European Parliament and of the Council of 25 October 2011 on consumer rights, amending Council Directive 93/13/EEC and Directive 1999/44/EC of the European Parliament and of the Council and repealing Council Directive 85/577/EEC and Directive 97/7/EC of the European Parliament and of the Council, [2011] *OJ* L 304, Art. 2; and Regulation (EU) 2022/2065 of the European Parliament and of the Council of 19 October 2022 on a Single Market For Digital Services and amending Directive 2000/31/EC (Digital Services Act), [2022] *OJ* L 277, Art. 3.

16 Paradigmatic: Case C-168/05, *Mostaza Claro v. Centro Movil Milenium SL* [2006] ECR I-1042, para. 36, with reference to Art. 6 Unfair Terms Directive 1993 (Council Directive 93/13/EEC of 5 April 1993 on unfair terms in consumer contracts, [1993] *OJ* L 95/29 (Unfair Contract Terms Directive): 'This is a mandatory provision which, taking into account the weaker position of one of the parties to the contract, aims to replace the formal balance which the latter establishes between the rights and obligations of the parties with an effective balance which re-establishes equality between them'.

general private law because important organising dimensions of private law relations are kept out of materialisation.

Take the example of Article II.-7:207 DCFR (Unfair Exploitation).[17] Pursuant to this provision,

> (1) A party may avoid a contract if, at the time of the conclusion of the contract:
> (a) the party was dependent on or had a relationship of trust with the other party, was in economic distress or had urgent needs, was improvident, ignorant, inexperienced or lacking in bargaining skill; and
> (b) the other party knew or could reasonably be expected to have known this and, given the circumstances and purpose of the contract, exploited the first party's situation by taking an excessive benefit or grossly unfair advantage.

This general European private law articulation says nothing more about 'the person'. All we know is that they were dependent on or had a relationship of trust with the other party, were in economic distress or had urgent needs, were improvident, ignorant, inexperienced, or lacking in bargaining skill. But how did they end up being dependent, in economic distress, or with urgent needs? Through what process are parties labelled improvident, ignorant, inexperienced, or lacking in bargaining skill? Whom does private law consider 'ignorant' and 'lacking in skill'? Why do they have to prove their own 'weakness' in order to be relieved from the exploitative contract?[18] And what and whose purpose do these private law dichotomies serve? Are members of privileged and dominant groups as likely to end up in predicaments that render them some version of 'less competent' than multiply marginalised contracting parties? Are structural oppression and marginalisation in society not likely to be reproduced also in contractual relationships? If so, then why does private law turn a blind eye to the structural dimensions of (pre) contractual exploitation?

What is more, the provision does not convey or reveal anything more about 'the other party' than that they knew or could reasonably be expected to have known about the predicament of the first party and that they exploited

17 The Draft Common Frame of Reference (DCFR) is meant as an academic restatement of European private law; it is not itself law in any formal sense. For positive law examples from some Western/hegemonic European jurisdictions, see e.g. Art. 1143 French Civil Code ('where one contracting party exploits the other's state of dependence'), Art. 138 German Civil Code ('a person, by exploiting the predicament, inexperience, lack of sound judgement or considerable weakness of will of another'), Art. 3:44 Dutch Civil Code ('he is under the influence of particular circumstances, like a state of emergency, dependency, thoughtlessness, an addiction, an abnormal mental condition or inexperience').

18 See C. von Bar, E. Clive and H. Schulte-Nölke (eds.), *Principles, Definitions and Model Rules of European private law: Draft Common Frame of Reference (DCFR)*, prepared by the Study Group on a European Civil Code and the Research Group on EC Private Law (Acquis Group), full edition, Vol. I, Sellier, Munich 2009, pp. 507–508.

the first party's situation by taking an excessive benefit or grossly unfair advantage. But are Black women as likely as white men to be in a position to exploit the other contracting party's situation by taking an excessive benefit or grossly unfair advantage? Does the capacity to contractually exploit correlate with cis-heteronormativity, with white supremacy, with ability? (How) does private law code and naturalise racial and ethnic power? European private law 'materialisation' does not provide any insight that would assist in answering these questions, and what is more, such answers would not be salient to private law's relation to justice.

In sum, contemporary private law doctrines, even when asserted as 'materialised', are blind to race, ethnicity, and gender – amongst others – and therefore necessarily and inherently incapable of allowing visibility and legibility of the ways in which oppression shapes multiply marginalised experiences in private legal relationships. As a result, the existing (European) private law is profoundly alienating. It ignores the fact, central to the lives of all private law subjects, that they come to relationships governed by private law, not with certain individual 'weaknesses' or 'strengths' that are commensurable and can be meaningfully expressed in the single currency of bargaining power, but with lived experiences with structural features of society that are profoundly unjust. What is more, this assertion of private law's neutrality may actually play a constructive, justificatory role in maintaining and reproducing injustice, thereby naturalising racial, gender, imperial and ethnic majority power through private law relationships.

## 3.3. THE EU'S STRUCTURAL BLINDNESS TO INTERSECTIONAL DISCRIMINATION

EU antidiscrimination law applies to a wide (but limited) set of relationships covered (potentially) by private law, including (self)employment, education, and the supply of goods and services. In other words, the pertinent EU Directives have horizontal effect (indirect, via transposition into Member State law), and thus are properly understood as (core) parts of EU private law even though they are often treated as a different subject.

However, EU antidiscrimination law contains structural obstacles to incorporating an intersectional approach.[19] The EU's patchwork of legislative instruments poses significant structural difficulties, as legislative instruments

19 We do not mean to imply that such structural obstacles are the *sole* reason why European approaches to antidiscrimination have not been attentive to multiple marginalisation. Notably, the European Court of Human Rights' jurisprudence is similarly unresponsive to intersectional harms: see the project 'Intersectional Rewrites: European Court of Human Rights Judgments Reimagined', https://intersectionalrewrites.org/.

vary in grounds, scope, legal bases, defences, and exceptions.[20] For instance, while the Race Equality Directive (2000) and the Employment Equality Framework Directive (2000) are both meant to implement the principle of equal treatment,[21] they each do so on different grounds (e.g., the latter does not include race and ethnicity) and only have a partial overlap in scope. The EU's legislative collage reflects clear, discrete distinctions between various one-dimensional grounds of discrimination and thus structurally resists intersectional analyses of discrimination that can capture multiple marginalisation. What is more, the same dominant legal paradigm of antidiscrimination critiqued by Crenshaw also drives EU legal analysis: parties must argue through the paradigm of sameness/difference to show that they have been treated less favourably than a similarly positioned comparator.[22] It is exactly this paradigm that produces a selective legal legibility of discrimination. It both forces multiply marginalised people to explicate their experiences only to the extent that they are comparable and similar to experiences of discrimination of more privileged others, and marks multiply marginalised people as exceptions because they are deemed too different from norm-setting privileged subjects.

As a result, EU antidiscrimination law is structurally blind in two distinct ways. First, the law is blind to discriminations at the intersection of different discrimination types addressed within one single Directive (for example, religion and age, or disability and sexual orientation, in the case of the Framework Directive). Second – and most relevant here – the law is blind towards discrimination that occurs at the intersection of these two Directives, such as the intersection between sex and race, which renders discrimination of women of colour invisible. This has become obvious in the infamous line of 'headscarf cases' where the Court of Justice privileges 'the right to conduct a business' over the right of Muslim women to wear a headscarf at work.[23] As has been pointed out by Nozizwe Dube, 'by concealing itself behind the single-axis framework that characterises EU non-discrimination law, the Court does not acknowledge the entirety and complexity of the disadvantage that victims of intersectional discrimination face'.[24] This in spite of attempts by some of

---

20 S. Fredman, 'Intersectional discrimination in EU gender equality and non-discrimination law', European Commission Report, May 2016, ch. 5, https://op.europa.eu/en/publication-detail/-/publication/d73a9221-b7c3-40f6-8414-8a48a2157a2f.

21 See Council Directive 2000/43/EC of 29 June 2000 implementing the principle of equal treatment between persons irrespective of racial or ethnic origin, [2000] *OJ* L 180, Art. 1; Council Directive 2000/78/EC of 27 November 2000 establishing a general framework for equal treatment in employment and occupation, [2000] *OJ* L 303, Art. 1.

22 See K. Crenshaw, above n. 6, 148–149; S. Fredman, above n. 20, ch. 5, p. 65.

23 See e.g. Joined Cases (C-804/18) *I.X. v. WABE eV* and (C-341/19) *M.H. Müller Handels GmbH v. M.J*, 15.072021, ECLI:EU:C:2021:594.

24 N. Dube, 'Not just another Islamic headscarf case: LF v SCRL and the CJEU's missed opportunity to inch closer to acknowledging intersectionality', *ELB Blogpost* 4/2023, 19.01.2023.

its Advocates General to point the Court in the right direction.[25] Moreover, as a general matter, in its interpretations of non-discrimination law, the Court seems to be particularly colour blind in that it privileges ethnicity discourse over race.[26]

Both directives are currently under review. And intersectionality has been tabled by the European Commission as a possible concern.[27] However, in the Commission's reading, like in much of the relevant European literature, intersectionality is understood as – and reduced to – the problem of multiple discrimination.[28] In this respect, the European Parliament has made a better attempt to acknowledge intersectionality in a recent resolution, which underlines that 'intersectional discrimination differs from multiple discrimination'.[29] In the resolution, the European Parliament acknowledges that 'in the case of intersectional discrimination, the grounds of discrimination are intertwined, which creates a unique type of discrimination', that 'applying an intersectional analysis allows us to address and understand social inequalities, exclusion and discrimination from a comprehensive, systemic and structural perspective, while overcoming a single-axis approach to discrimination', and that 'intersectional policies cannot be implemented without centring racialised people at the intersections of discrimination'.[30]

---

25 See Opinion of Advocate General Kokott (C-443/15 *Parris v. Trinity College Dublin*), 30.06.2016, ECLI:EU:C:2016:493 (with specific reference to Crenshaw). See also Opinion of Advocate General Medina, C-344/20 *LF v SCRL*, 28.04.2022, ECLI:EU:C:2022:328.

26 To be more precise, the Court follows the language of the directive of 'racial origin', as if somehow racialised persons *arrived* – and hence are newcomers. The Race Equality Directive, moreover, refers to racial *or* ethnic origin, structurally negating the reality that race and ethnicity can intersect to shape experiences of discrimination.

27 European Commission, 'Possible gaps in the legal protection against discrimination on grounds of ethnic or racial origin: factual summary report. open public consultation', Ares(2022)4818137 - 01/07/2022, p. 7.
See also Commission Communication 'A Union of equality: EU anti-racism action plan 2020-2025' Brussels, 18.9.2020 COM(2020) 565 final, pp. 2, 13.

28 This refers to the idea that discrimination grounds can be cumulative, such that discrimination is viewed and proven on separate but multiple grounds. This view still resists the idea of intersectionality, which identifies a qualitative shift in the experience of discrimination *vis-à-vis* a one-dimensional perspective.

29 European Parliament Resolution of 6 July 2022 on intersectional discrimination in the European Union: the socio-economic situation of women of African, Middle-Eastern, Latin-American and Asian descent (2021/2243(INI)), B-D.

30 European Parliament Resolution of 6 July 2022 on intersectional discrimination in the European Union: the socio-economic situation of women of African, Middle-Eastern, Latin-American and Asian descent (2021/2243(INI)), B-D.

# 4. INTERSECTIONALITY AND LIBERAL JUSTICE

## 4.1. LIBERAL SOCIAL JUSTICE

As an abstract matter, the injustice of structural social inequalities is widely accepted. And it is not difficult to see how intersectionality ought to be central to dominant accounts of social justice, such as John Rawls' 'Justice as Fairness'.[31] In Rawlsian terms, when a society is characterised by structural racism and other types of structural oppression then that society lacks a just basic structure. And if the second principle of justice as fairness (in its first part) holds that social inequalities are acceptable only if they work to the benefit of the least well-off groups in society, then this principle naturally needs to take into account the multiple marginalisation of members of society. In other words, what it means to be the least well-off must be considered in light of people's positionings at the intersections of multiple social oppressions. And Black feminists have long pointed out that women of colour are 'at the bottom'.[32] Similarly, the demand made by the second part of that same principle – that socio-economically relevant positions be open to all under conditions of fair equality of opportunity – makes sense only through a thoroughly intersectional reading. Finally, concerning the first principle, which requires equal basic liberties for all, Rawls was very clear that this demand should not be understood formally but in a substantive sense of the equal fair *benefit* of these liberties. In sum, mainstream understandings of social justice such as Rawlsian political liberalism are easily read as prohibiting the social injustices that are made visible and legible through an intersectional lens. As a result, these theories ought to be read as demanding special attention for social

---

31 J. Rawls, *Justice as Fairness: A Restatement*, E. Kelly (ed.), Harvard University Press, Cambridge MA/London 2001. The focus here will be on Rawls' as the pre-eminent mainstream account of social justice. However, much of what we have to say also applies to other social justice theories, in particular other liberal-egalitarian ones, such as the capabilities approach developed by A. Sen, *The Idea of Justice*, Belknap Press, Cambridge MA 2009 and M.C. Nussbaum, *Creating capabilities: the human development approach*, Belknap Press, Cambridge MA 2011.

32 See e.g. 'The Combahee river collective statement' (1977) by the Combahee River Collective, above n. 7: 'at the very bottom of the American capitalistic economy', 'being on the bottom' 'our position at the bottom'; K. Crenshaw, above n. 6, 169: 'most disadvantaged' and (with reference to the basement metaphor (p. 151): 'These people are stacked - feet standing on shoulders - with those on the bottom being disadvantaged by the full array of factors, up to the very top, where the heads of all those disadvantaged by a singular factor brush up against the ceiling'; bell hooks, 'Black women: shaping feminist theory' in bell hooks (ed.), *Feminist Theory: From Margin to Center* [1984], Routledge, Boston MA 2015, p. 16: 'at the bottom of the occupational ladder'.

injustices experienced by multiply marginalised persons, even if in fact this has yet to happen in most cases.[33]

## 4.2. DIVISION OF LABOUR

However, while the institutional responsibility of the basic structure of society for ensuring social justice necessarily seems to demand an intersectional approach even in mainstream liberal political thought, it is much more controversial among liberals that private law shares any of that responsibility. In this regard, dominant liberal accounts of social justice invoke the idea of a division of labour between private law and other institutions. On this view, which is widespread among liberal philosophers (e.g., Dworkin, Rawls, Ripstein),[34] private law is not responsible for ensuring social justice at all: while the basic structure of society has the task, in the words of Rawls, to ensure 'background justice' for transactions between private parties, private law has no part in that institutional responsibility. In other words, on this view of the division of responsibility, private law is not part of the basic structure of society, namely the main socioeconomic-political institutions responsible for social justice. And so, to the extent that the oppression of multiply marginalised persons is primarily, or even exclusively, a matter of social injustice as opposed to interpersonal justice (on which further below), private law bears no responsibility. For these liberals, the point is not that structural injustices and their intersections are not important. Rather, in their view, their importance is simply best addressed elsewhere. The reason may be either expediency, i.e., that it is impossible to properly assess the social inequality ramifications of private transactions, as Rawls thought,[35] or moral, i.e., that it is unjust to make individual private parties bear the responsibility for structural injustices in society, as Weinrib and Ripstein argue.[36] Both positions result in

[33] Our claim that Rawlsian social justice should centre intersectional oppression and marginalisation does not imply that all understandings of intersectionality could embrace Rawlsian justice. In particular, more identitarian strands are fundamentally at odds with liberal understandings of social justice.

[34] J. Rawls, *Political Liberalism* [1993], expanded ed. Columbia University Press, New York 2005, pp. 266–269; A. Ripstein, 'Private order and public justice: Kant and Rawls' (2006) 92 *Virginia Law Review* 1391; R. Dworkin, *Justice for Hedgehogs*, Belknap Press, Cambridge MA/London 2011, p. 287.

[35] J. Rawls, above n. 34, lecture VII ('The basic structure as subject').

[36] E.J. Weinrib, *The Idea of Private Law*, Harvard University Press, Cambridge MA/London 1995; A. Ripstein, above n. 34; A. Ripstein, *Force and Freedom: Kant's Legal and Political Philosophy*, Harvard University Press, Cambridge MA/London 2009. See also R. Dworkin, above n. 34, p. 43, where he uses the metaphor of 'swimming in your own lane' to illustrate the idea of a division of public and private responsibilities.

a liberal permissiveness that sets aside structural injustices as a concern for private law.[37]

There exist alternative responses, immanent to liberalism, to these liberal claims to private law exceptionalism. First, the expediency argument is contingent, and there are many cases in which we can be quite confident that the formal application of a private law rule will reproduce and exacerbate structural – and structurally intersecting – social injustices (see e.g. Bagchi, Shiffrin).[38] Secondly, the moral division of labour view relies on a natural law understanding of pre-political moral private rights, which private law must simply implement, while on a post-institutional view (as in Rawlsian justice), morally relevant rights are established through just institutions, such that private law would be complicit in the creation of oppressive, and therefore unjust, private rights under the division of labour view.[39] Finally, and most directly, private law is in fact part of the basic structure of society as understood by Rawls, because of its key role, at least in capitalist societies (and most certainly after the waves of massive privatisations) in distributing wealth, capabilities, and primary goods.[40]

---

37 For a critical discussion, see M.W. Hesselink, *Justifying Contract in Europe: Political Philosophies of European Contract Law*, Oxford University Press, Oxford 2021, pp. 300–306.

38 S.V. Shiffrin, 'Paternalism, unconscionability doctrine, and accommodation' (2000) 29 *Philosophy & Public Affairs* 205; A. Bagchi, 'Distributive justice and contract' in G. Klass, G. Letsas and P. Saprai (eds.), *Philosophical Foundations of Contract Law*, Oxford University Press, Oxford 2014, pp. 193–212.

39 A third response would be purely nominal. Private law could be kept 'pure' by calling instances of private law social justice 'public law', as often happens, for example, in the case of horizontal non-discrimination law. On EU non-discrimination law, see above section 3. Contrast DCFR, Book II, Chapter 2 (Non-discrimination), where the right not to be discriminated against is included in general contract law. See, in particular, Art. II.–2:101 (Right not to be discriminated against): 'A person has a right not to be discriminated against on the grounds of sex or ethnic or racial origin in relation to a contract or other juridical act the object of which is to provide access to, or supply, goods, other assets or services which are available to the public'. However, the provision does not address intersectional discrimination.

40 See e.g. A.T. Kronman, 'Contract law and distributive justice' (1980) 89 *Yale Law Journal* 472; K.A. Kordana and D.H. Tabachnick, 'Rawls and contract law' (2005) 73 *George Washington Law Review* 598; S. Scheffler, 'Distributive justice, the basic structure and the place of private law' (2015) *Oxford Journal of Legal Studies* 1; J. Klijnsma, 'Contract law as fairness' (2015) 28 *Ratio Juris* 68; M.W. Hesselink, 'Unjust conduct in the internal market: on the role of European private law in the division of moral responsibility between the EU, its member states and their citizens' (2016) 35 *Yearbook of European Law* 410; L.K.L. Tjon Soei Len, *Minimum Contract Justice: A Capabilities Perspective on Sweatshops and Consumer Contracts*, Hart Publishing, Oxford 2017.

## 4.3. LIBERAL INTERPERSONAL JUSTICE

Implicit (Dworkin, Rawls) or explicit (Weinrib, Ripstein) in the division of labour view is a formal understanding of private law. In other words, division of labour views vindicate, rather than criticise, the pre-materialisation understanding of private law. On this view, the specific characteristics of the parties, such as their vulnerabilities; their relationships – including their power dynamics – and their context – including how they are socially (dis)embedded in patterns of prejudice, denigration, and exclusion – should be ignored when determining the private rights, obligations, and remedies of the parties to a given relationship governed by private law.

Again, on this view, parties' social, economic and political positionings are ignored not on the libertarian ground that social justice is a mirage (Hayek),[41] but because such inequities should be addressed through different institutions than private law.

However, what about private law theories that vindicate and defend the materialisation of interpersonal justice? Until recently, interpersonal justice theories were as colour blind as the mainstream liberal theories of social justice. However, this is changing. Indeed, the relational theory of private law justice by Dagan and Dorfman, which is committed to substantive autonomy and equality, explicitly understands private law's responsibility for justice as directly horizontal, not merely indirectly and derivate from society's (vertical) social justice responsibilities.[42] Yet, so far, they have not taken up an intersectional reading of private rights and wrongs.

## 4.4. A LIBERAL FEMINIST VARIATION

Liberal feminists may see in intersectionality's encounter with European private law an opportunity for liberation.[43] For instance, the potential of contract – the normative force of interpersonal promise or agreement – promises a democratised way to shape distribution of social and economic goods between persons. With a broad space for contractual thinking (and contractual freedom) to roam, so the liberal promise goes, parties hold the

---

41 F.A. Hayek, *Law, Legislation and Liberty; A new statement of the liberal principles of justice and political economy* [1973], Routledge, London/New York 2003, Vol. 2 ('The mirage of social justice').

42 See H. Dagan and A. Dorfman, 'Just Relationships' (2016) 116 *Columbia Law Review* 1395; H. Dagan and A. Dorfman, *Relational Justice: A Theory of Private Law*, Cambridge University Press, Cambridge 2024.

43 See M. Ertman, 'Contract's influence on feminism and vice versa' in D. Brake, M. Chamallas and V. Williams (eds.), *The Oxford Handbook of Feminism and Law in the U.S.*, Oxford University Press, Oxford 2022.

power to give shape to their own ideas of desirable inter-personal relationships, whether they be intimate or at arm's length. In the context of feminist struggles for social justice, contract then holds – at least in theory – a radical potential to place formative power, for instance, of family structures, or of the scope of the 'economic', into the hands of multiply marginalised persons (e.g. countering heterosexist ideals of the family, expanding the gendered notions of economic activity).[44] In this sense, contract law can align more easily with the plurality of ways in which people engage in interpersonal relationships beyond, for instance, heteronormative patriarchal white supremacist restrictions. On this view, the radical potential of contractual thinking may allow contract to be an aid in struggles towards social justice and dreams of liberation. With the extension of contractual freedom to persons beyond formal exclusions of racialised and gendered difference, the liberal feminist view sees in private law, and contract more specifically, a potential for liberation and response to persisting and historical racial and gender injustice. Thus, on this account, intersectionality might – and ought to – be taken up in private law to further examine its liberatory potential for multiply marginalised people. However, this, too, has yet to happen in European legal scholarship.

## 5. INTERSECTIONALITY AND REPARATIVE PRIVATE LAW JUSTICE

### 5.1. NON-IDEAL THEORY

It is important to realise that most liberal social justice theories are ideal theories, and that the same applies for most private law theories. These are theories setting out what an ideal society and an ideal private law, respectively, would look like. In particular, the division of labour claim does not go further than stating what the ideal role of private law in a just society would be. And the idea is that private law would have no responsibility for social justice in a 'well-ordered society', to use the Rawlsian phrase, because social justice would be assured by a sufficiently just basic structure, which would provide a background for fair transactions among equals. As such, private law would have no responsibility for any injustice arising from multiple marginalisation,

---

44 In this liberal, individual choice-centred framework, contract represents the availability of expanded opportunities for plural family formation and recognition. Yet, other feminists critique this celebratory reading of contract as choice, and show how contract works to the detriment of multiply marginalised persons. See for instance, in the context of surrogacy contracts: D.E. Roberts, *Killing the Black body: race, reproduction, and the meaning of liberty*, Vintage Books, New York 1999; D.E. Roberts, 'Why Baby Markets Aren't Free' (2017) 7 *UC Irvine Law Review* 611.

and its encounter with intersectionality would have limited implications for general private law. Many people would consider these ideal theories utopian fantasies, detached from the bitter realities of intersectional oppression and marginalisation.

However, there exists a second way in which intersectionality may be taken up in European private law. This strategy remains internal to the liberal framework and addresses the failure of leading ideal liberal accounts of social justice to foreground actual historical and persisting structural injustices. European private law governs in a social context where background justice patently has never been assured because, in reality, the basic structure is profoundly unjust. In particular, the basic structure is characterised by deep historical persisting and exacerbating structural inequalities across gender, sexuality, race, ethnicity, ability, and class which impact multiply marginalised persons in various ways. This raises the urgent question of what private law's role should be under non-ideal, unjust circumstances – that is, our real circumstances here and now. This brings us to non-ideal theory. There exists a rich scholarship from critical feminist and critical race theorists who argue against ideal liberal accounts of justice, because their accounts *de facto* legitimate patriarchal and white supremacist social orders.[45] One response is to turn away from (or never to engage with) liberal justice (see below, section 6), while others have responded by proposing a process of more or less radical rethinking of liberal justice in a profoundly non-ideal world.

## 5.2. A PRIVATE LAW RIGHT AGAINST INTERSECTIONAL EXPLOITATION

Aditi Bagchi has argued that when background social justice is not assured by other institutions, then private law as a societal institution has a responsibility for social justice that it might not have under ideal circumstances. As she puts it, 'whatever the relationship between distributive justice and private law in ideal theory, a failure to meet our obligations of distributive justice destabilises our other rights and obligations toward one another'.[46] In particular, she argues for 'a negative right against conduct that exploits and exacerbates distributive injustice'.[47] She explicitly grounds this right not only in social justice but also in interpersonal justice. The idea is that our moral responsibilities for justice are not exhausted by the moral duty, affirmed by Rawls, to support just institutions

---

[45] Notably, C. Pateman, *The Sexual Contract*, Stanford University Press, Redwood City CA 1988; C.W. Mills, *The Racial Contract*, Cornell University Press, Ithaca NY 1999.

[46] A. Bagchi, 'Distributive injustice and private law' (2008) 60 *Hastings Law Journal* 105, 107–108.

[47] Ibid., 134.

where they exist. When just socio-political institutions are not in place, we retain what she calls 'imperfect social duties and rights' towards each other. These interpersonal or horizontal social duties obtain under circumstances of distributive (or wider, social) injustice, i.e., where society has not achieved social/distributive justice.

Taking up an intersectional understanding of injustice (a subject that Bagchi does not address) this means, it would seem, that any materialisation of private law should prioritise the spill-over effects of the main structural social injustices in a given society onto private law relationships. Very concretely, for European private law this could mean that a new EU-wide doctrine of intersectional exploitation should be centre stage rather than, say, consumer protection in the digital single market. Thus, instead of ensuring the wellbeing of 'average consumers', European private law would be concerned chiefly with what happens to people at the bottom of social hierarchies. As a very concrete example of what this might mean, the text of Article II.-7:207 DCFR (Unfair Exploitation) could be adapted to highlight and centre the moral significance of multiple marginalisation to contract exploitation.[48] It could run something like this:

> 'Article # (Intersectional exploitation):
>
> (1) A party may avoid a contract if, at the time of the conclusion of the contract:
>   (a) that party was oppressed by the combined effects of intersecting types of subordination, either individual or structural, such as sexism, racism, ableism, homo- and transphobia, ageism, and classism; and
>   (b) the other party knew or could be expected to have known this and, in the light of the circumstances and purpose of the contract, exploited the first party's situation by taking an excessive benefit or unfair advantage.

Following the example of Article II.-7:207 DCFR, a second paragraph could be added allowing for judicial adaptation of the contract at the request of the disadvantaged party, which could run as follows:

> Upon the request of the party entitled to avoidance, a court may if it is appropriate, adapt the contract in order to bring it into accordance with what might have been agreed in the absence of the intersectional exploitation.

48 The idea is not that the new article should replace the current Art. II.-7:207 DCFR, but rather that it should be added to the current DCFR in order to highlight and centre the moral significance of multiple marginalisation to contractual exploitation. Similarly, the proposed new provision should not be read *e contrario* as implying that the mere effect of a single type of subordination, as opposed to the combined effects of several intersecting types of subordination, should not give ground for contract annulment. Single vector oppression and marginalisation are simply outside the scope of the present chapter. Moreover, coordination issues may arise if intersectionality is going to be taken up in (EU or national) non-discrimination law.

This second paragraph may be of important practical relevance, as disadvantaged parties would probably prefer, in most cases, contractual adaptation (substituting the exploitative price with a fair one) as a remedy over contractual avoidance/annulment (which would make them lose access to the good or the service).

It might be argued, against the introduction of such a provision, that this would lead to great legal uncertainty. For how can the combined oppressive effects of these intersecting types of subordination possibly be proven? Our answer is that any such probatory difficulties do not seem to differ categorically from those arising in the context of the original Article II.-7:207 DCFR (Unfair Exploitation) (establishing e.g. 'economic distress', 'urgent needs', or 'ignorance') or Article 3, Unfair Terms Directive 1993 (determining 'unfairness, contrary to the requirement of good faith').

## 5.3. OCCUPYING LIBERALISM

A notable critic of Rawls, Charles Mills, criticised dominant liberal theories of justice, and specifically Rawls' theory, based on social contract theory.[49] To fixate on the minutiae of ideal theories of justice for a well-ordered society, Mills argued, means to ignore the structural injustices of existing ill-ordered – namely, racist anti-Black – societies that have impacted actual people over time. His critique exposed the racist nature of the social contract. However, rather than rejecting liberal justice altogether he argued for occupying it.[50] He proposed the retention of the liberal promise of liberty and equality through an exploration of a radically different account of justice (racial justice), i.e., one that seeks to correct and redress how liberal theorising of justice historically and currently excludes and structurally justifies racial domination.

Mills' critique is notably non-intersectional in the sense that it centres on racial justice alone, but the implications of his critique are patently relevant in the encounter of intersectionality and European private law. Mills' critique elevates the question of how liberal private law's promises of freedom and equality must be radically reconsidered to take account of its actual historical and current role in constructing, maintaining, and naturalising the oppression of multiply marginalised persons. This question demands a radical recentring and correction of private law's role in systemic exclusion and subordination of multiply marginalised persons: how can the theorising of European private law acknowledge, account for, and correct its complicity in injustice? Rather than leading to small or easy adjustments and reforms to European private

---

49 C.W. Mills, above n. 45.

50 C.W. Mills, *Black Rights/White Wrongs: The Critique of Racial Liberalism*, Oxford University Press, Oxford 2017, ch. 2 ('Occupy Liberalism!').

law doctrines and interpretations, it points towards a radical restructuring of its very foundations. In particular, Mills' work ensconces a radical approach to contract – one that uses contractual thinking to correct racial injustice. His account opens a different path for the radical restructuring of new (and likely unrecognisable) liberal private law that centres on the interests of multiply marginalised persons – as opposed to the interests of consumers – and the correction of the injustices that have structurally shaped their exploitation and subordination.

Concretely, a radical liberal rethinking of private law could include additional, punitive damages for racial, gendered, ableist, etc. private harms in tort, as well as unjust enrichment/disgorgement claims. Such structural changes could have made a difference, for example, in the recent Sanda Dia student 'hazing' death case in Belgium and similar ones marred by the combined effects of institutional racism and classism, potentially allowing for more effective civil law remedies (punitive damages) where the criminal law fails.[51] As another example, they could support protection against eviction of multiply marginalised tenants in cases where landlords own more houses than they would under a more just basic structure.

Moreover, as another very concrete example, the possible new DCFR provision discussed above could be made more radical by structurally excluding ignorance based on privilege as an excuse. The passage 'the other party knew or could be expected to have known this' could then be deleted on the ground that today, ignorance based on privilege (whether white, male, ableist, etc.) should not yield a private law legal advantage. As a baseline, private law could hold that all parties should be aware that our society is characterised by structural racism, sexism, ablism, homo- and transphobia and classism and their intersecting and compounding effects. The more radical first paragraph of a new Article # DCFR (Intersectional exploitation) could then run as follows:[52]

> Article # (Intersectional exploitation)
> (1) A party may avoid a contract if, at the time of the conclusion of the contract:
>    (a) that party was oppressed by the combined effects of intersecting types of subordination, either individual or structural, such as sexism, racism, ableism, homo- and transphobia, ageism, and classism; and
>    (b) the other party exploited the first party's situation by taking an excessive benefit or unfair advantage.

[51] Cf. 'Ex-fraternity members in Belgium found guilty over death of student', *The Guardian*, 26.05.2023, www.theguardian.com/world/2023/may/26/ex-fraternity-members-in-belgium-found-guilty-over-death-of-student; 'Students in Belgium hazing death are sentenced to fines and service', *New York Times*, 26.05.2023, www.nytimes.com/2023/05/26/world/europe/belgium-students-hazing-sentencing.html.

[52] The second paragraph on contractual adaptation could remain the same.

## 5.4. DECOLONISING EU PRIVATE LAW

This provision could become part of an EU directive on combating multiple marginalisation and oppression. Such a directive could find a solid basis in Article 114 TFEU, because an internal market where intersectional exploitation is allowed is clearly not functioning properly. Indeed, an EU directive that explicitly adopts an intersectional lens to market functioning would have a much more secure basis than much of the EU consumer acquis, which is also based, often rather artificially, on the same legal basis as for internal market integration (Article 114 TFEU).

It is important to note, however, that attempts to decolonise European private law must be attentive to the specific and multiple ways in which Member States have been complicit in historical and ongoing wrongs of marginalisation and oppression. Private law is situated in these specific national contexts and plays a role in maintaining and constructing gender and race within specific and varying European contexts. Yet, while Member States are responsible for private law complicity in injustice, that fact alone does not relieve the EU from responsibility. As Gurminder Bhambra has argued, 'the decolonization of Europe will only happen once the colonial histories of Europe are explicitly reckoned with and Europe itself is understood to have been constituted by those histories – in all their variety'.[53] As a matter of symbolism, this requires a change in the preamble to the Treaty on European Union (TEU), by which the current self-glorifying normative-historical account, expressing appropriating 'inspiration' and selective 'recalling',[54] is supplemented and partly replaced by a reckoning and taking of responsibility for Europe's colonial past and present. And as a matter of concrete steps, this should indeed include reparations, as Bhambra rightly argues.[55] Further, decolonising the EU, as a long overdue response to structural injustices and an act of taking responsibility, must be structural too. Therefore, it must include all sectors of EU law, including EU private law. And just like 'good governance' and 'digital Europe' can be horizontal EU programmes, stretching across various sectors and competences, so too could (and should) be the 'decolonising EU' project'.

---

53 G.K. Bhambra, 'A Decolonial Project for Europe' (2022) 60(2) *Journal of Common Market Studies* 229.

54 See the Preamble: 'DRAWING INSPIRATION from the cultural, religious and humanist inheritance of Europe, from which have developed the universal values of the inviolable and inalienable rights of the human person, freedom, democracy, equality and the rule of law, RECALLING the historic importance of the ending of the division of the European continent and the need to create firm bases for the construction of the future Europe'.

55 Ibid.

## 5.5. OCCUPYING PRIVATE LAW

But truly occupying or liberalising illiberal private law, to state it in Millsian words, entails more than rewriting preambles, or shifting private law rules, even if comprehensively across EU law.

Deep engagement with radical rethinking must start with reconsideration of private law's role in the oppressive, imperial, colonial histories, and present-day reality of Europe. It must start with structural revision – not of judgments and rules but – of the history of private law, of private law theory, of private legal scholarship. To occupy liberal private law, means to identify sanitising egalitarian accounts of Europe and its various private laws; to discard ideas of exceptionalism in the sexist, racist, colonial, imperial, oppressive nature of European private laws; to recognise Eurocentric, 'civilising' tendencies that impoverish intellectual life and appropriate and extract ideas – like intersectionality, like decolonisation – into existing private law discourse.[56] If intersectionality's encounter with European private law moves through the strategy of radical rethinking, there must be an intersectional paradigm shift that impacts not merely European patterns of private law freedoms, rights and obligations, but also who engages in the production of European law knowledge, its ground rules, and its evaluations.[57]

## 5.6. DEMOCRATIC (DIS)EMPOWERMENT

What would an intersectional paradigm shift entail for EU private law-making under profoundly non-ideal circumstances? Let's start from who gets to decide today on how to acknowledge intersectionality in European private law. Currently, EPL-making in the European Commission, Parliament, Court of Justice, and legal academia is predominantly a white affair. To put it in terms of deliberative democracy, the white (male) perspective, voice, concerns, and reasons are massively overrepresented, while the voices of multiply marginalised people are nearly absent, and their concerns made almost invisible.

Even recent initiatives to make EU law and policy more legitimate are blind towards the problem of the whiteness of EU law and policy-making. Notably, the Conference on the Future of Europe failed to address racism as a

---

56 In the European private law context, taking up intersectionality can easily become an intellectual project and extraction of ideas, while excluding those whose labour and lived reality of multiple marginalisation produced and produces the knowledge that undergoes European private law disciplining. See section 2.

57 See L.K.L. Tjon Soei Len, above nn. 2 and 3, and M.W. Hesselink, above n. 2.

core concern for Europe's and Europeans' future.[58] Similarly, the Commission recently proudly announced that 'building on the success of the Conference on the Future of Europe, citizens' panels are now part of the Commission's policymaking in certain key areas'.[59] This 'new generation of citizens' panels' will deliberate on initiatives on food waste, learning mobility and virtual worlds,[60] but absent attention for intersectional injustice (for instance, within chosen key areas) the experiences of multiple marginalisation are likely to be overlooked. This raises the question of what would have happened if the random selection of citizens for the deliberative panels had been stratified, not merely on the basis of five criteria to be 'representative of the EU's diversity', i.e. gender, age, geographic origin, socio-economic background, and education level,[61] but also of race and ethnicity.[62] However, even such more legitimate deliberative panels would remain toothless unless they were also given important agenda-setting powers. Only the combination of statistical overrepresentation of currently marginalised groups and genuine powers to set the deliberative agenda might be deserving of the label 'new generation of citizens' panels'. And only such panels might bring a switch from European private law's current fixation with consumer protection towards intersectional justice.

Yet, it is submitted, the problem of the democratic illegitimacy of the EU private law acquis runs much deeper. Statistical representation is not the same as democratic empowerment. The problem with the privileged access to EU private law-making is not merely the epistemic one that the preferences of multiply marginalised persons are not properly tracked.[63] It is also the social justice problem of the violation of the right not to be dominated by laws

58 The 338-page *Report on the Final Outcomes* of the Conference on the Future of Europe (May 2022), 15, mentions racism only once (under proposal 46 on 'Education', measure 2, item 8: 'Combating bullying and racism' see p. 89) and ethnicity also just once (in the Annex, p. 102).

59 Commission work programme 2023 'A Union standing firm and united' (Strasbourg, 18.10.2022 COM(2022) 548 final).

60 Ibid.

61 Conference on the Future of Europe, *Report on the final outcomes* (May 2022), 15. https://knowledge4policy.ec.europa.eu/news/report-final-outcomes-conference-future-europe-now-online_en.

62 Arguably, those who have been overrepresented and structurally enjoyed unjustified power ought to be kept out of the democratic deliberation altogether, at least as a temporary measure until their excessive power is overcome. Note that as a matter of non-ideal democratic theory the statistical *under*representation (or even exclusion) of those at the intersection of several privileges (ie white heteronormative men) in democratic deliberation under current conditions of structural social injustices would *increase*, not reduce, the legitimacy of EU (private) law-making.

63 Contrast H. Landemore, *Democratic Reason: Politics, collective intelligence, and the rule of the many*, Princeton University Press, Princeton NJ 2013; H. Landemore, *Open Democracy: Reinventing Popular Rule for the Twenty-first Century*, Princeton University Press, Princeton NJ 2020.

made by others.[64] Democratic agency is key here. Therefore, under non-ideal theory radical reform should aim at increasing democratic control for people belonging to multiply marginalised groups, while at the same dismantling the current structures of privileged access to European private law-making which have ensured domination through European private law. In democracy, nothing can replace actual political agency and democratic participation; there are no shortcuts.[65]

In sum, just like Rawlsian liberal justice, so too Habermasian deliberative democracy is liable to the radical immanent critique of not living up to its own emancipatory promises and, as a consequence, ending up being apologetic, rather than critical, of existing structures of intersectional oppression. Therefore, in our current profoundly non-ideal circumstances, occupying deliberative democracy – after the example of Mills' idea of occupying liberalism – is not only legitimate but necessary. This can take different shapes. But what they will have in common is that they will be discomforting, unsettling, and indeed disempowering for those whose unjustified structurally privileged access to EU private law-making currently undermines its democratic legitimacy. Yet, will the master's tools ever dismantle the master's house?[66]

## 6. INTERSECTIONALITY AND PRIVATE LAW ABOLITION

### 6.1. THINKING BEYOND PRIVATE LAW REFORM

The various shapes of occupying and radically rethinking private law under non-ideal conditions connect to intersectionality's deep engagement with attempts to critically rethink and reshape law. But if, through intersectional readings, European private law must be recast as a structurally oppressive institution (i.e. if private law is an oppressive tool that colludes with structural injustices) then radically rethinking private law may have to move from occupying private law towards the possibility of abolition.

Contract's legitimacy as an institution, for instance, is on shaky ground if private law itself is responsible for constructing gendered racial bargaining power. It is on shaky grounds if private law operates to shape structural injustices that it purports to take for granted, i.e., if contract constructs the 'flourishing'

---

64 M.W. Hesselink, 'Private law subjects in European mini-publics' (2024) 22(4) *International Journal of Constitutional Law* 971.

65 C. Lafont, *Democracy Without Shortcuts: A Participatory Conception of Deliberative Democracy*, Oxford University Press, Oxford 2020.

66 A. Lorde, 'The master's tools will never dismantle the master's house' in A. Lorde, above n. 5, pp. 103–106.

market-based economy in which gendered racialised 'others' are structurally exploited. If this *is* contract – the notion of agreement whose normative force and legally binding nature is abstracted and detached from the actual conditions of human lives that shape its conditions – perhaps contract needs to be so radically restructured that it amounts to its effective abolition. Attending critically to naturalising and justificatory manoeuvres in European private law discourses that turn a blind eye to private law complicity in injustice is one way to make space for abolition as a starting point. While intersectionality creates no normative necessity for abolition, intersectional analyses of contract may spark, attach to, and invite questions and practices of abolition. Abolition in this sense is not an end state (i.e., private law dismantled), but a commitment to processes that centre multiply marginalised people and dismantle private law and private law theory that is oppressive.

## 6.2. ABOLITION

Abolitionist critique is a powerful body of thought and activism that challenges oppressive structures.[67] Abolitionist critiques have focused on systems with expressed aims of ensuring safety, justice and equality, but which in practice create and maintain structural unsafety, injustice, and oppression. Notably, abolitionists have positioned themselves against reforms to legal systems and structures and instead argue that they are beyond repair and should therefore be abolished.[68] Abolitionism has a long history but is commonly tied to US-based movements and Black feminist struggles to abolish slavery. In its contemporary US context, it is chiefly pointed against 'carceral' systems, notably the criminal justice system under which Black people are subjected to mass incarceration as a continuant of racial oppression.[69] Abolition critique has also become vibrant in relation to European systems of incarceration (for instance those that respond to migrants, people with disabilities, etc.), as they are archetypes of oppressive systems.[70] A deep and critical engagement with

[67] See for instance, A. Davis, *Are Prisons Obsolete?*, Seven Stories Press, New York 2003; M. Kaba, *We Do This 'Til We Free Us: Abolitionist Organizing and Transforming Justice*, Haymarket Books, Chicago IL 2021; R. Wilson Gilmore, *Abolition Geography: Essays Towards Liberation*, Verso, London/New York 2022.

[68] See for instance, L. Ben-Moshe, 'The tension between abolition and reform' in M.E. Nagel and A.J. Nocella (eds.), *The End of Prisons: Reflections from the Decarceration Movement* (Value Inquiry Book Series), Editions Rodopi BV, Amsterdam 2013, pp. 83–92.

[69] See for instance, M. Alexander, *The New Jim Crow: Mass Incarceration in the Age of Colorblindness*, The New Press, New York 2010.

[70] For an examination of political and social organising across Europe see: A. Emejulu and L. Bassel, *Women of Colour Resist: Exploring Women of Colour's Activism in Europe*, University of Warwick, Project Report 2021, https://www.wocresist.com/wp-content/uploads/2021/12/Women-of-Colour-Resist.pdf.

abolitionism in European private law discourse is important for epistemic reasons, since abolitionist critique and movements have been from the outset a powerful Black feminist response to the lived realities of misogynoir.[71]

## 6.3. PRIVATE LAW ABOLITION

While policing, incarceration, imprisonment, and detention are at the core of abolitionist critique, all structures of oppression ought to be dismantled under an abolitionist framework. In this regard, it is noteworthy that there has been comparably less attention paid to private law in the abolitionist movements. The overt violence and dehumanisation of carceral state responses reasonably draw more attention than the covert violence of private law enforcement by means of state power. But indeed, if all structures of oppression ought to be dismantled under an abolitionist framework this raises the question: Is (European) private law beyond repair? If property and contract are intrinsically exploitative and oppressive along gendered, racialised and ethnicised lines, then they may not be worthy of a defence for reform, including radical reform. If so, what would private law abolition entail? And if abolition is warranted, what – if anything – should replace it?

Abolitionist scholarship and activism challenges the assumption that punishment and incarceration (through policing and imprisonment) make society safer. Similarly, the claim that a private law system and a system of civil procedure ensures interpersonal justice and protects interpersonal rights can be challenged. Thinking private law abolition,[72] and discussing it as a serious alternative, is a radical way of taking intersectionality seriously. Conversely, abolition, be it of criminal justice or of civil justice, must be thought intersectionally.[73]

Note that the private law abolitionism considered here is not a form of nihilism.[74] To the contrary, it is strongly idealist in its deep commitment to

71 M. Bailey, *Misogynoir Transformed: Black Women's Digital Resistance*, New York University Press, New York 2021. Here it is relevant to consider earlier questions about how and when European private law scholarship engages Black women's labour and knowledge. Critical reflection is required to assess how ideas such as intersectionality are taken up in sanitised, disciplined, forms, i.e., in accordance with white European comfort and sensibilities that render race almost unspeakable. See G. Wekker, above n. 3.

72 For a similar exploration for another field, i.e., international relations, see O.U. Rutazibwa, 'After inclusion. Thinking with Julian Go's "Thinking against empire: anticolonial thought as social theory"' (2023) 74(3) *British Journal of Sociology* 324.

73 A.Y. Davis, G. Dent, E. Meiners, B. Richie, *Abolition. Feminism. Now.*, Penguin, London 2022.

74 This chapter was submitted for publication to the *European Review of Private Law* (ERPL) and rejected there for its 'unworkable nihilism that is divorced from political and legal reality'.

justice. In particular, it is best understood as a way – perhaps the only viable one – to overcome the profound private law injustices resulting from existing forms of marginalisation and oppression through private law.

## 6.4. ABOLISHING CONTRACT

What does it mean to take up the idea of private law abolition? Taking up the possibility of private law abolition, requires a radical way of thinking about our social order and the role that private law plays in human lives and relations. Abolition, first and foremost, asks us to consider the idea that a more just future is possible without private law.[75] What then are we asked to let go of, if we consider private law abolition in the name of justice?

For starters, abolition could challenge firmly held ideas in contract law:[76]

- Abolition of the idea that contract is essential to the fulfilment of human needs and for human flourishing.
- Abolition of the bilateral structure of agreement, which shields private parties from considering other people's – and collective – interests.
- Abolition of the core ideas of contract that animate attempts to legitimise and justify state violence as a contractual consequence.
- Abolition of the idea that contract serves well-being by enabling self-interested private pursuits.
- Abolition of the idea that a person's acquiescence (theorised as 'will', 'consent' etc.) to a counter-party's bargaining power should count as morally transformative, such as to justify state violence.
- Abolition of the idea that a flourishing economy and social provisioning necessarily depend on contract.
- Abolition of the idea that the only way a person can create trust that they will keep their word is through contract's access to violent enforcement.
- Abolition of the idea that the world can only turn with the legal certainty of contract at the foundation of social and economic relations.

---

75 A post-revolutionary society without property law has been central to communist and anarchist thought. However, until recently those accounts tended to be non-intersectional (and structurally sexist and racist) focusing singularly on the oppression of the working class, *de facto* understood as white men. This is rapidly changing today. See e.g. C. Bottici, *Anarchafeminism*, Bloomsbury, London 2021.

76 As to tort law, a key question relates to the current private/public divide: if a post-abolition approach of interpersonal harm means a disarticulation of crime and punishment (see Davis et al. (n. 67)) and a shift from punishment towards repair, then in current categories this might seem to imply a shift from a public law (vertical justice) towards a private law (horizontal justice) approach, while in reality it would mean an approach that transcends the private/public divide.

- Abolition of the legal certainty of exploitation that contract secures.
- Abolition of the idea that struggles for justice of multiply marginalised people *must* engage with, build on, put their energies into, private law as it is produced in entanglements of capitalism, whiteness, patriarchy, and heteronormativity in order for them to be considered 'reasonable', 'feasible', worthy of consideration as opposed to too radical.

What it means to take up the idea of private law abolition is to allow creative legal discourse to engage alternatives to these core private law ideas, and encourage legal scholarship to question these private law assumptions, that are usually taken for granted, in favour of exploring alternative ways to fulfil human needs and support human flourishing.

## 6.5. HUMAN RELATIONS BEYOND PRIVATE LAW ABOLITION

Just like in the case of normative theory, here too we could distinguish analytically between private law abolition, while everything else remains the same, and private law abolition in concert with the abolition of all other institutions so actively engaged in – or deeply intertwined with – structural oppression that they must also be considered beyond repair. However, clearly, from the point of view of abolitionist critique, only the latter strategy makes sense, as private law would be but one of the structures of oppression that would undergo dismantling. In particular, private law abolition would go hand in hand with the abolition of global capitalism as the structure in which social provisioning takes place.[77]

Thinking private law abolition requires us to make assumptions about human interaction in a world without private law. These assumptions may have to draw on conceptions of the human person as situated in a post-abolition world. That may seem speculative. But remember that the same applies for ideal theories of social justice and of private law in a 'well-ordered society'. These are equally counter-factual and not necessarily more plausible or even acceptable. In particular, social justice theories grounded in social contract theory have contrasted the civic state following the conclusion of social contract favourably with the 'state of nature' (Hobbes, Kant), with doubtful colonialist connotations.

[77] On the constitutive role of law, in particular general private law, for a capitalist economy, see S. Deakin, D. Gindis, G.M. Hodgson, K. Huang and K. Pistor, 'Legal institutionalism: Capitalism and the constitutive role of law' (2017) 45 *Journal of Comparative Economics* 188; K. Pistor, *The Code of Capital: How the Law Creates Wealth and Inequality*, Princeton University Press, Princeton NJ 2019.

The central function of private law is commonly described in terms of its role in supporting social and economic relations. Contract, for instance, is commonly seen as the legal institution at the foundation of private exchange in market-based societies. In this context, private law thus serves its function in fulfilling basic human needs and allowing people to engage in exchange to obtain goods and services. Private law supports the mechanism, i.e., private exchange, through which the distribution of goods takes place under capitalism. Private law enables trust, confidence, and security so that persons can give up something in return for something else in a context of living among strangers. Its role can be restated as ensuring reciprocity. Thinking about private law abolition requires thinking about alternatives to social provisioning, the distribution of resources, the fulfilment of needs of the living world, et cetera.

## 6.6. ABOLITION AND COMMUNITY

Thinking private law abolition also requires being self-reflexive about possible critiques. One such possible critique is the risk of reproducing community oppression and marginalisation. Current abolitionist thinking explores community-based responses when it comes to imagining society after abolition. For example, when it comes to the core intersectional question of abolition feminism, ie how to build a world both without prisons and police and without gender and sexual violence – most concretely, what tools are available to hold someone accountable if we don't call the police? – then the answer tends to be found in community-based responses (addressing conflict and harm within organising communities; healing, accountability, and repair within communities; investing in communities).[78] Indeed, the core focus seems to be on making communities safer, not e.g. society in general (which may include many different communities) or interpersonal relations (between specific individuals).

This raises the question of whether this focus on communities within abolitionist thought and activism is susceptible to similar critiques to those raised in response to communitarianism, and if so, whether that is problematic. What counts as a community? What happens to persons who do not fit into any community, either in their own view or of the existing communities? Who gets to decide about membership and boundaries of the community? If the procedure is majority voting, then what does this mean for minorities within the community? What about violence from non-community members or across different communities? And more specifically, for questions currently dealt with by private law: Will everything be held in common, or will some things

[78] Davis et al. (n. 73), 13, and passim.

continue to be owned individually? What about conflicting legitimate needs in relation, e.g., to alternative uses of commons? Will priority rules develop over time, either on a case-to-case basis or through community deliberation, that are similar or even indistinguishable from those currently found in the common law or civil codes, respectively?

It will be clear that some of these questions are familiar from the liberal-egalitarian critique of communitarianism, and that others remind us of the questions raised by Marx' sketchy peeks into a communist society after the successfully completed revolution. Perhaps there exist very good answers, which could strengthen the paradigm of private law abolition. But it is clear that, both as a matter of theory and as a very practical question, the relationship between abolition and community should be central in(European) private law abolitionist thought and activism.

Crucially, however, in these debates, in light of its own structural unwillingness or incapacity to centre various types of structural oppression and their intersections, liberal thought is not in a position to claim the default. Thinking an intersectional (European) private law requires a paradigm shift. There is no turning back to liberal ideal theory, either because it is too complicit in – and compromised by – turning a blind eye to the fact of multiple structural oppression, or because it is too detached from a profoundly non-ideal reality, or both. Indeed, we suggest that the most promising strategy towards further thinking intersectionality in (European) private law might be to start from the radical premise of (European) private law abolition. Arguably, this reversal of the burden of proof could even be defended on Rawlsian grounds: pursuant to the difference principle in its procedural aspect, it must be proven to those at the bottom that society's current basic structure, including its system of private law, also works for their benefit. Until then, the normative case – in terms of social justice – for its abolition stands.

## 6.7. THE ABOLITION OF RIGHTS

Finally, another possible challenge to private law abolitionism comes from one of the founders of Critical Race Theory ('CRT'), Patricia Williams.[79] In a powerful rebuttal of the Critical Legal Studies ('CLS') critique of rights,[80] Williams argues that, unlike the white male leaders of the CLS movement, most Black people and in particular Black women, do not have the privilege of

[79] Cf. R. Delgado, J. Stefancic and A. Harris, *Critical Race Theory: An Introduction*, 4th edn., New York University Press, New York 2023, p. 5.

[80] For the CLS critique of rights, see D. Kennedy, *A Critique of Adjudication {fin de siècle}*, Harvard University Press, Cambridge MA 1997, ch. 13, esp. p. 332 ('Rights then function as no more than interests (perhaps with an exclamation mark)').

being able to rely on informal trust-based solutions; they need formally binding contracts, which provide them with legally enforceable rights.[81] Williams offers the illuminating story where she and Peter Gabel, a co-founder of the CLS movement, both newly arrived in California from New York, are hunting for apartments. Gabel pays a sizeable cash deposit without any formal contract or even a receipt. Williams observes that this avenue of informal trust would never be open to her as a Black woman: she needs the formal lease. As she writes, 'unlike Peter, I am still engaged in a struggle to set up transactions at arm's length, as legitimately commercial, and to portray myself as a bargainer of separate worth, distinct power, sufficient rights to manipulate commerce'.[82] More generally, she points out, the discourse of rights (first and foremost civil rights) has been central to Black political strategy of emancipation. 'Therefore', she remarks, 'one of the most troubling positions advanced by CLS is that of rights' *disutility* in political advancement'.[83] As she points out, to Black people in the US the prospect of attaining full rights under law has been 'a fiercely motivational, almost religious, source of hope'.[84] Historically, she explains, recounting her personal story of discovering the contract of sale for her great-great-grandmother Sophie, for the Black community the stake fundamental in rights is to be recognised as a *subject* with contractual rights rather than a mere *object* of a legal contract between two others.[85]

At first sight, Williams' convincing refutation of the CLS critique of rights and her defence of formal contractual rights seem to present a formidable challenge also to the idea of private law abolition; that is, the abolition of the current system of legally enforceable private rights and obligations. Indeed, when she writes that the 'failure of rights discourse, much noted in CLS scholarship, does not logically mean that informal systems will lead to better outcomes',[86] this seems to go directly against the idea of private law abolition and community solutions. However, upon further reflection, Williams' powerful critique of CLS' rights scepticism, applies most forcefully to a world *where other people have rights*; that is, our profoundly non-ideal world where the basic structure of society, established by the social contract, ensures rights for some (white people, in particular white men) but not, or much less so, for others (Black people, especially Black women). In other words, Williams' CRT critique of the CLS critique of rights is immanent to the current oppressive and marginalising system of private law rights. Put in normative terms, it offers

81 P.J. Williams, *The Alchemy of Race and Rights*, Harvard University Press, Cambridge MA 1991, ch. 8 ('The Pain of Word Bondage'), pp. 146–165.

82 Ibid., p. 148.

83 Ibid., p. 150.

84 Ibid., p. 154.

85 Ibid., pp. 17–19.

86 Ibid., p. 158.

a non-ideal theory of the kind discussed in section 5 above. Yet, this leaves open the real possibility that a society where no one has any legally enforceable private law rights, because a system of private law no longer exists, would be a better society for Black women and others currently at the intersection of various forms of oppression and marginalisation (but not – and here comes the redistributive bite – for those who currently benefit most from such rights). Put differently, in a society where private law protects the interests of some as legally enforceable rights,[87] and where abolition of that private law system is not on the cards, the best strategy may well be still to try to obtain formal contract and property rights wherever possible. However, a society where no one has any legally enforceable private law rights may still be a more just one overall, because it no longer offers a key tool for intersectional oppression and marginalisation.

## 6.8. ABOLITION DEMOCRACY

As Angela Davis underlined, 'it is not only, or not even primarily, about abolition as a negative process of tearing down, but it is also about building up, about creating new institutions'.[88] With her, we would like to draw on the DuBoisian notion of abolition democracy. Du Bois introduced this term to express a vision of American society after the abolition of slavery; that is, a vision about what it meant to effectively abolish slavery. As he argued, slavery would not be fully abolished until Black people had the same social, economic and political standing, and equal control over the future of the country, as white people.[89] Similarly, for the abolition of prisons, Davis proposes 'the creation of an array of social institutions that would begin to solve the social problems that set people on the track to prison, thereby helping to render the prison obsolete'.[90] In the same vein we propose to think through the abolition of contract through the creation of new institutions that better serve everyone. Doing so engages radical democracy and starts with centring those currently at the bottom of society, i.e., those currently multiply oppressed and marginalised persons. As Gayatri Chakravorty Spivak recently pointed out, Du Bois' account

87 On the key role of private law in creating and entrenching wealth and economic and political inequality, see K. Pistor, above n. 77.

88 A.Y. Davis, *Abolition Democracy: Beyond Empire, Prisons, and Torture*, Seven Stories Press, New York 2005.

89 W.E.B. Du Bois, *Black Reconstruction in America* [1935], The Free Press, New York 1998, pp. 182 et seq.

90 A.Y. Davis, *Abolition Democracy*, above n. 89, p. 92.

of the oppression of Black people was not yet intersectional.[91] But what we are arguing for here is, of course, intersectional private law abolition democracy. From this point of view, contract abolition doesn't mean the mere tearing down of the institution of contract but the democratic construction of a post-contract society. Key here is the self-empowerment of the currently intersectionally oppressed and marginalised. This is not a matter of merely 'including' the currently excluded within existing frameworks of white (European) private law-making but first and foremost the radical transformation of these frameworks themselves. This is also an important reason why in this section on abolition we have raised more questions that we have answered. What is needed is not a top-down reform of contract but a bottom-up process of self-empowerment of the currently oppressed and marginalised to build a society beyond private law as we currently know it.

## 7. CONCLUDING REMARKS

As shown in this chapter, a range of questions arise from intersectionality's travel within the sphere of European private law. Several strategies through which intersectionality can be taken on in European private law give their own shape to potential answers. We discussed three quite different such strategies, i.e., liberal ideal theories of social and private law justice, liberal non-ideal theories of reparation, and private law abolition. Through our critical discussion we showed how intersectionality's encounter with European private law yields insights about European, legal, and private law sensibilities, more so than about intersectionality as a concept.

Intersectionality comes to European private law without the European, legal, and private law sensibilities and assumptions that render it a race- and gender-neutral space. Instead, intersectionality allows European private law to become visible as a site where gendered, racial – and other forms of – power, are coded, organised, and expressed. As a lens, intersectionality can help to examine how private law constitutes gendered, racial forms of legal privileging, showing how it naturalises and justifies persisting gendered, racial and ethnic inequities.

Centring the predicament of multiply marginalised persons is what private law's encounter with intersectionality ought to do. And it matters how that work is done. From our analysis, it is obvious that it cannot merely consist of an intellectual exercise of redefining abstract private law subjects, because

[91] G.C. Spivak, 'W.E.B. Du Bois and Angela Davis on Abolition Democracy', *13/13 Seminar Series*, 2/13 (06.10.2020), https://blogs.law.columbia.edu/abolition1313/gayatri-chakravorty-spivak-w-e-b-du-bois-and-angela-davis-on-abolition-democracy/.

the stakes of intersectional work are not imagined; they are real. Taking up intersectionality as a lens in the space of European private law elevates root problems, inviting a self-conscious reckoning of private law's complicity in historic and ongoing oppression. At the same time, it helps to expose how mutually constitutive forms of oppression are formative – historically and presently – to private law and its theory.

This chapter has yielded insights and caution about the various ways in which intersectionality can be taken up, drawing on our familiarity with existing European private law discourse. For obvious reasons of legitimacy – both political (agency) and epistemic (positionality) – our analysis could not engender anything like a blueprint for an intersectional European private law. Indeed, we submit that thinking a genuine encounter between intersectionality and European private law cannot start from the premise that targeted reform will suffice, leaving European private law's current basic structure in place. We see more potential in addressing the social and political struggles of multiply marginalised people, which intersectionality brings forward, through a much more radical rethinking – one where the dominant liberal paradigm of social and interpersonal justice cannot claim the default either. Indeed, (European) private law abolition may be the best starting point for reimagining a more just future that centres resistance to intersectional marginalisation and oppression in (European) private law.

# CHAPTER 10

# THE STAKES OF CONTRACT LAW. IDENTITIES AND DISTRIBUTION IN CONSUMER CONTRACTS AND GENDER-RELATED TRANSACTIONS

Maria Rosaria MARELLA and Giovanni MARINI



## 1. A CRITICAL TOOLBOX TO ANALYSE POWER IN PRIVATE LAW

In the traditional view, bargaining power continues to be one of the most controversial problems of contract law, but has rarely been analysed in its deep genesis. Viewing bargaining power as a product of the pre-existing economic and social relations, the law can only be given the task of intervening later to modify, contain and correct its distortions and excesses in order to restore proper social relations.

The processes of harmonisation and standardisation of law have brought to light the possibility of choosing among several possible rules to carry out the project. Each of the different options theoretically available in the field, however, produces a different distribution of bargaining power among the parties, belying the neutrality usually attributed to this type of rule. As has already been made evident since the Social Justice Manifesto and in particular by one of its major promoters, Hugh Collins,[1] relative decisions are followed by a redistribution of power and resources among the parties to the dispute and thus among the groups to which they belong, that triggers further complex processes of incentive or disincentive for or against them.

Thus, when dealing with standard form contracts, we will agree with Professor Bianca when he says that the legitimate use of the state, whether in enforcing market rules or otherwise, requires 'some normative theory of what forms of coercion society wishes to prohibit and what forms it wishes to permit'.[2] There is no doubt that – just as happens in the relations between capital and labour – it is legal regulation that 'constitutes' the subjects to be regulated and makes some weaker than others, forcing them to accept a condition of subordination.

In this sense, the Foucauldian analysis, while containing a partial image of law, of which it captures only certain aspects, proves, in contrast, to be decisive for understanding the functioning of power. And this is certainly not because of Foucault's idea of law, linked as it was to a sanctioning and repressive view of the norm typical of criminal law, nor because of the recessive view of state power in favour of the plurality of emanating centres that make up the more complex network produced by 'the disciplines' in a Foucauldian sense. Instead, it is the careful analysis of the mechanisms of production and reproduction of power relations that proves fundamental. Modern power is a 'relational' power, that is 'exercized from innumerable points', is highly indeterminate in character and is never something 'acquired, seized or shared'.[3] These forms of power are neither negative nor unidirectional; they do not repress but, on the contrary, are positive, operating through a whole range of technologies and cultural tools to direct individual existences; they produce forms of subjectivity. Power is

1 H. Collins, 'La giustizia contrattuale in Europa' (2003) *Rivista critica del diritto privato* 659.
2 C.M. Bianca, *Diritto civile. Vol. 3 Il contratto*, Giuffrè, Milan 2019.
3 'The Subject and Power', in B. Wallis (ed.), *Art after Modernism. Rethinking Representation*, The New Museum of Contemporary Art, New York 1989, and M. Foucault, *Two Lectures Power /Knwoledge, Selected Interviews and Other Writings, (1972/77)*, Pantheon Book, New York 1980.

only a structural activity by which subjects are produced and in relation to which they can be considered anonymous transmitters.

In the discussion on the power/contract relationship four core themes need to be highlighted as a methodological premise.

## 1.1. DICHOTOMIC DISCOURSE IN LAW

Contrary to what is sometimes claimed, namely that law is operating only at the margins of society, the law plays a major key role in reproducing social and bargaining power; as such, it determines the rules of the game, but also the identity of the players.

Relationships which were normally thought of as non-legal, like relationships marked by belonging to a social class, are largely produced by the law.

Within the legal realm, a dualistic or dichotomic thinking (public/private, market/family, production/reproduction) is allied with a discourse of 'naturalisation' of social structures and equates to an apparatus of access/non-access, coercion/freedom, and interference/non-interference.

In legal orders, these distinctions are encoded in rules that construct distinct realms of private power (for example, through rules of property and contract) and a separate, insulated realm of state or public power.

The public/private dichotomy, although undermined in multiple directions and situations, continues to structure, directly or indirectly, the order of discourse in contemporary legal thought. It is on this (contingent) order that the order of other dichotomous patterns depends.

The deconstruction of these dichotomies, the emphasis on their unstable boundaries and their historical contingency allows one to dismantle the hierarchal order they establish between the terms of the opposition and their effect on the distribution of power within society.

In this chapter, we focus on some of the dichotomies, such as the rule/exception opposition, that structure legal discourse, by offering here a scheme to organise the various doctrines operating in contract law along a hierarchical order, with relevant implications for the respective bargaining power and identity of the contracting parties, which are differently affected by such hierarchies.

## 1.2. DISTRIBUTIVE ANALYSIS

Distribution in private law is not a new theme. It was first developed in the United States by legal realists,[4] and Robert Hale was their hero.[5] Later critical legal studies and particularly Duncan Kennedy took up where the realist project left off.[6]

The realist project highlights the way in which law constructs the institutional mechanisms that represent the framework within which economic and social relations between different groups are conducted: mechanisms that also determine the position of strength of group members and the outcomes that individuals can achieve.

Their reconstruction, generalising from the relations between capital and labour,[7] brings into full light the force of law which, through the various legal rules, constructs a complex series of prohibitions and permissions, which not only chooses who can play, but also determines the rules of the game, distributes the stakes to its players and thus configures their identity.[8]

Beginning with the very initial allocation of property titles and remedies, the law excludes all others from the possibility of appropriating the resources that it has allocated and that constitute the stakes with which the owner can sit at the bargaining table. Through the configuration of the rules (of the game) – that is, those rules that define the legitimacy of the behaviours or means by which the division of the joint product (of the exchange) is achieved – the law is also able to determine the outcome of exchanges.[9]

Thus, it is not so much the presence of an institution or its particular definition by a code or case law that determines the outcome of bargaining, but all the 'little' ground rules that accompany its application, because it is on their concrete configuration that the outcomes that the parties may succeed in achieving in individual bargaining depend.

This reconstruction clearly brings to the fore the problem of power in private relations and the role of the legal system in this regard. Robert Hale and other legal realists overturn the perspective of classical legal thought and present a different view in which private law can no longer be seen as the foundation of

---

4 J.W. Singer, 'Legal Realism Now' (1988) 76 *California Law Review* 465, 544.

5 R.L. Hale, 'Coercion and Distribution in a Supposedly Non-Coercive State' (1923) 38 *Political Science Quarterly* 470, 494.

6 D. Kennedy, 'The Stakes of Law or Hale and Foucault!' (1991) XV *Legal Studies Forum* 327, 366.

7 D. Kennedy, 'Distributive and paternalist motives in contract and tort law, with special reference to compulsory terms and unequal bargaining power' (1982) 41 *Maryland Law Review* 563.

8 D. Kennedy, 'The Political Stakes in "Merely Technical" Issues of Contract Law' (2001) 1 *European Review of Private Law* 7, 28; G. Marini, 'Distribuzione e identità nel diritto dei contratti' (2009) 1 *Rivista critica del diritto privato* 1, 66.

9 M.R. Cohen, 'The Basis of contract' (1933) 46 *Harvard Law Review* 553, 582.

the freedom of private parties, but on the contrary as a complex mechanism by which the state (primarily through the courts) simply 'delegates to private parties the ability to exercise coercion'.[10] Thus, it becomes possible to overturn the mainstream description of contract in terms of contractual freedom and to propose instead a different view, according to which contractual freedom is nothing more than a much more sophisticated regime that allows individuals to legitimately exercise forms of economic pressure on others.

In this framework, legal realism powerfully repudiated the classical description of the relationship between law and the market. There was a lie at the heart of *laissez-faire*: markets do not exist outside of the law, and state regulation is not a wrongful incursion into a natural order.

The realist insight aims at unveiling the state's powerful role in determining the background rules for social action and in maintaining an unequal distribution of wealth, particularly through the use of contract and property law. Realists argued that contracts are public, rather than private, because individuals ask the state to enforce them by using law to aid one party against the other. Even when they are seemingly the mere product of 'voluntary' agreements, the results of the relations of conflict and cooperation between the parties are always conditioned by the legal system.

Likewise, realists claimed that property is not a natural right protected by the state only in the rare event of a threat of dispossession, but a right created by the state to exclude others generally. By enforcing a right called property, the law, then, does not merely protect owners in their possession, but also creates both owners and non-owners.

The distribution of market power is thus only partly a function of private decisions of market actors; to a substantial extent, it is determined by the legal definition and allocation of property and contract rights. What is private is not revealed or guaranteed by the law; it is build and constructed by the law.

Thus, we move from the complicity of the law in the creation of power relations to the analysis of the concrete dynamics and apparatuses with which the law contributes to making certain individuals or groups particularly weak and/or vulnerable.

---

10 R. Hale, 'Bargaining, Duress, and Economic Liberty' (1943) 43 *Columbia Law Review* 603, 628: 'bargaining power would be different were it not that the law endows some with rights that are more advantageous than those with which it endows others. It is with these unequal rights that men bargain and exert pressure on one another'. See also M.R. Cohen, 'Property and Sovereignty' (1927) 13 *Cornell Law Review* 8.

## 1.3. INTERSECTIONALITY

The notion of intersectionality identifies the ways in which different regimes of inequality interact and/or combine to produce complex, multiple inequalities.

We should remind ourselves that intersectional analysis started from an analysis of legal materials.[11] Intersectionality is not only about recognition and/or cultural devaluation of identities, but also and overall, about distribution.

Intersectionality comes from leftist and race critical theory – oriented to stress conflicts on wealth and power distribution – rather than from identity politics, oriented to recognition. It was misappropriated as an argument that black women are denied their rights and social recognition in general because they have a different stigmatised identity. In reality, it was initially a critical analysis of the situation of black women, not understood as bearers of an essential or even a socially constructed identity, but as people who are differently treated by official legal actors by being denied remedies for race and gender discrimination. Within the legal regimes that respond to different kinds of discriminatory or oppressive treatments, Black women were marginalised not as a result of stereotypes about what they were like, but as the product of the way power is discursively organised and deployed by the law. They were made invisible: invisibility here meant legal invisibility.

Intersectionality is eventually a critique of identity politics and the role of law in marginalising some sub-groups within a given identity/category. It is also an analysis of the role of (contract) law in producing complex gender, class, and inter- and intra-race distributive outcomes. It suggests that the different legal solutions available must be scrutinised for their potential effect on different sections of women and/or different sexual orientations, according to their preferences. The basic idea underlying it is that there are no zero-sum outcomes; there are always winners and losers.[12]

## 1.4. MARX/PASHUKANIS (REVISED)

The law is a site of capitalist and (patriarchal) bargains, but the law can also be deeply incoherent both as a discourse and in its operation. Therefore, it may be an interesting move to help dismantle illegitimate hierarchies in all facets of social life. In doing so, we must emphasise the importance of legal rules not only in public law and criminal law but also, and particularly, in private law.

---

11 K. Crenshaw, 'Demarginalising the intersection of race and sex: a black feminist critique of antidiscrimination doctrine, feminist theory and antiracist politics' (1989) (1) *University of Chicago Legal Forum* 139.

12 G. Marini, above n. 8, 66.

These rules are the product of contestation between social forces and not the result of fidelity to the abstraction (abstract legal form of commodity). Each one is the crystallisation or result of a particular complex decision process in a particular political/economic conjuncture.

Marx,[13] and later Pashukanis,[14] emphasised in their writings the role of law as the background against which an economic conflict plays out. They emphasised the way in which private law (especially property and contract law) distributes the surplus to the advantage of someone (capitalists, but also landlords, banks, investors, insurance companies) at the expense of other 'weak' parties.

In line with classical legal thought and the dogmatic tradition, Karl Marx thought that the abstract legal concepts of property and contract had necessary specific meanings when implemented at the level of individual legal rules governing the production of commodities and the distribution of profits.

Later, Evgeny Pashukanis developed a Marxist theory of private law in which property and contract had their own internal commodity logic. The actual regime was produced by the abstract legal form and abstract legal ideas of property and contract, ignoring the actual power relations that the legal form necessarily embodied.[15]

We certainly agree on the importance of (private) law and the idea that there are systemic advantages and disadvantages generated by the legal regime and its complex set of background rules; we also admit that changes in the legal regime in a given direction will benefit some and disadvantage others. On the other hand, we disagree with the static reconstruction of legal form and the power of abstraction *per se*. There is a sort of fetishism of legal forms in Pashukanis's thought that we do not buy.[16] A realist analysis of private law shows that these rules are often vague or contradictory, and in any case open to conflicting but legally reasonable and sound interpretations.[17]

We are obviously referring to specific rules governing property rights and contract rules, to specific rules (of prohibition and permission) regulating bargaining behaviour, and to specific rules about what one can do, or threaten to do, to the other party even after a breach (remedies). Asymmetries, exploitation, and oppression seem to be produced mainly by the crystallisation

---

13 K. Marx, *Das Kapital*, 1867.

14 E. Pashukanis, *The General Theory of Law and Marxism*, (trans. B. Enhorn), Transaction Publishers, New Brunswick NJ 2002

15 G. Amendola, 'The Abolition of Law or Law of the Common(s)? Pashukanis and the Revolution' (2017) 116 *South Atlantic Quarterly* 707, 725.

16 D. Kennedy, 'Property as Fetish and Tool' (25.06.2014) *Grassroots Economic Organizing*, https://geo.coop/story/property-fetish-and-tool (accessed 14.04.2025).

17 M. Xifaras, 'The Role of Law in Critical Theory, Critique and Praxis', Columbia University website, 2018, http/blogs.law.columbia.edu/.

of these sets of rules, which constitute contingent and incoherent ensembles that are always open to revision.

Even alternatives to formal state law, according to a pluralist view of legal orders – informal laws such as grassroots rules, private ordering of market relations, etc. – are no less contingent and incoherent.[18] At every stage of economic development, multi-layered legal orders have survived within state law, with contradictory relationships to the rules enacted by state legislatures or judges. The ability of parties to appeal from one normative order to another may influence outcomes, but it is not clear that it will lead to better results.

All these rules (formal and informal) are contested between social forces and are only very marginally constrained by fidelity to the abstractions (of private law property and contract). These rules (of the game) are contingent, always in motion and always at stake. Just as contingent is the distribution of wealth and power that results from them.

It is important to trace historically and model analytically how this contingent and incoherent ensemble of (formal or informal) rules is shaped and operates in actual situations.

Obviously, looking at power relationships at this more granular level (trying to change or model actual rules and institutional practices) does not aim to change the whole of society, but only to achieve more modest but no less substantial local objectives. It is quite possible that a single attempt to equalise the distribution between groups, conceived as crosscutting and intersectional, will fail.

This approach leaves open the relationship with other forms of critique. What is still at stake is a strategic approach to separating what we need to think about law in general from what we need to do in a given moment. Our beliefs about the law should not prevent us from dismantling private law doctrines and private law theory that are oppressive to multiply marginalised people.

The aim is to identify how power operates in contemporary society, trying to change those background rules in the interest of those who are oppressed and exploited permanently and to defend the solutions developed in their favour against mainstream arguments. The question at hand is how the exchange surplus in the current regime is created and transferred back to the strongest individuals, enabling them to absorb the costs of protection.

---

[18] D. Kennedy, *A Critique of Adjudication*, Harvard University Press, Cambridge MA 1998.

## 2. CONTRACT, POWER AND THE ROLE OF THE RULE/ EXCEPTION DICHOTOMY IN GENDER ISSUES

In the complex interplay between contract and power, relations of power are primarily reflected in the hierarchies that liberal theories set up among different contract doctrines. Establishing a rule/exception relationship among rules, principles, and doctrines – far from being a neutral or merely technical move – is a 'classic' way of establishing a hierarchy among them. In the rule/exception game, what is meant to be the exception is marginalised and subordinated to what is fixed as the rule. As a result, the doctrine, principle, or rule that is considered the exception would be applied much less than the one that is considered the rule. Now, given that different rules and doctrines produce different distributive settings, since – as already noted – there are no zero-sum solutions, it is intuitive that rules and exceptions distribute power, resources, and wealth in different proportions and according to different logics and circumstances. In other words, rules and exceptions privilege different typologies of contracting parties. If we assume that the enforcement of one doctrine rather than another has different distributive consequences, the rule/exception hierarchy deriving from the classification of a doctrine as the exception rather than the rule, does not work only at a logical or abstract level. On the contrary, it affects and even constitutes relations of power between individuals and groups within society, insofar as individuals enter into contracts and take on the roles of contracting parties. Consideration v. reliance and promissory estoppel, procedural unconscionability v. substantive unconscionability, strict liability v. impossibility are examples of apparently neutral or technical rule/exception schemes that serve to govern hierarchical relations of race, gender, and class. For instance, feminist theorists have largely demonstrated the extent to which the enforcement of procedural unconscionability rather than substantive unconscionability and the consideration doctrine rather than promissory estoppel can disempower women plaintiffs in domestic contract cases. In this respect, the rule/exception dichotomy has a specific distributive outcome.

More generally, the rule/exception pattern epitomises the function of legal discourse in producing and reproducing dynamics of power in which genderisation plays a major role.

Drawing on feminist theories, in this section we articulate a critical analysis of the rule/exception conventional legal discourse through three examples that shed light on its capacity to produce discrete distributive effects, create/reinforce gender stereotypes, and be associated with a gendered legal language, producing genderised legal texts.

## 2.1. CAREWORK AND THE ROLE OF THE RULE/EXCEPTION DICHOTOMY

Over time, the consideration/promissory estoppel hierarchy has triggered and reinforced the subordination and marginalisation of unpaid reproductive work in cases where spouses agree on compensation and rewards for care work performed by wives. In two (in)famous cases, *Borelli v. Brusseau*[19] and *State of Minnesota v. Bachmann*,[20] the courts have argued that the spouses' agreements on remuneration for household and care work were not binding and enforceable because the work performed was due in fulfilment of a marital duty. According to both judgments, there was no consideration and no legal basis for an exchange, which 'seemed to resurrect what had once been a gendered assignment of marital obligations in which the wife owed the husband a duty of care in exchange of his financial support'.[21] In this line, the *Bachmann* court emphasised that 'The Bachmanns have not shown that their proposed wage agreement results in either gain or loss to either person; unlike the typical employment relationship, the economic exchange between the Bachmanns would be purely illusory'. In the background lies the peril that the *Borelli* court explicitly evoked, that such negotiations are incompatible with the institution of marriage as defined by the law.

Here the consideration doctrine shows its dark side: far from being a mere technical apparatus, it functions to perpetuate the divide between production and reproduction. It effectively excludes any single activity that does not directly and immediately identify with a commodity – that is, with the market sphere – from the realm of contract law. Furthermore, when informal care work is at stake, negotiations within the family, particularly between spouses, are perceived as having the potential to obscure the distinction between family

---

19 In *Borelli v. Brusseau*, 16 Cal. Rptr. 2d, 16, 12 Cal. App. 4th 647 (1993), a husband was very sick and wanted his wife to nurse him at home rather than be in a hospital. He promised to give her some of his personal property if she took care of him. She did and took care of him until he died. But he broke his promise and left his property to his daughter. The court concluded that there was no binding contract for lack of consideration.

20 Suzanne Margie Bachmann, who was sentenced to 90 days jail time in 1994, asked that she be allowed to leave jail on weekdays to perform housework and care for her four children. Because she had negotiated an hourly wage to be paid by her husband for her work, Bachmann argued that she satisfied the conditions of a Minnesota statute authorising work-release for employed individuals who receive a fair and reasonable wage for their work. A trial court nonetheless denied work release on the ground that homemaking is not 'employment' within the meaning of the statute. The Minnesota Court of Appeals affirmed: *State of Minnesota v. Bachmann* 521 NW 2d 886, 886 (Minn. Ct. App. 1994). S.K. Silbaugh, 'Turning Labor into Love. Housework and the Law' (1996) 91 *Northwestern University Law Review* 1.

21 J. Carbone and J. Carillo, 'Borelli v. Brusseau, 12 Cla. App. 4th 647 (1st Div. 1993), Commentary' in R. Rebouché (ed.), *Feminist Judgments. Family Law Opinions Rewritten*, Cambridge University Press, Cambridge 2020, p. 273.

and market. This, in turn, can be seen as a threat to the sanctity of marriage and the value of family solidarity as a fundamental component of the institution.[22]

Broadly speaking, the doctrine of consideration has been such as to exclude from the range of legally binding transactions all those agreements which, although binding according to the intention of the parties, directly or even indirectly impinge on the sphere of reproduction. Classic examples of this exclusion are cases where relatives agree that one party will move near to the other in exchange for a promise of land or free housing, but after the transfer, the promisor fails to honour the promise. In terms of consideration, the change in the promisee's situation has not been bargained for; nor, if there is a detriment, has it been requested or agreed upon. Moreover, the promise itself does not confer any concrete benefit on the promisor.[23] Ultimately, such agreements prove to be unenforceable with no regard to the detriment suffered by the promisee.

The result would be very different if courts applied the doctrine of promissory estoppel to these cases. If promissory estoppel is not viewed as an exception, but rather as a complement, a substitute for or equivalent to consideration, then the reasonable and foreseeable reliance of the promisee will rule the case. In *Borelli v. Brusseau*, the California Supreme Court held that the oral agreement between the spouses was unenforceable because it lacked consideration given spouses' duty to support each other.[24] Specifically, the Court treated the alleged agreement as an invalid contract because it would facilitate provision of the wife's nursing care in exchange for the husband's assets. Following a broader trend in case law, the *Borelli* court seemed 'to keep the judiciary out of family disputes'. It is no coincidence that 'feminists have long criticised these doctrines as upholding patriarchal authority and marginalizing women's ability to seek redress for family conflicts'.[25] In other words, these doctrines, and above all consideration, emphasise and reproduce the production/reproduction opposition within contract law, thereby favouring husbands and creating 'an insidious social norm of male dominance'.[26] In contrast by enforcing non-bargained-for promises and blurring the market/ non-market divide, promissory estoppel also mitigates the power imbalance

22 M.R. Marella, 'Critical Family Law' (2011) 2 *American University Journal of Gender Social Policy and Law* 721, 754; M.R. Marella, 'The Non-Subversive Function of European Private Law: The Case of Harmonisation of Family Law' (2006) 12(1) *European Law Journal* 78.

23 G. Marini, *Promessa e affidamento nel diritto dei contratti*, Jovene, Naples 1995, pp. 31 et seq.

24 The Court also found the agreement unenforceable because it violated public policy by destroying the social meaning of the institution of marriage and its foundation in unconditional love, affection, and solidarity.

25 J. Carbone and J. Carillo, above n. 21, pp. 278 et seq.

26 J. Carrillo, 'Borelli v. Brusseau, 12 Cla. App. 4th 647(1st Div. 1993), Judgement', in R. Rebouché (ed.), above n. 21, p. 282.

between the parties[27] as it contributes to the empowerment of subjects marginalised because of their social class, gender, race, and/or their status as reproductive workers. Indeed, the plaintiffs/promisees in the cases of agreements that were disregarded due to the application of the consideration doctrine were the weaker parties to the transactions. Social norms, especially gender norms, are implicated in contractual relationships and influence the social context in which transactions (and human interactions) take place. By taking into account a broader and more complex background in which agreements are made, 'a fuller view of the parties',[28] promissory estoppel allows for a different appreciation of the power relations involved. In *Borelli*, the court held the wife's care work performed in favour of her husband to be something she could not exchange for an equivalent value. Similarly, the *Bachmann* court maintained that the wife's care work could not be the subject of employment. The courts argued this for two different reasons: because caregiving is a marital duty and because it has no market value. Instead, 'the enforcement of the promise using promissory estoppel would give the care work value and importance',[29] without devaluing the couple's love relationship, but with due acknowledgement of the power dynamics within it. The enforcement of promissory estoppel brings to the fore aspects of social life that can be ascribed to the realm of social reproduction and which are usually disregarded in their economic value. Moreover, assuming that contracts are not made in a void, but in the context of specific power relations, promissory estoppel has the effect of highlighting power imbalances between the parties and possibly correcting them in favour of the weaker or disempowered party.

My conclusion on this point is that the rule/exception scheme, with reference to the relationship between consideration and promissory estoppel, operates ideologically to exclude social reproduction from the law of contract, with the effect of marginalising those who provide it and of denying its economic relevance.[30]

## 2.2. LEGAL DICHOTOMIES IN PRE-MARITAL AGREEMENTS

When premarital agreements in contemplation of divorce are at stake, the main question that arises is no longer whether such contracts are binding

27 O. Gan, 'A Feminist Economic Perspective on Contract Law: Promissory Estoppel as an Example' (2021) 28 *Michigan Journal of Gender and Law* 1.

28 Ibid., 41.

29 Ibid., 23.

30 Similarly, in Continental jurisdictions, functional equivalents of consideration (*cause suffisante*, *causa*, etc.) are the rule in the legal regime of contractual transactions, marginalising the role of reliance protection with the same kind of distributive effects on promisors and promisees.

and, therefore, enforceable, but rather whether the recognition of freedom of contract in this field tolerates claims of contractual (and gender) justice. In particular, with the diffusion of prenups, feminists have raised the question of whether freedom of contract is a possible answer to issues of self-determination in family law, or whether it would instead magnify women's subordination and exploitation. Indeed, the recognition of the validity of prenuptial agreements seems to establish a 'norm of male dominance' – mirroring and reversing the perverse negotiation of care/consideration dynamics discussed above: while the possibility of binding marital agreements on care work – usually denied – would empower caregivers, i.e. women, the enforceability of premarital contracts in contemplation of divorce – normally accepted – typically benefits men,[31] or wealthier parties because they usually derogate from the default regime of joint marital property. In other words, freedom of contract – the way it is usually enforced in the home – does not appear to promote a fair distribution of family wealth between the genders.

The courts' responses to the gendered outcomes of freedom of contract in family relations have varied over time. Premarital agreements have been evaluated, alternatively, from the perspective of substantive fairness or from the perspective of freedom of contract in its classic version, as will theory. Hence, problems of unfairness have been generally addressed by enforcing the unconscionability doctrine, interpreted according to a dual standard: substantive and formal (or procedural). While procedural unconscionability focuses on the circumstances surrounding the contract's execution, substantive unconscionability concentrates on the contract's terms.

When United States courts began to recognise the enforceability of prenuptial agreements, they generally adopted the 'fairness approach', which involved the implementation of protective doctrines such as duress, misrepresentation, and substantial unconscionability. This meant to articulate the contractualisation of the family in accordance with claims of substantive justice.[32] Over time the will theory perspective has prevailed: whatever each party has bargained for is presumed to result from their own rational choice in the light of individual wealth maximisation. Women's formal equality in the labour market has played a major role here as a persuasive argument to dismiss protective doctrines, which have become tendentially exceptional in the courts' rationale.[33] In particular, under section 6(a)(2) of the Uniform Premarital Agreement Act (UPAA), broadly adopted in the country until the approval of a new uniform act, the UPMAA (Uniform Premarital and Marital Agreements Act) in 2012 – unconscionability alone was not a sufficient defence against

31 J. Carbone and J. Carillo, above n. 21, p. 273.

32 In some State jurisdictions – such as New Jersey – a prenuptial agreement was qualified as unconscionable if it left one of the parties without reasonable means of support.

33 *Simeone v. Simeone* 581 A. 2d 162 (Pa. 1990).

enforcement. The agreement would have been enforceable no matter how unconscionable it was if a party had received reasonable financial disclosure, waived the right to disclosure, or had reasonable knowledge of the other party's property.

Which means that substantive unconscionability *per se* does not affect the enforceability of the contract. In other words, not the substantive fairness of the agreement, but procedural unconscionability regulates the matter.[34]

Now, in the rule/exception interplay, when the doctrine presented as the exception is seen as preferentially applicable to a particular social group – identified on the basis of class, gender or race – the recipients of the exceptional rule are 'naturally' endowed with the social identity of the weaker, marginalised party. In other words, the hierarchy intrinsic to the structure of dichotomies is mirrored in the hierarchy established among the identities that the dichotomies construct.

In the case of prenuptial agreements, for instance, the formal unconscionability option, framed within an ideology of prenups as 'just' contracts, goes with a specific women's identity that is characterised by a sense of empowerment and autonomy, celebrating the 'modern', liberated woman, able to self-determine herself with no constraints, uncertainties or insecurities. In contrast, the 'exception', i.e., a substantive notion of unconscionability correlated with an idea of contractual fairness and even a 'second look' option,[35] is associated with paternalism and a feminine stereotype that is considered outdated because of its intrinsic inferiority and subalternity to men, a woman in constant need of the support of the state.

Similarly, in Italian law, the two solutions proposed by the Supreme Court for the enforceability of matrimonial agreements in the context of divorce – both of which impose nullity, but with different degrees of intensity – reflect two different stereotypes of women. The rule of general nullity,[36] insofar as it renders voidable any agreement, even if it favours the supposedly weaker spouse, is compatible with formal gender equality and the emancipated woman, while the doctrine of relative nullity[37] is enforceable only in favour of the spouse made worse off by the agreement, that is, the subaltern woman.

---

[34] Compared to the UPAA, the UPMAA introduces a seemingly different regime for unconscionable terms but rejects a return to pre-UPAA 'paternalism'. It recognises a role for substantive unconscionability but adopts an 'unconscionability-at-execution' standard – not at the time of enforcement, i.e., divorce – that places a heavy burden of proof on the party seeking to void an agreement. The challenging party must generally prove both substantive unconscionability – a grossly unfair term, and procedural unconscionability – a grossly unfair process.

[35] A.M. Caulley, 'Policing the Prenup: When Love at First Sight Deserves a Second Look' (2017) 39 *Women's Rights Law Reporter* 1.

[36] Cass. civ., 26.04.2021, n. 11012.

[37] Cass. civ., 14.06.2000, n. 8109.

Both the doctrine depicted as the rule and the doctrine applied as an exception produce discrete distributive effects. Depending on the different groups of women they will affect, both can be empowering or disempowering.

An intersectional gaze is implied here.[38] The intersection of class, gender, and race will determine who will be advantaged or disadvantaged by each of them. The argument becomes strikingly clear if one considers the impact of both categories of doctrines at the symbolic level. This brings the issue of identity to the fore once more. The ultimate distributive outcome concerns not only economic and social power but also symbolic power. This result might seem to be intertwined with the so-called difference dilemma. Doctrines that enforce formal equality promote the liberated woman model, but at the same time, they preserve the *status quo* with substantial inequalities within it. Doctrines that push forward an ideal of substantive equality are more likely to remove obstacles to a more just society at the price of depicting women as victims of male power and to end up disempowering them. The intersectional approach can help to dismantle the difference dilemma and escape another dichotomic trap. We must assume, first, that low-income, disadvantaged women in the family/contract pattern are worse off not because of the way they are, but because of the way power is discursively organised and deployed by the law; and second, that the various legal solutions available need to be examined for their potential impact on different groups of women, according to their preferences, and in terms of the complex gender, class, inter- and intra-racial distributive outcomes they can achieve.

## 2.3. THE MALE/FEMALE DICHOTOMY AS THE MATRIX OF ALL LEGAL DICHOTOMIES

Feminist legal theory has also highlighted the masculinity of the mainstream legal discourse in marginalising certain doctrines in relation to others. This in turn constructs the identity of the legal interpreter and theorist, the law professor – and the jurist's mainstream identity more generally – as white and male (and elitist).

In an unfinished article (published posthumously), Mary Joe Frug shows 'how conventional analytical devices are deeply implicated in the construction of our current gender system'.[39] Debunking the idea that 'the male bias of

38 K. Crenshaw, 'Demarginalising the intersection of race and sex: a black feminist critique of antidiscrimination doctrine, feminist theory and antiracist politics' (1989) (1) *University of Chicago Legal Forum* 139.

39 M.J. Frug, 'Rescuing Impossibility Doctrine. A Postmodern feminist Analysis of Contract Law' (1992) 140 *University of Pennsylvania Law Review* 1029, 1046.

our society ... has not had important consequences for contract law',[40] she emphasises the role of language, including legal language, as a mechanism of power – a mechanism in which gender relations are intimately entangled, so that identifying the gendered character of discourses becomes a feminist strategy for contesting 'the extensive and complicated network of social and cultural practices which legitimate the subordination of women'. And this begins with the recognition that the relationship between dichotomies in opposing discourses often reflects cultural stereotypes of men and women.

The dichotomy she addresses in her article is a doctrinal one, namely the strict liability/impossibility dichotomy or, more precisely, the male/female stereotyping in the conceptualisation of the doctrine of impossibility in legal literature, where impossibility can be more or less the exception as opposed to full performance (or strict liability) as the rule, depending on the masculine or feminine attitude adopted by the author under consideration. The hierarchical nature of dichotomies is crucial here. Namely, the hierarchical dimension of gender relations sheds light on the ordering of opposing discourses: usually one argument is understood as the dominant approach, while 'the second line of thought is perceived as exceptional or subordinate to the first',[41] mirroring the male/female pattern.

In highlighting the gendered nature of doctrinal discourse, Frug also suggests that legal rhetoric can assume sexual overtones, suggestive of stereotypical 'sex talk', perhaps unconscious *double entendre*. In this framework, the idea, asserted by some scholars,[42] that impossibility can only be enforced when the promisee is the superior risk-bearer offers not a clue for parties already in contractual relationships, but an abstract standard designed to facilitate efficient contract planning, presenting itself as 'singular, daunting, rigid, and cocksure ... like a phallus'.[43] In fact, it proposes an on/off remedial system based on the full performance/discharge dichotomy, which resonates with 'stereotypical male virtues'.[44] Suggesting a sexual *double entendre*, these scholars criticise the conventional legal categories in this field as *empty* and *sterile* and promise to *give content* to a different analysis, recalling the erotic imagery of alpha-maleness. Frug then presents an opposing discourse that rejects the superior risk-bearer standard and promotes values of mutual fairness in light of a 'pluralistic, context-sensitive model of contract relations, ... in which the parties rely on good faith, forbearance, and sharing, rather than insisting on a literal interpretation of their contract texts'. The performance/discharge

---

40 Ibid., 1030.

41 Ibid., 1032.

42 Frug refers here to R.A. Posner and A.M. Rosenfield, 'Impossibility and Related Doctrines in Contract Law: An Economic Analysis' (1977), 6(1) *The Journal of Legal Studies* 83.

43 M.J. Frug, above n. 39, 1035.

44 Ibid., 1036.

dichotomy is abandoned in favour of a duty of adjustment and conventional remedial options that can take into account the *actual harm* being caused to a party. This discourse displays all the arguments typical of cultural feminism's ethic of care, celebrating a supposedly feminine attitude to justice. Its language is not cocksure, but 'unintimidating, accommodating, and unassuming'. The impossibility doctrine is presented as supplemental to freedom of contract, moulded on the desires of the parties, applicable where the parties have left gaps in their contract. For Frug, all of this evokes 'a stereotypically female description of sexual relations'.[45] In developing her argument, Frug also shows that both narratives suffer from the stereotypical weaknesses associated with their respective genders of reference: the *masculine* arbitrariness, rigidity and authoritarianism, in one case, the *feminine* terror of confrontation, argument and autonomy, in the other.[46] In both versions, the genderisation of legal language ends up reproducing the same dynamics of power that construct the hierarchy between men and women. From the point of view of post-modern feminism that Frug embraces, it is necessary to escape this pattern, which means to collapse the male/female opposition and to disrupt the relationship of mutual segregation of strict liability and impossibility doctrine, by recognising their reciprocal distance, but, at the same time, their relationship of reciprocal dependence. Maleness cannot be defined other than in relation to femaleness, just as strict liability and full performance cannot be defined except in relation to impossibility and discharge. Hosting the '*différance*' (à la Jacques Derrida)[47] within each term of the opposition means overcoming the opposition itself and deconstructing the discursive practices that build social hierarchies.

---

45 Frug refers here (ibid., 1038) to R.A. Hillman, 'An Analysis of the Cessation of Contractual Relations' (1983) 68(5) *Cornell Law Review* 1, 617.

46 Ibid., 1038 et seq.

47 The reference here is to Derrida's coinage of the term différance, which plays on the fact that the French verb *différer*, like the Italian 'differire', refers both to the concept of 'difference' and to that of 'postponement', to indicate the dynamic process of creating meaning in language, where each sign acquires meaning only in relation to other signs, referring to something else and not possessing its own stable meaning. The 'a' in the word 'différance' has a crucial value: with respect to the temporal dimension, it indicates deferral, postponement in time, the suspension of meaning that is never fully present, but precisely 'deferred'. In spatial terms, it indicates the interval, the distance between signs, the separation that allows their differentiation. The term was first used by the French philosopher in J. Derrida, 'Cogito et histoire de la folie' (1963) 68(4) *Revue de Métaphysique et de Morale* 68:460–494; its use is then explored in depth in J. Derrida, 'Différance' (1968) *Bulletin de la Société francaise de philosophie*, LXII, 3, 73-101. Frug's use of it in the text is clear: to highlight the mutually constitutive relationship between the terms of the opposition between non-fulfillment and impossibility—to indicate in the doctrine of impossibility the différance in contract law—serves to deconstruct the hierarchical order of rule/exception that is generally attributed to them, and in an infinite chain of references to signifiers and dichotomies, to arrive at the deconstruction of the fundamental opposition, that between masculine and feminine.

## 3. BARGAINING POWER AND BACKGROUND RULES: THE ROLE OF THE LAW OF SOCIAL REPRODUCTION

Critical analysis demonstrates that the distributive outcomes of transactions are not merely influenced by the legal doctrines or rules in the foreground – that is, those rules directly applied to the contract – but also by background rules, which are significant determinants of the relative bargaining power of each contractual party. As far as gender-related contracts are concerned, the potential for an unequal balance of bargaining power is one of the most critical issues.

Once more, the case of domestic agreements, including prenuptial agreements, is of paramount importance in testing the influence of the imbalance of bargaining power on contract fairness. However, the question remains as to where this imbalance originates. Is it a matter of culture? Of social justice? Or is it a legal issue? In gender-related transactions, the way in which the law regulates social reproduction is a significant factor in the unequal distribution of bargaining power between the parties. In particular, the family law discipline of the core of reproductive labour, i.e., care and housework performed for free for a spouse, children, elderly parents, disabled members of the family and the like, represents the matrix of the inequalities that arise from the marginalisation of social reproduction in the public discourse.

Because modern family law regulates caregiving as a marital duty of contribution to the household, it cannot be waived, nor can it be contractualised: in other words, it cannot be bargained for or paid for.[48] Its relevance emerges in various places in the law of marriage: 1. As an essential part of marriage, it represents a duty to contribute to the household; 2. It is rewarded by joint marital property in legal systems that enforce this regime model (but opting out usually requires no justification, so it's quite easy to waive the default regime); 3. In the event of family breakdown, care work performed during marriage can be rewarded through alimony or division of marital property (with many limitations, depending on the balancing considerations of the courts as to whether and how much alimony is due, whether it is permanent or temporary, whether or not it rewards so-called investments in human capital, whether it is valued on the basis of living standards during marriage or on opportunity costs, or on the idea of individual autonomy and self-determination, viewing marriage as a temporary partnership).

As a matter of fact, the legal treatment of informal, non-waged care and housework in the home (i.e., in the context of marriage and unmarried couples) serves as a background rule, with caregivers disadvantaged by a legal regime that

[48] See above section 2.1.

structures care work as unpaid work and ultimately as non-labour. In keeping with this regulatory framework, legal discourse obscures the performative and gendered nature of unpaid care work and reinforces genderised identities: in divorce cases, lawyers typically talk about the weaker spouse and never link this weakness to unpaid care work for the family. According to this narrative, the weaker spouse is such by nature, not because she performs unpaid work for the family. The conjugal regime of care work just described affects the power relations within married couples and exerts its influence in relation to unmarried couples too (a different paradigm for them is hardly recognised), because it constitutes a (set of) *background rule(s)* that affects the whole law of social reproduction, influencing the bargaining power of caregivers and defining the position of women in society and the market. In fact, on the one hand, the non-work model established by family law influences the availability and desirability of alternative options that informal caregivers can find in the market, to the extent that the burden of care work renders them structurally less appealing in the marketplace and weak in bargaining; on the other hand, this same weakness affects the possibility and desirability of leaving marriage to pursue an independent life. As Carol Rose has observed, this phenomenon also plays out at the symbolic level. First, the fact that women are the predominant or exclusive providers of care work creates a presumption of willingness to cooperate as a social actor. This, in turn, leads to the perception that women are more cooperative than men, which disadvantages them in the marketplace. Given that the household is 'a woman's domain', solidarity is the predominant attitude of women, both within the family and in the market. This presumption can influence their overall contractual experience in the market (and in the family). In other words, it diminishes women's bargaining power. Secondly, this social stereotype extends far beyond family law, domesticity, and the sphere of informal care work. It contributes to the production of subaltern subjectivities and to the creation/reinforcement of a commodified sphere of genderised jobs (including sex work and, to some extent, surrogacy), which lie at the margins of the regulated market and have specific characteristics: unregulated activities, womanly labour, unskilled work, and social isolation.[49] Third, this complex pattern specifically affects, directly and indirectly, the way waged care work is socially perceived. The commodification of care (wage care labour) is generated at the global scale by the desire of women in the Global North to be freed from the unpaid gendered care work in the family that makes them economically vulnerable and socially marginalised. The reverse is also true: migrant care workers inserted into global care chains are mostly women from the Global South aspiring to get better earning opportunities by working

[49] P. Kotiswaran, 'Laws of Social Reproduction' (2023) 19 *Annual Review of Law and Social Sciences* 145.

in households in the Global North. Paid and unpaid care work are, therefore, mutually constitutive and share the same social perception, the two polarities of which are romanticisation on the one hand and devaluation on the other. Both the romanticisation and the devaluation of care derive from commonplaces about unpaid family work, which in turn are grounded in its legal regime: women's ethics of care, women's presumed inclination to cooperate, are reflected in the legal construction of housework as non-work. To sum up, the model of unpaid family work exerts a symbolic hegemony in the field of social reproduction, since it influences the social perception and the economy of care and reproductive work available in the market. On the other hand, it acts as a background rule that affects the bargaining power of caregivers in whatever employment or social activity they undertake, disempowering them.

## 4. AGAINST THE EU AVERAGE CONSUMER: CONSUMER VULNERABILITY AND THE CONSTRUCTION OF SPACE

A process of 'socialisation' of private law profoundly affected European legal systems at the end of the 1800s, recalibrating the private/public divide and enhancing a new idea of private law as another tool to redistribute power and resources among different groups in society in response to urgent social problems that had emerged because of inequalities among formally free and equal citizens.

The legislation (and, more rarely, the judge through general clauses) took a primary role through the legal protection of specific categories of weaker parties and designed a new private law articulated in two bodies: the individualistic and static, dogmatic core of the civil codes and a vital, democratic and social law in the periphery, marked by *ad hoc* statutory laws.

To these developments consumer law should be traced back . The consumer was considered a weaker market actor and as such they required protection by means of regulation, mostly in the form of compulsory laws to regulate and drive the whole national market.

In this framework, until the 1960s, in Continental Europe, consumer law was tied to compulsory terms and price control, disclosing the substantial link between public intervention and private law.

In the current perspective, the inequality of bargaining power – which was one of the main concerns of this first stage of consumerism – has been somehow metabolised and translated into a physiological phenomenon. By now the main issue has become the presence of pathological factors that may affect the process by which the contract is completed and do not allow contractual autonomy to perform its function properly.

The asymmetry of contractual power is no longer the result of unequal relations of the parties, but the result of so-called *market failures*, a range of situations that prevent the market from operating correctly. This *ex-post* control of transactions emphasises private law autonomy over public intervention because the courts are supposed to only remedy market failures instead of regulating the contract to prevent them.

Even standard contracts fit into this pattern, because by excluding individually negotiated contracts, it is taken for granted that consumers who bargain for their contracts negotiate terms that match their needs and are aware of the consequences.

If the regulatory nature of the intervention is no longer denied, then (public) interference is made much less problematic for the (private) market, since it now serves to restore the conditions for its proper functioning.

In Continental law, very often the allocative efficiency motive that characterises this type of intervention has been disguised and harnessed to bring it more in line with what is considered to be the European tradition from a perspective that combines market protection and personal values.[50]

A discourse of identity became, then, slowly dominant. In any legal system claimants of rights are organised according to their plural, cross-cutting 'identities'. 'Identity represents at once an extension of and a total transformation of the categories – social class and national minority – through which the social jurists disintegrated the Savignian "people"'.[51] Identity is the offspring of the social concerns with subordinated or discriminated-against identities.

At the core of identity discourse are the 'weak parties': the antagonistic subjects of the former stage – whose interests had to be coordinated in order to ensure the general interest – become 'weak parts' to be protected also through a private law regime that takes into account their weakness and tries to mitigate it by defining legal relations in which the 'strong' are called on to take care of the 'weak'. Some actors are forbidden to discriminate against some identities. Some actors may be compelled to deal on more favourable terms with others.[52]It is difficult however to identify the distributional consequences

50 The literature of behavioural economics that suggests patterns of over-optimism and mis-estimation of certain risks in decision-making provides additional autonomy-based arguments for doctrines that are often characterised as paternalistic (and therefore slightly suspect) interventions in contractual freedom.

51 D. Kennedy, *Three globalizations of law and legal thought: 1850–2000*, Cambridge University Press, Cambridge 2010, p. 66.

52 Weak parts as opposed to strong parts: worker and employer, landlord and tenant, consumers and professionals, women and men, and then – depending on the different national contexts and various feelings – mentally disabled and 'normal', disabled and able, children and adults and among them elderly and younger people, unemployed and those in employment, and with them now illegal immigrants compared to legal immigrants and citizens. Even the poor tend to be considered a category compared with the middle class and the wealthy.

of such interventions.[53] Identity becomes the site of conflict. Some identities conflict with each other and further (internal) conflicts may occur within any form of identity. This is also the case of consumer law, in which it is not easy to understand the distributive effects it may have within different consumer groups ('poor consumers', 'risks consumers', 'disadvantaged consumers'). It is possible, in fact, that the benefits of protection are not distributed evenly within the group: the impact on all those who are included can be different, hitting the weakest within the group or impacting unilaterally instead on the stronger ones (the most informed and responsible members may end up subsidising the most opportunist and venal ones). A more refined distributive analysis can produce a more articulated vision, clarifying too the different ways in which vertical (class) differences cross and are combined with horizontal (cultural) differences.

In competitive market situations, these regulatory interventions most often induce the strong party to *pass on* the costs of protection to the beneficiaries, but it compels them to pay higher prices. The objection is the so-called 'backfiring': the increase of the price affects the marginal consumer, placed at the lowest level of income, excluding him from the market or forcing him to turn to the black market, where protection is lower still or non-existent.[54]

However, another and more complex version of this phenomenon has also been revealed: the cross-subsidy effect would operate from the group of the most responsible or competent (consumers) to the group of the least responsible and competent (consumers). With the increase in protective measures, the price increase will burden more the prudent or informed consumer (who would not need protection and would probably not pay for it) and now must pay as much as the inattentive consumer. Protection is turned into a real subsidy from the former to the latter. In any case solidarity is all among the 'weak party' group and the distributive effect operates only within this section.The goal of 1960s consumer politics to guarantee the protection of the weaker members of the consumer society gradually disappeared and it was replaced with a different view in which the consumer is a competent market actor who operates in a multinational market. From this perspective the object of the protection is the average consumer – 'reasonably well-informed and reasonably observant

---

53 R.X. Hale, above n. 5, 470; D. Kennedy, 'The Stakes of Law, or Hale and Foucault' in D. Kennedy, *Sexy Dressing Etc. Essays on the Power and Politics of Cultural Identity*, Harvard University Press, Cambridge MA 1993, p. 83.

54 The case is very well known and should call for more attention to the way in which consumer protection operates in so-called ghetto markets.

and circumspect'[55] – who is able to protect herself through active and well-informed choices in the marketplace.[56]

Consumer empowerment has become so crucial that all European legislation relies on the consumers' ability to use and process market information to foster competition and drive the European economy. The law of consumer protection has turned into consumer law 'without protection'.[57] The European model has undergone a significant transformation, ranked as one of 'access justice' and different from the national models of social justice. It mainly gives consumers a chance to access (the internal market) through fair and non-discriminatory access conditions.

Even in the United States, which lacks a comprehensive vision of consumer law, there has been a similar trajectory in unconscionability cases, which are the main venues for the realisation of consumer protection.[58] It is still in 1965, in the *Williams* case, that Judge Skelly Wright may define unconscionability as a pillar of a real 'law of the poor, a response against the old rules that

---

55 Recital 18 of the Preamble of the Unfair Commercial Practices Directive.

56 For various critiques of the empowerment-through-information approach in the EU cf. V. Mak, 'The Consumer in European Regulatory Private Law' in D. Leczykievicz and S. Weatherill (eds.), *The Image(s) of the Consumer in EU Law: Legislation, Free Movemenr and Competition Law*, Hart Publishing, Oxford 2016, p. 382; H.-W. Micklitz, 'The Expulsion of the Concept of Protection from the Consumer Law and the Return to Social Elements in the Civil Law: A Bittersweet Polemic' (2012) 35 *JCP (Journal of Consumer Policy)* 283, 296; G. Howells, 'The Potential and Limits of Consumer Empowerment by Information' (2005) 32(3) *Journal of Law and Society* 349, 370. For the difficulty in dealing with consumers' information overload and their limited information processing capabilities, see B.B. Duivenvoorde, *The Consumer Benchmarks in the Unfair Commercial Practice Directive*, Springer, New York 2015; H. Schebesta and K. Purnhagen, 'Island or Ocean: Empirical Evidence on the Average Consumer Concept in the UCPD' (2020) 28 *European Review of Private Law* 293, 310.

57 '[A] legal model which does not primarily guarantee social justice through redistribution, but especially ensures access to the market, to enable him to benefit from the advantages of the plethora of products and services on offer in an expanded European or global environment: "access justice" (*Zugangsgerechtigkeit*)'.
H.W. Micklitz, above n. 56, 'The consumer shall take advantage of the economic benefits of the single European market by using [the] internet in an active way (to search for the cheapest provider and order products regardless of all territorial social and linguistic limitations (efficiency) with negative effect on local providers and social structures at neighbourhood level)'.

58 Under the unconscionability provision of the American Uniform Commercial Code, s 2-302, courts decline to enforce contracts where the terms are grossly unfair in circumstances where the purchaser was illiterate or naive in business matters (*Frostifresh Corpn v. Reynoso* 54 Misc. 2d 119 (1967), or on the broadest statement of the test of unconscionability, where there is 'an absence of meaningful choice' (*Williams v. Walker-Thomas Furniture Co.* 350 F. 2d 445, 449 (DC Cir., 1965). Although disputed (see A. Leff, 'Unconscionability and the Crowd – Consumers and the Common Law Tradition' (1969) 31 *University of Pittsburgh Law Review* 349, 354, and R. Epstein, 'Unconscionability: a critical reappraisal' (1975) 18 *Journal of Law and Economics* 293), the doctrine found its way into the system, applied by analogy to all types of contracts: E.A. Farnsworth, W.E. Young and C. Sanger, *Contracts. Cases and materials*, Wolters Kluwer, New York 2020.

co-operate in creating and perpetuating the injustice involved in the way many poor people are forced to live in the nation's capital'; however, after 10 years, there are almost no more precedents where the remedy is invoked in favour of the poor. In casebooks, the use of unconscionability for these purposes has been curtailed to a mere historical curiosity, a sort of remnant to be remembered just to legitimise a legal landscape where unconscionability is now mainly, if not only, used to counter the consequences of informational asymmetries in the standard form contracts or adhesion contracts by setting aside unfair terms.[59]

## 5. VULNERABILITY IN THE DIGITAL SPACE

This has brought to light again many of the criticisms that followed the emergence of consumer law in the '60s about the selectivity and opacity of the consumer category and therefore its ideological role. Consumers are not a uniform category: diversity and heterogeneity better characterise consumers as a group – for they do not share the same abilities, characteristics, social circumstances, and economic position.

In such a context, the first critique is reminiscent of the 'poor pay more' phenomenon because information and transparency benefit those already in a privileged position.[60] The second critique is that in this way it flattens the poor and the rich within the same space. A richer understanding of the act of consumption and what it involves is needed, one that takes into account the social and cultural context within which consumer preferences are channelled.[61]

With this comes back to the fore again the possibility, too, of promoting a different type of consumer, the vulnerable consumer, i.e., that consumer incapable of self-care and due diligence, who finds little solace in European regulation. But who are the 'vulnerable'?

---

59 The doctrine seeks 'the prevention of oppression and unfair surprise' and is directed against the 'disturbance of allocation of risks because of superior bargaining power'. Courts continue to apply the unconscionability doctrine to refuse to enforce extremely high interest rates, even when consumers are well aware of them when signing.

60 D. Caplovitz, *The Poor Pay More: Consumer Protection of Low-Income Families*, The Free Press, New York 1963.

61 On the way in which the concept of consumption becomes an instrument of social integration and control through atomisation and individualisation of behaviour in modern capitalist society, I. Ramsay, 'Consumer Law and the Search for Empowerment' (1991) 19 *Canadian Business Law Journal* 397; I. Ramsay, 'Framework for Regulation of the Consumer Marketplace' (1985) 8 *JCP* 353.

The idea of the 'vulnerable consumer' – as it is usually conceived – singles out certain groups of consumers that are more susceptible to being deceived and less able to protect themselves.[62]

Digital markets remind us that vulnerability describes a universal state of defencelessness and susceptibility to (the exploitation of) power imbalances that are the result of increasing automation and datafication of commerce.[63]

If the use of digital technology and data analytics can certainly be useful in optimising commercial practices by helping the consumer to find and remember goods and services they are looking for, and by personalising the relationship between trader and consumer, on the other hand their use can be the source of new power imbalances between consumers and traders, and new forms of unfair commercial practices.

At the heart of the new targeted advertising is the creation of personalised 'persuasion profiles' that operate in connection with adaptive strategies that deliver the right message at the right time and place to the right consumer.

Persuasion profiles are only part of the problem. On a more structural level, the platformisation of e-commerce and the creation of an architecture of the site enable choices that benefit an online service by coercing, steering, or deceiving users into making unintended and potentially harmful decisions.

In such digital choice environments, technology is used more generally to shape the very relationship between advertisers, sellers, and consumers and give it continuity and enduring knowledge of the consumer 'commercialisation potential' that increases over time and with time. Large commercial tech platforms have enjoyed broad opportunities to shape the digital marketplace. Within the boundaries of the GDPR and competition law, they were essentially free to build digital choice architectures and to develop a flourishing App economy.

The conditions the consumer encounters in the choice architecture of digital markets create new forms of vulnerability. Thus, vulnerability is not

---

62 On vulnerability see T. Wilhelmsson, 'The Informed Consumer vs the Vulnerable Consumer in European Unfair Commercial Practices Law – A Comment' in G.G. Howells, A. Hordhausen, D. Parry and C. Twigg-Flesner (eds.), *Yearbook of Consumer Law*, Ashgate Publishing, Farnham 2007, p. 211, pp. 212–213; see S. Weatherill, 'Who is the "Average Consumer"?' in S. Weatherill and U. Bernitz (eds.), *The Regulation of Unfair Commercial Practices under EC Directive 2005/29: New Rules and New Techniques*, Hart Publishing, Oxford 2007, p. 136; V. Mak, above n. 57, p. 386; P. Cartwright, 'Understanding and Protecting Vulnerable Financial Consumers' (2005) 38 *JCP* 119, 138. N. Reich, 'Vulnerable consumers in EU law' in D. Leczykiewicz and S. Weatherill (eds.), *The Image of the Consumer in EU Law: Legislation, Free Movement and Competition Law*, Bloomsbury Publishing, London 2018. For a layered understanding of vulnerability, see F. Luna, 'Elucidating the Concept of Vulnerability. Layers Not Labels' (2009) 2 *International Journal of Feminist Approaches to Bioethics* 121, 139, and F. Luna, 'Identifying and Evaluating Layers of Vulnerability – A Way Forward' (2019) 19 *Developing World Bioethics* 86, 95.

63 N. Helberger et al., 'Choice Architectures in the Digital Economy: Towards a New Understanding of Digital Vulnerability' (2022) 45 *JCP* 175.

an unfortunate by-product of digital consumer markets, but the system's purposeful product.

With digital practices, vulnerability is about the power or ability of commercial actors to affect the decisions, desires, and behaviour of the consumers in ways that they cannot prevent. It is created through the interaction between sellers and consumers within digital environments that can learn about them and be adapted accordingly.[64] Against these practices, it is unlikely that the remedies provided by the Unfair Commercial Practices Directive (UCP) and, where relevant, the General Data Protection Regulation (GDPR) will succeed.[65]

On the one hand, the choice of the average consumer as the benchmark to assess a commercial practice's fairness represents a serious obstacle to the adequacy of the remedy. On the other hand, the use of the concept of vulnerability does not secure a better outcome.[66]

According to UCP the vulnerable consumer is a member of a 'clearly identifiable group of consumers who are particularly vulnerable to the practice or the underlying product because of their mental or physical infirmity, age or credulity in a way which the trader could reasonably be expected to foresee' (Article 5(3)). Under the UCP, be the list exhaustive or not,[67] vulnerability is traceable only to personal or internal characteristics and the effect that these characteristics have on the consumer's ability to deal.

Again, this is a case where an inherent tension at the heart of consumer protection law can be observed between enabling consumers to play their role as active and autonomous market participants and protecting the weaker party, a party that requires special regulatory or policy attention due to lack of

64 V. Mak, 'A Primavera for European Consumer Law: Re-birth of the Consumer Image in the Light of Digitalisation and Sustainability' (2022) 11 *Journal of European Consumer and Market Law* 77, 80. N. Bol et al., 'Vulnerability in a Tracked Society: Combining Tracking and Survey Data to Understand Who Gets Targeted With What Content' (2020) 22(11) *New Media & Society* 1996, 2017; G. Malgieri and J. Niklas, 'Vulnerable Data Subjects' (2020) 37 *Computer Law and Security Review* 1, 16.

65 N. Helberger, 'Profiling and targeting consumers in the Internet of Things – A new challenge for consumer law' in R. Schulze and D. Staudenmayer (eds.), *Digital Revolution: Challenges for Contract Law in Practice*, Nomos, Baden-Baden 2020, pp. 135–162.

66 B. Duivenvoorde, 'The protection of vulnerable consumers under the Unfair Commercial Practice Directive' (2013) 2(2) *Journal of European Consumer and Market Law* 69 A survey of the way in which the concept is used to allow differentiation in situations in which uniform treatment of all would lead to unfairness for some (D. Leczykiewicz and S. Weatherill (eds.), above n. 57, and L. Peroni and A. Timmers, 'Vulnerable groups: The promise of an emerging concept in European human rights convention law' (2013) 11(4) *International Journal of Constitutional Law* 1056, 1085, with special reference to European Court of Human Rights' case law).

67 B. Duivenvoorde, above n. 67; G. Howells, C. Twigg-Flesner and T. Wilhelmsson, *Rethinking EUconsumer law*, Milton Park, Routledge 2018. H.G. Micklitz and M. Namyslowska, *Münchener Kommentar Zum Lauterkeitsrecht*, C.H. Beck, Munich 2020, Art. 8 Rdnr. 22.

bargaining power, structural inequalities and other market or social conditions that make them more vulnerable to forms of discrimination or unequal treatment.[68]

In the European landscape the two categories end up reinforcing the default standard of the 'average consumer'. First, consumer vulnerability is conceived as an exception from the norm of the 'average consumer' and to justify its protection is not enough to allege a status of consumer, but it is necessary to add further substantial considerations; and secondly, using the 'average' consumer as a benchmark makes it the parameter against which the vulnerabilities are to be assessed.

The categorical approach invites different kinds of criticisms. First, personal characteristics are too narrow and flat as characteristics to enable us to grasp the dynamic dimension of vulnerabilities. Vulnerability depends on the circumstances (or contextual setting) in which consumers find themselves. Second, the person-based categorisations not only stigmatise groups of consumers but also prevent us from identifying those groups within the vulnerable category that are worse off than others. Thus, it prevents the operators (judges, lawyers, and state) from directing their attention to the factors that undermine consumer decision-making and that call for special and differentiated protections from the state.

Recent advances in vulnerability literature have questioned the rigidity of the distinction between the average or the vulnerable consumer due to the risk of framing consumer protection law as something that only certain 'weak' categories of people need, a destabilising departure from the 'average' consumer, something that depends only on your personal characteristics and not on the overall structure of the market.[69]

The digitalisation of consumer markets is further feeding these concerns. It has triggered entirely new forms of personalised persuasion strategies that find out, and build on, individual biases, weaknesses, preferences. They can be targeted, very knowingly, at making consumers – even those that do not belong to the typical categories of vulnerable consumers – vulnerable, in the sense of affecting their ability to rationally deal with a particular marketing practice. Thereby consumer vulnerability becomes a goal that the systems can optimise for.

The focus should shift to the properties of digital choice environments and the way in which sellers are allowed to detect and exploit digital vulnerability.

---

68 A. Cole, 'All of us are vulnerable, but some are more vulnerable than others: The political ambiguity of vulnerability studies, an ambivalent critique' (2016) 17(2) *Critical Horizons* 260, 273: 'Vulnerability has to be reframed as a claim about injustice'.

69 G. Howells, C. Twigg-Flesner and T. Wilhelmsson, *Rethinking EU consumer law*, Milton Park, Routledge 2018, 28-29.

In its turn, the universal approach has been criticised as well, because it leaves no room for individual differences related to identity and social status.[70] It forgets how vulnerability is significantly affected by the quality and quantity of resources available to each of us.[71] As such it would reproduce – but in reverse – the same the dichotomy between vulnerable/non-vulnerable that vulnerability theory sought to abolish.[72]

To take account of these inequalities, it is necessary to acknowledge and analyse in depth the specific factors that turn the theoretical possibility of being vulnerable into a real condition of unfairness:[73] a different approach, certainly more attentive to the role played by external and societal factors which 'originate, sustain, and reinforce vulnerabilities'.[74] From this perspective, an important contribution has emphasised "the interaction of individual states, individual characteristics, and external conditions within a context where consumption goals may be hindered and the experience affects personal and social perceptions of self".[75] Another view points out that it is not so much belonging to a group of particular consumers that marks these individuals as vulnerable, but 'it is the circumstances that consumers face that determine their vulnerability'.[76] In a similar vein, some have focused on contextual, relational, and situational factors, and drawn a useful distinction between informational vulnerability (as in the UCP) and impact vulnerability (pressure, supply,

---

70 The European Commission itself re-affirmed the individual dimension of vulnerability, affected very much by situation: 'a consumer can be vulnerable in one situation but not in others' and 'some consumers may be more vulnerable than others': European Commission, Understanding Consumer Vulnerability in the EU's Key Markets, Factsheet (2016).

71 F.R. Cooper, 'Always already suspect: Revising vulnerability theory' (2015) 93 *The North Carolina Law Review* 1339, 1379.

72 A. Cole, above n. 69: 'The concept has been rendered so broad as to obscure the needs of specific groups and individuals, undermining its premise as a conceptual frame to understand and challenge systemic inequalities' (p. 267).

73 L. Peroni and A. Timmers, above n. 67.

74 L. Peroni and A. Timmers, above n. 67. Consumer literature relates to two main streams of thought: vulnerability as a result of disadvantages and of marketer manipulation. Regarding disadvantages, research in this stream focuses on individuals disadvantaged through their individual characteristics, socio-economic status, and available resources (R.P. Hill and E. Sharma, 'Consumer Vulnerability' (2020) 30(2) *JCP* 4). In the case of manipulation, researchers have, for example, examined why and how interpersonal influence can make consumers vulnerable to marketing scams (J. Langenderfer and T.A. Shimp, 'Consumer vulnerability to scams, swindles, and fraud: A new theory of visceral influences on persuasion' (2001) 18(7) *Psychology & Marketing* 763, 783).

75 See S.M. Baker, J.W. Gentry and T.L. Rittenburg, 'Building Understanding of the Domain of Consumer Vulnerability' (2005) 25(2) *Journal of Macromarketing* 128, 129, emphasising the broad range of factors affecting vulnerability, such as individual characteristics (e.g., age, race, physical capabilities), social phenomena (e.g. stereotyping), business practices (e.g., store layouts, marketer manipulations), and environmental forces (e.g. natural disasters).

76 R.P. Hill and E. Sharma, above n. 75, 4.

redress).[77] Or, finally, some focus on a clear distinction between vulnerabilities and capabilities in which the latter should be considered individual, internal vulnerability drivers, and the former external, contextual, relational, and situational vulnerability drivers composed of markets' varying consumer conditions not related to the capabilities of a single individual.[78]

Indeed, to acknowledge that vulnerability is the product of 'systems of power and privilege that interact to produce webs of advantages and disadvantages'[79] means to shift the focus on those market structures and configurations that make some people vulnerable or exploit their vulnerabilities.

Thus, vulnerability depends on one's relation to the world and the different forces (social, physical, technical) that can affect anything one deems important, and one's (lack of) control or power over those forces.

The universal condition of vulnerability is particularly true for digital markets: an important goal behind digital market practices is to identify all those different circumstances under which persons can be made vulnerable, as well as the points beyond which they become vulnerable.

In practice, this means that to truly understand and conceptualise consumer vulnerability, it is necessary to explore market practices, systemic and institutional conditions that create vulnerability in the first place. In this system vulnerability is dynamic; it is the product of an 'adaptive persuasive system'.[80] It is precisely people's ongoing involvement in various digital markets and services that makes them increasingly vulnerable to having their (economic) behaviour manipulated. Its typical features are (a) architectural, because digital choice architectures are designed to infer or even create vulnerabilities; (b) relational, because people's relational ties with others make them vulnerable to other actors and influences: and (c) partly independent of lack of privacy, because digital vulnerabilities can only be reinforced by 'optimising' the privacy settings environment for maximal data flows, and platforms can further strengthen their position of power by gaining even more

---

77 P. Cartwright, 'Understanding and protecting vulnerable financial consumers' (2015) 38 *Journal of Consumer Policy* 119.

78 I. Berg, 'Consumer vulnerability: Are older people more vulnerable as consumers than others?' (2015) 39(4) *International Journal of Consumer Studies* 284.

79 M. Albertson Fineman, 'The Vulnerable Subject: Anchoring Equality in the Human Condition' (2008) 20 *Yale Journal of Law and Feminism* 1, 16. Indeed, as Albertson Fineman (p. 9) has argued, vulnerability theory can be a 'powerful conceptual tool with the potential to define an obligation for the state to ensure a richer and more robust guarantee of equality than is currently afforded under the equal protection model'.

80 C. Mackenzie, W. Rogers and S. Dodds, 'Introduction:What is vulnerability, and why does it matter for moral theory?', in C. Mackenzie, W. Rogers and S. Dodds (eds.), *Vulnerability: New Essays in Ethics and Feminist Philosophy*, OUP, Oxford 2018, 1–29.

insight into the behaviour and psychology of their users.[81] With respect to this feature, not all kinds of vulnerability materialise for everyone, and not all potential vulnerability ('dispositional vulnerabilities') necessarily translates into 'occurrent vulnerabilities'. Even when actual vulnerabilities *do* often materialise in certain circumstances, it does not follow that all consumers will be rendered *equally* vulnerable, since vulnerabilities have differentiated impact on different persons in different situations.

At the same time, dispositional vulnerabilities should not be underestimated. In our contemporary digital marketplaces, data-driven dynamically adjustable digital choice architectures can not only identify inherent vulnerabilities, but they can also reveal the way in which different consumers can be rendered vulnerable under different conditions.

It would be necessary to extend situational monopolies, so far typically discussed only in relation to uncompetitive pricing or coercing choice, also to situations in which users are induced to divulge more data than they would normally do and which abuse our inherent vulnerabilities to make us take decisions that we would otherwise not have taken.

A more holistic and contextual understanding of consumer vulnerability necessarily leads to a different strategy that rules out any understanding of consumer protection in terms of information tools and at the same time goes also beyond the needs of individual consumers.

Since structural as well as relational imbalances are involved, individual remedies – such as more information about parameters used to single them out – are not enough, particularly when data-driven strategies are used to create relational dependencies or digital situational monopolies.[82]

In the light of those digital market practices, it is necessary to imagine new professional duties and obligations of professional diligence (Article 5(1) and (2) UCP) and to retrieve a concept such as undue influence under Article 9 of the UCP.

The approach to vulnerability as a complex phenomenon also requires amechanism to be devised to counteract it, mitigate its impact and to take into account the collective dimension of the phenomenon.

Finally, it should also be added that consumer-related data are combined in extraordinary ways to be used outside the commercial sphere in different areas

81 N. Hellberger *Profiling and Targeting Consumers in the Internet of Things – A New Challenge in Consumer Law* (2016), in R. Schulze & D. Staudenmayer, *Digital Revolution: Challenges for contract law in practice,* Nomos, Baden-Baden, 135-162. R. Calo, 'Privacy, vulnerability, and affordances' (2017) 66(2) *DePaul Law Review* 591, 604.

82 It is the combination of data-driven insights into the user, a service platform geared to establishing lasting relationships with users, and certain architectural choices that reduce the likelihood of users moving outside the service universe and thereby reducing autonomy and choice.

of our life, politics, health, and work.[83] Through those practices it is possible to determine who gets access to which commercial/public services, at what price, and who is refused access or is given access on less favourable conditions.[84]

Neither consumer law, with its focus on economic decision-making, nor data protection law, with its emphasis on individual cases and rights of individual users *vis-à-vis* digital market practices, seems to be prepared to deal with these broader societal issues.

Once again, we might ask the questions of the EU's competence, legitimacy, and suitability to regulate a digital European society through the backdoor of Article 114 TFEU.

## 6. INTERLUDE: LEARNING FROM BROOKLINE.[85] CONSTRUCTING A RACIALLY SEGREGATED URBAN SPACE THROUGH CONTRACTS[86]

The production of urban segregation in US metropolitan areas has been a major factor in the construction of racial identities – and particularly in the construction of African American identity as inferior and inherently degrading. Private agreements contributed significantly to the efforts of federal and local governments to create a racially segregated urban environment in the first half of the twentieth century, at least until the presidency of John F. Kennedy.

The racialisation of urban neighbourhoods was as much the result of contracts and public regulations as it was of targeted development strategies supported by a strong public–private partnership. So-called 'white flight', i.e., white people fleeing from inner cities and moving to the suburbs, was due to a combination of a number of factors: a strong policy of zoning across the country, a mechanism of federal financing of construction loans to developers, and the inclusion of racially restrictive covenants in suburban property deeds.

At the core of this policy was the idea that opening up property to the middle class would prevent social uprisings along the lines of the Russian Revolution of

83 In the digital society, the distinction between the consumer as economic actor and the citizen as social actor is further eroded (M. Scammell, 'The internet and civic engagement: The age of the citizen-consumer' (2000) 17(4) *Political Communication* 351, 355).

84 S. Rodotà, *New Technologies and Human Rights Facts, interpretations, perspectives A report for a Fundamental Rights Agency's discussion* (2020), 11 *Comp. L. Rev.* 2; S. Barocas and A. Selbst, *Big Data's Disparate Impact* (2016), 104 *California Law Review*, 671; R. Fisman and M. Luca, *Fixing Discrimination in Online Marketplaces, in Harv. Bus. Rev.*, 2016/12.

85 Brookline, Massachusetts, was the first American city where title deeds, already at the end of the nineteenth century, forbade the resale of property 'to any negro or native of Ireland'.

86 This section depends to a large extent on the reading of R. Rothstein, *The Color of Law. A Forgotten History of How Our Government Segregated America*, Liveright Publishing Corporation, New York 2017.

1917. Home ownership would make citizens loyal to the capitalist system. This took place at a time when both the federal and local governments had begun to carry out racial segregation campaigns that affected the distribution of the population on the territory along the lines of race (sometimes along with class and nationality). Both strategies were supported by zoning regulations that designed white neighbourhoods as racially segregated single-family residential districts, with the further goal of protecting white homes from loss of value.

Initially, local zoning regulations were explicit in excluding non-Caucasian people from areas destined for whites' dwellings: local ordinances prohibited African Americans from buying homes on blocks where whites were the majority, and *vice versa*. In 1917, however, the Supreme Court forbade racial segregation by zoning ordinances (*Buchanan v. Warley*)[87] because it violated freedom of contract protected by the Fourteenth Amendment: racial zoning ordinances interfered with the owner's right to sell property to whomever he pleased. In order to evade *Buchanan*, zoning ordinances then took an economic route (in disguise of racist motives) by distinguishing single-family neighbourhoods from multifamily districts, the former being unaffordable to most African Americans (and to low-income families of all races). A federal campaign pushed white middle-class families to move out of apartments into single-family homes. But middle-class African American families could now also afford single-family homes. To promote homeownership along with racial segregation, the federal government instituted a series of mortgage insurance and amortisation programmes, available only to white neighbourhood owners and suburban developers[88] on the condition that they not sell to blacks, while promoting individual home deeds that prohibited the future resale of whites' homes to African Americans. The rationale was that federal investment in non-exclusive 'white' properties was risky because of the likely rapid decline in property values that would inevitably occur if African American families lived nearby.

Contractual arrangements proved strategic to this policy. Over time, restrictive covenants banning resale to people of colour turned out to be hardly effective because of privity of contract: agreements could not exert their binding strength on third parties like new purchasers, and in case of violation of the prohibition clause, original contracting parties like developers were unlikely to sue counterparts for breach of contract because of lack of interest.[89] Under these circumstances it was difficult to have the black family evicted.

---

87 *Buchanan v. Warley* 245 US 60 (1917).

88 On the interplay between single-family zoning and Federal Housing Administration policy, see also L. Gallagher, *The End of the Suburbs. Where the American Dream Is Moving*, Penguin Group, New York 2013, pp. 39 et seq.

89 A more complex picture of these dynamics is offered by B. Ross, *Dead End. Suburban Sprawl and the Rebirth of American Urbanism*, Oxford University Press, Oxford 2014, pp. 19 et seq.

So increasingly, throughout the twentieth century, segregationists adopted a different contractual strategy: contracts among all the owners of white neighbourhoods. But even this solution proved unsatisfactory to them. Anyone who did not sign the agreement could sell to African American families without fear of being successfully sued. The next step was then to institute a community in each new neighbourhood and bind owners to racial restrictions through associative contracts. Subdivision developers established such community associations prior to the initial sales, made membership a *conditio sine qua non* of purchase, and included 'whites-only' clauses. The association racial policy could not be modified without the vote of home owners representing a majority of the whole area. Based on such restrictive covenants, lawsuits against African American occupants – whether owners or tenants – usually resulted in their eviction. Courts generally saved these clauses by reasoning that they were private agreements.

In 1948, the Supreme Court stated that State court enforcement of racially restrictive covenants was unconstitutional (*Shelley v. Kraemer*).[90] The Court acknowledged that private individuals could discriminate, but State courts could not order black families to vacate homes they had purchased in white neighbourhoods because this would violate the Fourteenth Amendment, which prohibits State governments' involvement in racial segregation. The Supreme Court also banned federal complicity in racial discrimination, which included the federal loan-financing programme. Resistance to the *Shelley* ruling, even at the federal level, was again based on financial grounds: the depreciation of property values. As a result, restrictive covenants were turned into 'gentlemen's agreements' that required neighbours or a community board to approve any sale, with no explicit reference to race. In addition, despite *Shelley*, deeds often included liquidated damages clauses in the event of sale to African Americans, the total amount of which was often much greater than the value of the house. Later, the Supreme Court also outlawed the practice of using liquidated damages for discriminatory purposes, by prohibiting State courts from enforcing them, but it didn't go as far as to declare such contracts unlawful.

The federal programme did not cease to fund developers who openly refused to sell to black buyers until 1962, by virtue of an executive order issued by President John F. Kennedy.

Nevertheless, the long series of segregation policies continued thereafter to affect the modes and features of urbanisation, reinforcing and reproducing the racial division of urban space: African American families were still reluctant to buy into white neighbourhoods because – even though restrictive covenants no longer had legal authority – recorded deeds went on to spread 'the message

90 *Shelley v. Kraemer*, 334 US 1 (1948).

that the purchasers should not live where they were not wanted'.[91] In this complex framework, discriminatory contracts proved perfectly functional to the relational dynamics of power we have outlined above: both the well-off and subaltern people showed their willingness to continue following the same route of power distribution that had made them what they were.

The combination of public and private law through the various policies and apparatuses that produced the racial segregation of urban space in the United States was a major factor in the construction of African American identity as inferior, degraded, socially suspect, and marginal for further specific reasons.

The policy of residential segregation through zoning ordinances was not limited initially to explicitly banning people of colour from isolated all-white neighbourhoods, and later on to separating single-family residential subdivisions (for whites) from multi-family or rooming house neighbourhoods (for blacks). It also aimed to situate industrial plants, landfills, automobile junkyards, even toxic waste dumps, and other polluting sites in or near African American neighbourhoods, while zoning single-family, all-white neighbourhoods as first-residential areas to protect them from deterioration. This helped drive up property values in the latter neighbourhoods, making them unaffordable for people of colour and, at the same time contributing to the degradation of African American neighbourhoods into urban slums. In fact, not only were these neighbourhoods zoned for polluting industries, but they were also zoned to allow saloons, nightclubs, houses of prostitution, and all kinds of businesses that were prohibited in white neighbourhoods. In addition, residential subdivisions were proscribed in single-family neighbourhoods, while they were allowed in industrial (black and poor) neighbourhoods, encouraging the proliferation of rooming houses for an overcrowded population. Finally, the exclusion of African American housing from federal financing (through the insured, amortised mortgages mentioned above) made its effective cost much higher than its counterpart in white neighbourhoods, with the result that owners had fewer resources to devote to upkeep, encouraging decay and worsening slum conditions in their neighbourhoods.

The association of African American identity with slum conditions resulted in a pervasive imagery of a degraded and perverse social group. To this picture, the contractual narrative entailed in restrictive covenants of the sort we have described added the idea of people of colour as a threat to the peaceful enjoyment of property and to the prospect of rent from the expected increase in value.

Even today, racial segregation and environmental injustice due to the location of polluting facilities in racialised neighbourhoods are the legacy of

[91] R. Rothstein, above n. 87, p. 90.

this public–private partnership. And this is not just true of urbanisation in the US. Similar patterns can easily be observed in European urban areas.

## 7. CONSUMERS IN THE GHETTOS

Nothing more than virtual space reminds us of the importance of 'spaces' as places that are able to determine the conditions of possibilities of the various subjects who 'inhabit' them. These spaces, as is well known, are not given but are in many ways the product of social interaction, ideological conceptions, architectural theories and, of course, law.

Spatial organisation has always been a mode of social control and differentiation. The line is a regulatory technology; it marks a boundary – the line between the city and suburbs, between centre and margins

In many analyses (racially) segregated space both creates and perpetuates (racial) segregation. (Racially) identified space results from state action rather than being an unfortunate but irredeemable consequence of purely private or individual choices.

The unique spatial isolation of the Black poor is a crucial factor in establishing their social, economic, and political situation in the contemporary United States. Strictly limited to this particular social context (the city and the Black people) it would be dangerous to generalise this analysis beyond the United States. But, even though it would be incorrect to presume that the operation of space may be identical or analogous in other countries and situations, nonetheless it seems a fruitful way to problematise the issue of power and link it with space.

As a matter of fact, unequal consumption is likely to be related to issues of class, gender, and race and to the organisation of living spaces.

Recent literature has pointed to the existence of closed spaces that function as 'states of exception', or of particular spaces, such as 'borders', as places of passage where legal regulation is weakened or becomes less effective. While these situations tend to be more widespread than in the past, there is no doubt that the condition of the places where one lives (e.g., cities, neighbourhoods, ghettos) or virtual spaces in which one acts (e.g., the internet) generates complex, inter and intra-race, gender, and class redistributive outcomes.

Long considered a purely public phenomenon of territorial government, land use planning by allowing diversification between different urban areas within the same city, has had complex consequences. While it has allowed for preservation of the homogeneity of individual districts and their cultural fabric, it has also contributed heavily to segregation and marginalisation of others. The latter exerts a decisive influence on the patterns of life and the economic and social relations that can be developed within it; the complex web of public and private law often puts the matter beyond the reach of conventional consumer laws. To what extent should we factor into the analysis the harsh economic realities of the ghettos consumers and the subversion of middle-class rules?

There is indeed a great deal of concern about the global or transnational dimension of consumer protection and its excessive emphasis on the goal of reducing the costs of inter-state transactions at the expense of other (social justice) objectives, but not as much about the local dimensions. Yet, beyond incorporating contract doctrines such as unconscionability and related remedies, there is very little consumer law that recognises the aggregate peculiarities and deprivations of low-income consumers, as individuals or parts of the city. These protections assume the primacy of meaningful consumer choice, which itself assumes choice. They assume that market failures can be corrected by minor, equitable adjustments in contracts litigated by individual consumers against private vendors.

The quintessential situation is displayed by the famous US case of *Williams v. Walker-Thomas*,[92] in which the Court of Appeals for the District of Columbia declined to enforce an unfair contract for the reason of unconscionability.

The seller, Walker-Thomas, offered credit to customers – many of whom were not regularly employed and would not be granted credit otherwise – on outrageous terms (interest rates were high, security was retained in all goods purchased, and goods were repossessed after even trivial defaults). The buyer Mrs. Williams was – known to seller – a welfare recipient with many children. After Ms. Williams had already paid more than two-thirds of the complete purchase price and then defaulted, Walker-Thomas sought to repossess all goods purchased. The Court of Appeal decline to enforce the contract because of Ms. Williams's lack of bargaining power due to her personal characteristics.

These kinds of remedies focus on the individual transaction and often sketch a scenario in which a strong individual is taking advantage of the weakness of another. The problems are located in consumers' individual behaviour, drawing most of the time on sexual and racial stereotypes, a construction which often involves a measure of victim blaming.[93] This individual focus tends to shade out the broader structural constraints (such as gender, race, or class) and places within which an individual is living.

Ghettos reinforces vulnerability that limits consumer agency. Those spaces are characterised by racial/ethnic housing- and job-segregation, concentrated poverty, economic isolation from the mainstream economy, and oligopolistic (a small number of sellers and lenders) household goods markets with widespread 'low road' practices.

---

92 *Wiliams v. Walker-Thomas Furniture Co.*, above n. 59.

93 U. Reifner, 'Collective consumer redress: The use of consumer protection law in out-of-court dispute resolution' in T. Bourgoignie (eds.), *Proceedings of the Seventh Workshop of Consumer Law*, Bruylant, Brussels 1992, pp. 283–315.

Ghettos can be considered anti-markets; that is, places where the rules and preferences of middle-class life are suspended, and the landscape has been systematically stripped of the private and public resources that sustain economic stability and create wealth. Increased consumerism inside and outside anti-markets makes a reliance on some articulation of consumption dynamics unavoidable in the context of existing consumer law. It is necessary to identify those structural elements that differentiate it and, relatedly, to identify legal principles of consumption that may empower profoundly weakened neighbourhoods.

The concept of 'situational monopolies' is useful in describing this situation in which products or services are marketed to a 'captive' audience that can then be charged higher prices than would be reasonable in different places.

In this situation, by digging into the context, it is not difficult to find overcharge[94] and to shut down at the very least the neoclassic argument that protection measures 'hurt the people they are supposed to help'. There is no hindrance, then, to the use of private-law background rules to redistribute transactional surpluses from strong to weak parties or to recurring to regulation; with only a proper warning, however, to take into account the possible – in that context – relative vulnerability of the person who is subject to the remedy.

Further problems arise because existing consumer law is largely ineffective either because it fails to reach these types of transactional deficiencies, because protection costs too much to pursue through individual litigation (we can also doubt that they trust official forms of protection) or because the deficiencies are collective and pre-contractual (redlining), putting them beyond the reach of established legal claims.

It is important, though, to find further mechanisms to counteract these shortcomings, to mitigate their impact on consumers and ultimately to try to come somewhat closer to equality in those living spaces.

To sum up, it is not necessary to drop altogether European law and its multiple goals (prevention of consumer frauds and aggressive market practices, fease and control of consumer credit). It is necessary instead to follow the different costs and benefits of the processes of harmonisation of the law and their repercussions (also outside of contract law) in order to identify the 'losers' and to correct, as far as possible, its perverse effects.

Analyses of this kind are able to reveal how no transformative project is really at zero sum: there is always conflict and there is always someone who wins and someone who loses.

---

94 They typically compete not on price but on factors like location, branding, advertising, discounts, and sales. They use their high prices along with these devices to raise their revenue above cost up to the point where the additional revenue for each unit sold to loyal customers is less than the reduction of revenue from lost customers.

This is undoubtedly a difficult exercise: it requires us to choose, to be able to disaggregate or to consider separately the consequences of the rules with respect to different components of each category, without moving from positions that assume homogenous identities, and to avoid excessive standardisation or fragmentation. It leads us to take into account the complexity of the groups targeted for legal intervention; it leads us to examine their various components and the multiplicity of their interests, because these interests can also be placed at cross purposes.

# INDEX

www.ingramcontent.com/pod-product-compliance
Ingram Content Group UK Ltd.
Pitfield, Milton Keynes, MK11 3LW, UK
UKHW051906290926
8980IPUK00018B/1797

9 781839 706028